Planning the development of universities
A series of reports based on an IIEP research project

Vol. I.   IIEP seminar on planning the development of universities, Paris, 7-11 July 1969 (Basic discussion paper/ Summary report of the seminar/ Case study on Leningrad State University/ Case study on the University of Sussex)

Vol. II.   Analysis of the questionnaire of the project 'Planning the development of universities'
(Summary of the findings from the questionnaire/ Introduction and the structure of the sample/ The state of replies/ University growth/ University autonomy and the involvement of different bodies in the internal decision-making process/ Trends of change in university structure (1958-68)/ Structure of the student body/ Teaching staff/ Innovation in the teaching work/ Evaluation of teaching programmes/ Research in the universities/ Source of university finance/ Use of indices for university planning/ Past and future factors of change in the university/ University functions and their priorities/ The tables/ Appendix I. Method of analysis of the questionnaire/ Appendix II. The questionnaire/ Appendix III. Glossary of terms)

Vol. III. Final report of the project / Summary report of the Seminar / Summaries of case studies / Guidelines for the preparation of case studies

Vol. IV. Case studies: Methodology of planning of the university system in the USSR / Planning the teaching work at Humboldt University, Berlin, German Democratic Republic / State University of New York at Buffalo: case study of teaching and research / System of indicators and criteria for planning and management at the Western Australian Institute of Technology / A university information system: case study carried out at the Catholic University of Louvain, Belgium

International Institute for Educational Planning

Planning the development of universities—IV

Edited by Victor G. Onushkin

Paris 1975 The Unesco Press

The IIEP research project on 'Planning the development of universities' has been carried out with financial assistance from the Swedish International Development Authority (SIDA), the Canadian International Development Agency (CIDA) and the Ford Foundation.

Published in 1975 by the Unesco Press
Place de Fontenoy, 75700 Paris
Printed by N.I.C.I., Ghent
ISBN 92-803-1068-2

Preface

This fourth and final volume in the series of publications of the research project 'Planning the development of universities' contains five selected case studies covering different aspects of university planning. Two case studies analyse university planning in countries—the USSR and the German Democratic Republic—where overall national social and economic planning exists and where planning of higher education forms part of the developed planning system. The other three case studies analyse some aspects of university planning, management and the information system, in countries where there is no national socio-economic planning system.

The study written by the President of the USSR Academy of Pedagogical Sciences, Professor V. Stolyetov, on the methodology of planning of the university system in the USSR contains an interesting description of the systematic and comprehensive approach to higher educational planning which has been adopted in the USSR. It gives the principles underlying the development of the university system and shows how planning takes account of the interactions of such aspects of university activity as student enrolment and employment of young graduates, the training of university teaching staff and subsequent improvement of their qualifications, and so on. One of the most important parts of this study is that dealing with the system of indices used in the Soviet Union for planning the development of higher educational institutions and for evaluating their effectiveness.

The study on planning the teaching work at Humboldt University in the German Democratic Republic deals with one of the two basic functions of the university and shows how the teaching work is linked with other university activities such as the admission of students, teaching staff formation, utilization of facilities, etc. The traditional function of teaching has been transformed by this university into a teaching-learning process in which both the teaching staff and the students have an active rôle to play. A particularly interesting aspect covered by this study is the methods used for evaluation of the work of the teaching staff.

An example of university management in a situation where there is no overall economic or manpower planning is given by the case study written at the State University of New York at Buffalo. Here the activities of the university are coordinated within the state system and the study shows how different interested parties at departmental, faculty and other levels participate in university planning and organisation of the teaching and research work.

The Western Australian Institute of Technology is, in comparison with the universities where other case studies were carried out, a relatively new institution and has, since its inception, paid a great deal of attention to the question of organisation and management. In this study an attempt was made to present the Institute as a working system, and a detailed analysis has been made of the decision-making and planning processes, the flows of information and the indicators and criteria used for planning and management. On the basis of this analysis, a model has been constructed for planning and managerial purposes.

In this IIEP research project, it was assumed that efficient university planning and management can exist only when an adequate information system has been developed and it was therefore important that we give an example of an attempt to build up such a university information system. The University of Louvain was chosen for this purpose since a major attempt was made at this institution to introduce modern management techniques based on the use of a computer. The study provides some general information concerning the concept of an information system as well as details of the sub-systems for students, finance, etc. The study is interesting from the point of view of analysing the major problems and difficulties which universities are likely to encounter when introducing new techniques of processing information, and points out some of the advantages gained from such innovations.

The five different case studies collected together in this volume constitute an interesting comparative survey of how universities plan their activities within different socio-economic contexts. However, all of them substantiate that the use of modern methods of planning and management, supported by an adequate information system and a system of criteria for the evaluation of university activities, can make a very important contribution towards improving university planning and management and towards a better orientation of university activities to the socio-economic needs of their respective countries.

RAYMOND POIGNANT

Contents

1. Methodology of planning of the university system in the USSR
   by Professor V. Stolyetov, President and Member of the USSR Academy of
   Pedagogical Sciences, Moscow 9

2. Planning the teaching work at Humboldt University, Berlin, German Democratic Republic
   by H. Lehmann, H. J. Schulz and a group of staff members of the Research
   Institute for Higher Education, Humboldt University 59

3. Planning the development of universities: State University of New York at
   Buffalo, case study of teaching and research
   by T. A. Razik and a group of research associates and assistants . . . 103

4. System of indicators and criteria for planning and management at the Western
   Australian Institute of Technology
   by H. W. Peters, Assistant Director (Administration and Finance), WAIT . 213

5. A university information system: a case study carried out at the Catholic University of Louvain, Belgium
   by L. Boxus, A. Dodet, A. Gysels and P. Walckiers. 317

Methodology of planning of the university system in the USSR

V. N. Stolyetov
President and Member of the USSR Academy of Pedagogical Sciences

Contents

Introduction 11
I.   Principles underlying planning the development of the university system   .   12
II. Planning of student enrolment 17
III. Planning employment of young graduates on termination of university educa-
     tion 26
IV. Training of the teaching staff of institutes of higher education and improve-
     ment of their qualifications 29
V.   Types of institutes of higher education 34
VI. Planning of teaching and evaluation of teaching standards 40
VII. System of indices for planning the development of an institute of higher
     education and evaluation of its effectiveness (basis of an information system)   44
Appendixes 49

Introduction

Scholars and scientists in the Soviet Union are constantly paying more and more attention to planning in connection with the development of the university system and, as a logical consequence, to the methodology to be adopted. As the problems which need to be solved by the universities become more and more complicated, so the degree of attention given to planning increases. The practical experience at present being accumulated is a constant aid to the improvement of planning methods.

Let us begin by looking at the matter from a negative standpoint and ask what are the processes and developments which are not planned. What is not planned is the 'production' of talent, the timing of scientific discoveries and the emergence of radically new basic theories. These are not planned, and no attempt is made to do so, because the conditions for the emergence of talent and the timing of scientific discoveries are still almost quite unpredictable. Soviet scholars and scientists strive for better planning of events, processes and objectives which are amenable to either direct or indirect quantitative appraisal and evaluation. In doing this, it goes without saying, they select for planning the events, processes and objectives which exercise a determining influence on such conditions as will promote on the one hand, the fullest and most comprehensive development of the capacities of young people anxious to take an active part in industrial production or in the advancement of science and, on the other hand, the greatest possible success in the development of scientific research undertaken by university scientists of every age-group and degree of qualification.

I. Principles underlying planning the development of the university system

How can one define the work which is involved in planning? In our opinion, planning is an activity which is common to all mankind. Any right-thinking person setting out to accomplish some kind of work endeavours to establish clearly the aim he wishes to achieve, the way he might reach it and the means which will be necessary to him. On investigating the type of work involved in planning the development of universities, we find that general commonsense is the starting-point.

First of all, the head and the teaching staff of a university try to envisage what will be the aim of the university in a year and in five and in ten years' time. It is here that planning begins, for if planning is to be in some measure successful, there must be a solid basis.

Planning the development of universities rests first and foremost on: (1) the lessons of the past; (2) the social purpose of education; (3) considerations of the present state of learning, identification of its trends and how it will develop in the near future; and (4) methods of ascertaining and calculating demand for experts and scientific workers from industry, teaching and culture. There are other basic factors which will be brought out when we come to deal with planning in practice.

1. The lessons of the past

The history of higher education goes back many hundreds of years and a thorough investigation of it can throw light on the prospects for the development of higher education in the near future. The historical approach to dealing with the problems of planning is one which we consider not only useful but indispensable. There are two variants of this approach. One of them, earlier in date, would have us think on these lines: 'thus it was, thus it is and thus it is to be preserved in future'. The second variant derives from a work for progress and would have us think 'thus it was, thus it is, but this not how we will do it in future'. We believe the second variant to be more fruitful and to correspond more closely to the aims of planning. Yet, the historical method involves still more; methods based on comparisons.

We are studying how various universities and various institutes developed and in the course of our investigations, we have found that certain universities developed more rapidly (i.e. they rapidly built up a highly-qualified teaching body, achieved important scientific results, and reached a high standard of training of young specialists, etc.) than did other universities. A thorough investigation of the causes of the differing rates of development from one university to another provides highly valuable information which is most useful to those working out planning methods. The same may be said of the differing rates of progress seen in the various university chairs and in faculties inside a particular university.

How a young man or woman enters upon scientific research work and progresses as a scientific worker is a matter of great interest. As we look at what goes on in universities, specialised research institutes, design establishments and industrial undertakings, it is not difficult to come across many cases where, after a successful university career, a man in the course of the next five or at most eight to ten years achieves great successes in the scientific or technical field, rises to the management of important departments or whole enterprises, or in the same space of time presents theses for his Ph. D. and D.Sc., or sometimes achieves the honour of being elected to the Academy of Sciences. In the USSR, the overwhelming majority of young men and women terminate their university studies at the age of about 22 or 23. Consequently, a man may reach the stage we have just mentioned at about the age of 32 or 33.

However, in the same sectors of science or industry, one may often come across cases where a man, after completing his university education, will take not 8 to 10 but as much as 20 to 30 years to reach such a level of personal creative advance. Where are we to find the reason for such a considerable difference in the rates of individuals' creative progress?

It has been usual to regard the young graduate's individual amount of talent as the explanation for his rapid creative progress. This is an explanation which is believed to be an indisputable truth. But what is talent after all? No-one today is in a position to give anything like a convincing answer to the question. Sometimes the emergence of talent is put into the category of natural phenomena for which there is no explanation, or an explanation is put forward which serious men of learning are unable to accept. There are some researchers who put forward explanations which are not based on objective facts but on the prejudices of our grandfathers' time, and in so doing fall into the realms of mysticism and mythology where scientific judgments and conclusions are unknown.

Observations which have been made in universities lead us to the conclusion that in the *present* state of scientific knowledge (we will not take it upon ourselves to predict what it will be in fifty or a hundred years' time) rapid and super-rapid progress on the part of young men and women is not to be attributed to some natural possession of talent which is beyond the grasp of the scientific mind, but is rather to be explained by the prevailing state of the teaching process, in the degree of a person's individual self-discipline, his application to work, his degree of desire for knowledge, the extent to which his personal willpower is developed and a number of other circumstances capable of being studied and accounted for.

An inclination for hard work, a desire to know more and willpower are qualities brought out by education. At the various levels of progress in life, education is imparted and acquired by varying means. A child of six or seven receives his first precise objective, which is set by his parents; that of getting through primary school in three to four years. At ten or eleven, the young fellow faces his second precise programme, that of getting through secondary schooling in seven to eight years. At seventeen or eighteen, the boy or girl comes (if he or she so wishes) up against the third programme, that of completing university studies in four to six years.

At 23 or 24 the university graduate, if he or she wishes to train for independent research work, sees a fourth programme opening up, that of completing an academic post-graduate period and programme in three years and submitting a Ph.D. thesis, after which he is entitled to carry out scientific work on his own. Therefore, up to the end of the fourth programme, it is evident that life is subject to precise planning by annual stages, but when the stage of independent work is reached (which is not the case with everybody), the young man or woman begins to plan his or her scientific work less precisely and with less external demands. And this is where the qualities gradually brought out in each of the preceding periods begin to make their influence felt most strongly.

At the fourth stage, a man must show that he is capable of discovering new truths and knowledge and of entering the fifth stage of actually making new discoveries of significant importance. Each succeeding stage on the ladder is more complex than the one before and he is not free to carry out his programme as he sees fit. Therefore, a man must set his own aims and truths or he will run the risk of seeing his whole life as an investigator rendered unfruitful. Such self-limitation requires a great measure of personal willpower.

One man will begin to work out this personal plan for advance as a creative investigator at the end of the third stage and another in the course of the fourth. Experience tells us that the earlier a man defines his personal plan the sooner and better it will be fulfilled.

A strictly scientific study of past individual creative progress made by large bodies of university students provides valuable information for the planning of young men's and women's careers and can help them in the working-out of their personal plans.

Finally, research into the past experience of universities will provide valuable information about the level of costs of training individual graduates. Costs vary very considerably from university to university. Variations depend in the first place on the number of students at a given university, in a given faculty, etc.

Research into universities' historical experience brings us to the next subject-division of the principles underlying planning, i.e. the definition of the social purpose of education.

2. The social purpose of education

What is the social purpose of education? To be brief, it may be said that there are two variants of the answer. The first is that education trains qualified workers, employees and specialists; here, pragmatic and utilitarian aims are the determining factors. The other variant is that the imparting of instruction serves as the instrument of true education, of the development of the human personality, of awakening and developing a man's creative capacities. Here the determining factor is that of all-round personality development, the training of young people not only to fill this or that function in the industrial world or in the many facets of culture but also to play an active part in the life of the country and in solving the problems of society. It is this second variant that guides the schools and universities of the USSR in the definition of their purpose.

Whether the first or second answer to the question is taken as the right one determines the methods to be followed for planning the teaching work and evaluation of standards achieved. It also determines the type of teaching staff and long-term objectives for many other areas of university activity including admission plans, the regulations for admission and for transfer from one university to another, the structure of curricula and course programmes and procedures for employment of graduates completing their university courses.

3. Consideration of the present state of learning and identification of trends and future developments as one of the foundations of planning the development of the university system

The second half of the 15th century is considered to have seen the beginnings of the Renaissance. This is a period of history which is marked by the emergence of capitalistic systems in a number of Western and Central European countries. In the same period we see the beginning of the development of modern science in relation to nature and human society (not the beginnings of science *per se*, for which we have to go back to earliest antiquity, but the beginning of a new era in the growth of science as related to nature, society and thought). In the 15th to 18th centuries differentiation of branches of knowledge proceeded very slowly. The 18th century was marked by the powerful movement of the encyclopaedists. As D'Alambert saw it, the 'encyclopaedia' was to reveal the essence of all human knowledge, provide a detailed account of each of the sciences and show up the close connection existing between them. Unquestioning belief, such as prevailed in the middle ages, now found itself confronted with experimental analysis of nature and man. Intellect and reason were now the only yardstick with which to measure anything existing. The encyclopaedists and their movement contributed very greatly to the advancement of science as applied to nature, human society and thought, and even today men of learning contrive to turn to the spiritual riches amassed by the encyclopaedists.

At the height of the encyclopaedists' activity the process of differentiation of the various branches of knowledge began, especially where natural sciences were concerned. This process was at its most intense in the 19th and the first decades of the 20th century. Differentiation of the natural sciences overshadowed and pushed the encyclopaedists' aims into the background. This did not however mean that their aims of revealing the essence of all human knowledge and the close connection between individual sciences had lost significance for the men of the day and become merely a step along the road of history. Modern science confirms this, for the first years of the 20th century have seen the beginning of a process of integration of individual sciences which in its first stages found expression in the birth of such subjects as biochemistry, biophysics, physical chemistry and others. A high degree of integration is to be seen in cybernetics and its even more numerous ramifications such as technical cybernetics, neurocybernetics, etc. and, of course, with cybernetics we have not seen the end of integration.

In the last century an expression became current to the effect that 'the age of the encyclopaedists is over'. It obtained wide acceptance among research workers and achieved the status of a commonplace truth. But we can see a time coming when this 'truth' will be suspect for all naturalists and then discarded. More and more problems are coming forward which can be solved only by making use of the achievements of a number of sciences (for instance, the building of space vehicles, space flights, the conquest of cancer, the treatment of vascular heart troubles, etc.). Nowadays, the solution of the biggest and most significant problems calls for the application of encyclopaedic knowledge. The outstanding achievements of our time in scientific, technical and industrial fields have all been made possible only by synthesising the achievements of a large number of branches of knowledge which had become differentiated.

Quite obviously no one on earth is capable of mastering the whole accumulated body of scientific, technical and economic knowledge, nor were there such people in the past. We shall do well to recall how the disciples of Saint-Simon, the great French socialist and Utopian, defined 'encyclopaedism'. They posed the question: 'What is the encyclopaedia of knowledge?' and answered to the effect that the true meaning of the word 'encyclopaedia' is 'the significance of the interconnection of branches of human knowledge'. School and university must acquaint pupils and students with basic knowledge of the channels linking the various scientific disciplines. This is an obligation which influences the organisational structure of universities and their programmes and curricula and, as a consequence, the way in which questions concerning planning the development of universities are met and solved. The way in which science will develop in the very near future, the nature and direction of its development, can be defined and forecast only by those carrying out active scientific research. It therefore follows that scientific research is an indispensable element in the structure of a modern university and an indispensable part of planning its development.

4. The methods of ascertaining and calculating demand for graduates and scientific workers by industry, teaching and the world of culture

This is a fundamental part of planning the development of institutes of higher education. It is a highly dynamic process, evolving with the changing conditions of the national economy and culture and with the increased complications of the tasks set before us by the life and development of our society.

The following section of our report is devoted to an analysis of this complex question.

II. Planning of student enrolment

It is the size of the student body that determines a good number of the planning indices for development of higher education. The size of professorial and other teaching staff, the scope and extent of scientific research, the number of institutes of higher education (there is a minimum, optimum and maximum for the number of students at a given university) the numbers of post-graduate students, the amount of floor-space for classrooms and living purposes, expenditure on teaching materials and libraries are all derivatives of the size of student enrolment. The greatest attention is, therefore, being paid to the planning of student numbers.

In the first years of the history of the Soviet State, the number of students was determined by the *annual admission to universities and institutes of as many as could be accommodated at the time in lecture-rooms and laboratories*. The October Socialist Revolution unleashed among the workers and peasants a great desire for scientific knowledge, and as a consequence the original principle had to suffer some modification. A beginning was made with the establishment of new universities in a number of big cities that previous to 1917 had no institutes of higher education. The new universities were allotted many of the best buildings which were previously used for other purposes (assembly rooms for the nobility, businessmen's clubs and houses owned by capitalists for investment purposes, etc.). In 1967 the Soviet State celebrated its 50th anniversary, and in 1968-69 many Soviet universities and institutes in turn celebrated their fiftieth anniversaries.

In the years 1918-22 the number of universities and institutes showed a very rapid rise, but the rise is not so rapid when compared with the numbers of students. In the period 1922-25 smaller and weaker universities and institutes were amalgamated and the number of institutes of higher education fell slightly. Organisational changes brought changes in the staff-student ratio, as can be seen from Table 1. In the years that followed the number of institutes of higher education and the number of students in them rose steadily, with fluctuations in some years brought about by the reorganisation of the system of higher education and by causes connected primarily with the international situation, e.g. the war of 1941-45.

After the ravages of war (the first world war of 1914-18 and the civil war of 1918-21) on industry, transport and agriculture had been made good, the country began its first five-year plan for the development of the national economy, which

TABLE 1. Student/teacher ratios, 1921 to 1925

Per institute of higher education	1921	1922	1923	1924	1925
Students	887.9	806.5	874.0	1 163.6	1 034.0
Teachers	77.2	84.5	81.9	103.1	111.8
Students per teacher	11.2	9.5	10.7	11.3	9.2

was beginning to require more and more young experts. In the years 1928-30 a large number of new institutes of higher education were established and student numbers increased rapidly.

Table 2 gives a summary of numbers of institutes of higher education and numbers of students.

TABLE 2. Student enrolment in institutes of higher education

Years	Number of institutes of higher education	Number of students (thousands)	Years	Number of institutes of higher education	Number of students (thousands)
1914/15	105	127.4	1958/59	766	2 178.9
1927/28	148	168.5	1959/60	753	2 267.0
1932/33	832	504.4	1960/61	739	2 396.1
1937/38	683	547.2	1961/62	731	2 639.9
1940/41	817	811.7	1962/63	738	2 943.7
1945/46	789	730.2	1963/64	742	3 260.7
1950/51	880	1 247.4	1964/65	754	3 608.4
1951/52	887	1 356.1	1965/66	756	3 860.6
1952/53	827	1 441.5	1966/67	767	4 123.2
1953/54	818	1 562.0	1967/68	785	4 310.9
1954/55	798	1 730.5	1968/69	794	4 469.7
1955/56	765	1 867.0	1969/70	800	4 549.6
1956/57	767	2 001.0	1970/71	805	4 580.6
1957/58	763	2 099.1			

The increase in numbers of schools and students demanded that more attention be given to planning the system, and as experience was accumulated a system of planning student enrolment was gradually evolved. The basic criteria are:

(1) Demand from industry in general and from the transport, communications and buidling industries. The leaders in the industries concerned, basing themselves on technological considerations and on forecasts of quantitative and qualitative changes in the volume of production, estimate their needs of young graduates and submit their claims to the planning bodies.

(2) Demand from agriculture. The leaders of agricultural enterprises take much the same steps as the leaders of industry, they define their demands and submit them to the planning bodies.

(3) Demand from the health service. Government bodies identify the prospects for expansion and improvement of the national health service as regards hospitals, out-patient clinics, sanatoria, etc. over the next five to ten years. This forecasting enables the planning bodies to estimate the numbers of specialists that will be needed (doctors, chemists, engineers, etc.) for the health services.

(4) Demand from education. The Supreme Soviets in the republics and the ministries of education define the prospects for expanding and improving the primary and secondary school systems during the next five to ten years. This forecasting enables the planning bodies to estimate the numbers of teachers and other specialists (physical culture instructors, librarians, etc.) which the national education system will require.

(5) Demands of scientific research. The specialised departments in scientific institutions (the Academies of Sciences, the scientific research institutes and the laboratories serving various branches of the national economy, etc.) forecast the development of science over a longer period (of 10 to 15 or 20 years) and define the specialists they will require and the numbers of young graduates they will need. The requirements of these specialised scientific research bodies are also reflected in the overall State plan.

(6) Demands of higher education. The institutes of higher education, basing themselves on forecasts of their own development, define their own needs for young graduates and notify them to the planning bodies. In submitting notifications they have an eye, as do the specialised scentific research bodies, to longer-term requirements on the basis of forecasting developments in science and technology. Thus, provision is made here for the training of specialists in fields not yet reflected in the demands put in by industrial and agricultural enterprises which are based on short-term requirements.

In the current (ninth) National Five-Year Plan provision is made for the rounding-off of the overall system of secondary education. This, of course, will call for a further increase in the number of teachers and consequently require expansion of training work. At the same time, the increased numbers of young people completing their secondary education will mean increased pressure from those wishing to go on to higher education in the universities and institutes. This is also being taken care of in the process of planning. Our country is gradually coming nearer *to the aim we set ourselves, namely, to provide specialised secondary or higher education for all those deserving it.* This is in accordance with the previously stated aim that education should be the means to ensure all-round development of a man's personality. As the requirements of industry and branches of culture for specialists are more and more fully met, the fundamental mission of school and university, the all-round development of a man's personality, will come to be the principal criterion for determining the size of student bodies.

Nowadays, all demands for graduates received from industry and from different branches of culture are collated and analyzed by the planning bodies, who take into account the past history of higher education and the actual possibilities of the institutes of higher education (their material resources and teaching staff availabilities) and make amendments as necessary. The final plan for the five-year period is then broken down by years and forwarded to the institutes of higher education to be put into operation.

How the student admissions are allotted to universities and institutes is a matter for decision by the authorities supervising the system of institutes of higher education. The rectors of universities and institutes play an active part here. *It is the rector who has the most exact and thorough knowledge of the possibilities of the university under his charge* (material resources, professorial and other teaching staffs, etc.). *Consequently, his decision on the numbers of students to be admitted and how they are to be allotted to faculties is the final determining factor.* Planning for the size of student enrolment must be practicable and workable and guarantee a high standard of training for the students admitted. This is the reason for the decisive role of the rector in planning the numbers of students to be admitted.

Each university or institute prepares its own five-year development plan, based on the State economic plan for the period. The point of departure is the student admission plan for the next five years, broken down by annual periods. At the same time, based on investment funds received from government and industry, the university or institute prepares a five-year plan for the development of its material resources, covering the building of new lecture rooms, laboratories, students' hostel accommodation, refectories, clubs and stadiums and the acquisition of all kinds of material and equipment, etc. Once this plan for the development of its material resources has been completed, a university or institute may receive additional investment funds from government and industry; in this case, the student admission plan is amended (to permit an increase in the numbers of students to be admitted) together with, as a logical consequence, all other planning indices, including those concerning size of teaching staff and numbers of post-graduate students, etc. A great deal of attention is paid to expansion of the university or institute's material resources, as it has a great influence on the growth of the university and its increased capacity to satisfy the aspirations of young people for higher education. (One of the planning indices for the development of an institute of higher education which are outlined in Part VII of this paper is: 'Percentage of capital investment approved for the institute of higher education, actually utilized during the year under review'. Universities and institutes compete to get their figure under this head as high as possible.)

All those who complete their secondary education, irrespective of sex, social position or ethnic origin, have an equal right to enter a university or institute. There is no restriction due to material circumstances since tuition at universities and institutes is free and students receive a grant from the State for their keep during their studies. The only test for entry is the standard of the applicant's knowledge. With the number of university places for the time being lower than the numbers of those seeking higher education, the universities and institutes are obliged to set competitive examinations. (The author is convinced that a time will come when the necessity of competitive examinations will disappear, without the standard of higher education declining.)

Each university makes its own arrangements for student admission. Admission is granted to those boys and girls who get the highest marks in the competitive examination and the highest marks on their secondary-school leaving certificates, which of course serves as a stimulus to them to absorb what they are taught at secondary school. The results of examinations for admisson to normal (day-time) faculties are shown in Table 3 (average for the USSR) covering a number of recent years.

TABLE 3.   Student applications and examination passes (day-time)

Year	Per hundred places	
	Applications made	Examination passes
1965	294	158
1966	368	173
1967	339	163
1968	313	157
1969	291	146
1970	279	142
1971	270	140

The fluctuations from year to year in the number of applications made per 100 student places have occurred while the numbers of those completing their secondary education have been on the increase from year to year. The reason for these fluctuations is to be found in the constant increase in the numbers of universities and institutes in the USSR and the rapid increase in the numbers of those admitted to institutes of higher education and to secondary vocational schools (technical colleges and schools). Any young person completing his or her general secondary education may enter a secondary vocational school (technical college or school) and attain a qualification after a year-and-a-half's or two years' tuition. The total number of those following courses at technical colleges and schools is the same as that for the total university-level students. Any young person completing his course at a secondary vocational school (technical college or school) has the right to continue his education in the future at an institute of higher education.

The slight drop in the years 1965-71 in the numbers of those passing competitive examinations has occurred at a time when the standard of work in the general secondary education system has been gradually rising. The fall in these numbers has been caused by professors and other teaching staffs in institutes of higher education, faced with the rapid advances taking place in science and technology and anxious to raise the standards of training of young graduates-to-be, very naturally putting up the demands they make on the level of knowledge of those seeking admission. It may be asked by what means they increase their demands. The number and selection of study-subjects set in entrance examinations varies according to the branch of knowledge the faculty (or faculty department) is concerned with. In the case of most of the humanities, there are no mathematics or physics examinations but more examinations in history and literature. The syllabus for all university entrance examinations is the same; it is the syllabus of the secondary school system. But, as is well known, examining on the same syllabus can be done in varying ways. Some examiners will concentrate on the formal knowledge acquired, others on the capacity shown of actively utilising the knowledge imparted in school, others again on the ability to find more than one solution to one and the same problem, and an examination on the same syllabus may turn out very differently.

Pressure in the competitive examination (i.e. the numbers of those competing for each available place) varies from one institute of higher education to another, primarily because the question of choosing which university or institute to apply to is a matter for the candidates themselves. Needless to say, secondary school teachers give a lot of guidance to their pupils, advising them where to apply to according to the gifts they display. Every year also the institutes of higher education distribute to schools large quantities of printed information to make clear their structure and the subjects they teach, with details of professorial chairs, who holds them, and so on. Each year they hold an 'open day' when future students can meet the professors and other teachers. Information is given by the daily press and radio, and of course, advice is available to the young people concerned from parents, relations, friends and students. But in the end, the final choice is left to the young man or young woman who is seeking higher education.

Professors and teaching staffs of institutes of higher education make an annual analysis of the results of competitive examinations. These show up the strengths and weaknesses of the work done in secondary schools. The conclusions reached are published in journals for teachers in secondary schools and, revealing as they do the weak points in the teaching given in the general secondary school system, help to remove them in the future. The strong points brought out are an aid to making useful experience more widely available. Certain institutes and universities make an annual analysis and comparison of competitive examination results for a cross-section of schools and for schools in certain districts and cities, and this shows up which are the strongest and which are the weakest schools and promotes exchanges of experience gained in the course of teaching work.

Professors and other teaching staff show a continuing interest in what happens to the boys and girls not admitted to a university or institute on the results of the competitive examination. The following examples, based on real life, indicate some of the various ways they may continue their education:

1. The rector of a university or institute must make a report to the superintending bodies as to how the admission plan has been carried out. But he has the

possibility (and many frequently take advantage of it) of enrolling, in addition to the planned admission, a number of young people who have successfully passed the examination but not won through in the competition. These additional students attend lectures and laboratory courses and take examinations, but as and when official places become free (as places constantly do for a large number of reasons) they are transferred to the basic student body. And even if there is no official transfer for them, it is of no consequence. There have been cases of young people graduating from university who were still not part of the planned admission quota. This is reassuring as a sign of flexibility and humanity in the university admission system.

2. The overwhelming majority of Soviet universities and institutes have, apart from their regular day-time courses, evening and correspondence courses. Over the last decade and a half the system of catering for students on part-time release from industry has become firmly established in all the institutes of higher education in the USSR. Co-operation between three systems of teaching (day-time, evening and correspondence) in institutes of higher education creates some complications in their organisational structure and administration. But what might be called the negative side is fully compensated for by the advantages to be found in co-operation. The following are some of these advantages:

(a) Students following correspondence and evening courses have given the universities and institutes a channel of communication to life outside and to industry. It has been found in practice that this channel of communication has a favourable influence on day-time students and on the teaching work of the professors. We are convinced that education which is divorced from real life and the production of goods brings negative results.

(b) The institutes of higher education have met the needs of students on part-time release from industry. How did this come about? Correspondence courses in Soviet universities and institutes were organised and set up long ago. The young men and girls taking these courses were scattered over wide areas. When it was necessary to sit an examination they had some fairly long journeys to make. On the way from where they worked (and lived) to their university or institute they were passing many a day-time institute of higher education. But the 'travellers' had no chance of enjoying the teaching services of the day-time institutes of higher education they passed.The separation of one type of teaching from another resulted in the correspondence-course students losing time on journeys while day-time institutes of higher education were deprived of a pro-portion of their potential student enrolment. Co-operation between the three forms of teaching, day-time, evening and correspondence, has put an end to such disadvantages.

(c) The co-operation that has been forthcoming in each institute of higher education from those concerned with each of the three systems of teaching, day-time, correspondence and evening, in the instruction of students on part-time release from industry and in dealing with the problems connected with drawing up the necessary high-class manuals for them, has gathered together a whole body of professors and other teachers, numbering many thousands.

This leads to an improvement in the supply of literature to students and in the possibilities for them to utilise technical means of learning.

(d) The higher-education system is given a greater degree of flexibility, both at the time of admission to the first-year course and when the time comes to appoint new graduates to jobs. Better conditions are created both for the flexibility of planning the development of higher education and for each student and his personal circumstances. We shall speak later of the appointment of young graduates to jobs. Here we shall touch on the connection between flexibility in the system of education on the one hand and the personal circumstances of the student and planning of tuition on the other.

Students' personal circumstances can vary widely. A man for various reasons (family circumstances, the attraction of some practical activity, illness, etc.) may be deprived of the possibility of studying at day-time courses but still wish and be able to take advantage of evening and correspondence courses. The laws governing the system of higher education in the USSR give a man during his period of higher education the right and possibility of choosing as he wishes this or that of the three systems of tuition and also of switching from the one initially chosen to another which turns out to be more convenient for him. The course programmes of all three systems (day-time, evening and correspondence) are co-ordinated in such a way as to make possible a switch from one to another. This ensures flexibility of the system of organisation of higher education in catering to the convenience of students.

At the time of student admission, the rectors of institutes of higher education have the possibility (and many of them take advantage of it) of enrolling, in evening or correspondence courses, some of those who failed the competitive examination for entrance to day-time courses. Subsequently, in his second or third year, any such student wishing to do so has the possibility of switching from one system to another.

Evening and correspondence courses at universities and institutes are very popular with young working people. Every year a large number of young men and girls apply to sit for entrance examinations, as is shown by Table 4 (averages for the USSR).

Admission to evening and correspondence courses means making decisions between a great number of applicants who have a great desire for knowledge. But here the degree of satisfaction given to young people's aspirations for higher education is greater than in the case of day-time courses; the vast majority of those passing the competitive examination are enrolled.

3. A proportion of those who complete their general secondary-school education and for some reason take no steps to go on to an institute of higher education go direct into everyday work, in the main into manufacturing industries. Those also who did not succeed in the competitive examination and those not admitted to the university or institute or to specialized secondary educational establishments (technical colleges and schools) do the same. But these are not forgotten by the institutes of higher education who organise twelve months' courses to prepare young people for university entrance. These courses aim at improving

TABLE 4. Evening and correspondence courses

| | per 100 places | | | |
| | evening courses | | correspondence courses | |
Years	applications made	examination passes	applications made	examination passes
1965	265	127	218	124
1966	277	127	224	119
1967	309	133	239	123
1968	280	130	220	119
1969	272	124	218	117
1970	250	119	216	119
1971	239	120	199	118

the standard of general secondary education received by boys and girls. They may be attended by anyone with secondary education and wishing at some time in the future to sit for the competitive examinations. Good teachers are in charge of the courses and many of the students following them succeed at the end in passing the competitive examinations of institutes of higher education.

Four years ago the institutes of higher education also set up special 'preparatory faculties'. The enrolment for these is from young people, workers, farmers and soldiers demobilised at the end of their period of military service. Most of those enrolled for 'preparatory courses' are released from work and given a grant for their upkeep during the period of the course. Some of those taking these courses do so under the system of part-time release from industry. All those successfully completing the 'preparatory faculties' and passing the final examination secure admission to institutes of higher education without having to sit and pass the competitive entrance examination. These preparatory faculties for young people from industry and farming make up for shortcomings in secondary education, which varies from school to school, and contribute to ensuring conformity of the social structure of the student body with that of society.

There are a number of centrally-situated and highly-qualified institutes of higher education in Moscow, Leningrad, Kiev and some other cities (where competition for entry is particularly keen) which offer enrolment *hors concours* to a certain number of young men and women from Union republics who have been studying at secondary schools in their own languages. There are difficulties of course for such young people competing with those who have completed their secondary education in the Russian language but enrolment *hors concours* ensures equal rights and opportunities.

III. Planning of employment of young graduates on termination of university education

Not all those admitted to a university or institute complete their studies in the regulation time (which varies from 4 to 5½ years according to the subject being studied and the type of institute concerned). The official statistics take into account only those who have completed their course of studies at an institute of higher education in the regulation time. The annual percentage of drop-outs from the student body is shown in Table 5 (average for the USSR).

TABLE 5. Student drop-outs

| | Percentage of drop-out | |
| | From all three systems of courses (day-time, evening and correspondence) | From day-time courses |
Academic year		
1965/66	5.6	3.8
1966/67	6.1	3.4
1967/68	5.5	2.6
1968/69	5.9	3.5
1969/70	6.3	3.7
1970/71	5.9	3.8

The biggest percentage of drop-outs is to be observed in the first and second years; it is notably lower in the later years. On average, 88.5 to 90% of those admitted to first-year day-time courses complete their studies in the regulation time. What happens to those who do not complete their studies at an institute of higher education in the regulation time? A good number of them finish by taking advantage of evening or correspondence courses, or even of day-time courses; those who do not complete their courses take up work mainly in sectors of the economy corresponding to the training they have been receiving in university or institute, usually in posts calling for skilled work of one kind or another. Persons who have started and not completed a course of higher education are usually included in statistics under the heading of practical workers.

The plan for allocation of employment to young graduates of day-time courses is usually set up eighteen months before the expected completion of the course. The first draft of the plan is drawn up by the institutes of higher education which take into consideration the actual numbers of students in their pre-final year and put the final touches to it just before it is necessary to make appointments.

The numbers involved in the employment plan are obviously less than those in the admission plan of four or five years ago, and they are deliberately not linked together, since professors and teaching staffs must make a free assessment of students' progress in learning, and deans and rectors must have the possibility to weed out those who are not keeping up. The reasons for student drop-out before the end of their university or institute studies are the subject of study only for academic purposes and to eliminate weaknesses in tuition practice.

Each institute's plan is forwarded to the higher education administrative bodies, which then set up an overall plan for appointments and forward it to the planning bodies. These allot the numbers planned to the departments and bodies which have put in their demands for young graduates, and the departments, etc. notify the institutes of higher education (via the higher education administrative bodies) what are the localities of the jobs and conditions of work attached to them. Each graduate, under the rules in force, makes his own choice as to where he wishes to work.

Each institute of higher education then sets up a number of boards (according to the number of men and women graduating) to deal with the questions involved in appointments to jobs. Those who sit on the boards are customarily representatives of the rector and faculty dean, of the professorial chairs and of public bodies. In good time (three or four months before graduation) the boards inform the graduates-to-be where they are being appointed and of their conditions of work. (Undertakings and institutions offering jobs to young graduates are under an obligation to provide each one with living quarters and pay for his journey from the university to the place of work and also inform him of pay and conditions). Graduates freely choose their future job among several possibilities and the best students get a wider and better choice. Cases of dispute between the appointments board and the graduate are rare and even so eventually such disagreements are resolved to the full satisfaction of both parties. If the new graduate because of family circumstances, such as ailing or very old parents or various other family circumstances, is not able to leave the place where he lives and there is no job there at the time in question, he is given the right to obtain a job by his own efforts. Such cases however seldom occur.

There is no system of appointment to jobs for graduates from evening or correspondence courses. In fact, each student following these courses is as a rule working in the sector for which the courses are training their students. These, as they go on from one course of study to the next, are steadily raising their degrees of skill and are obtaining promotions at their places of work. When the time comes for them to complete their studies they are already as a rule working at a job corresponding to their skills, but there are exceptions to this rule.

It happens from time to time that some sector of industry, transport, communications, agriculture or culture, begins to feel a great need of specialists of one kind or another (as happens particularly frequently when new technological methods are introduced or new branches of industry spring up) and the need had not been foreseen five years ago, and it is desirable that it should be met as rapidly as possible. When such a situation arises, steps are taken to increase admissions to the first-year course for the subject in short supply and to increase the number of older students taking it. But the shortage is met mainly by transferring day-course students from related courses less affected by shortages. Day-time students are found to be very amenable and willingly of their own accord transfer to such subjects. At the same time, it has been found that following the plan of courses devised some time ago according to long-term forecasts of the future of science and engineering, any switches of teaching staff required are quite painless.

At the same time, enquiries are made among evening and correspondence-course students and some are found to be willing to transfer to day-time courses and so obtain their degree in the subject in short supply more rapidly. The co-operation existing between the three systems (day-time, evening and extension) which has already been touched on and the flexibility it gives to the system of higher education enables succeeding demands for young graduates from sectors of the national economy to be met rapidly.

Cases also arise, and the number of them is increasing, where graduates from evening and correspondence courses express a wish (for personal reasons of the most widely varying nature) to be allocated a job under the State plan for employment of graduates. The authorities of the institutes of higher education are always in a position to meet such requests, since there are always more jobs offered than there are graduates from day-time courses.

IV. Training of the teaching staff of institutes of higher education and improvement of their qualifications

It is right and proper to preface an explanation of the system of training of teaching staff and improvement of their standards by looking first at two questions, namely, how the teaching staff requirement is calculated and the basis for the system of training and improvement of qualifications.

1. Calculation of teaching staff requirement

The number of teachers required is determined by the size of student enrolment. The table in Part II of this report shows the fluctuations experienced in the staff/student ratio. There were big changes in the first decade of the history of Soviet universities, swinging between 9.2 and 11.3 when the system had not yet settled down. It has become stabilized in the last twenty years with a staff/student ratio in day-time courses of 1:12.5—13.0 and higher ones of course in the case of evening and correspondence courses, the amount of independent work the student does being bigger here.

The ratio of 1:12.5—13.0 quoted is one very much averaged out—over more than four million students. It varies very greatly from one university or institute to another for a variety of reasons which are not taken into consideration when the overall plan for the university system is being prepared. There can be considerable variations of the ratio also inside a given university depending on the subject in question, how much teaching is done in a department and so on. Variations inside a university are a matter for the rector after consultation with the university council.

There are two noteworthy features here of importance to planning. The first is that the staff/student ratio in each individual university has been stable over the last two decades; secondly, the possibility of varying the ratio inside a university enables its authorities to look into any serious variation in the conditions in which its work is being done and reach a decision which will bring about improved activity on the part of the university.

A stable staff/student ratio in each university is a matter of importance for planning. Universities have an interest not only in maintaining the level of student enrolment but in increasing it. Stability in the numbers of students is a condition of stability in the numbers of the teaching staff; an increase in student numbers is a condition for increase in the numbers of staff.

2. *Basis of the system of training teaching staff and of improving qualifications*

In the case of the higher educational system, the answer to this question is of course the day-to-day scientific research and teaching work of the professors, teachers and assistants of the university. The universities train teachers for the secondary-school system. Teachers for the universities are trained by the universities themselves. A university needs scientific research work in order:

1. To determine with full knowledge of the facts what should be the direction and prospects for the development of science and, based on this, the direction of and prospects for the development of the university;
2. to carry out the teaching work in accordance with modern scientific standards;
3. to instil habits of research into the students and develop in them scientific modes of thought;
4. to ensure further generations of university teachers by means of expert surveillance of the work of the post-graduates; and
5. to carry on fundamental scientific research to meet the needs of science.

Training of young teachers for higher education is done principally by means of a system of post-graduate studies.

Universities and institutes with a big academic staff have the limit to the numbers of post-graduates who may be taken fixed for them each year by the planning authorities. When the limit is decided on, account is taken of: (a) the given university or institute's requirements for young teachers; (b) the requirements of new universities and institutes recently established and not yet having a big teaching staff; and (c) the requirements of scientific research institutes also recently established.

Those accepted for post-graduateships are those persons who have finished their university course and show capabilities for scientific research work. In a number of subjects corresponding to certain sectors of engineering and technology, post-graduateships are awarded to young graduates who have worked for a year or more in industry. Applications for post-graduateships are put forward by their academic supervisors-to-be and by departmental councils. Each would-be post-graduate submits a paper on the subject he proposes to research in during his stay at the university and the potential academic supervisor makes a critical assessment of it. If this assessment is favourable, the candidate sits two or three examinations on the relevant subject matter, the examinations being set by special committees representing the chair and the dean. The examination results are reviewed by the council which makes a decision for or against the candidate. Its decision is final. It can happen that two or three are competing for a given post-graduateship and preference is given to the candidate who has put in the most worth-while initial paper and receives the highest marks in the examinations.

A post-graduate course lasts three years, during which the student is called upon to prepare for two or three examinations of Ph.D. standard on subjects set by the council, also to gain teaching experience (post-graduates supervise laboratory practical work and seminars and lectures, among other duties), carry out scientific research on a chosen subject and submit a Ph.D. thesis to the council. A good proportion of post-graduates meet these requirements and end their studies with a Ph.D. In 1970 26.2% of them in institutes of higher education in the RSFSR did so, the figure for 1971 being 32.4%. If to these are added those who met the requirements except for being four or five months late with the submission of their thesis, the figures for 1970 and 1971 go up to 60.3 and 64.4% respectively. Post-graduates not meeting the requirements, which principally means that they did not finish their thesis, are taken off the list of post-graduates at the end of the three-year period and directed to practical work. Some submit their thesis later on.

It can be seen from statistics over a longish period that 40 to 50% of the teaching staff of institutes of higher education are trained under the post-graduate system and the remaining 50 to 60% in other ways; of these, the two most important are the following:

1. A young graduate is attached to a department as an assistant or laboratory assistant—in big universities, he will usually do both. He carries out his teaching duties and at the same time does his share of scientific research work. When he has assembled sufficient material, he turns to the preparation of his Ph.D. thesis and takes the relevant examinations. At this stage the university authorities have the right to grant him a year's leave on full pay.
2. A young graduate after his university course goes to work in industry and investigates on the spot some technical or technological problem and prepares a Ph.D. thesis. A man working on these lines for his Ph.D. may be exempted from some or all of the examinations which others have to sit.

In the training of young teachers for higher education, university or institute authorities are accountable to the planners for one thing only, namely the observance of the limit set for acceptance of post-graduate students. Responsibility for directing their work and for the level of their training is entirely a matter for those supervising them and the university council, as is recruitment of academic staff and their level of qualification. All members of the academic staff are elected and re-elected in a secret ballot by the university council, which proceeds only after a thorough discussion of each candidate's qualities and failings.

After achieving his Ph.D., and provided he has behind him an adequate practical teaching period approved by the university council and a list of published scientific works to his name, the person concerned has the right to apply for the post of university reader. This is granted by the university council or faculty council and is confirmed by the Supreme Attestation Board which is attached to the USSR Ministry of higher education and includes among its members the most eminent and well-known academics of the Soviet Union.

The next step along the young academic teacher's road is the preparation of his D.Sc. thesis. Having his Ph.D. degree and the title of reader, he may choose between two methods; (a) having, in consequence of his own personal scientific research work, his six-hour working day being devoted half to teaching and half to research, accumulated an adequate amount of scientific material and having published a considerable number of scientific works, he may apply to the University Council for a post as senior scientific worker in order to proceed to finish off his D.Sc. thesis. The Council considers his application and makes a decision. If he obtains a post as senior scientific worker (for one to two years), he is completely relieved of teaching work; (b) some of the readers do all the basic work for their D.Sc. thesis without giving up their teaching work and only towards the end take the three or four months' leave permitted by law on full pay to finish off their D.Sc. thesis.

What is it that provides the incentive to the post-graduate to submit his Ph.D. thesis and a Ph.D. his D.Sc. thesis? There are a number of factors to stimulate him: (a) the title of reader is rarely and only as an exception given to one not holding a Ph.D. or that of professor to one not having a D.Sc., while those having the degrees get the titles as a matter of course; (b) only readers and professors are entitled to give a course of lectures; (c) promotion (in universities and institutes) to a chair is a right enjoyed by professors and only exceptionally by readers, and then only for five years; (d) only professors have the right to post-graduate assistants (readers only in exceptional cases); (e) only professors (and readers only in exceptional cases) have the right to become members of the faculty and university councils; (f) holding a degree and a title results in a reduction of obligatory teaching duties and a corresponding increase in time for scientific research work; (g) holding a degree and a title makes it more possible to get your works published, since publishing houses are more ready to publish the works of professors and readers than those of people not holding degrees and titles.

The planning of teaching for the academic year is done by the chair and the faculty council. Professors and readers are allowed to complete all their teaching work in three to four months and devote the rest of the time to research. The result is that holding a degree and a title means more freedom to plan your working time. Finally, a degree and a title enhance the authority of the teacher concerned.

Some years ago, in addition to the procedure of submitting Ph.D. and D.Sc. thesis, a further method of raising academic staffs' qualifications was brought in. Every five years, each one has the right to four months' paid leave which he may use as he considers best by: (a) attending courses to attain higher teaching qualifications in his own subject; (b) scientific research work in a laboratory of interest to him under an eminent scientist; (c) a training period with major technically advanced industrial undertakings; (d) scientific work in a library; or (e) finishing off a textbook, a monograph or a thesis. Of these, the most popular are work in scientific research laboratories, training periods in major industrial undertakings and periods of creative leave for finishing off some scientific work or other, including theses.

In all universities and institutes in the RSFSR each member of the teaching staff has his own personal five-year plan for raising his standards of teaching and in his own subject. The plan sets out his projected activities year by year and how he proposes to use the four months' leave which he is granted every five years. The individual plans are collated in an overall plan for the faculty. There is an annual review of what has been done during the past year at which plans for the next year are launched. In this way, five-year-period planning is a continuous process and the plan itself proceeds smoothly.

Planning for higher standards in teaching and qualifications in a subject is an internal university matter and must serve the purposes of university life and its improvement. Courses to help teaching staffs of institutes of higher education to attain higher standards under both heads are arranged in the leading universities and institutes and those giving the lectures are professors of the greatest experience.

Many universities and institutes have continuous courses to provide higher qualifications for engineering and technical staffs employed in manufacturing industry and in administrative sections. These post-experience courses are very popular with those teaching in institutes of higher education; they lead to a strengthening of relations between the university or institute and those engaged in production. University professors inform those from industry about the latest achievements of science and the participants impart their on-the-job experiences. Both the professors and the participants are enriched by this exchange of information. Also, in the course of his encounters with the participants, a professor will often come upon interesting people capable of working on some current problem in production conditions or of taking part in the department's teaching work, etc.

There is one further source of recruitment of university teachers, namely, industry, these persons being experts with a great deal of production experience. Faculties of technology, management and industrial economics are glad to welcome these experts from industry. The courses run by institutes of higher education for raising the qualifications of men from engineering works are one way of coming across and selecting such experts.

A production expert having been so selected (selection being made by the faculty council) and having successfully taught for one year, the Supreme Attestation Board of the USSR (already mentioned) has the right on the submission of the aforementioned council to award him the title of reader or professor.

V. Types of institutes of higher education

The type of university or institute which evolves depends on a number of factors; on its traditions, the direction in which its teaching has developed, the composition of its faculties, the requirements of society and the economy, its geographical location, etc. In each one the interaction of these factors produces distinctive features and imprints a specific stamp. It might be said that each university and institute largely stands by itself. And yet, if we examine the immense variety that results, we shall perceive characteristics which are common to all.

In pre-revolutionary Russia there were institutes of higher education of the university type, with faculties for natural sciences and the humanities; engineering institutes of the polytechnic type; commercial institutes of broad syllabus; and agricultural schools and institutes with a full range of agronomic, livestock, forestry and engineering subjects.

At the end of the twenties and the beginning of the thirties the national economy of the USSR began to feel a grave shortage of higher-grade specialists and steps were taken to set up rapidly a large number of narrowly specialised institutes. Education departments were divorced from universities and some dozens of colleges of education were set up. The medical faculties of universities organised a large number of schools of medicine. Departments of engineering institutes were separated to form a series of narrowly specialised institutes devoted to steel, textiles, machine-tools, chemical engineering, aviation instruments, motor vehicles, building, motorways, etc. These narrowly specialised institutes made a big contribution towards supplying the country with the specialists it needed for carrying out industrialisation plans. But as science and engineering develop, big industrial undertakings are becoming more complex in their form and nature. This trend in its turn is affecting the institutes and there is a tendency for them to lose their narrowly specialised character and become more like polytechnical institutes.

In 1930, for instance, a number of electric-power institutes were set up and turned out specialists in the building and running of thermal and hydro-electric power stations. As time went on, these institutes brought in subjects covering radio-engineering, the electronics industry, computers, electronic instrumentation, etc., and gradually became electric-power polytechnical institutes; in the same way, many other specialised institutes turned into polytechnical institutes with a considerably wider range of subjects. The national economy is making ever greater demands for specialists of university grade. Universities and polytechnical institutes (technical universities) have now become the dominant type of institute of higher education. This can be seen in the following table.

TABLE 6.   Universities and polytechnical institutes in the USSR (by number)

	1960 USSR	RSFSR	1965 USSR	RSFSR	1970 USSR	RSFSR	1971 USSR	RSFSR	1972 USSR	RSFSR
Universities	40	19	42	19	51	27	52	28	58	33
Polytechnical institutes	31	19	50	29	52	31	53	33	55	34

The increases seen above are a reflection of the current scientific and technological revolution, which is causing a rapid increase in the demand for specialists with a broad mental outlook and a capacity to switch when necessary from work on one sector to work on a contiguous one. For a number of years some polytechnical institutes, e.g. the Leningrad Polytechnical and Electrical-Engineering Institutes, have been studying the question of consolidating subjects of courses being followed by undergraduates and the possibility of unifying a number of narrowly-defined subjects into one single broader one. Investigations show that consolidation is not only possible but necessary. The Novocherkassk Polytechnical Institute has conducted an enquiry, by sending out questionnaires to industrial undertakings asking them to state the requirements they look for in a graduate, that is, what engineering, management and research duties he will be called upon to carry out. When the questionaires were received, they were compared with the programmes for a number of related subjects and it was found that a single demand from a firm could be met by a number of closely-related subjects, and *vice versa*, one single subject could meet a number of closely-related demands. In other words, it turned out that closely-related subjects overlap and can be successfully amalgamated. University and polytechnic subject groups are more and more dominating the breakdown of studies in institutes of higher education. Table 7 shows the breakdown for students following day-time courses. The proportion of university subjects and polytechnic subjects is the biggest and remains quite stable from year to year. This will remain so in the foreseeable future and in the two groups in question it is expected that later on there will be a degree of amalgamation of subjects. This is a conclusion suggested by trends observed in science, technical subjects, technology and industry. We feel that the future belongs not to graduates of narrow specialisation but to those with a degree of 'universalisation' in some wide field of activity. Any narrow specialisation will appear only over and above relatively 'universal' training gained by means of a spell of practical activity in some sector of the national economy. This is a feeling which today is shared by quite a large number of Soviet teachers, and it is in accordance with this that the structure of universities and institutes will evolve.

TABLE 7. Breakdown of subject-groups being studied in day-time courses: all students in the USSR (in percentages)

Subject-groups	1967	1968	1969	1970	1971
University[1]	45.7	45.6	45.1	45.0	44.9
Polytechnic[2]	35.6	35.1	35.3	35.7	35.7
Building	2.5	3.0	3.3	3.3	3.5
Transport	3.7	3.7	3.7	3.7	3.7
Communications	1.0	0.9	0.9	0.9	0.9
Agriculture	9.7	9.8	9.7	9.4	9.2
Physical culture and sport	0.7	0.8	0.8	0.8	0.9
Arts	1.1	1.1	1.2	1.2	1.2

1. University subjects: natural science, humanities, medicine, law, economics.
2. Polytechnic subjects: engineering subjects related to basic sectors of industry.

A further matter of interest is the size of institutes of higher education, as determined by the number of students enrolled.

Universities show great variations in the numbers of students they enrol (see Appendix VII). In 1970, 26,769 students were following courses at Moscow University, the biggest in respect of numbers of students, while at the same time 2,384 were studying at Krasnoyarsk University, one of the recently established universities where the student body will increase.

A breakdown by size of student population of all institutes of higher education in the USSR is given in Table 8.

TABLE 8. Breakdown of institutes of higher education (USSR—1971 statistics)

Total number of students in institutes of higher education	Number of institutes of higher education
up to 500	32
501— 1 000	42
1 001— 2 000	70
2 001— 3 000	124
3 001— 4 000	144
4 001— 6 000	168
6 001— 8 000	107
8 001—10 000	49
10 001—15 000	47
15 001—20 000	17
over 20 000	11

As can be seen, institutes of higher education exhibit very wide varieties in their numbers of students. The size of the student body has a very great influence on the amount of money spent on the training of each student. In the USSR, with tuition gratis and all services rendered by the university or institute to the student also gratis, the amount of state expenditure per student (with a student body considerably exceeding four millions) is a matter of no small importance. Preliminary investigations show that the amount spent per student goes down as the size of the student body in a given institute of higher education increases. The limits to such an increase are set not by economic considerations but by the possibilities of effective administration of the university or institute.

It may be asked why, with the development of higher education in the USSR planned as it is, such a wide variation (from 500 to more than 20,000) is permitted in the numbers of students at institutes of higher education. Would it not be better to have a majority of establishments with 15,000 to 20,000 students each, rather than a large number with 500, 1,000 or 2,000 per establishment? There is no doubt that from the point of view of expenditure, it would be of greater advantage to have less institutes each with a bigger number of students. But the fact is, when planning the future of institutes of higher education, we take into account not only financial costs but a number of other vital indicators. Some of these are as follows:

1. Planning of long-term development of higher education *aims at an even distribution of institutes of higher education all over the territory of the Soviet Union.* Up to 1917 the vast majority of universities and institutes, and, as a result, the vast majority of students were concentrated in Petrograd, Moscow, Kiev, Kharkov and a very few other cities. The whole territory of Siberia had only two institutes of higher education in Tomsk. In what today are the Kazakh, Uzbek, Turkman, Tadzhik and Kirghiz Republics there was not a single institute of higher education, and none in Transcaucasia. Today they exist in every Union Republic and in every large city of Siberia.

2. The USSR has extremely diversified natural conditions. Consequently, when agricultural institutes are set up, endeavours are made to get them close to the regions for which the agronomists, livestock experts and engineers are trained. Agricultural specialists for Central Asia are trained on one set of lines, those for Siberia on another, and there are others for the Black Earth Region and for the areas of European Russia outside that region. Most of the agricultural insttutes have a relatively small student body.

3. Triining of teachers for the primary and secondary school systems is also done cloae to the regions in which the future teachers will have to work, and for this reasson every district and regional capital today has its own education institute.

4. Institutes of higher education training graduates for work in the artistic field (theatre, cinema and the applied arts) by definition cannot be large in terms of numbers of students. Where institutes of higher education for the arts are established account is taken of ethnological and regional features and also of the availability of qualified teachers of the subjects in question.

There are other quite important factors deserving mention. Universities being centres of science and culture, all the Union Republics long ago set up their own. Until recently only a very small number of the autonomous republics which form part of one or other Union Republic had their own university, but with the advance of industry, science and culture all the autonomous republics previously without universities have established universities in the last twenty years. Here we find the reason for the rapid increase in the number of universities.

Each university, in planning its future development, takes into consideration the economic, scientific and cultural special features of its own republic and endeavours to meet to the fullest extent the demands which the local economy and culture make on it.

When we come to look at the structure of various universities, it is immediately obvious that each differs essentially from the other (see Appendix I). In Moscow University there are no engineering faculties. This is because they are unnecessary. In Moscow, we have a number of very old-established engineering institutes which are polytechnical by type, for instance, the Moscow Higher Technical School which in the full sense of the word is a polytechnical institute for machine-building and the Moscow Power Institute, a polytechnical institute for electric-power subjects, radio-engineering and electronics. The same is true of Leningrad University, for Leningrad is a centre of engineering education. Both Moscow and Leningrad universities have close links with engineering institutes of polytechnic type, particularly between the faculties teaching mathematics, physics, chemistry, etc. The Moscow K. A. Timiriazev Agricultural Academy and the Leningrad Agricultural Institute are both academies in the full sense of the word, turning out graduates in the full range of subjects connected with agriculture. Chairs of general science in these two institutes of higher education are also 'university Chairs'.

The position with the universities in the Yakut and Chuvash is different. Each of these has a faculty of medicine (the Moscow and Leningrad Universities do not —in Moscow and Leningrad big medical schools to train doctors exist side-by-side with the university and closely collaborate with it). The Yakutsk University has an agricultural faculty while the university in the Chuvash ASSR does not, Cheboksary, the capital of the autonomous republic, having a specialised agricultural institute. Each of these universities has an engineering faculty, training engineers for industries which are developing in the republics. Most of the students graduating from these two universities obtain jobs in their own republics. Naturally, if the graduate wishes it, he is free to work in any part of the Soviet Union, as is the case with graduates of any institute of higher education in the country. In appointing young graduates to jobs the appointments boards endeavour, in order to avoid long journeys, to select jobs in the area nearest to the university or institute. But modifications may be made to meet personal wishes expressed by graduates; they have a right to choose where they want to work. A degree from any university or institute carries identical legal weight in any part of the USSR.

Not all universities have philosophy and journalism faculties. The reasons for this are that there are not sufficient highly-qualified teachers and also that in universities such as those in the Yakutsk and Chuvash ASSRs the numbers of students would be very few, amounting to less than the minimum levels required for setting up normal working faculties and chairs. Young people in the Yakutsk and Chuvash ASSRs wishing to study philosophy or journalism join universities where these subjects are taught.

In 1972 there were 824 universities and institutes in the Soviet Union. Each of them has its own specific characteristics. Such diversity is very desirable, for it allows the system of higher education to retain its flexibility and achieve greater success in meeting national problems while at the same time it is able more fully to meet the demands of young people. While retaining this diversity and flexibility, University academic councils take care to ensure that a high standard of tuition for students is maintained.

VI. Planning of teaching and evaluation of teaching standards

The planning of teaching is seen as the most important sector of planning the development of a university. It is teaching that shapes the future of both the university and the society which it serves.

The standard of teaching depends on the teaching staff's qualifications in the domain of pedagogics and field of study. The methods used to build up teaching staff in universities and institutes in the Soviet Union have been described in Part IV of this paper. The standard of teaching depends very much on the state of the scientific research being done by those charged with teaching and therefore we will include a few words about the planning of scientific research.

Planning of scientific research is done entirely by the departments. Each department selects subjects for scientific research and sets the time by which work on them is to be concluded. The free choice of subjects is no easy matter. A chair will select subjects it feels able to cope with. In itself the choice of a subject or a group of subjects conveys the research potential the chair possesses. Inside the same faculty, you may find some departments researching on the most complex and topical subjects, whereas others may choose quite simple subjects. Obviously such a difference in standards cannot be avoided and the facts of university life are not slow to show it up. The weaker department inevitably suffers some criticism in the university's scientific councils and at student gatherings and perhaps even in the scientific press. This sort of criticism has its effect and serves as a stimulus. But there are other most important factors. Departments carrying out research on complex and topical subjects attract grants from the State Committee for Science and Technology or from industry and agriculture, etc. Together with such grants come further supplies of equipment and additions to operative and auxiliary staffs. Departments doing successful work find their reputation increasing inside the university (or institute) and also outside. Such research also acts as a magnet for students and post-graduates.

Departments' annual work records are compared and contrasted inside the university and also within the framework of the university system (see Part VII). This procedure is a matter of lively interest and leads to greater intensity of scientific activity.

It often happens that for a number of years little is heard from departments working on big fundamental problems. But a time does come when what they have been working on becomes clear, perhaps in the shape of a new original manual, a significant monograph or big new theoretical solutions, and these, of course, do not pass unnoticed and are hailed by the academic world (See Part VII).

Where a university has highly qualified teacher-scientists and its departments are scientifically very active, a high standard of teaching is assured. (To which may be added: where modern teaching equipment and high-quality manuals are available, although here it might also be argued that modern equipment and high-class manuals are a direct function of the teaching staff's qualifications and of the level of their scientific activity.) What has been said here of course does not rule out the necessity of teaching being planned. Planning is necessary both in strong and in weak universities.

In Soviet universities and institutes, teaching is organised on the basis of curricula. A model curriculum is devised for each subject by working parties consisting of highly-qualified scholars and scientists working in a particular branch of knowledge in various universities and institutes. The model curriculum prepared is submitted for expert examination by the most outstanding scholars and scientists attached to universities and institutes. Having successfully passed this expert examination, it goes up to the Scientific and Technical Council attached to the USSR Ministry of Higher Education. When the Scientific and Technical Council gives its approval, the procedure of preparing the model curriculum is concluded.

The council of each university and institute, on receiving the model curriculum, adapts it to the conditions of their establishment, making the necessary modifications and refinements.

However, the most highly qualified universities and institutes with big teaching staff prepare their own individual curricula, which may differ from the model curricula. These are also examined by the Scientific and Technical Council, but the prestige of these highly-qualified universities and institutes is sufficient to ensure that scrutiny is completed rapidly and favourably.

The programmes of courses of each general science and each general engineering subject covered by the curriculum are devised, scrutinised and approved along the same lines as the model curriculum. Each department, as it puts the course programmes into effect, may, with the agreement of the university council, introduce such changes as are made necessary by actual conditions in the university. Many programmes for mandatory (special) courses and also optional courses (of which the older-established universities and institutes have quite a large number) are devised by a high-powered working party and confirmed by the university council.

A continuous check on compliance with the curriculum is carried out by the faculty deans and faculty councils. Checking on course programmes is in the hands of the department giving tuition in the subjects in question. The heads of the faculty and the university have complete confidence in the staff of each department and society has the same confidence in the university. But basically, checking of tuition is ensured by the responsibility of the professors and the teaching staff towards the students, towards the rest of the professorial and teaching bodies and towards society as a whole. A Soviet professor has no responsibility other than his own personal moral responsibility and of course any other responsibility in the world of education is unthinkable. Planning of the details of teaching (lectures, seminars and practical work) is done by the departments and faculties in line with the curriculum.

Before the young finalist graduates there is a session of the State Examination Board in the department. The student is examined orally on his degree thesis or project, and on his performance in this the Board awards the student a degree. Membership of the Boards consists of professors from other universities and from the university concerned, well-known experts working in industry and representatives of public bodies. The Boards enjoy high moral esteem and their assessment of the student's level of accomplishment is final. The fundamental aim of the Board is to ensure a uniform standard of higher education in all universities. The degrees awarded to graduates by the various universities and institutes of the Soviet Union have the same legal weight anywhere in the country. The Boards aim at ensuring that degrees are also of equal value. The finalists who are not considered to have reached the required standard are given time for further work and a second appearance before the board (either with degree project or as examinees).

The State Examination Boards have a number of other important functions to carry out. Paragraph 20 of Appendix II dealing with the statement on quantitative indicators of the work of institutes of higher education speaks of 'the number of students' degree theses and projects, recommended by the State Examination Board for implementation...', from which it may be seen that the Boards not only examine the finalists on their degree theses and projects but also select those which are of practical utility and recommend them to industry for use. The number of such theses and projects is increasing year by year.

After a survey of all the oral examinations, the State Examination Boards draw up the conclusions they have reached about the theoretical training of the finalists they have examined and make recommendations for improving parts of the course programmes and for introducing new courses. This is all notified to the university council and much importance is attached to it by rectors and faculty deans, who are aware that it assists the improvement of curricula and course programmes. Things today are moving at such a rapid pace that curricula and course programmes, and textbooks and manuals, have to be constantly improved. This work is done by faculty councils, inter-departmental methodological committees and by the university councils. Matters affecting a single department are dealt with by the department's staff and the results of their discussions are reported to the council which then makes a decision. A *faculty council* consists of all heads of departments and other older professors of great prestige. The *university council* consists of the heads of all basic faculties and professors of experience and prestige. In this way, curricula and course programmes in force, as well as improvements made in them, are the results of the thinking of all the professors and teaching staff of the university.

It sometimes happens that the opinion is voiced that if there is no precise method for assessing the state of teaching (i.e. the effectiveness of what teachers and students are doing) then no planning is possible. This is a concept which merits attention.

Teaching (in the primary, secondary and higher education systems) is an activity where there has to be some aid for the assessment of results. There are many systems of current, on-the-spot assessment, for instance the results of examinations taken by students and the papers they write during their courses and for their examinations, etc. There is of course much that is subjective in this kind of assessment and it is one that has to be used with very great care and withal inside your own university only. Such on-the-spot assessments are quite inappropriate for any comparison of the results of work in more than one university. Every university has its traditions which inevitably influence on-the-spot assessments.

The most objective evaluation of the standard of teaching and education is the contribution which graduates make to society after they have left school or university. This can be made only after some time has passed.

When we speak of criteria for evaluation, this may be understood to be achievement of university objectives as to the kind of graduate produced. We prepare the patterns of graduates (formulate our purpose), then work out a curriculum and course programmes, plan the teaching (lectures, seminars, laboratory practical work, individual work, obligatory and supplementary reading for students, etc.), we plan the utilisation of technical aids to teaching, student participation in scientific research etc.

And when the teaching planned has been carried out, we stand back and look at the result and ask ourselves whether we have or have not achieved the purpose we set ourselves.

VII. System of indices for planning the development of an institute of higher education and evaluation of its effectiveness (basis of an information system)

The indices set by the government for a Soviet university or institute are few in number. Account has to be rendered of fulfilling the first-year student admission plan, plan for appointments of graduates to jobs, acceptance of post-graduate students, finance and capital investments. Decisions on the vast majority of questions affecting the internal life of the university and academic life are left to the heads of universities (rectors) and university councils and no official report is needed in connection with these questions.

How the numerous questions affecting the internal life of the university, which each university decides on for itself, are to be answered has always been planned and of course still is being planned, in one way or another, by government authorities and the council of the university. Some years ago, with a view to furthering exchanges of information, a group of leading members of universities and institutes in the RSFSR analysed and synthesised their accumulated experience in methods of planning and evolved a set of indices (see Appendix II). Only indices which can be expressed numerically, and which have reference to essential aspects of the life of an institute of higher education, are used.

Section I of Appendix II deals with professors and the rest of the teaching staff. What should be the qualifications of a man heading a department? Is he to be a Ph.D. or a D.Sc., or can he be a man with teaching ability but without a degree? The standard of teaching and of scientific work is dependent on how this question is answered. Rectors and university councils endeavour to ensure that the majority of the departments are headed by man with a D.Sc., and plan how and when this can be brought about.

Paragraph 2 of Section I deals with organising the plan for raising the standards of the teaching staff. This we have already touched on. What is actually observed in carrying out the plan for the past year serves as a basis for the plan for the following year.

Paragraph 3 of Section I deals with a most important question, i.e. how people prepare themselves for their D.Sc. Here the relative indices are of particular importance, namely, the annual numbers of those submitting a D.Sc. thesis out of the hundreds who proposed to do so. This is a figure which makes it possible (a) to make a comparison between universities; (b) to define the success of each university in its endeavours to advance and develop: and (c) to make plans for the future on the basis of the present facts.

Paragraph 4 of Section 1 deals with the question of preparing for a Ph.D. It follows the same lines and has the same purpose as that for a D.Sc. In Appendixes IV and V, figures are given for a number of years for four universities and four institutes by way of illustration. The biggest number of Ph.D. and D.Sc. theses submitted was to be seen at Leningrad University. The latter has long been turning out Ph.D.s and D.Sc.s not only for the needs of its own departments but also to meet the requirements of new universities and institutes, of Academies of Science and scientific research institutions in industry and agriculture. Exchange of information between universities on how their members have prepared for their Ph.D. and D.Sc. and what the results have been helps them to profit by the best experience and to improve on what they themselves are doing. The rapid increase in the numbers of doctors of philosophy to be seen in all institutes of higher education promises an increased rate of output of doctors of science in the near future.

Exact planning of the number of theses to be submitted each year is not possible, nor do universities and institutes aim at any such arithmetical precision, but lessons drawn from practical experience allow the university to organise this activity in such a way as to increase the rate of growth in the numbers of theses and quicken the rise in the level of the teaching staff's qualifications.

Paragraphs 5 to 8 of Section I are devoted to the question of the post-graduate student system. As stated, a university under the official statistical system must fulfil the plan for acceptance of post-graduates. But this index, important as it is, does not bring out how much organisational work of importance to the life of the university or institute needs to be done. The universities try to ensure that every scholar or scientist (the doctors of science first and foremost) has post-graduate students attached to him. This is dealt with in Paragraph 5.

Paragraph 6 deals with the results of the post-graduate work, how many of them reach the end of their post-graduate study period and submit a Ph.D. thesis. Information on the degree of success attained makes it possible to plan for improvements in the system.

In the biggest and strongest universities, a good number of the post-graduates are working towards the definite aim of (a) meeting the teaching-staff requirements of departments in a given university: (b) meeting the teaching-staff requirements of departments in new universities now being built; or (c) meeting the needs which scientific research institutes and laboratories inside industry have for scientific workers. Planning of special post-graduateships has been shown in practice to produce very good results and for this reason an index is retained for them. They are dealt with in Paragraphs 7 and 8.

Paragraph 9, concerning the 'numbers of teaching staff in general science departments of the institutes who have a university education, as a percentage of the total number of teaching staff in the same departments' touches on a matter to which very particular attention is being paid by engineering, agronomic and other similar institutes. In mathematics, physics, chemistry, biology, geology and the social sciences teaching staff with a university education are a guarantee of the highest standards of tuition. The institutes endeavour to ensure that their staff in all general science departments have a university education.

Section II of the statement on the system of indices is devoted to questions of planning in connection with scientific research work. In institutes of higher education this is financed from two sources, either out of the State budget or by industry under agreements. The amount of financing per member of teaching staff, scientific worker or engineer does not of course indicate the quality of research being done but it does give an indication of the amount being done and the degree of activity. This index makes it possible to compare one university or institute with another and such comparisons stimulate a constant increase in the volume of research being done in institutes of higher education.

The value of scientific research carried out is judged by the scientific public and the scientific press. Determination of the economic impact (where this is possible) of completed scientific and technical research also serves in a certain measure as an index of the value of what is being done. The scientific and technical standard of research being done is also indicated by the volume of commissions received by a university from government bodies in connection with scientific and technical problems of the highest significance for science, for the national economy and for culture. Only the most highly qualified bodies of scientists are able to accept such commissions, and consequently the volume of commissions received serves as a quite objective indication of the state of scientific research in a university.

Numbers of scientific works published and numbers of author's attestations, certificates and medals received from the USSR Exhibition of the Achievements of the National Economy are also indirect but objective indices.

The scientists in charge of departments in universities and institutes constantly endeavour to bring students showing an interest in scientific work into their research work. It can be seen in practice that these are students capable of good scientific work which is published in the scientific press. In order to assess the value of the scientific work they do, competitions and exhibitions are periodically arranged in regions or republics, and expert committees, composed of highly-qualified scientists, make an appraisal of the work submitted. The authors of the best work are awarded special medals, attestations and money prizes.

Universities differ one from another in the number of students carrying out scientific research and in the results achieved. But examination of the results and the exchanges of information that have taken place have promoted an increase in the volume of scientific research activity on the part of students. (See Table 9)

The figures vary from year to year, as is quite natural; a university does not always succeed in getting first place or anything like it in a competition, and consequently the indices show changes. But general trend is towards an increase in the number of prizes per thousand students and the tendency enables planning for the near future to be done with a degree of probability.

Section III of the statement on indices deals with teaching methods, and we will look at two paragraphs of this section. Paragraph 19 provides for figures on the number of students working to individual study-plans. The basis for this is

TABLE 9. Changes year by year in numbers of medals, attestations and prizes awarded to students for scientific research (per thousand students)

University	Years					
	1966	1967	1968	1969	1970	1971
Voronezh	11.6	1.2	13.6	39.2	44.2	29.47
Perm	6.9	10.0	27.8	34.7	51.9	34.6
Saratov	43.4	28.9	3.1	31.4	54.0	34.43
Tomsk	18.5	37.7	51.1	30.0	31.8	28.36
Bashkir ASSR	4.1	7.2	7.4	6.1	10.9	9.13
Iskutsk	10.7	11.4	21.5	21.9	30.7	15.86
Mordovian ASSR	7.0	28.9	36.0	33.4	54.9	53.0

that institutes of higher education are authorized to transfer students to individual study-plans, which enable a student to make a more thorough study of a group of subjects of interest to him and included in the general curriculum or to study additionally any subject not included in the general curriculum. In order to transfer to an individual study-plan, a student in his first or second year, while taking general courses, has to demonstrate that he is hard-working and personally wishes to do this. The number of study-hours and the volume of studying to be done in the case of an individual study-plan are higher than for the general curriculum. The departmental council, if satisfied about the student's application to work and his desire to transfer, usually grants the request.

The number of students working to individual study-plans is an index of the standard of tuition being imparted and of the sucess of students' work. The planners aim at increasing the number of these students.

Paragraph 23 of Section III deals with the average number of hours of lecturing done by a professor. Each professor decides for himself how many hours he will lecture, but sometimes, due to the attraction of the scientific research he is doing, he will give only the minimum number of hours of lecturing. The university council has an interest in seeing that students receive lectures from the professor rather than from other categories of teachers. Reports on the number of a professor's lecturing hours help the council to arrange that this number should be the optimum one, i.e. not to the detriment of either students or the professor, and bearing in mind that the latter has both teaching and research responsibilities.

Section IV deals with social sciences departments. Institutes of higher education in the USSR are well aware of the importance of the education of students on the humanities side, and therefore a separate section of the statement on indices is devoted to them.

Section V deals with extra-curricular activities. Under this, results of readers' study-groups, in which students can develop their speaking abilities, are reviewed as well as results of the activities of amateur clubs for those interested in theatre, music and choral singing, etc. Much attention is also paid to physical culture and students' sporting activities, to the organisation of leisure time, etc.

Evening and correspondence courses have their own system of indices (see Appendix III), adapted to conditions of teaching students under part-time release from industry.

The results of teaching activities are analysed on the basis of the system of indices; by comparing the results of the activities of all faculties and departments, the university council and rector's office are able to see which faculties and departments have been working most successfully. Further analysis brings out the conditions that have led to greater success. Exchanges of information between universities and institutes make possible further analysis at inter-university level, and with this knowledge it becomes possible to plan what is required of faculties and departments in the future. All planning of future development is founded on the professorial and other teaching staff, their meeting of moral responsibility towards young students and doing all that is needed to ensure that they grow to be highly-qualified graduates capable of justifying all the hopes of society, at whose expense they have been educated.

University faculties

Moscow State University
1. Mechanics/mathematics
2. Applied mathematics
3. Physics
4. Chemistry
5. Biology/soil-study
6. Geography
7. Geology
8. History
9. Philology
10. Philosophy
11. Economics
12. Law
13. Journalism
14. Institute of Oriental Languages
15. Preparatory faculty

Leningrad State University
1. Mathematics/mechanics
2. Applied mathematics
3. Physics
4. Chemistry
5. Biology/soil-study
6. Geology
7. Geography
8. Economics
9. History
10. Law
11. Oriental faculty
12. Philology
13. Psychology
14. Philosophy

Yakutsk University
1. History/philology
2. Foreign languages
3. Physics/mathematics
4. Biology/geography
5. Medicine
6. Engineering/technology
7. Agriculture

Chuvash University
1. History/philology
2. Economics
3. Chemistry
4. Medicine
5. Physics/mathematics
6. Electrical engineering
7. Electrification of industry
8. General engineering (extension)

Indices of the activities of institutes of higher education in the RSFSR

Section I: Staff

1. The number of the institute's departments headed by professors and doctors of science, as a percentage of the total number of departments (excluding departments of Russian and foreign languages and drawing and design).
2. The number of teaching staff sent by the institute on courses to raise their qualifications as a percentage of the total number of members of professorial and other teaching staff.
3. The number of D.Sc. theses submitted during the year, per hundred members of professorial and other teaching staff having Ph.D. degrees.
4. The number of Ph.D. theses submitted during the year under review by members of the institute's teaching staff on a competitive basis, per hundred members of professorial and other teaching staff not having a degree of that level.
5. Number of post-graduates in the institute as at the end of the year under review, as a proportion of the number of scientific teaching staff having a second degree or higher.
6. The number of post-graduates having submitted theses inside the regulation period, as a percentage of the total number of post-graduates having completed the regulation study period during the year under review.
7. The number of post-graduates detached by the institute during the year under review to special post-graduateships in other institutes of higher education and establishments, and also the number of post-graduates accepted by the institute with special assignments for their own institute of higher education, as a percentage of the total number of scientific teaching staff not having a second degree and title.
8. The number of post-graduates accepted during the year under review for special post-graduateships for other institutes of higher education and establishments, as a percentage of the total numbers admitted under the post-graduate plan.
9. The number of teaching staff of general sciences departments with a university education, as a percentage of the total number of teaching staff of the same departments.
10. The number of teaching staffs in departments of economics and industrial management having had experience in industry corresponding to their subject, as a percentage of the total number of those teaching in the same departments.

Section II: Scientific research work

11. Amount (in thousands of roubles) of work done during the year and financed by agreements with industry and the state budget, per member of teaching staff, post-graduate and scientific worker (senior scientific worker, junior scientific worker, senior engineer, engineer).
12. The economic impact (in thousands of roubles—and supported by statements from industry) registered during the year under review by sectors of the national economy

of incorporating the scientific research work done by the institute of higher education both the year under review and in preceding years, as a proportion of the annual amount received under agreements with industry and from the state budget (in thousands of roubles).

13. The volume (in thousands of roubles) of scientific research work financed under agreements with industry and from the state budget and done during the year under review in pursuance of commissions from the Council of ministers of the USSR and the Council of ministers of the RSFSR, under co-ordinated plans or by individual commission of the State committee of the Council of ministers of the USSR for Scientific and technical matters, or under co-ordinated plans of the Academy of Sciences of the USSR, as a percentage of the total amount (expressed in thousands of roubles) of scientific research work done during the year by the institute of higher education and financed from funds received under agreements with industry or from the state budget.

14. The number of scientific articles published by members of the scientific teaching staff of the institute of higher education in Moscow scientific and technical journals and also the number of reports published in the papers of All-Union and republic conferences and seminars, per hundred members of scientific teaching staff of the institute.

15. The number of author's attestations, diplomas and medals of the Exhibition of achievements of the National economy of the USSR received by the institute as a whole during the year, per hundred members of teaching staff, post-graduates and scientific workers.

16. The number of students' papers (including degree and in-course projects), medals awarded, attestations and prizes at regional, republic and Union exhibitions and competitions, per thousand students following day-time courses.

Section III: Tuition

17. The number of textbooks, manuals and monographs published during the year by members of the teaching staff at state publishing houses, per hundred members of professorial and other teaching staff.

18. The volume (in printed pages) of intra-institute publications on teaching methods for the year under review, per hundred members of professorial and other teaching staff.

19. The number of students having worked during the preceding year to individual study-plans, per hundred students following day-time courses.

20. The number of students' degree papers and projects (from all three course systems) of the preceding academic year recommended by the State Examination Board for use in industrial pratice, per hundred students graduating during the preceding academic year.

21. The number of graduates of the preceding year from all three course systems awarded degrees with distinction, as a percentage of the total number of graduates of the preceding academic year.

22. The number of students graduating from all three course systems during the preceding academic year, as a percentage of the total number due for graduation under the relevant admissions plan.

23. Number of hours of lectures for students of the institute given by professors and doctors of science, per professor and doctor of science.

Section IV: Social sciences departments' activities

24. Numbers of doctors of science or professors, as a percentage of total numbers of the departments' teaching staff.

25. Numbers of Ph.Ds or readers, as a percentage of the total numbers of the departments' teaching staff.

26. Numbers of teaching staff having published monographs or chapters of collective monographs, as a percentage of total numbers of the departments' teaching staff.

27. The number of post-graduates having submitted theses inside the regulation period, as a percentage of the total number of post-graduates having completed their regulation period during the year under review.

28. Numbers of papers on social science subjects prepared by day-time course students and discussed in seminars, as a percentage of total number of students attending seminars.

29. Numbers of students taking part in student study-groups on social science subjects, as a percentage of total numbers of day-time course students.

30. Numbers of students taking an active part in student discussion panels on problems of social sciences and having submitted reports, as a percentage of total numbers of day-time students.

Section V: Extra-curricular activities

31. Numbers of students taking part in activities of readers' working-parties, junior-readers' and social-worker-profession groups, per hundred day-time course students.

32. Numbers of students awarded certificates and diplomas, etc. at city, regional, republic and Union amateur art exhibitions and competitions, per hundred day-time course students.

33. Numbers of students working in vacation time in students' construction-squads, per hundred day-time course students.

34. Annual number of sportsmen produced with special rating, per hundred day-time course students.

35. Numbers of prize-winning placings of students of the institute of higher education competing in regional, republic and All-Union sporting contests, per hundred day-time course students (for institutes of higher education in Moscow and Leningrad district contests are equated to regional contests).

36. Numbers of students taking treatment and convalescent leave of absence of various kinds (sick-bay, sanatoria, holiday hostels) on passes issued by the institute of higher education during the year, per hundred day-time course students.

37. Numbers of persons taking preparatory courses of the institute of higher education during the preceding academic year, per hundred first-year course students in all three course systems of the current academic year.

38. Numbers of young persons of worker and rural background taking day-time courses at the institute of higher education during the current academic year, as a percentage of the total number of students following day-time courses.

39. Percentage of capital investment approved for the institute of higher education actually utilised during the year under review.

Indices of the activities of evening and correspondence institutes of higher education (and faculties)

Section I: Staff. See Appendix II, 1-10.

Section II: Scientific research work. See Appendix II, 11-16

Section III: Tuition

17. The number of textbooks, manuals and monographs published by members of the teaching staff at state publishing houses, per hundred members of professorial and other teaching staff.
18. The volume (in printed pages) of intra-institute publications on teaching methods for the year under review, per hundred members of professorial and other teaching staff.
19. Number of teaching staff of the institute of higher education with academic degrees and titles sent to branch-establishments, tuition-consultation centres and also to outlying faculties to assist with teaching methodology, per hundred members of professorial and other teaching staff.
20. Number of degree papers and projects of students following correspondence and evening courses during the preceding academic year recommended by the State Examination Board for use in industrial practice, per hundred students graduating during the preceding academic year.
21. Number of graduates of the preceding year following correspondence and evening courses awarded degrees with distinction, as a percentage of the total number of correspondence and evening-course graduates of the preceding academic year.
22. Number of students graduating from correspondence and evening courses during the preceding academic year, as a percentage of the total number of correspondence and evening-course students due for graduation under the relevant admission plan.
23. Number of hours of lectures for students of the institute given by professors and doctors of science, per professor and doctor of science.

Section IV: Social sciences departments' activities

24. Numbers of doctors of science or professors, as a percentage of total numbers of the departments' teaching staff.
25. Numbers of Ph.D.s or readers, as a percentage of the total numbers of the departments' teaching staff.
26. Numbers of teaching staff having published monographs or chapters of collective monographs, as a percentage of total number of the departments' teaching staff.
27. The number of post-graduates having submitted theses inside the regulation period,

as a percentage of the total number of post-graduates having completed their regulation period during the year under review.

28. Number of papers on social science subjects prepared by evening-course students and discussed in seminars, as a percentage of total number of students attending seminars.

29. Number of evening-course students taking an active part in student discussion panels on problems of social sciences and having submitted reports, as a percentage of total numbers of evening-course students.

Section V: Extra-curricular activities

30. Numbers of persons taking preparatory courses of the institute during the preceding academic year, per hundred first-year students of the current academic year.

31. Numbers of students accepted for a first-year course and working on their subject, as a percentage of total enrolment.

32. Percentage of capital investment approved for the institute of higher education actually utilised during the year under review.

Number of teaching staff submitting Ph. D. theses in the course of the year, as a percentage of teaching staff having a Ph. D.

Institute of higher education	1966	1967	1968	1969	1970	1971
1. Leningrad University	3.0	4.6	4.2	4.2	3.2	3.76
2. Rostov University	2.0	2.6	1.7	1.9	1.2	1.5
3. Tomsk University	2.8	4.4	1.7	3.3	1.6	2.25
4. Saratov University	3.0	1.2	1.0	0.7	1.0	1.94
5. Leningrad Polytechnical Institute	1.2	1.0	0.7	1.8	1.4	1.94
6. Saratov Polytechnical Institute	0.5	1.0	1.4	0.4	0.4	0.6
7. Leningrad Chemical-Technology Institute	0.8	3.5	1.3	2.6	3.1	3.4
8. Leningrad Electrical-Engineering Institute	1.8	1.1	1.3	1.2	1.3	1.22

APPENDIX V

Number of teaching staff submitting Ph. D. theses in the course of the year, as a percentage of number of teaching staff not having obtained Ph. D.

Institute of higher education	1966	1967	1968	1969	1970	1971
1. Leningrad University	9.0	14.4	15.9	18.0	14.2	16.34
2. Rostov University	15.2	13.1	11.5	10.1	12.2	12.45
3. Tomsk University	6.0	6.1	8.7	6.0	5.6	4.05
4. Saratov University	12.1	8.5	3.8	4.1	6.3	4.9
5. Leningrad Polytechnical Institute	3.6	4.0	7.0	7.6	8.6	4.83
6. Saratov Polytechnical Institute	3.8	5.4	4.8	4.6	7.1	5.9
7. Leningrad Chemical-Technology Institute	6.4	5.9	9.3	2.7	5.7	1.9
8. Leningrad Electrical-Engineering Institute	5.2	5.2	4.1	3.9	6.2	5.16

Secondary vocational schools (technical colleges and schools) and numbers of students

Year	Number of schools	Number of persons attending (thousands)	Year	Number of schools	Number of persons attending (thousands)
1914/15	450	54.3	1958/59	3 346	1 875.9
1927/28	1 037	189.4	1959/60	3 330	1 907.8
1932/33	3 509	723.7	1960/61	3 328	2 059.5
1937/38	3 496	862.5	1961/62	3 416	2 369.7
1940/41	3 773	974.8	1962/63	3 521	2 667.7
1945/46	3 169	1 007.7	1963/64	3 626	2 982.8
1950/51	3 424	1 297.6	1964/65	3 717	3 326.0
1951/52	3 541	1 368.9	1965/66	3 820	3 659.3
1952/53	3 604	1 477.4	1966/67	3 980	3 993.8
1953/54	3 726	1 645.5	1967/68	4 075	4 166.6
1954/55	3 795	1 838.7	1968/69	4 129	4 261.5
1955/56	3 753	1 960.4	1969/70	4 196	4 301.7
1956/57	3 642	2 012.2	1970/71	4 223	4 388.0
1957/58	3 498	1 941.1			

Students enrolled at universities in the USSR, 1970 (by number)

University	Union Republic	Number of students	University	Union Republic	Number of students
Bashkir	RSFSR	7 016	Yakut	RSFSR	6 498
Voronezh	RSFSR	11 717	Dnepropetrovsk	Ukraine	12 311
Gorki	RSFSR	10 111	Donbass	Ukraine	13 204
Far-East	RSFSR	6 351	Kiev	Ukraine	19 036
Dagestan	RSFSR	8 092	Lvov	Ukraine	12 075
Irkutsk	RSFSR	10 084	Odessa	Ukraine	11 333
Kabardino-Balkar	RSFSR	9 039	Uzhgorod	Ukraine	10 780
Kazan	RSFSR	9 007	Kharkov	Ukraine	12 992
Kaliningrad	RSFSR	4 307	Czernovits	Ukraine	9 533
Kalmyk	RSFSR	2 541	Belorussian	Belorussian	16 941
Krasnoyarsk	RSFSR	2 384	Gomel	Belorussian	4 825
Kuban	RSFSR	7 403	Samarkand	Uzbek	12 305
Leningrad	RSFSR	19 785	Tashkent	Uzbek	15 498
Moscow	RSFSR	26 769	Kazakh	Kazakh	10 008
Mordovian	RSFSR	16 043	Tbilisi	Georgian	16 019
Novosibirsk	RSFSR	3 805	Azerbaidzhan	Azerbaidzhan	11 466
Perm	RSFSR	9 993	Vilnius	Lithuanian	15 682
Petrozavodsk	RSFSR	6 802	Kishinev	Moldavian	8 056
Rostov	RSFSR	9 452	Latvian	Latvian	8 702
Saratov	RSFSR	9 366	Kirghiz	Kirghiz	13 996
Northern Ossetin	RSFSR	6 908	Tadzhik	Tadshik	12 300
Tomsk	RSFSR	9 965	Erevan	Armenian	11 871
Urals	RSFSR	6 384	Turkmen	Turkmen	9 880
Chuvask	RSFSR	6 897	Tartu	Estonian	6 273

Planning the teaching work at Humboldt University, Berlin

H. Lehman *and* H. J. Schulz,
*and a group of staff members of
the Research Institute for Higher Education, Humboldt University*

Contents

I.   Some basic data on the University and the system of higher education within which it operates 61
II. Place and importance of planning the teaching work in the University . . 68
III. Planning of studies 74
     The different types of courses offered by the University 74
     Elaboration of the curricula 78
     Planning the activities of the teaching staff 80
     Planning the work of students 84
     Planning of classroom assignment, timetables and the production of textbooks and teaching aids 89
     Planning of the teaching process 94
     Methods of evaluating teaching activities 97
Conclusions 99
Appendixes 101

I. Some basic data on the University and the system of higher education within which it operates

Humboldt University of Berlin, founded in 1810, is the university of the capital of the German Democratic Republic. Like other educational institutions, it is an essential part of the socialist order and of the integrated educational system of the country. Due to the radical transformation of the country's social system after 1945 and three university reforms, the university's position and function have greatly changed within the last 27 years.

The *first university reform* brought about basic changes in higher education which assured:

1. Equal rights to education: the system of privilege in education which existed formerly was abolished. Children of the peasant and working class, as well as female students, were given favourable opportunities for admission to all educational institutions, including universities and colleges.
2. Education given in the spirit of peace, humanism and mutual respect between peoples, based on Marxism-Leninism.
3. Integration of progressive scientific education and research into the socio-economic life of the country. These changes were made possible by the socialist system under which the means of production are publicly owned, a leading role is taken by the working class and its Marxist-Leninist party, and there is central management and planning of social development by the State with the participation of all citizens.

When the University of Berlin was re-opened in 1945 the proportion of students from workers' and peasants' families was already 8.4% higher than before the second world war, but this percentage did not by any means meet demands. The Berlin Institute of Preliminary Studies, founded in 1946 and transformed in 1949 into the Workers' and Peasants' Faculty of Humboldt University, was of special significance in promoting the studies of working-class children. In 1951 the proportion of students from working-class families in the University had reached 40% of the total.

The *second university reform* was launched at the beginning of the 1950s, at a time when construction of the socialist system was being initiated and the First Five-Year Plan implemented. Its fundamental concerns were, on the basis of Marxism-Leninism, to raise the level of training; to put into practice the principles of planning and integration of higher education into the socialist system, and to significantly enlarge the training capacity of higher educational institutes. In 1951 obligatory teaching programmes were introduced in the universities which required all students to study Marxism-Leninism and a foreign language, as well as to take part in sports activities. During the years 1951 to 1955 the number of universities and colleges increased from 21 to 46 and the number of full-time students from 27,822 to 60,148

The *third university reform*, introduced in the mid-1960s, was designed to further the building of a fully developed socialist society. It was concerned with raising the material and cultural standards of the people and with promoting scientific and technological progress. Higher education is an integral part of the unified system of social education which ensures the education and training of highly qualified socialist persons capable of performing creative work and the systematic development of scientific work at universities in accordance with socioeconomic needs. Science as a productive force in our society is being promoted by means of the teamwork of scientists and students, universities, institutions of social practice and the economy as a whole. At Humboldt University new teaching programmes were begun which aimed at achieving a higher quality of education and training. An increasing number of students are working independently on projects for the Student Competition, fairs and exhibitions and to contribute generally to scientific and socio-intellectual life.

Also in the course of the implementation of the third university reform new mechanisms of administration have been introduced to democratize higher education and satisfy new demands and conditions. In 1968 the traditional faculties and institutes of Humboldt University were replaced by twenty-four sections and the Social and Scientific Councils were set up as advisory bodies to the Rector.

In 1970 the Gross Product[1] of all branches of the economy amounted to 275,000 million marks, giving an equivalent of 16,130 marks *per capita*. The National Income[2] almost quadrupled from 1950 to 1970:

TABLE 1.   National income and income *per capita,* 1950, 1960 and 1970

Year	National Income in millions of marks	Marks *per capita*
1950	27 200	1 480
1960	73 600	4 130
1970	108 700	6 350

An increase of between 136,000 and 138,000 million marks in 1975 is envisaged, corresponding to a rate of increase of about 5 per cent per annum.

1. The gross social product *(gesellschaftliches Gesamtprodukt)* represents the total gross product values produced in the sphere of material production of society (industry, building industry, agriculture and forestry, transport, postal and telecommunication services, trade and other producing branches).
2. The national income produced is the difference between the gross social product and the value of the means of production consumed, i.e. that part of the value of the gross product created by productive (living) labour.

The increase in National Income as well as improvement in the material and cultural standards of the population has been achieved despite demographic decreases from 18.388 million inhabitants in 1950 to 17.057 million inhabitants in 1970. At the same time, the proportion of the working age-group relative to the total population has decreased from 64.1% in 1950 to 57.8% in 1970, while the percentage of old-age pensioners has risen from 13.8 to 19.5 during the same period.

At present 8.7% of the population are in the age-group most likely to enter institutions of higher education, between 18 and 25 years of age.

Population density in the German Democratic Republic is 158 people per km^2.

The basic principle of the German Democratic Republic Constitution, 'Man is the centre of all efforts of socialist society and its state' (Article 2), establishes the objectives of science and education and consequently the basic criteria for the planning of education.

The GDR's universities and colleges play an important role as institutions for the training and further education of a highly qualified socialist manpower, as centres for the promotion of science and research, and as centres of intellectual and cultural life in their particular areas. They carry out their tasks on the basis of the GDR Constitution, which states in Article 17:

"(1.) Science and research, and the subsequent application of their findings, are the essential foundations of socialist society, and should be fostered by the State.

(2.) The German Democratic Republic assures all citizens a high standard of education, in accordance with constantly increasing social requirements, by means of an integrated socialist educational system. It enables citizens to shape society and to participate creatively in the development of socialist democracy.

(3.) The German Democratic Republic promotes science and education in order to protect and enrich both society and the life of its citizens to make full use of the scientific and technological revolution and to guarantee the constant progress of socialist society.

(4.) Any misuse of science, for example against peace, international understanding, and against the life and dignity of man, is prohibited."

The integration of the socialist educational system (with the universities and colleges at its peak) is shown particularly by the common objectives of all stages, in their identical principles, and in the organizational structure of the system.

The general aim of the educational system is the same as that of socialist society —to develop educated socialist personalities, and each educational level contributes to achieving this aim. Particular emphasis is given to raising the educational standard of the greatest possible number of young people. The system includes socialist education and special training in the ideologies of the working class.

The Law on Integrated System of Socialist Education (1965) sets out the following tried and tested principles for all educational institutions: (a) education and training should be integrated with the daily life of society; (b) theory should be combined with practice; (c) learning and study should go hand in hand with productive activity.

TABLE 2. State expenditure on education (in millions of marks)

	Year					Rate of increase	
	1960	1967	1968	1969	1970	1960 = 100	1968 = 100
National income	73 641	93 043	97 830	102 900	108 700	147.5	111.5
Expenditure on education	3 856.0	4 779.0	4 825.6	5 161.9	5 689.3	147.0	118.0
General schools	1 897.9	2 411.6	2 454.0	2 625.8	2 943.6	155.0	119.5
Vocational education[1]	583.4	868.8	849.2	848.9	887.8	152.0	103.5
Technical education	330.6	305.8	284.0	344.0	312.1	95.0	110.0
Higher education	676.0	687.4	710.6	786.6	928.3	138.0[2]	130.5
Education expenditure as percentage of national income	5.2	5.1	4.9	5.0	5.2	—	—

1. These numbers give only an incomplete picture of expenditure on vocational education since public enterprises also give funds for this purpose. However, there are as yet no complete data on this additional expenditure.
2. The core of the educational reform introduced by the 'Law on the Integrated System of Socialist Education' was the setting-up of a ten-year general polytechnical secondary school and subsequent vocational training for all young people. This resulted in a more rapid increase of expenditure for general schools and vocational training, particularly up to 1967/68. After this aim had largely been achieved, a comparatively greater proportion of the budget was spent on expanding higher education.

It is possible to progress from each stage of education in the system to the one above—there are no educational 'dead ends' (see Appendix I). Since all educational institutions are maintained by the State, their development is administered and planned by it, and care is taken to maintain co-ordination and balance both between the individual branches of education and between it and the demands made by social development.

Development of universities and colleges is planned by the Ministry of Higher and Technical Education *(Ministerium für das Hoch- und Fachschulwesen)* according to the principles of democratic centralism, e.g. centralized administration and planning of the whole of society by the State, with active democratic participation by the majority of the working people, scientists and students.

In 1970 State expenditure on education totalled 5,689 million marks, including 928 million marks for universities and colleges of higher education.

Growth of spending on education is shown in table 2. Integrated and comprehensive secondary education for all children has made it possible to considerably increase the percentage of those enrolled at and graduating from universities and colleges of higher education as table 3 shows.

TABLE 3. Universities and colleges of higher education: enrolments and graduates (percentage of the corresponding average age-group[1])

Year	Enrolments	Graduates with a first academic degree
1950/51	5.0	2.1
1960/61	10.5	5.2
1969/70	16.7	12.5

1. Under the method of calculation used, which is most likely to facilitate meaningful international comparisons, numbers of newly-enrolled full- and part-time students are correlated with the average for the age-group 18 to 21 years, and in the case of graduates from 22 to 25. If full- and part-time studies are calculated separately, the percentages for this period are somewhat lower owing to the demographic situation.

Approximately 50 % of all students come from the working classes; about 90 % of all full-time students are granted State scholarships and for this type of study no fees are charged. Scholarships and allowances are awarded in accordance with the parents' income, the students' achievements and other social considerations.

In the German Democratic Republic there are now 54 universities and colleges of higher education, providing an education up to academic degree level as a pre-requisite for taking up a specific occupation. In 1951, there were 21 and in 1960 44 such institutions. The numbers of students have risen continuously and the past three years have seen a particularly large expansion; in 1970 the number of those enrolled as full-time students was 70 % higher than in 1967.

The number of graduates employed (including those in agriculture) almost doubled from 1961 to 1970, increasing from 129,949 (1961) to 257,835 (1970).

TABLE 4. Numbers of students, newly-enrolled students and graduates holding a first academic degree

Year	Students		Newly-enrolled students		Graduates	
	Total	Full-time students	Total	Full-time students	Total	Full-time students
1950/51	31 512	27 822	—	9 555	4 631	4 631
1960/61	112 929	74 205	29 648	18 332	13 978	9 382
1969/70	138 666	100 204	41 597	31 084	20 416	14 854

This corresponds to an increase from 21.8 to 41.8 graduates per 1,000 persons employed.

Humboldt University, which has at present 17,994 students, including 11,472 full-time students, is the largest university in the country. It admits not only the inhabitants of the City of Berlin and surroundings, but also those of other districts. The ratio of full-time teachers to full-time students at present averages 1:5.4[1] throughout the German Democratic Republic.

Central administration and planning by the State involves the participation of all universities and colleges and other social forces in discussing and deciding questions concerning the development of higher education, and the principles which shall apply to each university.

The head of Humboldt University is the Rector, who is assisted by various advisory bodies (see Appendix II). He is elected by the Scientific Council *(Wissenschaftlicher Rat)* of the University and his nomination is approved by the Minister of Higher and Technical Education. At least once a year the Rector will summon the Conference *(Konzil)*, which is an assembly of elected scientists, students, office and other workers, where he gives an account of the achievements of the University and outlines the tasks that lie ahead. The Rector is assisted by two advisory bodies: the Social Council *(Gesellschaftlicher Rat)* and the Scientific Council, which help him to determine and carry out the main tasks of the University in teaching, education and the promotion of science and research.

The Social Council is composed of 50 members among whom are directors and representatives of public enterprises and scientific institutions; deputies of parliamentary bodies; heads and officials of State organizations; the Rector and the Prorectors of the University; representatives of local and university political organizations; university teachers, research workers and students; and workers and technical university personnel.

Those members of the Social Council who belong to the University are elected by the University Conference for a term of three years. All the others are appointed by the Minister of Higher and Technical Education on the recommendation of the Rector after consulting the political organizations of the University.

1. The total number of students and teaching staff was converted into full-time equivalents, three part-time students corresponding to one full-time student.

The Social Council meets twice a year. Standing committees or *ad hoc* committees are formed for special tasks. It is both the right and the duty of the Council to advise the Rector on the administration and planning of the University; to collect information for implementing the work of the University as laid down in the State plan; to demand the convocation of the University Conference by the Rector if this is necessary for the solution of important problems; and to submit recommendations to the Minister of Higher and Technical Education.

The Scientific Council advises the Rector on the basic questions of research, training, education and refresher courses and all that promotes scientific knowledge. It supports the Rector in carrying out long-term planning in these areas, in the development of socialist co-operative work within and outside the University, and in the planning of academic departments.

According to State regulations, the Scientific Council awards academic degrees and the *facultas docendi*. It also advises on the appointment of university teachers.

Distinguished university teachers, research workers and students are elected for a term of three years to the Scientific Council by the plenary assemblies of the sections. The Council, of whom the Rector is the Chairman, has 100 members and is composed in such a way as to ensure that the most important scientific disciplines of the University are represented and that it includes among its members prominent researchers and outstanding university teachers, scientists with many years of teaching experience, as well as young university teachers, students of various disciplines, leading members of the University administration and representatives of scientific institutions co-operating with the University. The executive committee of each political organization (Socialist Unity Party - SED, Confederation of Free German Trade Unions - FDGB, Free German Youth - FDJ) may send a delegate. The Scientific Council established four Faculties, each of twenty members, headed by Deans. Its work, between the plenary sessions, is organized by the Senate, which consists of the Rector, the Pro-rectors, the Deans of the Faculties of the Scientific Council, distinguished university teachers, research workers and students as well as a representative of each political organization of the University.

The University is sub-divided into twenty-six Sections *(Sektionen)* which are the teaching and research units corresponding to the principal fields of learning. These are headed by Directors who are assisted by the Council of the Section. The Council includes representatives of social organizations and relevant enterprises, State officials and also outstanding scientists, students, workers and office workers of the Section concerned.

II. Place and importance of planning the teaching work in the University

The continuity of administration and planning is guaranteed by long-term plans for the development of the national economy. These five-year plans are established on the basis of the Directives of the congresses of the Socialist Unity Party of Germany (SED). The Directive adopted at the Eighth Party Congress for the 1971-75 National Economic Plan states that the further development of universities and colleges should conform to the requirements of the national economy. Children of workers and co-operative farmers should receive special attention and educational and training patterns *(Profil)* should be drawn up in accordance with the requirements of scientific and technological development.

As far as the students are concerned, uniformity of socialist class-oriented education in the fields of social sciences, natural sciences and technology must be brought to a high level. In this process, the creative capacities of the students must be comprehensively developed and effectively utilised for productive purposes. This basic orientation of training and education is also reflected in the orientation of university research work, which, being a component part of the entire national research potential, is guided so as to provide the scientific basis for a higher level of education. The emphasis here is on harmony of research with education and training, so as to further the development of the scientific content of teaching throughout the educational system.

On the basis of the five-year plans, national economic plans are drawn up for each year, which include targets for higher and technical education. Both five-year and one-year plans are subject to approval by the People's Chamber of the German Democratic Republic, which entrusts the Council of Ministers with their implementation.

The Minister of Higher and Technical Education is responsible for working out long- and short-term plans for higher and technical education (including postgraduate training, science development, research, improving the qualifications of young scientists). These activities are comprehensively planned taking into account their mutual inter-relationships[1]. The Minister issues instructions and directives,

1. Regulation on the Methodology of Drawing up the National Economic Plan for 1972, 16 April 1971, Law Gazette of the GDR, Separate print no. 703, pp. 150-151.

based on his long-term plan for the development of higher education, to the Rectors of the universities and other institutions which then serve as the basis for the individual institutional planning.

The Directive of the Minister of Higher and Technical Education for the academic year 1971-72 stated that in order to improve the level of training in the basic mathematical, scientific, technological and agricultural disciplines *(Grundstudienrichtungen)*, the following steps are to be taken:

1. In the Chemistry and Chemical Engineering Sections the results of their two years' experience with the detailed 'Chemistry' and 'Chemical Engineering' syllabuses *(präzisierte Ausbildungsdokumente)* are to be closely analysed. The results, together with proposals for raising scientific standards still further, are to be submitted to the Minister by May 1972.

2. Draft syllabuses of the basic disciplines in the fields of mathematics, biology, engineering (machine-building) should be discussed in the Scientific Councils of the universities and colleges concerned by December, and preparations are to be made for the introduction of the new curricula from 1 September, 1972.

3. The detailed syllabuses in the basic disciplines of physics, electrical engineering, constructional engineering, architecture and agricultural engineering must be worked out by December. Thorough preparation must be made for their introduction on 1 September 1973.

The Rector, the Directors of the Sections, scientists and students submitted their proposals for the above. This is only one example of their contribution to the elaboration and discussion of central plans for, besides this, representatives of Humboldt University are also members of the following central bodies:

People's Chamber *(Volkskammer)* of the GDR	— 3 representatives
Council of Universities and Colleges *(Hoch- und Fach-schulrat)*	— 5 representatives
Council of Academic Degrees *(Rat für akademisch Grade)*	— 7 representatives
Central Committee of the Scientists Trade Union *(Zentralvorstand der Gewerkschaft Wissenschaft)*	— 4 representatives
Central Council of Free German Youth *(Zentralrat der Freien Deutschen Jugend —* FDJ)	— 2 representatives

The Rector has the responsibility of working out long- and short-term plans for his university or college on the basis of the Regulations and Directives issued by the Minister. After these plans have been approved by the Minister, the Rector is responsible for their implementation; he directs activities in the fields of training, education, post-graduate training, science development, research and improving the qualifications of young scientists.

Having fixed the number of staff for undergraduate and post-graduate training in each basic discipline, the Rector entrusts the Directors of the Sections with the administration and planning of the teaching process in accordance with the syllabuses. The Rector ensures the proper allocation of material and financial resources (payment of wages, salaries and scholarships, the allocation of fixed assets and investment funds, lecture rooms, laboratories, workrooms including libraries, training aids and appliances, living accommodation, dining-halls, sports facilities and cultural centres). With the support of the Directors of the Sections, social organizations and above all of the Trade Union of Scientists and the Free German Youth (FDJ)[1], the Rector seeks to ensure rational utilisation of these resources to achieve the best results in training and education and to continuously improve the working and living conditions of all people belonging to the university.

In the administration and planning of teaching the Rector relies on the Director of Education and Training *(Direktor für Erziehung und Ausbildung)*, who is in charge of a Methodological Department (see Part III, E), and on the Director of Post-graduate Training. He receives additional support from the Scientific-Methodological Council *(Wissenschaftlich-Methodische Kommission)* which helps to popularise effective methods of training and education as well as the rational use of new training aids and appliances, and to make experience gained in university pedagogics known. An important instrument at the disposal of the Rector in this respect is the Chair of University Pedagogics *(Lehrstuhl Hochschulpädagogik)* which, on his instructions, organizes training courses for staff members.

This programme was worked out according to the plan (adopted in July 1971) for solving problems of university-level pedagogics at Humboldt and of the national syllabus for training and improving qualifications in university-level pedagogics for the years 1971-1975.

Using all resources available in the various Sections of the University, particularly in the Pedagogics Section, a training system is being gradually implemented to ensure a high standard of university-level pedagogics.

The following measures are to be introduced in the near future: (1) basic training for young scientists; (2) courses in university-level pedagogics covering the utilization and development of teaching and learning aids; (3) colloquies organized by the Scientific-Methodological Committee for utilizing and generalizing the teaching experience gained in the Sections. The content of the course includes:

1. University policy of the GDR, particularly after the Eighth Party Congress (1-2 hours).
2. Psychological, didactic and educational aspects of the pedagogical process at university level (11-12 hours).
2.1 Concept, nature and characteristics of the pedagogical process (1-2 hours).
2.2 Psychological aspects of the pedagogical process at university level (4 hours).
2.3 Fundamental didactic relations characteristic of all forms of teaching and learning in socialist society (3 hours).
2.4 Educational aspects of the pedagogical process at university level (3 hours).
3. Teaching arrangements of the socialist university, their functions, guidance to effective organization (5 hours).
4. Current tasks of university-level pedagogics; didactic and methodological guidance for their realization (30 hours).
4.1 Socialist study rationalization—a contribution to increasing the standard of training and education.

1. The FDJ is the centralized socialist youth organization of the GDR, in which young scientists, students, workers, apprentices and office workers are politically organized.

4.2 Problems arising for students on transfer from a lower stage of learning (secondary school, vocational school) to the university and the consequences for university teachers.

4.3 Planning of studies at Section level.

4.4 Development and utilization of teaching and learning aids.

4.5 Individual study in the system of socialist university training.

4.6 The analysis of teaching activities, especially by guest listeners, as a means of improving education and training.

4.7 Evaluation of students' performance in the process of university training.

Training and improvement of qualifications is mostly provided by intensive courses of about 50 hours. All participants write an examination paper whose theme should be relevant to their particular work in order that teaching and training in their own Sections may be improved. After the successful conclusion of training and the writing of the examination paper, the participant receives a certificate of qualification.

Everyone engaged in the work of the University—academic staff, students, workers and office staff—exercises an active influence on the administration and planning of university training. Not only do they have an active part in the work of the Conference, but in addition have a continuous indirect influence by submitting proposals, discussing topical problems and undertaking control functions in different organizations such as the Trade Unions, the Free German Youth, the Scientific Council and the Social Council.

The activities of the Rector are also supported and controlled by the public, the people's representatives and their organs (People's Chamber, City Council of Greater Berlin) and by the press, radio and television. For example, during the traditional 'Berlin Students Days' *(Berliner Studententage)* the University, by exhibitions of the work of students and young scientists, gives a public account of the results achieved in teaching, science development and research.

Of special importance, to ensure continuous links between the universities and social life, between theory and practice, and between training, education and research, is the support and advice on curricula given to the Rector by national industries. This may take the following forms: discussion of syllabuses in the presence of representatives from various branches of the national economy; students completing certain parts of their training courses in industry, etc.; lectures and courses given by representatives from different branches of the national economy; defence of diploma papers in the enterprises themselves; and provision of educational aids and appliances.

The *Directors of the Sections* guide the training and education of students enrolled in their Sections according to the syllabuses, in the elaboration of which they have taken part.

Implementation of particular syllabuses is undertaken by the Section where the students enrol initially, as well as by other Sections, for instance that for Foreign Languages. Each Director of a Section requests his own divisions to prepare and carry out lectures and courses for the Section concerned, as well as for other Sections, on the basis of teaching programmes. In addition, he is responsible for co-ordinating the whole complex of education and training for students enrolled in his Section.

It is his responsibility to organize the students by years of study into groups[1] of about 15 to 25 students and to appoint tutors for them. These tutors, chiefly assistants and senior assistants, advise the groups throughout their stay at the University on the most effective methods of study and on scientific work, and generally help in their education. This includes group discussion to organize mutual help, to encourage political and moral development and the establishment of relations with other student collectives, in particular working-class youth in socialist industry and young farmers' collectives. The tutor closely co-operates with the group's elected Free German Youth official and with all other members of the teaching staff participating in the education and training of his students.

In the administration and planning of the teaching process the Director of the Section is assisted by the Deputy Director for Education and Training and the Head of the Department for Further Training and Part-time Study *(Leiter der Abteilung Weiterbildung/Fernstudium)*. The latter two are aided by the Commission for Education and Training which is composed of experienced teaching staff and selected students.

Maintenance of the level of socialist education and a high scientific standard is the responsibility of each member of the teaching staff. Various Sections, such as those for Mathematics and Chemistry, now regularly analyse their results with the close co-operation of all members of the teaching staff and of assistants working in that particular year of study. The results are evaluated with an eye to further improving the teaching process and they are discussed in the Section Council.

At least once a year the plenary assembly of the Section will meet to hear the report of the Director of the Section and there are subsequent discussions of results achieved in education, training, and the promotion of young scientists.

A number of problems have arisen in the development of the teaching process at Humboldt University which can only be solved by a gradual process over a period of years. One group of problems results from the increasing numbers of students, as shown in Table 5.

TABLE 5. Increases in the number of students at Humboldt University

Year	Total number	Full-time students	Correspondence students
1965	14 330	10 247	3 451
1966	13 504	9 918	2 905
1967	13 901	9 780	3 447
1968	13 538	9 983	3 555
1969	15 191	10 436	4 755
1970	17 994	11 472	6 089
1971	20 445	12 382	6 578

1. These groups are at the same time the smallest organizational units of the Free German Youth.

Although the number of those admitted to the University will remain constant until 1975, the problem of effective utilization of available lecture-rooms, class-rooms, other working facilities and hostels, in order to guarantee higher standards of education and training, remains to be solved.

In spite of this, achievement of further improvement in the quality of study is possible since the ratio of teaching staff and other scientific workers to students is very favourable. This is due to the long-term staffing policy. Thus at Humboldt University—with the exception of the School of Medicine—the ratio between professors or senior lecturers and students is 1:26.5 and when all academic staff are taken into account (professors, senior lecturers, senior assistants, teachers in higher education and lecturers) the ratio is 1:6.2.

A further problem with regard to the organization of education, training and research stems from the different sizes of the Sections and their different rates of growth. They vary in size from 425 staff members, including 137 academic staff, to 30 members of whom 26 are academic staff. Also there are some Sections with only one special subject, such as that for Law, and often Sections with over ten special sub-divisions, such as the Section for Philology and German Language and Literature.

III. Planning of studies

A. The different types of courses of study offered by the University

Humboldt University offers all types of courses existing in higher education in the German Democratic Republic: full-time courses, correspondence courses, evening courses, post-graduate courses, part-time study *(Teilstudium)* and research courses.

The number of students to be admitted to university-level study is fixed for all the above-mentioned types of study, taking into consideration the population's growing desire to attain a high educational standard and the demand for graduates.

Admission to university-level study is conditional upon a secondary-school leaving certificate, which can be obtained in various ways (see Appendix I). Admission to university-level study is granted according to the level achieved in the certificate and social considerations. Applications are made for courses in the primary subject chosen by the applicant.

In their efforts to meet the ever-growing needs of socialist society, Humboldt University and all other institutions of higher education in the country have succeeded in making good progress in the reorganization of studies, in terms of both content and methodology. This refers, above all, to the close relationship of subject-based studies with working-class ideology, their practical application, and to the integration of teaching, learning and research. Progress manifests itself in an increased sense of social responsibility in the individual, and an increased scientific potential.

The objectives and the content of studies were reconsidered and further developed on the basis of the predictable main trends of development in society, in science, and particularly in the national economy. In this process, new academic chairs, those of industrial sociology, engineering psychology and information electronics for example, and new Sections such as the Section of Food technology, have come into being.

In addition, the necessity for the establishment of inter-disciplinary courses has emerged. Thus, some of the specialized courses of study required in the Horticultural Section need complex training in the fields of technology, constructional engineering techniques, economy, horticulture, and mathematics as well as in measurement and control engineering. Training in these subjects is given by the teaching staff in the Mathematics, Biology, Animal-breeding and Veterinary medicine, and Food technology Sections, and by the German Building Academy *(Deutsche Bauakademie)* and the Academy of Sciences *(Akademie der Wissenschaften)*. In addition, scientists employed in industry or agriculture have been appointed to conduct parts of the course. Similar tendencies can be observed in other Sections in the field of Natural Sciences.

Following its terms of co-ordination with other institutions of higher education, Humboldt University concentrates its training especially in Mathematics, Physics, Economic sciences, Food technology and Teacher training.

The organization of full-time studies

As a rule a course of full-time studies lasts four years. It is sub-divided into basic and specialized studies *(Grund- und Fachstudium)*. Basic studies consist of a fundamental course in Marxism-Leninism (including philosophy and political economy), instruction in the essential foundations of a specific subject, foreign language training and compulsory sports instruction[1].

Later, the student continues his theoretical and practical training in a more specialized manner, together with the study of Marxism-Leninism. There is no sharp division between basic and specialized studies; certain parts of basic traning may, to some extent, be continued in the course of specialized studies, and specific specialized aspects may already be started on during basic studies.

The extent of compulsory instruction for all students is fixed on the basis of the teaching programmes, and students are expected to spend (including individual studies) 50 to 60 hours per week on their studies, of which about 30 hours are covered by lectures and tutorials.

The academic year for full-time courses starts on 1 September, and teaching activities cover 40 weeks. Scholarships are, however, paid monthly over the whole year. The students have a holiday of four weeks duration each year, but following an initiative of the Free German Youth many of them take up social and political activities, for example working in industrial enterprises or on agricultural co-operative farms.

On the basis of national regulations and in co-operation with the leading committees of the FDJ the Rector fixes, within an overall time schedule, the dates that are of importance for the general timing of the academic year. In accordance with the teaching programmes, the Directors of the Sections set up the schedules for students in the different years and courses. This is done in co-operation with all the other Sections involved.

The most common forms of training in full-time courses are lectures, seminars, tutorials and classes *(Übungen)*, laboratory work, practical periods inside and outside the university, and different forms of individual studies. Whereas lectures are usually given to all students in the same year of study, seminars and classes as

1. The proportion of Marxism-Leninism, foreign languages and sports amounts to about 25% of the total time during basic studies.

well as practical periods inside the university are generally conducted in groups *(Seminargruppen)*.

During the courses, tests are set which, together with the results of examinations, contribute to the general assessment of the student's achievements. In addition, the overall development of the student's personality is evaluated at longer intervals (see section G below). The students conclude their studies with the 'Diplom', the first academic degree.

The organization of correspondence studies (Fernstudium)

Correspondence courses allow working people to obtain a university education without giving up their jobs. This type of student should already have gained sufficient practical experience in the subject of study chosen, and the conditions they have to comply with are the same as those for full-time studies. As a rule applicants are delegated by their firms, but individual applications are also possible. However, all firms have a legal obligation to grant paid leave every year to participants in university correspondence courses. The fee for such courses at all universities is 120 marks per academic year.

The teaching programme of correspondence studies is equal, in its essential points, to the full-time schedule of a given subject, but it takes into consideration that correspondence students, due to their occupations, have valuable experience in the application of science and in administration.

Individual studies organized on the basis of special manuals, study guides and other teaching materials are the major activity. Each student is required to spend about 800 to 1,000 hours per year studying. There are also on average 20 days of consultations of 8 hours each per year. These consultations are given at the institution where the student is enrolled or in a branch of the Section concerned. Such branches exist in big cities or industrial areas for the basic disciplines of Law, Finance, Economy and for refresher courses in Pedagogy, and serve about 14% of the students enrolled.

After at least four years of correspondence studies, the student is granted six months to prepare for the first academic degree, the diploma, which is equivalent to that awarded for full-time studies.

The organization of evening studies

The regulations governing correspondence studies also apply to evening studies. This form of study is preferred by people living and working in the locality of the university. It exists as a combination of evening and correspondence courses in the Section for Philology and German Studies *(Philologien/Germanistik)* at Humboldt University. In contrast to correspondence courses, evening courses involve consultations with teaching staff at weekly intervals.

The organization of post-graduate and supplementary studies

Graduates of universities and colleges are given the opportunity to take up post-graduate or supplementary studies to deepen their specialized knowledge or widen it by studying related subjects.

The organization of these types of courses resembles that of correspondence courses, the various forms of instruction covering between 200 and 500 hours. All enterprises are obliged to grant at least 60 working days of sabbatical leave, with full pay, during post-graduate studies and for supplementary studies 80 working days are granted. In addition, enterprises may grant further paid leave on an individual basis. Courses usually last two years and on their successful completion the relevant State Certificate of Higher Education is awarded. The fee for a course of this type is 10 marks per month.

The organization of part-time studies and research courses

Part-time studies *(Teilstudium)* are usually open to university or college graduates who want to acquire additional job-related qualifications; it is unusual for a correspondence student to take up such studies. The courses include specific subjects, provided within the full-time correspondence and evening courses. Admission is usually dependent on the applicant having accomplished some major scientific achievement, such as a publication, patent or having taught at technical school level. The content of the individual teaching programme is determined by the Section, which also appoints the tutor. Part-time studies last two or three years, with successful graduates receiving the relevant State Certificate at the end.

Among the various kinds of further education for graduates there are also certain forms of training for a Doctor's degree, one of these being research studies, introduced in 1968. The main aim of the courses on research studies is to educate young scientists who will, after obtaining their Doctor's degree, join the staffs of universities, colleges, scientific academies, or enter socialist industry or agriculture[1]. Completion of these courses confers a Doctorate in a particular field of research *(Doktor eines Wissenschaftszweiges)* and studies cover a maximum of three years following immediately after the specialized full-time studies.

The following criteria are essential for admission to a course of research studies:
1. Success in the diploma examination (in the case of especially gifted students, research studies may be taken up before this examination).
2. Excellent results in the basic course on Marxism-Leninism.
3. Very good results in the study of the subject in question and the ability to acquire independently knowledge of the latest findings, experiences and methods of scientific work necessary for research and development.
4. Lively social and political activity; a firm standpoint on all questions shaping student life; creativeness and initiative in scientific work, and a lively interest in teaching and research.

1. Cf. Verordnung über das Forschungsstudium vom 1 Juni 1970, Gesetzblatt, Teil II, p. 410.

The number of research students and the subjects they should pursue are determined by the figures of the National Economic Plan. There were 541 research students at Humboldt University in 1971.

The Rector authorizes the Directors of Sections to select prospective research students from among the candidates. On the basis of constitutional principles, this selection is made according to the above criteria taking into consideration the social structure of the population and the need for special advancement of women.

Within the framework of a fixed plan, each research student constructs his individual working schedule, and seeks the confirmation of the Director of the department in which he works. The training of research students consists mainly of co-operation in the research work of their Section, and in research work collectives *(Forschungskollektive)* under the guidance of experienced scientists. The responsibility for supervision rests with the collectives in which they work or with a scientist especially entrusted with this task. The work of research students is to contribute to the solution of practical problems and for this reason studies are undertaken in the laboratories of industrial plants and enterprises. To this end, agreements are concluded between the Rector and the head of the institution concerned.

Marxist-Leninist further education during research studies is aimed at a substantial deepening of the knowledge acquired in the preceding courses and at further developing ability to apply Marxism-Leninism effectively in both social and scientific work. In addition, each research student must further develop his knowledge of two foreign languages and teach in his subject for two hours a week. In all, Marxism-Leninism, foreign languages, teaching and the consequent individual studies necessary for them take up about 40% of total working time during research studies.

Research students are expected to continue their extensive social and political activities, such as filling elective offices in social organizations and representative bodies, working as group instructors *(Zirkellehrer)* in social studies in the socialist youth organization and co-operating in youth projects. Every research student receives a State scholarship while at the University.

Since research studies are a relatively new form of training, there are quite a number of problems that are now the subject of scientific research. Among them the principal problem is that of how to ensure the correct combination of theory and practice.

As well as research studies, there are other types of training leading to the Doctorate, e.g. the *Aspirantur*, to which able and interested employees of enterprises and institutions outside higher education establishments can also be admitted.

B. Elaboration of curricula

Studies at the universities and colleges of higher education in the German Democratic Republic are pursued on the basis of compulsory syllabuses *(Ausbildungsdokumente)* issued by the State. These include a catalogue *(Nomenklatur)* of special and basic disciplines *(Fach- und Grundstudienrichtungen)*, characteristics of requirements *(Anforderungscharakteristik)*, programme of studies *(Studienprogramm)*, and general teaching programme *(Rahmenlehrprogramm)*.

The *catalogue* lists the special fields of studies, which are combined in groups to form basic disciplines.

The *characteristics of requirements* list details of the professional specifications needed to meet present and future social, scientific and technical requirements for graduates of various disciplines.

Programmes of studies specify object, content, and methods of studies, including the time schedule, in the form necessary for elaborating basic and special curricula at the universities (general planning) and for the immediate preparation of classes by the university teacher (detailed planning). These include:

1. Objectives of each discipline.
2. Outline of total number of hours to be devoted to subjects (sub-divided into instruction and private study) and their precentage share in the total time budget.
3. Schematic representation of courses indicating duration and position of subjects.
4. Teaching programmes of subjects (objectives, content, including time allowance, approximate criteria for use of different teaching methods, educational aids and materials, content and time of examinations).

In working out programmes of studies, links with secondary education and with courses for improving qualifications are taken into account. General teaching programmes cover subjects which are a compulsory part of all or of a number of basic disciplines, such as Marxism-Leninism. They guarantee the necessary uniformity of the educational process in specific fields.

The Ministry of Higher and Technical Education is responsible for elaborating and approving syllabuses. It appoints standing or temporary working groups which include university academic staff and students from the respective field of studies as well as representatives of such relevant concerns as the ministries, industry and scientific academies, for this work. The syllabuses are the basic tools for controlling and implementing university studies. They supply teachers with the scientific foundations of their work and enable them to make responsible decisions in the right direction. They also make it easier for students to follow their courses in a planned, purposeful and systematic manner.

The planning of studies is influenced principally by scientific developments and the demands which will be made on the graduate in his practical working life. Whereas the objectives of studies have to remain unchanged for at least the duration of one course of studies in the interest of continuous development, the actual content of studies may change more rapidly. This can lead to substitutions or even result in a re-shuffle of fields.

Revision or adaptation of syllabuses is therefore necessary after a certain period of time has elapsed. At present the whole system of higher education in the German Democratic Republic is going through a phase of checking its syllabuses. The following specifications derived from the objectives of higher education, the laws of study processes, and the principles of university pedagogics have been drawn up:

1. Objectives, content and method of study are to be set in accordance with socio-economic demands, while at the same time ensuring integration of social-ist education and scientific knowledge, of theory and practice, of teaching, learning and research.
2. A framework of the aims of study including intermediate aims and levels and covering the complete course of studies is to be drawn up.
3. The content for the whole period of study is to be established according to these aims.
4. General planning of teaching methods to be carried out taking the aims and content as methodical variants of study processes.
5. The content of study is to be determined on the principle of inter-changeability of content units.
6. Teaching methods are to be decided according to the basic demand for an in-crease in independent student activity.
7. Independent studies are to be planned as a guided and checkable form of study.

Whether university and college graduates can stand the test of practical working life remains the supreme criterion of the quality of education. Researches on the planning of studies and analyses of the way in which university graduates adapt to practical working life contribute to the further development of the syllabuses and their function within the study process. This also involves questions concern-ing the economics of education, but researches into the economic effectiveness of higher education have, however, to take educational aims defined in terms of society as their starting-point.

C. Planning the activities of the teaching staff

The academic staff has a set working week of $43\frac{3}{4}$ hours[1]. Moreover, there are legal regulations governing their duties. In 1969 two groups of university personnel (full-time university teachers and scientific personnel) were newly defined to corres-pond more exactly with their teaching, research and management responsibilities.

Full-time university teachers are Professors (appointed to a departmental chair) and Associate Professors *(Hochschuldozenten)*. They are appointed to their posts by the Minister of Higher and Technical Education and their duties are:

1. To guarantee a high level of teaching based on a high research performance.
2. To take part in planning and managing the process of development, especially in regard to scientific and teaching work.
3. To estimate trends and developments in their own fields of science and to make conclusions as to their impact on research and teaching.
4. To maintain high standards in selecting the contents and methods for training and education.
5. To supervise scientific personnel in their research and teaching work.

1. Verordnung über die wissenschaftlichen Mitarbeiter an den wissenschaftlichen Hochschulen—Mitarbeiterverordnung (MVO) vom 6 November 1968 (Gesetzblatt Teil II Nr. 127).

6. To take an active role in all forms of studies including examinations and courses to further improve qualifications.

In addition, there are *part-time university teachers*, i.e. representatives from particular spheres of practice (industry, agriculture, etc.) who may act as Professors or Associate Professors on a part-time basis.

The scientific personnel consist of:

1. Assistants *(wissenschaftliche Assistenten)* who may be employed for a limited length of time and work in research, training and education as well as in the field of medical care supporting the university teachers. At the same time, they improve their own knowledge and abilities.
2. Teachers in higher education *(Lehrer im Hochschuldienst)* who are in charge of seminars, classes, practica and similar forms ot study during the basic training. On an average they hold 20 lessons per week, may give lectures up to 2 hours per week and contribute to research work.
3. Lecturers *(Lektoren)* who are in charge of seminars, classes, practica and similar arrangements in all forms of study usually in a specialized field. On an average they hold 16 lessons per week, may give lectures up to 4 hours per week and carry out research projects.
4. Senior Assistants *(wissenschaftliche Oberassistenten)* who work in research, training, education and post-graduate education, being responsible for work with the students in seminars, consultations and in special forms ot training. They guide the scientific activity of the students and assistants, may give lectures up to 4 hours per week or may be engaged entirely in research.
5. Scientific Secretaries *(wissenschaftliche Sekretäre)* who are responsible for work connected with the planning, administration and organization of scientific work.

The Director of the Section is responsible for his university teachers and scientific staff, whose work is defined by the legal provisions covering the rights and duties of the s⁺aff of institutions of higher education. He must guarantee the economic use of the workforce and basic funds and must attempt to make them more and more effective. At present, investigations on this subject are being carried out at Humboldt University and at other institutions of higher education.

In planning the teaching and research work for the above staff, the following indices are used:

1. Number of students to number of scientific personnel (full-time equivalents)
2. Number of students to number of university teachers (full-time equivalents)
3. Number of university teachers to scientific personnel (full-time equivalents)
4. Amount of time devoted to research by academic staff (full-time equivalents) as a percentage of their total activities.

With regard to the third index, at Humboldt University this has been subject to some change over the period 1965-70 as is shown in table 6. These figures show that within a short period the composition of the academic staff has changed in favour of university teachers.

At Humboldt University the Directors of certain Sections carried out some investigations to analyse the time and work of academic staff. Here we present

TABLE 6. Ratio of university teachers to scientific personnel

Year	University as a whole	Non-medical groups
1965	1:4.9	1:4.7
1970	1:4.3	1:3.3

some details of investigations in the Sections of Biology and Chemistry. The analysis was made for three groups of people: (a) University teachers (professors and senior lecturers); (b) Senior assistants, lecturers, teachers in higher education; and (c) Scientific assistants.

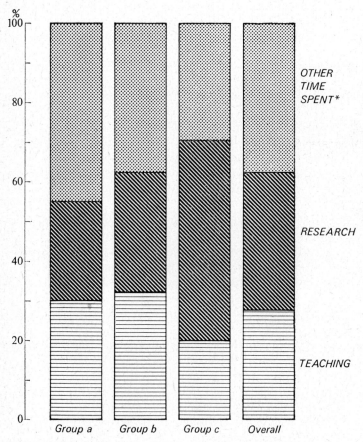

*This includes time spent on administrative work, own further education, legal holidays, illness, etc.

FIGURE 1. *Humboldt University, Section of Biology: use of working time (43-hour week) by different groups of staff in October 1970.*

Figure 1 shows that in October 1970 all three registered groups of persons spent about 27% of their working time on teaching. The percentage is lowest in group (c), which comprises assistants, because many of them are still working on their theses. According to the investigations of the following months, the ratio of time spent on instruction, research and 'other' became 1:1:1 in the Section of Biology; that is, one-third of time is spent on teaching. A breakdown of the time devoted to different forms of teaching was also investigated in the Section of Biology.

TABLE 7. Time spent on different types of teaching by groups of staff in October 1970 (hours and percentage)

| Group of staff | Types of activity[1] | | | | | | | | |
	1	2	3	4	5	6	7	8	All
Group (a)	183	180	38	41	100	355	48	6	936
Group (b)	376	221	77	13	3	183	120	28	1 021
Group (c)	238	252	3	136	—	98	28	93	848
Total hours	797	653	103	190	103	636	191	127	2 805
Group (a)	19.2	18.9	4.0	4.3	10.5	37.5	5.0	0.6	
Group (b)	36.9	21.6	7.5	1.3	0.3	17.9	11.8	2.7	
Group (c)	28.1	29.7	0.4	16.0	—	11.6	3.3	10.9	
Total per cent	28.2	23.2	4.2	6.7	3.7	22.5	7.0	4.5	

1. Types of Activity: 1: giving lectures etc.
2: preparation of and evaluation of lectures
3: examinations and tests of performance
4: tutoring
5: academic entrance examinations
6: time spent on management and organization
7: elaboration of teaching material
8: other

Over 50% of all time devoted to teaching by all academic staff of the Section was used for giving, preparing and evaluating lectures. The amount of time spent on this by professors and senior lecturers is 38%. Compared with the other two groups, they spent the largest amount of time on management and organization of teaching (38%), as much as for giving, preparing and evaluating lectures. The staff of groups (b) and (c) spent equal amounts of time on giving, preparing and evaluating instruction—59% and 58%. After carrying out the investigations over a longer period, the staff of this Section consider that at present the amount of time spent on preparing and evaluating lectures is too low, compared with the amount of time spent on giving lectures. On average, a ratio of 1 for giving a lecture to 2 for preparing and evaluating it is considered desirable. There should be differences according to the character of the lecture, to the scientific degree and qualification of the lecturer and so on. For instance, a ratio of 1 to 3 is looked upon as adequate for lectures dealing mainly with theoretical problems, and a ratio of 1 to 4 seems to be necessary for lectures which include experiments.

In the Chemistry Section investigations into the general work-load of academic staff were carried out in 1969/70, which provided information on the general structure by groups of teaching staff (professors, associate professors and assistants), breakdown and use. Supplementary studies were carried out to plan the time necessary for teaching. The time required for various types of teaching activities (experimental and theoretical lectures, seminars, practical courses, consultations given to students during their practical work, guidance of diploma-students, etc.) was calculated by interviewing selected representative staff (interviews and questionnaires) with due consideration of all factors influencing working time, such as availability of special literature, frequencies of lectures, seminars or classes per term, and closeness of links between the contents of research and teaching tasks, etc.

On the basis of the results obtained, a catalogue of teaching load characteristics was established. After defining the main factors affecting time spent on the respective types of teaching activities (e.g. lectures, seminars, classes, supervision of diploma papers) average values were established which could be used for planning. For the supervision of diploma papers the three levels of average values, depending on the various tasks to be performed, amount to 50, 100 and 150 hours.

By means of such average values the time needed for various teaching activities was established, and alternatives were calculated on the basis of the syllabuses (e.g. changes in the structure of courses, possibilities for conducting parallel courses, investigations into contents and methods of research and teaching). These results were taken into account in devising the syllabuses. In 1970/71, the Chemistry Section at the Technical University of Dresden carried out working time analyses and, with the experience of the Chemistry Section of Humboldt University, is now establishing average values to be used as standards for planning.

The results of these preliminary investigations do not in general indicate the need for an increase in the number of scientific personnel. On the contrary, a comprehensive improvement in the organization of work is the main necessity together with some streamlining of the processes This should achieve a steadily improving balance of teaching and research and ensure the most efficient use of the scientific work-force at the university's disposal.

D. Planning the work of students

Co-operation between university teachers and students is a prerequisite for the successful organization of studies. This also necessitates the student receiving detailed information on the envisaged course of study and providing information on the aims and methods of pursuing a particular course at the university.

If we take it as a generally accepted fact that teaching and learning are inseparable, we can assume it is necessary to apply planning to the activities of the university teacher as well as to those of the student. It is this which has led, among other reasons, to reconsideration of the teaching programmes which are currently in force at Humboldt University (see section B above). The scientific work which is done independently by the student outside the courses of instruction at the university will be incorporated into the new programmes.

Investigations conducted at the university by both university teachers and students have shown that the way in which students carry out their independent studies decisively influences the results obtained in their course of study and that attainments of students clearly improve if individual studies are planned and guided in much the same way as academic instruction. This refers to both content and time available for independent study. It is therefore essential that all the requirements which students are expected to fulfil should be carefully balanced.

The teaching staff makes every effort to improve the effectiveness of students' independent studies through the provision of:
1. Classes giving an introduction to the organization of independent scientific work.
2. Programmes for certain subjects that may be used as a guide to independent study.
3. Programmed guides for individual studies.
4. In lectures and seminars, clear and detailed statements are given of the work it is expected will be done by independent study.

The students themselves attribute great importance to their work in study groups— these usually number 4 to 5 persons. Inquiries among students of different years of study have shown that 86% of those questioned supported the idea of doing work in study groups and, as a rule, they meet for 3 to 5 hours a week.

The success of study-group work depends to a large extent on the ability of the university teacher and tutor allocated to the student's group to organize, direct and guide the work on a particular subject. This form of collective work also provides better opportunities for the Youth Organization to take an active part in the shaping of university courses. This, in turn, will lead to closer co-operation between the teaching staff and the Free German Youth.

In order to establish criteria for planning the time available for independent study, some Sections of Humboldt University are currently making a time study of student activities. Interim results indicate that generally the time allocated to courses of instruction at the university and to independent studies should be in the ratio of 1:1 or 1:2. This is also in agreement with the wishes of students to increase the amount of time for independent study to about 60% of the total available in a course of study.

In order to achieve this aim, certain difficulties have yet to be overcome. For example, under the present conditions of accommodation at the University, students need about 30 minutes to change classes. This represents a large amount of misused time if compared with the situation at other universities in the German Democratic Republic. It also means that it is not possible for students to devote more than an average of 50 hours per week to study. At present, classroom activities still take up 28 to 30 hours a week of the total time, so that the amount remaining for independent study is too small. Changes are envisaged to provide a continuous period of several weeks free of instruction to be used for independent study.

At Humboldt University, as at all other universities and colleges of higher education, students of all levels are expected to take part in various forms of organized research work. Over the past four years the governing bodies of the university have made particular efforts to ensure that each student, within his individual course of study, should do a certain amount of research work in addition to the scientific work required for writing his diploma paper. This aim has to a large extent been achieved.

Both experience and scientific investigations have shown that the carrying out of research by students under proper guidance greatly contributes to better results in their work and in the shaping of their personalities. Thus, the main aim is not to expand the scope of research, but rather to encourage students, particularly in higher courses—the third year and later—to take an active part in organized research studies. In this context the 'integrated students' groups' existing at Humboldt University should be mentioned.

In these groups the putting together of students from the same year of study (horizontal groups) has been abandoned as far as research is concerned. New groups have been formed of students doing research work on a particular subject from low as well as high levels of courses, including first-year students. Senior students partly act as tutors to the junior students and help them to acquire the necessary knowledge, abilities and skills required to take an active part in research. New working methods for these groups are at present being developed.

There are various ways in which students may take part in solving scientific problems, such as participating in contract research, working on specific 'youth projects', attending research seminars (predominantly in the university sections for arts and social sciences), joining a students' circle, or performing minor research tasks during their periods of practical training ('practicals') in factories, schools and laboratories.

In 1971 approximately 3,500 students, 75% of whom were in their third year—the remaining 25% being students of the first or second year—were engaged in contract research, mostly in the field of natural science and medicine. Another 1,700 students worked on 35 youth projects, which were mainly concerned with the improvement of the teaching process, including rationalization of courses and test and examination methods. Since one of the aims of socialist education is the firm integration of the individual student's research work in the general teaching process, the importance of research tasks for students collectives is obvious. There are many educational advantages to be gained by taking part in joint work on scientific problems. It is of special importance for the strengthening of the ideological attitude of the students and teaches them to be responsible to their collectives; they learn how to organize their work efficiently and acquire the ability to head a collective.

The governing bodies of universities support the development of creative scientific work by students in every possible way, particularly by public recognition of and by granting awards for outstanding results. One example is the foundation in 1963 of the Fichte Prize, which has since been awarded annually to students and young scientists for outstanding results achieved by either collective or individual research[1].

Another important problem, which still requires closer investigation, is how to combine the students' research work with the teaching programmes within the framework of the curricula.

In accordance with official legislation (paragraph 73 of the Law on the Integrated Socialist Educational System; the Regulation for Vocational Orientation in Schools and the corresponding Regulation of the Minister of Higher and Technical Education) Humboldt University carries out long-term and systematic job orientation.

Up to 3 February 1971, when the new Regulation on the guidance and employment of university and college graduates *(Absolventenordnung GBl. II, p. 297)* became effective, the work done by Humboldt University in the field of orientation of graduates towards employment was to prepare students for their subsequent occupations in the final stage of their studies and to advise them on their decisions about place of work.

The University participated in arranging employment of graduates by co-operating with nation-wide co-ordinating centres for mathematics, food chemistry, Germanic languages, Slavonic languages, etc. With the help of a computer, these centres co-ordinated the number of positions offered with the number of graduates leaving the universities.

In future, the responsibility of the university for the occupational guidance and employment of graduates will increase. Preparation for the various occupations will begin at an earlier stage and later the graduate will be helped in his transition from university to practical work and with further education. The students must make use of all possibilities offered by the university and enterprises which regard their future occupation. Even at the beginning of their course, State plans providing information on central economic objectives and possibilities of employment are at their disposal.

The successful co-operation of university and industry in the preparation of employment contracts will be continued. According to paragraph 20 of the Labour Code *(Gesetzbuch der Arbeit)*, enterprises conclude employment contracts for at least three years with graduates who are in their final year at university. Conclusion of a contract is, in each case, subject to the approval of the Commission for Graduate Distribution. Discussions are also held with each student about his future place of work.

It is the duty of the Rector to implement the stipulations of both the Five-Year Plan and the annual Economic Plans which concern requirements for graduates. In this he works closely with the Free German Youth.

Members of the teaching staff and other scientific personnel arrange that students shall have systematic content with their future places of work, especially by organizing the teaching process appropriately and by selecting suitable subjects for test and examination papers (diploma paper) and Doctorate theses. In this

1. The Fichte Prize was first awarded on the occasion of the 200th anniversary of the birth of the German philosopher, J. G. Fichte, who was the first Rector of Humboldt University.

regard, special attention and support is given to female students both during their studies, in the development of their careers, in their further education and in preparing them for responsible posts.

It should be noted particularly that those Sections and special disciplines which worked out, together with representatives of industry, a clear concept of the requirements a graduate is expected to meet, proved to be the most successful in job orientation. In these cases, the conclusion of employment contracts, the distribution of graduates and their further education presented very few difficulties. This concept, however, must be clearly defined or long-term occupational orientation and employment of graduates will run into difficulties. These can be overcome by improving co-operation between university and industry.

It has been the practice for some time to arrange periods of practical work in socialist enterprises and institutions, and these have proved most useful in preparing the students for their future social and professional careers. Students become acquainted from their first year at university with the requirements of their future work in industry and society; they get to know not only the place of work and working conditions, but the prospective development of their particular field.

In the Section for Food technology, for example, the curriculum for the first year of study includes a 4-week practical in an enterprise. Groups of two or three students work together in solving definite problems. Up to the fourth year the duration of these practical periods, as well as the demands made on the students, steadily increase. The last period, which may be of more than 6 months, has the aim of providing experience in administration and management: as an assistant to top management officials, the student is able to gain experience in heading working collectives and in the joint solution of problems, and also plays a leading role in the social and political activities of the enterprise. The students usually write their diploma papers in the course of the final period of practical training. As a rule, the subject of this paper is the result of a long-term agreement between the enterprise and the respective university section, and it is chosen so as to help the student in his later work in industry.

During each period of practical work, a university teacher or a scientific assistant visits each student at least twice at his place of work. Furthermore, there are regular discussions about problems and results of the 'practical' between groups of students and university teachers at consultation centres, which are in the neighbourhood of the enterprise.

Since this practical work *(Betriebspraktikum)* helps the students test, consolidate and apply their theoretical knowledge, the university bears the main responsibility for its success. The work should be closely linked with aspects of the particular student's scientific discipline, as well as with relevant aspects of technology, economy and industrial management and, at the same time, enable the students to practise solving problems independently under working conditions. It is therefore the aim of the university to establish close co-operation with both the manager of the enterprise and with the tutor appointed by him.

During a period of practical work extending over more than 12 weeks, the students—in compliance with the Regulation for organization of practical training

(GBl. II, S. 243, 1 March 1970)—are entitled to a basic pay of 300 marks a month. In addition to this, the enterprise may pay up to 70 % of the normal starting salary for a university graduate, provided that the student's performance is adequate. The university tutor gives an evaluation of the work performance and personal development of the student during the period of practical work. He works closely with the tutor appointed by the enterprise, who is usually a university graduate. This evaluation, in addition to that of the tutor of the enterprise, is considered to be of great significance. Both university and enterprise strive jointly to achieve a high standard in these personal evaluations. The university wishes to ensure the continuous development of the student both during his studies at the university and during the periods of practical work. Of special note in this regard is the Animal Breeding Section, where university teachers and assistants act as tutors to students' groups from the beginning to the end of their study, not only at the university, but also in the enterprise. There are special conferences of tutors with a university teacher in the chair for evaluation of each period of academic training and practical work. The results of these discussions are submitted to the Director of the Section, its Council or its Commission for Education and Training, in order to decide on measures for further improvement of teaching and training.

E. Planning of classroom assignment, timetables and the production of textbooks and teaching aids

Humboldt University uses electronic data processing (EDP) for classroom assignment and time-tabling, which greatly facilitates the administrative work of the Rector and the Section Directors. The following work has already been carried out in this connection

1. A comprehensive and detailed survey has been made of the total teaching load within the university; the interconnections between the teaching activities of individual Sections; the number and type of parallel activities of similar character the teaching load of each Section; the study load of each seminar group; and the teaching load of each teacher.
2. Basic data for teaching and time-load analyses and for measures to rationalize the teaching and training processes have been assembled.
3. The maintenance of a constant classroom and time reserve for better continuity of social and political work has been assured.
4. Exact information has been gathered on the total use of available rooms in the University as a whole, as well as on the assignment and utilization of each individual classroom, and a survey was made of actual room reserves or room shortages specifying the room types.
5. Exact data have been assembled for planning the admission quota for intramural and extramural studies; investments and equipment; reconstruction work; and teaching time and room reservoir, sub-divided as per section, student enrolment year, and student group.
6. Exact information was collected on the structure and size of teaching groups

(Unterrichtsgruppen) in each Section and on seminar and teaching group structure in the university as a whole.

Given the rapidly increasing number of students, and an unchanged number of available classrooms, it was considered that EDP would be the most expedient method for room assignment and time-tabling. The situation can be seen in table 8.

TABLE 8.   Number of teaching activities (lectures, seminars, classes) for the period 1970-72

	Number of weekly teaching activities per term	Net increase	Percentage increase
Autumn term 1970/71	3 000	—	—
Spring term 1971	3 454	454	15
Autumn term 1971/72	3 932	932	31

It will be seen that even though the number of classrooms remained static, space for an additional 932 courses had to be provided in the autumn term 1971/72. (These figures do not include courses of the Foreign Language Section, amounting to about 1,000 per term.) The principal cause of this remarkable increase in the number of teaching activities was the expansion of admissions to intramural and extramural studies in the enrolment period 1971-72, amounting to a net increase of 1,458 students.

Table 9 gives two examples of the time load recently attained in room assignment. In evaluating these figures it should be borne in mind that the maximum admissible time load is approximately 58 hours per week.

TABLE 9.   Time load per room, autumn term 1971/72

Time load per room in hours per week	Room complex A: number of rooms	Room complex B: number of rooms
66 — 63	6	
62 — 60	17	
61		1
59		1
up to 59	47	
up to 56		44
Number of assignable rooms	70	46

In one planning period, about 5,000 teaching activities (including foreign language classes), 2,000 instructors and lecturers, 1,000 seminar groups, and 500 classrooms have to be co-ordinated in such a way that each teaching activity is given its place in the timetable without overlapping any others. EDP is, for this immense planning task, indispensable.

The aim of using EDP is to work out such timetables for students and teaching staff, given the constraints of the actual room reservoir, as will:

1. Provide connected periods of instruction and thus connected periods of individual study for the students.
2. Ensure a continuous and well-balanced teaching load for the teaching staff.
3. Avoid, as far as possible, unassigned hours between classes, i.e. unproductive periods for students and teachers.
4. Provide sufficient time for the social and political activities of students and teachers.
5. Avoid loss of time through frequent unnecessary moving to places of instruction at a distance.

All these will contribute to effective teaching and training. Therefore, EDP room assignment and time-tabling should meet the following requirements:

1. Optimum utilization of the time reservoir of all university classrooms available; the periods to be used for teaching activities are as follows:

Monday	7.00 a.m. — 4.00 p.m.
Tuesday through Friday	7.00 a.m. — 7.00 p.m.
Saturday	7.00 a.m. — 1.00 p.m.

2. The size of the room assigned to a class should correspond to the number of participants; in other words, large rooms should not be occupied by small groups of students, which would result in waste of room capacity.
3. Continuous and connected instruction periods per seminar group and day, classes and teaching load being limited to a maximum of 6 hours per day.
4. Assignment of classrooms in a certain order of precedence; for this purpose teaching activities are ranked according to their importance, type (lecture, seminar, class), and the number of students participating.
5. At least one hour per day should be guaranteed for lunch,
   (i) for all student groups, between 11.00 a.m. and 2.00 p.m.
   (ii) for all teachers, from 12.00 to 2.00 p.m.
6. Assignment of hours to teachers in accordance with their own requests to the greatest possible extent. An effort is made to meet reasonable individual demands for specific hours and rooms, in other words, precautions are taken that invalid colleagues, teachers with young children, and those having to travel a long way to work, etc., are assigned classes at certain hours, in accordance with their own requests. In addition, it is possible in certain justified cases (and in general for all leading staff of the Sections) to 'set' their classes, that is to say that rooms and hours are assigned to them as required.
7. Provision of a sufficient time reserve for social and political activities (all university classrooms are made available for such activities on Mondays after 4.00 p.m. and on other days only if not used for teaching purposes).

It was not unfortunately possible to satisfy all demands in full for room assignment and time-tabling this term.

The use of EDP for this work involves the development of new methods. In order to ensure use of the remaining room reserves, for example, it is necessary to evolve a central plan on a uniform basis for the University as a whole, which in turn requires clarity of concept and continuity and exactness in the curriculum planning of Sections. Lastly, it is necessary to a certain extent to subordinate the specific interests and wishes of individual Sections to the common aims and objectives of all Sections and, indeed, of the University as a whole.

In order to ensure better utilization of the technical teaching and learning aids which are available and so improve the efficiency of teaching and training, an operational plan based on an analysis of all rooms used for teaching was elaborated. This analysis covered those rooms having or requiring little or no special equipment, such as lecture halls and seminar rooms. Laboratories and related types of rooms were not included. The following data were collected: seating capacity, present installation of technical teaching and learning aids, state of repair, conditions for the installation of equipment—window shades, dimmer control, projection screens or surfaces, power outlets—and blackboard surface. An inventory of technical teaching and learning aids in the various departments was made. By checking the equipment available in the departments against the number of teaching rooms to be equipped and the demands forwarded by the departments, it was found that it would be immediately possible to supply 70% of all rooms with the necessary equipment by transferring the existing available aids, particularly into the large lecture halls. This measure is already enabling a larger number of departments to use audio-visual teaching and learning aids this term and to make teaching more instructive and effective. According to the specific requirements established for lecture halls and seminar rooms, the basic inventory includes: slide projector, tape recorder, cassette projector, sound film projector and daylight overhead projector.

Equipment in excess of the basic inventory must be ordered from the Department of Teaching Methods and Study Rationalization in the Directorate for Education and Training *(Direktorat für Erziehung und Ausbildung)*. The transfer of existing technical teaching aids and the further installation of new equipment will take place in scheduled stages for different teaching room categories, according to seating capacity, and will be completed by 1975. In the first stage, teaching aids available in the departments will be transferred into rooms with a capacity of over 100 seats. In the following two stages the remaining rooms will be equipped, and older installations will be replaced by more efficient equipment capable of being linked together. To ensure that continuous use of stationary technical teaching and learning aids is possible, maintenance and repair services will be improved.

In this connection, a further study is being prepared on the efficient use of available facilities for the production of information media. These include prepared foils for writing projectors (including all folding foils); slides; films: 16 mm films (the majority with sound, and in colour), 8 mm films (usually film loops in cassettes), 35 mm films (sound films); tapes; and television recordings. These information media are partly prepared by members of the staff for use in their teaching activities and are continuously being developed. A high proportion of the total information media available is produced at the university centre for educational films *(Hochschulfilm- und bildstelle)* of Humboldt University, but an increasingly important role in the development of such media is being taken by the German Institute for Audio-Visual Teaching Aids *(Deutsches Institut für Film, Bild und Ton)*. On behalf of the Ministry of Higher and Technical Education this Institute, assisted by experts or groups of experts, is responsible for planning the production of audio-visual aids in universities and other institutions. The Institute itself actually produces only a limited amount.

In order to help students reach the goals laid down in their syllabuses, all teaching and learning aids are made available to full-time students free of charge. This applies to technical teaching and learning aids such as different types of projectors, language laboratories, laboratories with special equipment, the audio-visual centre, the pedagogical laboratory, as well as accommodation for independent study, printed material such as literature (libraries), textbooks, programmed courses, compendia, chemicals, and special equipment for specialized studies.

Students at the beginning of their courses or at some particular part of a course are told about the institutions where information may be obtained and the working materials which are necessary. Textbooks are available at moderate prices, since publishing is subsidized by the Government.

Problems of the aims and content of teaching and learning aids, and other questions connected with the evaluation and propagation of teaching experience gained in university education, are dealt with by the Department of Teaching Methods and Study Rationalization. The members of this department work under the Director of Education and Training, and are at the same time members of the various working groups of the Scientific-Methodological Committee attached to the Senate of the Scientific Council (see Part II, above). The Department endeavours to co-ordinate work in the fields of study rationalization and intensification, in particular the development, testing and general introduction of new and effective teaching methods and teaching material. It organizes co-operation between the Working Groups for Study Rationalization which exist in all Sections, and whose chairmen are also members of the Scientific-Methodological Committee.

The function, duties and working methods of the University Library of Humboldt University were re-organized, as in all other universities in this country, in 1969. At this time all the various libraries and documentary centres were united in one library under the direct control of the Rector. Its duties are to collect, evaluate and make accessible to university members scientific literature for teaching and research, for information and documentation work, and for further education. In addition, being a part of the library and information system of the whole country, it serves all citizens of the German Democratic Republic.

The University Library is sub-divided into the central library and the subsidiaries, which are the libraries in the Sections and other institutions of Humboldt University. The Director of the University Library is assisted by the Library and Information Council, which consists of the library commissioners of the Sections and student representatives. By keeping close contact with the University Library, the library commissioners ensure the necessary supply of special literature required for the teaching and research purposes of their respective Sections and for other library services. The University Library has frequently supplied from 20 to 50 copies of one textbook when required by the Sections. Books are lent out for periods of up to one year. The Section libraries also provide students with literature that is not easily accessible, lending them textbooks in larger numbers and for longer periods.

Central administration and co-ordination of library work has increased the efficiency of the University Library. The staffs of the central library and the subsidiaries endeavour to increase efficiency further by organizing introductory sessions for students. Lectures are held on subjects such as working with books, using the library, dealing with scientific literature, keeping card files and using information facilities.

TABLE 10. Use of the University Library

	1970	1971
Users (total)	15 094	16 649
Users belonging to universities and colleges	12 836	13 198
Students	*8 790*	*6 970*
University teachers, scientific personnel	*4 046*	*3 528*
Other users	2 258	3 451

NOTE Readers of Section libraries have not been included in this survey.

A great many students frequent the public libraries: the German State Library *(Deutsche Staatsbibliothek)*, the City-Library of Berlin *(Berliner Stadt-bibliothek)* and the Library of the Trade Unions *(Bibliothek der Gewerkschaften)*, since these are particularly well equipped.

F. Planning of the teaching process

The teaching process is planned by the Rector, assisted by the Director for Education and Training. It is the duty of the Director to analyse the basic problems which occur in the teaching process and to submit draft proposals in order to help the Rector in decision-making. He has the right to issue orders and instructions on behalf of the Rector to the Directors of the various Sections and to check on their work. To this end, he periodically summons the Deputy Directors for Education and Training of the various Sections for discussions of problems involved in planning and operating the teaching process. His duties comprise:
(a) planning and operating the teaching process on the basis of the approved syllabuses;
(b) organization of students' competitions and encouragement of particularly talented students, in close co-operation with the Free German Youth;
(c) guaranteeing high standards and the effectiveness of the teaching process;

(d) organizing studies efficiently;

(e) giving career advice for prospective students, arranging admission of students, and providing jobs for graduates;

(f) awarding of scholarships;

(g) organization of research studies;

(h) care and supervision of students at students' hostels.

The Deputy Director for Education and Training of a particular Section is responsible for planning and operating the teaching process of all the basic and special disciplines taught in the Section and is accountable to the Director of that Section. Therefore, his duties at Section level correspond closely to those of the Director for Education and Training at university level. The Deputy Director is assisted in his work by the Commission for Education and Training of the heads of the various divisions, the tutors of students' groups, and representatives of the Youth Organization.

This co-operation in the organization of studies clearly shows the new relations between lecturers and students in socialist society, and the fact that the student is no longer simply an object of training but plays an active part in organizing his own education and development. The student has all the rights and duties of a citizen and this determines the relations between the teacher and himself. Studies can be successful only if lecturers and students co-operate closely in mutual respect and confidence. This does not reduce the responsibility of the teaching staff for the educational process but puts it on a higher level.

However, it is not sufficient just to give the student a say in university affairs; appropriate rights and duties must be given to all those engaged in scientific work and university studies. An example of this is the scientific projects assigned to the Youth Organization. The projects outlined by the governing bodies are assigned to groups of students after consultations with the Youth Organization, and are chosen with the aim of actively involving students in the implementation of approved syllabuses.

In 1970, Humboldt University placed 28 such projects in the care of students. They were, in the main, priority projects concerned with changing content and methods of education, rationalization drives, and examinations. 2,270 full-time students—approximately 20% of the student body—were involved in youth projects *(Jugendobjekte)* and the results achieved by them were checked at Section or university level. After being approved by the University Administration and the Executive of the Youth Organization, they were incorporated in the plan of studies. For example, since 1969 in the Physics Section 248 students have actively co-operated in collecting data about the actual process of studies. Data covered both the contents and the timing of the process of studies and enabled quantitative and qualitative conclusions to be drawn which contributed to improving existing syllabuses.

Youth projects also provide a means for the further development of education and self-education in the various students' groups. The degree of maturity of the Free German Youth groups exercises a most important influence on study discipline and the attitude of the students and helps towards their successful graduation.

Twice a year the Executive of the Free German Youth and the teaching staff assess the progress made by students.

Detailed planning of teaching activity

On the basis of teaching material available the heads of divisions plan the teaching process for the different study years of their respective basic and special disciplines. In doing so, they take into account the specific conditions prevailing in the Section, for example the qualifications and pedagogical training of the teaching staff in the various subjects, the degree of maturity of the students, and economic conditions. Following this they collectively draw up the teaching programme for the lecturers in which they are assisted by the Free German Youth. The lecturer takes the responsibility for planning in detail intermediate objectives, subject matter and methods to be applied in the lectures and seminars stipulated in the teaching programme. Here, it is important to determine the sequence of events, measures and organization forms of the studies. Three basic principles must be observed:

1. The organizational and structural methods and their sequence must be comprehensively planned and carried out, taking account of the aim, contents and didactic functions (motivation of aim, introduction transmission, revision and inculcation, application and control) to ensure all-round personality development during studies. All organizational structures must fully integrate such complex units as lectures, tutorials[1], seminars[2], independent studies, practical work both on and off University premises.
2. The structure of the organization of studies must aim at increasing the independent work of the students.
3. The proportion of private studies must be greater than the total number of lessons.

For two years research has been undertaken at the University to establish indices for the distribution of the total number of study hours into instruction and private studies (see section D above) and to determine the proportions of lectures to seminars/tutorials. These investigations started from the premise that the objective of the studies is decisive for the choice of organizational methods and measures. Only when the sequence of steps has been determined from the point of view of the aim to be achieved can questions concerning the proportion of lectures to seminars or tutorials be tackled. Drawing on current studies, a ratio of 1:1.5 can be regarded as an index. This would mean the following distribution for the Physics Section:

1. Tutorials at seminar group level are mainly aimed at encouraging the student to cope purposefully and independently with his subject, on the basis of experience already gained, while employing an appropriate and specific approach (e.g. laboratory work).
2. It is the over-riding purpose of the seminar to harmonize individual conclusions and insights by way of synthesis with the overall system of learning. The active participation of students has a vital bearing on the methods applied throughout the seminar.

20% lectures
25% seminars/tutorials
55% independent studies *(Selbststudium)*
The current practice in this Section is:
35% lectures
25% seminars/tutorials
40% independent studies
and clearly reveals some problems in this respect.

G. Methods of evaluating teaching activities

Teaching is considered to be successful if it helps to produce socialist graduates, well-qualified in their subjects and familiar with all the vital issues which affect them. Successful teaching is also evident when graduates give a good account of themselves in the various spheres of socialist production. It may be gauged by the following general yardsticks: high scientific level of content based on successful research work consistent with social and scientific requirements; application of efficient and meaningful teaching methods; participation in the administration and planning of educational work; and practical application of the principle of socialist collective work. The teaching activities in all Sections of the University are subjected to a critical analysis by the Council at the time when an account of the University's performance in fulfilling its plan is given to the governing bodies.

In the Sections also teaching activity is appraised in public by the Director of the Section. As a rule, the work and teaching abilities of every lecturer and scientific assistant are assessed every two years. If the work has been carried out well, he or she can be promoted to the following grade within a statutory sliding scale of remuneration. Outstanding work in teaching and education is acknowledged and encouraged by the awarding of Government distinctions and distinctions given by social organizations such as the Free German Youth. Financial incentives also play a part since the Rector may pay bonuses out of a special fund set up to show appreciation of excellent work done in training and education. Taking the analyses of the Free German Youth as a base, the governing bodies, the Socialist Unity Party and the Trade Unions co-operate closely in order to arrive at a just decision for the award distinctions.

It has been a useful practice for lecturers to sit in on their colleagues' lectures and to evaluate them jointly. This is done, for instance, in the Sections of Philosophy and Chemistry. In this way efficient teaching methods are made known and are used on a wider scale more quickly, thus increasing the general efficiency of teaching.

The effect of teaching is reflected in students' achievements, which in turn are reflected in examination results. There are oral and written examinations at the end of each study year and at the close of a course of studies. Very often in these examinations the results of mid-term proficiency tests such as test certificates, short talks, and written papers, which are sometimes part of the lectures, are taken into consideration. In the Medical School, for example, attempts are being made to programme proficiency tests partly by audio-visual means. In some cases the results of such tests are evaluated by means of electronic data-processing.

The ability of students to apply scientific knowledge is of increasing significance. Therefore, the guidance university teachers and their scientific staff give the students in this work must be considered of great importance when quality of teaching is assessed. In this, representatives of the enterprises and institutions where students are doing practical work take part.

The governing bodies of the university and the various Sections continuously seek to analyse the attainments of the teaching staff as reflected in the achievements of students and the development of students' personalities and to draw the conclusions necessary for further improving the quality and effectiveness of studies. At the close of each year of study an analysis is made and the results are taken into account in the preparation of the following year's programme of study. These analyses are made by all universities and colleges of the German Democratic Republic on the basis of a limited number of questions which are reviewed and generalized by the Ministry of Higher and Technical Education to give results for the whole system of higher education in the German Democratic Republic.

Conclusions

The University is concentrating on further improving the standards and efficiency of education, in accordance with the recommendations of the Eighth Congress of the Socialist Unity Party of the German Democratic Republic. The improvement of standards and efficiency may be assessed by comparing total social effort and the benefits derived from it by society as a whole. One of the benefits can be seen in the standards attained by graduates in practical life as well as in their study performance and behaviour. From a quantitative viewpoint, it can be seen in the ratios of university graduates to skilled workers and graduates from technical colleges applied to society as a whole as well as to the various branches of national economy, science and culture.

A complex of interlinked factors is involved in the improvement of the standards and efficiency of studies. In the years to come the University will give its attention to the following factors (these being within the scope of this case study): planning and organization of studies, didactic and methodical elaboration of studies and improving the qualifications of the teaching staff.

The main tasks to be accomplished in the sphere of planning of studies are: further elaboration of qualitative and quantitative indices for university graduates to serve as a pre-requisite for planning the teaching objectives as well as the proper selection of subject matter best suited to achieve these objectives. A major concern of the organization of studies is to secure a more continuous course of studies by the provision and application of central regulations to a variety of institutional conditions.

With regard to the elaboration of didactics and methods, the University will concentrate its efforts on the effective integration of those forms and methods of teaching that have proved successful for many years with new forms, methods, working and teaching aids, trying at the same time to establish an optimum combination for longer teaching periods—several weeks at a time. With regard to improving the qualifications of the teaching staff, the major tasks are to intensify the continuous exchange of pedagogical experience (including publications), to arrange guest courses by experienced members of the teaching profession, to demonstrate new teaching methods as well as teaching aids, to conduct courses for improving the pedagogical qualifications of the teaching staff, and to further develop research in the field of university-level pedagogics.

In attempting to fulfil these tasks, the University can firmly rely on the continued efforts of the teaching staff and students to improve study courses so as to meet the growing social demand for higher standards and efficiency.

Structure of the centralised socialist education system

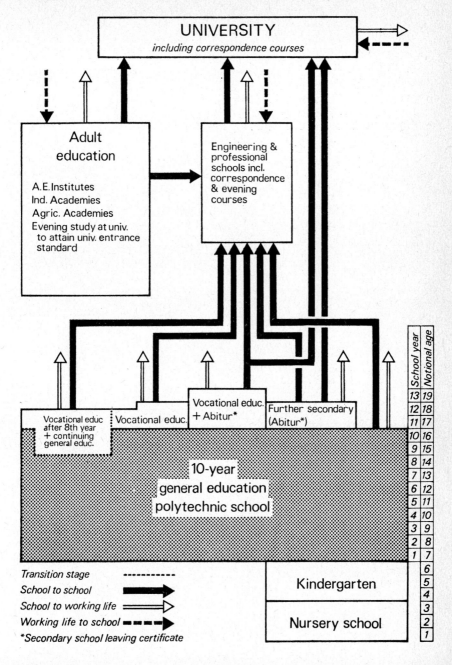

APPENDIX II

Structure and management of a university

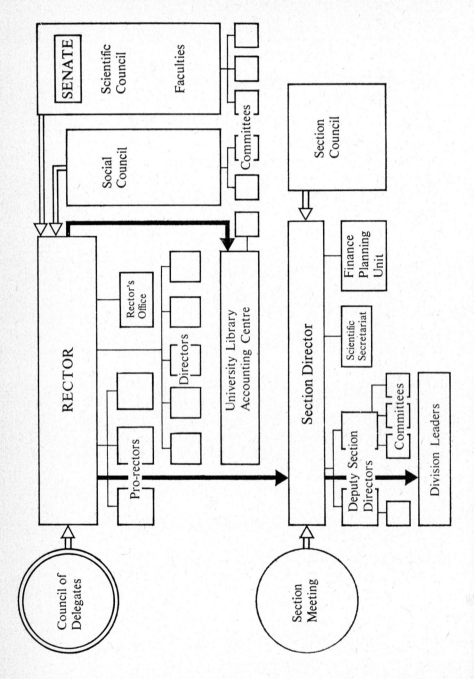

102

State University of New York at Buffalo: case study of teaching and research

Taher A. Razik
assisted by a group of research associates and assistants

Contents

Preface 105

Methodology 106

I. Background
   A. The Country, State and Community 107
   B. New York State and the University: a discussion of the 1962 merger and
      the inter-institutional relationship 109
   C. Levels of decision-making and planning between the State and SUNYAB 113

II. Teaching
   Introduction 120
   A. Administrative and academic organization of SUNYAB 121
   B. Types of educational programmes offered 134
   C. The teaching staff at SUNYAB 137
   D. Students at SUNYAB 147
   E. Space utilisation 155
   F. Information and Library resources and auxiliary academic units . . 161
   G. The budget system 168
   H. Evaluation: an objective overview 182

III. Research
   A. The research environment 188
   B. Research organization: the research proposal selection process . . . 195
   C. Research resource funds management 197
   D. Research facilities 203
   E. The students' rôle in research 206

Final comments 207

Glossary of terms 210

Preface

by Robert L. Ketter
President, State University of New York at Buffalo

Particular problems associated with the planning and management of different institutions of higher education can more or less dispassionately be observed, compared and analysed. Solutions to those problems, however, evolve from a consideration of the 'real world' alternatives which are unique to a particular institution. The State University of New York at Buffalo has and continues to have problems similar to those at many other institutions: increasing enrolments, lack of space, constraining finances, and the need to anticipate and serve the constantly changing demands of society. Although this case study describes concerns in the context of this specific University at this particular time, it does not maintain that they are necessarily applicable or desirable in the differing environments of other institutions or times. Nevertheless, it is our sincere hope that the study will suggest alternatives which other universities can consider as they view the mechanisms we used in analysing our problems, the processes we employed in coping with them, and the measures we took to anticipate future problems.

During the past ten years the State University of New York at Buffalo has passed through a transition unparallelled in its 126-year history as an institution of higher learning. Formerly a private University, it joined the State University of New York system of two- and four-year colleges and university centres in 1962. The rapid growth of the institution since that time reflects the conscious planning of many persons who have sought to further this institution's goal of becoming a pre-eminent university centre.

The former University of Buffalo, as a private institution, responded primarily to the needs of the immediate community. The merger with the state system broadened and significantly altered this mission. We now respond not just to the needs of the immediate community and the State of New York, but indeed recognize our national and international obligations.

Methodology

This case study, conducted for the International Institute for Educational Planning, details the planning, development, and management procedures routinely applied by the State University of New York at Buffalo (SUNYAB).

This study is divided into two major segments, teaching and research. In order to fully describe the scope of the planning and management aspects of these prime educational functions, data were collected from a number of sources. Personal interviews were conducted with approximately 64 people in key operational positions with either the State University central administration in Albany, or locally, at SUNYAB. This was followed by the distribution of a questionnaire investigating the teaching, research, planning, and management methods of 85 University departments. Finally, the most important documents issued by SUNYAB during the past 15 years were collected and studied.

This case study is designed to be descriptive in order to insure objectivity. Noticeable trends are acknowledged, and their implications are discussed in the final comments.

Greatest emphasis is placed upon the period following the incorporation with the State University system, as these findings are more current and deal with a far larger institution than the formerly private University of Buffalo.

The components of teaching and research

The functions of teaching and research are determined by the academic, financial and physical plant university sub-systems as analysed together with the inter-active processes of decision-making/participation, information, and human-flow. It is necessary to understand the inter-relationships of these sub-system elements and inter-active processes when defining the scope and limitations of SUNYAB's planning and managerial mechanisms.

I. Background

A. The Country, State, and community

The former role of the university as a somewhat isolated repository of knowledge available to a relatively élite few is changing as the result of pressures from many sectors of society. A university education is now considered to be more of a right than a privilege. The current view is that any student with ability and ambition should be provided with the opportunity to avail himself of a university education. However, due to cost and entrance requirements, the majority of those enrolled still come from the upper and middle classes. Nevertheless, education in the United States is considered a dynamic force which is largely accountable for societal improvement and preservation. As such, a college education today is felt to be a necessity, while only a few years ago a high school education was considered sufficient.

To this end, universities have attempted to establish skill-developing programmes for disadvantaged students, adopt more flexible admission policies, and revitalise curricula in order to prepare the students to fill many kinds of rôles in a rapidly changing society. Attempts have also been made to evolve a programme which not only facilitates a transfer of past knowledge but prepares the university student for a dynamic, evolving society.

Free and compulsory tax-supported elementary and secondary education has been historically provided throughout the United States. Higher education, however, is not universally available, although many states have constitutionalised an open admissions policy for all high school graduates desiring it. In recent years this provision has been tempered by a lack of facilities and funds. Each state is constitutionally responsible for its higher education but has delegated the power in large measure to localities.

The higher education structure in the United States is supported by public taxes, tuition (or fee charges), endowments, grants from individuals, industry, the Federal Government, churches, and foundations. There are approximately 2,525 institutions of higher education in the United States, of which 1,060 are publicly and 1,465 privately supported.

In New York State the University of the State of New York, established in

1789, controls both private and public education at all levels. The State University system typifies the form of public higher education in many states.

Structure and organization of higher education

The agency in the United States which most closely resembles a centralised education authority is the United States Office of Education, in the Department of Health, Education and Welfare. Essentially, the Office of Education serves as a clearing-house for educational information as a basis for understanding the country's overall educational problems. This Office also administers certain programmes authorised and funded by Congress. It is only at this point that the Federal Government has an opportunity to determine the direction of higher education.

Statistics show that in the autumn of 1969 5,8 million students were enrolled in public and 2,1 million in private institutions of post-secondary education. All these institutions are under the jurisdiction of their respective states.

The administrative structure of all education in New York State is headed by the Board of Regents of the University of the State of New York, consisting of 15 members appointed by the state legislature. The Board of Regents is the governing body for 64 four-year institutions and 165 two-year institutions of higher education, both public and private. Sub-administrative categories directly or indirectly responsible to the Board of Regents are presented in Part II, Section A.

The community and the University

The eight counties comprising Western New York are populated by nearly two million people. The Buffalo metropolitan area (Erie and Niagara Counties) accounts for approximately one and one-half million of these, of whom some 450,000 live within the Buffalo city limits.

Buffalo, the commercial centre of the area, ranks 30th in size in the nation. The area supports over 2,000 manufacturing companies. Similarly, Buffalo harbour ranks as a major distribution centre, located within 500 miles of ten of the eleven major U.S. industrial centres.

Currently, area public and private schools number over 320, from nursery to high-school levels, special education, and 17 public and private colleges and institutes. There are now 18 hospitals and medical centres, six of which are affiliated to the University. The city supports over 57 public and private social agencies. The Buffalo-Niagara Frontier area can be considered typical of any large American metropolitan area.

The State University of New York at Buffalo (SUNYAB) is the largest of the four State University of New York (SUNY) Centres, enrolling 24,635 in the autumn of 1970.

B. New York State and the University: a discussion of the 1962 merger and the interinstitutional relationship

The University at Buffalo is part of a very complex educational system operated by the State of New York. The University's relationship to this system was drastically altered as a result of the merger of 1962.

The New York State educational system

The American Federal Constitution contains no legal provisions for establishing or maintaining public education. The organization and administration of education, therefore, is legally reserved as a function of each of the 50 states. At the highest level the New York State educational system is run by a super-coordinating body that formulates and administers official educational policies. This body is called the 'University of the State of New York' (see Figure 1). It is not a university in the usual sense of the word, but rather a legal unit under which all institutions of higher education, as well as elementary and secondary schools, both public and private, have been incorporated. Included are other public educational institutions such as public libraries, museums, educational organizations and agencies. The University of the State of New York is governed by the Board of Regents made up of private individuals elected by the Legislature.

In higher education the Regents' functions are limited to receiving, critically reviewing, recommending and approving long-range master plans describing development, problems and expectations submitted every four years by the member institutions. These plans are then presented to the State Legislature and the Governor for approval, whereupon they become effective as law.

Next in the hierarchy of the New York educational system, and still under general supervision of the Regents, is the 'State University of New York' (SUNY), similar in name to, but very distinct in character from, the 'University of the State of New York'. It is this 'State University' that is the direct concern of this chapter. Created by an act of the Legislature in 1948, the State University of New York is governed by a Board of Trustees which is appointed by the Governor and then confirmed by the State Senate. Its chief official is a Chancellor, who is appointed by the Board of Trustees and approved by the Governor.

The State University System is under the jurisdiction of the State of New York and is created by and subject to the laws of the Legislature. Fiscal operations are controlled by the Executive Office of the Governor, the Legislative Committees and the Legislature.

The relationship of the former University of Buffalo to the State prior to 1962 was simply as a private, incorporated, institution belonging to the 'University of the State of New York' (see Figure 1). It was affected by the Board of Regents only in matters of accreditation.

As a result of the merger, the University of Buffalo, thereafter designated the 'State University of New York at Buffalo' (SUNYAB), became absorbed and

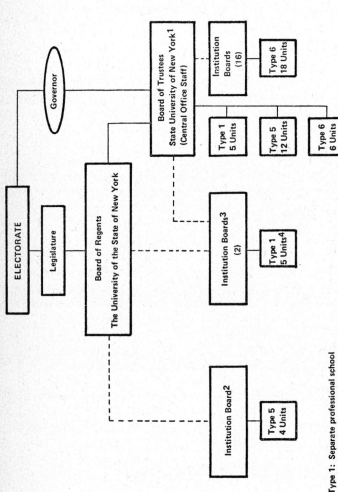

Type 1: Separate professional school
Type 5: 4-year (or more) college
Type 6: 2-year college

1 Governor appoints members but the board is supervised by Board of Regents, the University of the State of New York.
2 This is the Board of Higher Education of the City of New York, which governs four municipally controlled colleges comprising the College of the City of New York. It also governs three junior colleges shown in the 18 units under the Board of Trustees, State University of New York.
3 Privately controlled university boards. The Board of Trustees, State University of New York, is responsible for that portion of the budget of each of these two institution boards which deals with the contract colleges, since these colleges obtain State funds.
4 Four contract colleges are institutional units of Cornell University, a land-grant institution.

FIGURE 1. *Organization of New York State higher education system.*

affiliated as one of four graduate and professional centres of a centrally administered state system of higher education.

The philosophy of the State planners had been to avoid what they called the
'flagship concept' of university development, i.e., one major campus with a number
of satellite campuses; instead they intended to provide the conditions that would
develop a balanced parallel growth within each type of member campus with no
'star' institution.

*The ways in which the merger affected
the functioning of the University*

Financial planning and management
As a private institution the University of Buffalo was easy to operate. The academic community would set up the budget according to their needs and the
Business Office would provide, within the limits of available funds, the services
and operations required to meet those needs. Income from student tuition and
fees accounted for 80% of the University's support and the endowment fund and
gifts contributed the rest. These sources enabled the University to 'get along',
but it could never be a first-rate university without some new source of funds.

For many years the Office for Business Affairs had been run in a simple and
comparatively casual fashion. It was not organized as a modern business office
until a Vice-chancellor of Business Affairs was appointed in the mid-1950s, when
the different departments of purchasing, accounting, personnel and bursar were
created.

From 1962 to 1970 a critical shortage of money was no longer a significant
item in the University's endeavour to meet its goals. Its improved financial position enabled it to add substantially to its staff by placing its salary range in competition with major universities in the country. (See Part II, Section G). The
University, however, was not without problems, for it did suffer the early frustra-
tions of having to learn the intricacies of operating through the State Department
of the Budget. Purchasing difficulties produced serious interruptions in research
activity and some truly critical delays in the initiation of needed improvements.

Academic planning
With the merger, the size of departments increased which, in turn, fostered differentiation; e.g., geology from geography, linguistics from anthropology, political
science from history. Each department in the former College of Arts and Sciences
developed at a rapid pace. Practically every department became engaged in programmes of research. Three new schools were established: Health-Related Professions (1965), a graduate-level School of Information and Library Science (1966),
and a School of Architecture and Environmental Design (1968).

One of the original suggestions for coping with the needs of space limitations
and increased enrolment was the revision of the academic structure itself; towards
the end of the 60s the development of a system of seven newly-organized academic
Faculties was initiated, along with a system of separate colleges within the Uni-

versity to be essentially independent from the 'Faculties'[1] Thus, disciplines were shaped into clusters, and the theoretical combined with the applied. The new Faculties of Arts and Letters, Social Sciences and Administration, and Natural Sciences and Mathematics were carved largely out of the former College of Arts and Sciences. The Social Sciences Faculty also includes the former Schools of Social Welfare and Business Administration,[2] while Arts and Letters has taken over administrative responsibility for the new School of Architecture and Environmental Design. The Law and Jurisprudence Faculty now incorporates both the professional School of Law and undergraduate jurisprudence studies. The Faculty of Engineering and Applied Sciences has combined the School of Engineering and the School of Information and Library Sciences, while the Educational Studies Faculty is responsible for the undergraduate and graduate programmes of the former School of Education. Similarly, the Health Sciences faculty now administers the Schools of Medicine, Nursing, Dentistry, Health-Related Professions and Pharmacy as well as the academic and research-oriented programmes of the basic science departments.

To remove barriers between disciplines and to build bridges among Faculties, administrative Divisions for all undergraduate and graduate level degree-granting programmes were formed, drawing upon all Faculties for their instructional programmes. The previously mentioned College System also serves this end.

The reorganization has been paralleled by an equally drastic change in both undergraduate student and faculty governance and character; both adopted forms of governance by the 'whole', with each person of faculty rank a voting member of the Senate at large and every member of the undergraduate student body a voting member of the Polity.[3]

An important factor during this period was increased student activism, which developed particularly in terms of demands for greater self-determination and an increasing rôle in the University decision-making process. Consequently, SUNYAB began to divest itself of its *in loco parentis* responsibilities which had been an established principle in America since the origins of higher education.

SUNYAB has survived the changes that were reshaping its future as an institution of higher learning. However, from 1969 to 1971 various campus indicators signalled that the time had come for a slower pace. It was felt by some that SUNYAB was suffering from 'change fatigue'.

1. See Glossary, p. 210.
2. Effective September 1972, the School of Management (formerly the School of Business Administration) became an independent unit.
3. Recently changed to a 'representative' senate both in the Faculty and Student Governance bodies; the 'town meeting' proved unwieldy.

C. Levels of decision-making and planning between the State and SUNYAB

Levels of decision-making[1]

Since the State University of New York is organized as a system of campuses under a single Board of Trustees there are presumably advantages to be gained from co-ordination. Such co-ordination, it is normally expected, improves planning, promotes economy in the use of material and human resources, and enhances response to public need.

Campus type and purpose

The basic nature and purpose of each campus is determined centrally, i.e., by SUNY and not by the local institution. Whether an institution is to be a university centre, a college of arts and science, a two-year agricultural and technical college, or a specialised campus such as the College of Forestry in Syracuse is a matter for Trustee decision. No campus can unilaterally change its nature or purpose. In the case of SUNYAB, it was originally made part of the State system on the basis of needs determined by the Trustees of the State University of New York.

Programmes to achieve purpose

The academic programmes by means of which a campus carries out its purposes are determined locally in most cases, but centrally in certain others. The basis for the distinction is fairly clear.

The areas of local decision include those broad programme areas which are generally considered to represent the basic components of the particular type of campus in question. For example, it is to be expected that each of the four university centres will offer a broad range of degree programmes in the arts and sciences, from bachelor's to doctoral degrees.

The SUNY central administration's responsibility extends here only to identify the *procedures* which a campus shall follow in initiating such degree programmes, and not to question *whether or not* it will offer them. In such cases, it might be said, the internal argument alone is sufficient justification for the programme: the University centre needs to be free to offer these programmes simply because it is a university centre.

Central decision is required, however, in the establishment of more specialised programmes such as professional degree offerings at the university centres or colleges of arts and sciences, and such as arts and science offerings at the agricultural and technical or specialised colleges.[2] The establishment of a professional

1. Adapted from a paper presented by Harry W. Porter at the February 1968 meeting of State University Presidents, "The locus of decision-making in academic affairs in State University of New York."
2. Until recently there has been a moratorium on new programmes as well as an evaluation of on-going programmes.

school, in fact, requires Trustee action. In some instances, problems such as professional categorisation as in fine arts or sheer expense as in nuclear equipment may demand central decisions.

Curricula, instruction, and research
Matters of curricula, instruction, and research within the basic programmes offered by the State University campuses are almost completely a local responsibility. As suggested above, there are review procedures for certain types of new degree programmes, but these involve the professional judgments of specialised scholars more than central administrative review.

Library support for specialised, advanced programmes presents a problem. While the State University must develop appropriate depth of holdings to support its offerings on each campus, it seems obvious that the campuses should not compete among themselves for rare and highly specialised research collections, and thus, require some central supervision.

Arrangements for study abroad and the location of certain area studies programmes involve central supervision and decision. These controls, it should be noted, are quite separate from the questions of academic content and credit for study abroad programmes which remain matters of local determination, subject only to co-ordination and general review by the central staff in order that there be as much university-wide sharing of opportunity as is feasible.

The establishment of research centres, institutes, etc., follows prescribed procedures including approval by the Chancellor of the State University. Fiscal management of research is a central responsibility accomplished through the Research Foundation (See Part III, Section C).

Faculty affairs
In what might be termed faculty affairs, salary schedules, basic procedures for appointment, re-appointment, tenure, promotion, and dismissal, and other general faculty personnel rules, decisions are determined by State University Trustee policy. Appointments of administrative staff at salaries above $18,000 require central approval, as do certain faculty appointments at high salaries. Otherwise, except for certain general guarantees of faculty participation, faculty affairs are matters for local determination.

Student admissions and enrolment
While the total enrolment and the application processes of each campus are determined centrally, student admissions policies have been almost entirely products of local determination.

In summation, Figure 2 schematically describes where responsibility lies, centrally or locally.

Levels of planning
The theme of this case study is centred around the mechanisms for planning and managing teaching and research at SUNYAB. At the State level, there are offices

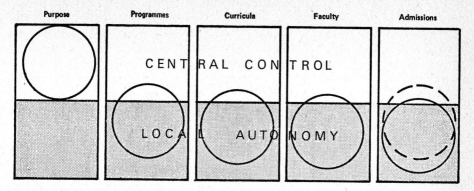

FIGURE 2. *A graphic summary of the locus of decision-making patterns.*

designed to help create the type of climate that is conducive to meeting the goals and objectives SUNYAB establishes, as well as broadening the educational perspective of the member units in the State University System.

There are, however, no effective *university-wide mechanisms* on the local campus that are designed specifically for planning the type of output and direction upon which SUNYAB intends to focus. It seems that what do exist are agencies designed to cope with the existing issues and in doing so plan enough ahead to avoid such pitfalls as over-spending, severe under-staffing, over-enrolment, and inadequate resources for administrative operations.

A clarification of the planning process must be presented here before going further into the teaching and research sections of the report. The kind of planning upon which the case studies were proposed is one in which a thorough rationalizing of procedures for the development of the University was anticipated. The notion of a university fully and immediately responsive in an integrated manner to the various tendencies within a rapidly changing socio-economic environment could be misleading with regard to the general sense of planning within American universities. It is necessary to be aware of the relatively autonomous development of American universities and the nature of political processes within the individualistic tradition of the country. Given these, much of the sense of planning at the University has depended upon a level of assumed agreement, of shared presuppositions, about the general direction of the University. This is a level of consciousness not easily described. Perhaps the nearest term for this foundation of planning would be that of consensus-building. The decision-making process at SUNYAB involves a large portion of those concerned and this very number would, on the one hand, belie any sense of specific unity about the direction of the University, while on the other, indicate the real, already present, agreement in the responses of those involved. For one criterion, a somewhat unspoken one, is exactly this vague sense of 'fit' in raising certain members of the faculty to the more proximate positions of decision. This is the consensus at work; the planning is already there in the sense that the hierarchy of reviewers of policy have to a large extent previously passed through the discrimination of their adherence to the

115

vaguely perceived, yet felt, notions of what constitutes the consensus. Admittedly, such a basis for planning is not easily discernible behind the seemingly inadequate formal mechanisms, yet it is precisely its vagueness which allows for a considerable amount of leeway and mix of more rationalized opinions on a given item. Persons with differing opinions may argue, within limits, that *their* definition more truly partakes of the consensus than that of another.

What makes this situation of consensus-building rather critical is that the notion of planning introduced from recent styles of business management does not allow, relatively speaking, for such an informal system of planning to be fully acceptable. Within the concept of totalisation of a system—the thorough rationalising of administration—there is the necessity for explicit articulation of goals; and this is much more difficult with regard to the University and the consensus upon which planning rests.

Thus, the following discussion outlines only the formal mechanisms in which SUNYAB participates that collectively decide the stated directions of the University. These established agencies for planning are briefly discussed at three levels: State-wide, local campus, and regional.

Planning at the State level
When the State University of New York was established by the State Legislature in 1948, high among the important powers and duties assumed by the newly-appointed University Trustees was the responsibility for planning the over-all development of state-supported higher education.

Specifically, the founding legislature required the Trustees to develop a long-range *Master Plan*. By an act of the Legislature in 1961 the State Education Law was amended, requiring the University to submit a quadrennial Master Plan to the Governor and the Board of Regents, with the first to be submitted in 1964. The Plan was to set *guidelines* for University growth and expansion. Progress reports were to be compiled during intervening years.

The 1964 Plan was prepared substantially within the Chancellor's office; the 1966 Interim Revision and Progress Report was developed within the Central Staff of SUNY Administration Office in Albany with some input from individual campuses. In 1968 an attempt at a wide-spread involvement was made. Because of the tremendous growth of SUNY over the years and the accompanying complexity of the problems surrounding its structure, governance and educational mission, the preparations for the 1972 Master Plan have emerged as the most comprehensive involvement of the SUNY system yet experienced. The process for developing the 1972 Master Plan has been devised to encourage the participation of all members of SUNY community, with the intention of indicating basic directions of the University system for the next decade.

The initial focus of the process has been on University-wide concerns. In addition, a major emphasis has been placed on providing an open and rather informal set of guidelines to ensure a maximum opportunity to transmit opinions and ideas to the Chancellor for his consideration in incorporating them in the 1972 Master Plan.

Secondly, during the summer and autumn of 1971 six symposia and a research panel were conducted to formulate a variety of questions, ideas, opinions and alternatives about the future directions of the University.

In the third phase of the 1972 planning process the campuses were asked to provide their own reactions, alternatives, and analyses on these same issues in a University-wide perspective.

Phase IV of the Master Planning process is for the presentation by each campus President of his campus' views on the University-wide issues raised by the symposia and the Research Panel for drafting into the final document.

The prime advantage of the Master Planning process is that it allows the member campuses of the SUNY system to reflect upon themselves.

It is important to note that the Central Administration Office that co-ordinates the entire process takes the position that the function of planning in SUNY is the 'creation of the future, not the prediction of one'.

Normally, specific planning is thought of in a budgetary context; narrowing down of options so that it is more predictable as to what the occurrences and the requirements might be at a specified time in the future. The Master Plan, as the State Planners see it, is considered a long-range document with developed options of which the State may or may not choose to take advantage when the time arrives.

The concept of educational planning in New York State is fundamentally different from that in countries where great emphasis is placed on determining manpower needs for the future and developing programmes around that predicted need. New York State planners attempt to assess within the State what kind of a future the people in the State want. There is no planning concerned with specific *analysis designation prediction*.

Peripherally, the SUNY Central Office for Planning assists other people in assessing and assembling information. They then try to help create the means to accomplish the objectives that the units establish.

In addition, the SUNY Office for Educational Development was originally intended to be the State-wide agency responsible for academic innovation and change throughout all SUNY campuses, but because of the budgetary crisis, the office has assumed a slightly different role to change with the times. By instituting 'venture finding',[1] the State has established a mechanism to determine whether a 'venture' has been successful or unsuccessful. Two examples of planning that attempt to couple the need for innovation and the wise use of available funds and resources are the Empire State College and Regionalism.

The Empire State College is a 'college without a campus'. It is built on the assumption that learning is an individual experience and that the highly motivated student can pursue degree study without spending full time at a campus. Students using books, correspondence courses, television, and occasional classes and semi-

1. Two or three-year grant containing the terms of its own wholeness so that one knows when one begins that venture and what are the standards on which to base the success or failure of the project.

nars study largely on their own. Emphasis is on individual study under the guidance of master teachers. It is an attempt to extend the opportunities for increasing the effectiveness of higher education, by adjusting the place, the content and the length of study time to the student.

Regionalism is another effort to curtail economic expenditure and to provide greater educational opportunities for students. This new policy divides the State University geographically into eight regions and four co-ordinating areas. The basic objectives of this organization are:

1. The sharing of educational resources and administrative services between institutions in the SUNY in the designated areas.
2. Improving the student admissions and transfer programmes in the University.
3. Co-ordinating the University's community service programmes and focusing more sharply on regional needs.

In effect, the programme places geater emphasis on the central administration role of formulating policy, improving fiscal management and developing public communications and accountability, while minimising its role in the actual operation of educational programmes and in day-to-day campus supervision.

Planning at the local campus level

It has been previously stated that matters of curricula, instruction and research within programmes offered at SUNYAB are the responsibility of the local campus.

Part II, Section B, will discuss the general process of academic decision-making that takes place at SUNYAB. It is at the departmental levels that most of the activity is focused. The Faculty Senate Committee on Educational Planning and Policy, a University-wide agency, reviews educational issues and, in making recommendations to the chief administrative officers, acts as a liaison between the faculty and administration.

The Faculty Senate Committee on Educational Planning and Policy is one mechanism for co-ordinating campus-wide planning. Another is the Office for Facilities Planning, which articulates University-wide needs for space. While the Educational Planning and Policy Committee exists as a standing committee within a legislative campus body, the Faculty Senate, the Office for Facilities Planning is part of the official administrative structure of SUNYAB. Section E of Part II, 'Space Utilisation', discusses the breadth of its functions and the decisive impact of its role on SUNYAB.

Planning at the regional level[1]

There is a trend in higher education in the United States toward inter-campus co-operation as a device to promote interchange among institutions for mutual benefit in a given region, both public as well as private. SUNYAB is a member of the Western New York Consortium for Higher Education, which includes 16

1. Note the distinction between the State-sponsored regional centres for learning and the Consortia. They are both attempts to co-ordinate resources within a geographic area, but the Consortia engages private institutions and is under a different auspice.

charter members among whose incorporated purposes are: to carry out their separate corporate purposes and aims including those which may be beyond the means or abilities of any one college or university, and to enlist the co-operation of other area institutions in educational programmes. Further, it attempts to plan for effective improvements in all those non-academic areas in which universities are involved.

Since its inception in 1967 its effectiveness has been difficult to ascertain, because the energies of the consortium have been devoted to organization and chartering procedures.

II. Teaching

Introduction

A more appropriate sense of the justification and rationale behind the decision-making that affect the academic, physical plant-facilities and fiscal elements can be gained by a familiarity with the goals the University has set. These goals provide the over-all guidelines on which priorities are set—the allocation of the budget, the recruitment of faculty and staff, library acquisitions and the nature of research and public service activities. In March 1972 the President of SUNYAB submitted the following as the present goals and objectives of SUNYAB:

1. The University will continue its evolution into one of the nation's pre-eminent graduate and professional centres with a firm commitment to the advancement of knowledge through teaching and research in selected academic and professional disciplines;
2. The University will continue to accept the obligation inherent in its graduate centre aspirations of creating both an outstanding undergraduate division with a rigorous academic orientation which challenges the individual to test the limits of his intellectual and personal development, and an outstanding continuing education division dedicated to the concept of education as a life-long pursuit;
3. In each of its major divisions—undergraduate, graduate, professional and continuing education—the University will act to maintain existing academic strengths, to strengthen areas of promise, and to develop new areas which possess indications of future importance to the University and to society;
4. The University will remain unequivocally committed to academic freedom; it will simultaneously insist upon a commitment to academic responsibility;
5. In its academic programmes, policies and organization, the University will remain open to innovation and sensitive to the needs of faculty and students, both present and prospective; but it will never lose sight of its academic purpose and of the need to determine and discriminate in favour of the most effective methods of advancing and transmitting knowledge, understanding and abilities which are significant and valuable to mankind;
6. The University will recognize the importance of an environment conducive to

learning, teaching and research; and it will seek to provide facilities, services and personal examples which create such an environment;

7. The University will continue to recognize a special relationship with the community and region, and it will serve in this relationship according to its academic interests and abilities;

8. The University will never be bound to the traditional forms of higher education; it will be willing to act alone or co-operatively in using its resources to create new forms which will further the realisation of its aspirations, purposes, and goals; and,

9. The University will strive to organise and govern itself in such a manner as to make the most productive use of those resources entrusted to it by society for the achievement of these goals.

A. Administrative and academic organization of SUNYAB

Institutions of higher learning should constantly evaluate their changing environment. They should then adjust their strategy to fit the environment, and choose an organisational structure that best supports it. Essentially, the academic organization under which SUNYAB currently operates was implemented in 1967 after receiving advice from educational consultants and *ad hoc* committees.[1]

When SUNYAB implemented its new plan, it was felt that it would:

> . . . allow (the University) to combine the virtues of American universities' emphasis on strong departments, the Continental European reliance on a communality of faculties, and the British approach which emphasises a collegiate environment.[2]

1. Administrative organization

As part of the State University of New York, SUNYAB is charged with fulfilling its mandated purpose as a state institution. The President of the University is responsible for the fulfilment of the State mandate. It is he who grants all academic degrees upon recommendation of the faculty on behalf of the SUNY Trustees. The President is assisted by a staff of vice-presidents. They are headed by an Executive Vice-president who co-ordinates all operations of the University and acts for the President in his absence. In the academic administrative hierarchy, the Vice-president for Academic Affairs reports to the Office of the President, (i.e., to the President and the Executive Vice-president) and co-ordinates all academic activities. (See Figure 3).

---

1. See Glossary, p. 210.
2. SUNYAB, *Character of the future university: basis for a flexible and changing physical development*, Buffalo, New York, State University of New York at Buffalo, 27 June 1967.

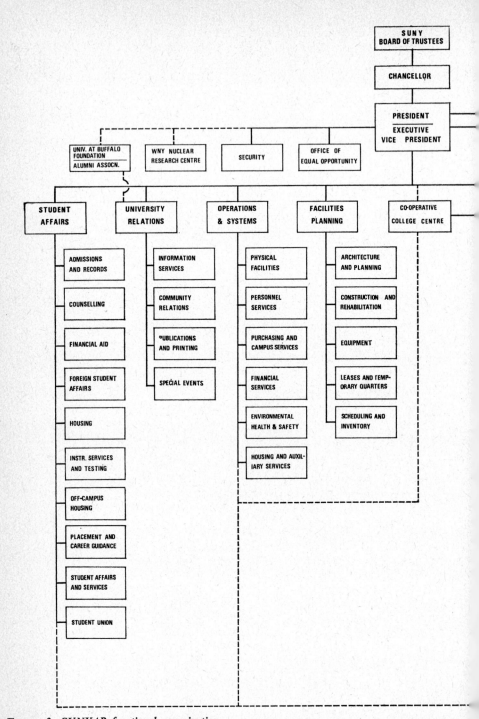

FIGURE 3. *SUNYAB functional organization.*

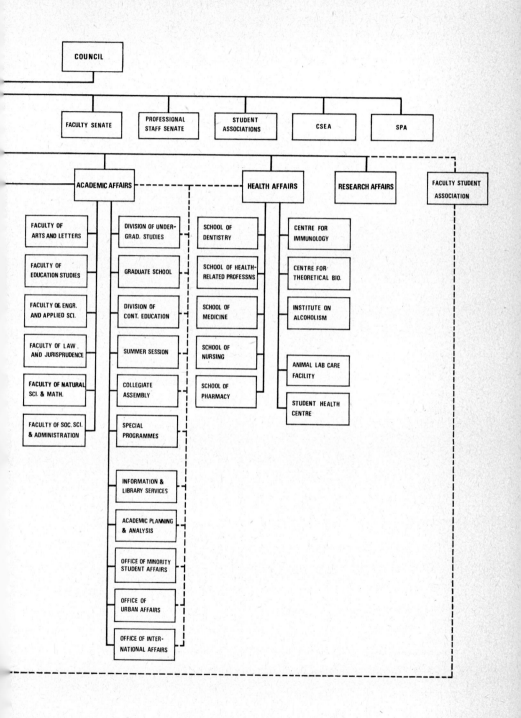

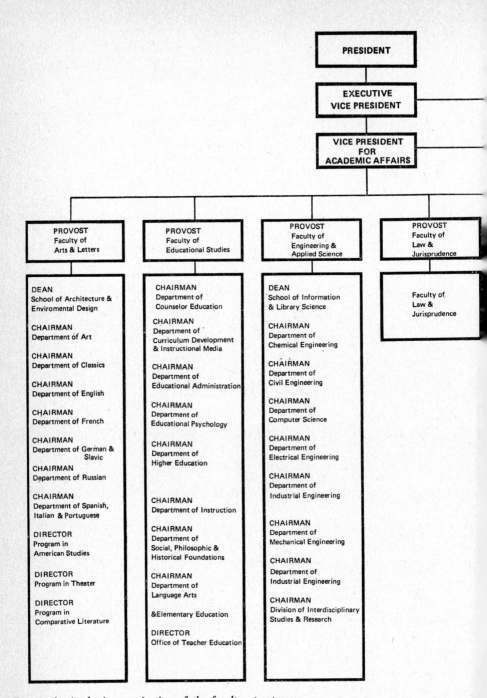

FIGURE 4. *Academic organization of the faculty structures.*

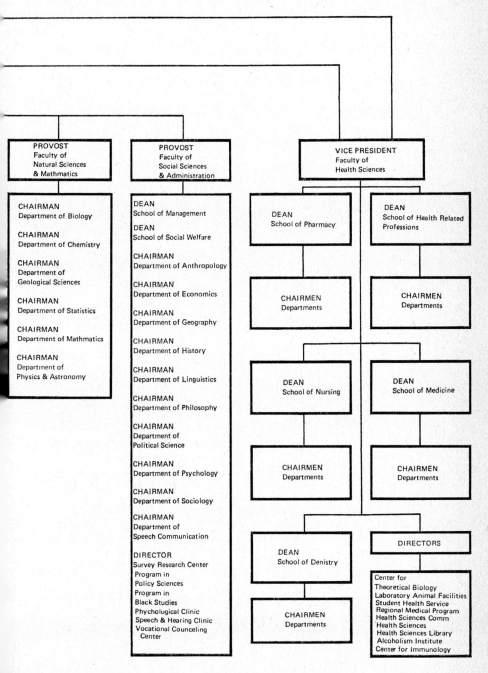

```
┌─────────────────┐        ┌─────────────────┐              ┌─────────────────────┐
│ PROVOST         │        │ PROVOST         │              │ VICE PRESIDENT      │
│ Faculty of      │        │ Faculty of      │              │ Faculty of          │
│ Natural Sciences│        │ Social Sciences │              │ Health Sciences     │
│ & Mathmatics    │        │ & Administration│              │                     │
└─────────────────┘        └─────────────────┘              └─────────────────────┘
```

PROVOST
Faculty of
Natural Sciences
& Mathmatics

CHAIRMAN
Department of Biology

CHAIRMAN
Department of Chemistry

CHAIRMAN
Department of
Geological Sciences

CHAIRMAN
Department of Statistics

CHAIRMAN
Department of Mathmatics

CHAIRMAN
Department of
Physics & Astronomy

PROVOST
Faculty of
Social Sciences
& Administration

DEAN
School of Management

DEAN
School of Social Welfare

CHAIRMAN
Department of Anthropology

CHAIRMAN
Department of Economics

CHAIRMAN
Department of Geography

CHAIRMAN
Department of History

CHAIRMAN
Department of Linguistics

CHAIRMAN
Department of Philosophy

CHAIRMAN
Department of
Political Science

CHAIRMAN
Department of Psychology

CHAIRMAN
Department of Sociology

CHAIRMAN
Department of
Speech Communication

DIRECTOR
Survey Research Center
Program in
Policy Sciences
Program in
Black Studies
Phychological Clinic
Speech & Hearing Clinic
Vocational Counceling
Center

VICE PRESIDENT
Faculty of
Health Sciences

DEAN
School of Pharmacy

CHAIRMEN
Departments

DEAN
School of Nursing

CHAIRMEN
Departments

DEAN
School of Denistry

CHAIRMEN
Departments

DEAN
School of Health Related
Professions

CHAIRMEN
Departments

DEAN
School of Medicine

CHAIRMEN
Departments

DIRECTORS

Center for
Theoretical Biology
Laboratory Animal Facilities
Student Health Service
Regional Medical Program
Health Sciences Comm
Health Sciences
Health Sciences Library
Alcoholism Institute
Center for Immunology

125

2. Academic organization

The academic component of the University is organised around two main structures, the Faculty System and the Collegiate System. (See Figure 4). Through these agencies the substantial portion of full-time courses are offered. The mechanism that co-ordinates the activities of the Faculties and Colleges is the Divisions, primarily the Division of Undergraduate Studies and the Division of Graduate Studies. Each is headed by a Dean who is responsible to the Vice-president for Academic Affairs. The Division of Continuing Education and the Division of Summer Session also co-ordinate academic activities but to proportionately fewer students. They are headed respectively by a Dean and a Director who have slightly different responsibilities from the Deans of other Divisions. Each Division is assigned to a particular academic level except the Division of Summer Sessions, which offers both graduate and undergraduate courses.

3. The Faculty system

The faculty System is by far the broadest and most sophisticated of the structures. There are seven Faculties, organised according to the disciplines within each. These Faculties, which are both teaching and research units, with many specialised but co-ordinated departments and schools, provide the greatest portion of full-time courses. Each is governed by a set of by-laws which have been reviewed and approved by the respective unit and the Faculty Senate. (See Section B of this Part, Faculty Senate). Six of the Faculties are headed by Provosts; the Faculty of Health Sciences, however, is headed by its own Vice-president because of its numerous professional schools which have Deans and departments within. (See Figure 4).

Each Provost is assisted by Associate and Assistant Provosts and usually by an Executive Committee as well as by the Council of Department Chairmen. The Council of Chairmen meet to discuss matters related to the well-being of the Faculty as a whole, guided by the policies which emerge from the faculty meetings and the rulings of the Executive Committee. They discuss all matters related to students, faculty, curriculum, research and any other items which call for recommendation or approval by the Faculty. Figure 5 outlines the administrative organization of the Faculty of Educational Studies with a description of the duties of its administrators. Even though every Faculty has developed its own by-laws, the similarity among the decision-making participation procedures is striking. Since the Faculties operate similarly, the Faculty of Educational Studies will be used as an example of the internal mechanisms that describe the structure and functions of the 'Faculties' in general.

4. General process of academic decision-making

Most of the reviewing and advising on academic issues is done by a representative committee composed of elected faculty members and, in some cases, the Provost.

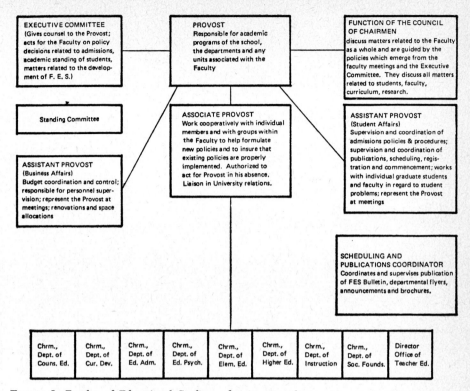

FIGURE 5. *Faculty of Educational Studies: administrative chart.*

Although the size of the committees varies, each is basically a representation of the department and the faculty constituency. With the exception of some explicit powers of the President and the Central Administration, the ultimate power for making most of the decisions on academic issues which affect the Faculty resides collectively in their hands. With the help of his assistants and budgetary specialists, the Provost serves as a facilitator and administrator of policies and programmes.

The actual foundation for the academic decision-making process is at the departmental level at SUNYAB, and is built around a cyclically hierarchical system of check-points, each step in the process representing a portion of the reviewing-evaluating mechanism that ensures both educationally valid curricula as well as sound use of funds and resources. The planning that occurs at this level is very loosely structured. Accordingly, the standing Curriculum Committees within the units of the Faculty and Collegiate Systems review programmes and courses offered in their respective units. The process resembles the schematic diagram presented in Figure 6.

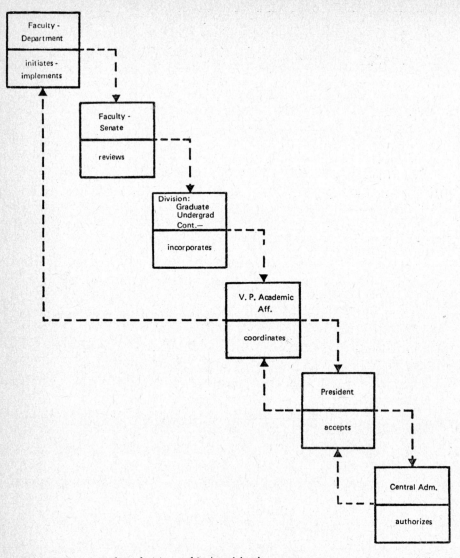

FIGURE 6. *The curriculum decision-making/participation process.*

Any planning and reviewing that occurs at the department-Faculty-Senate levels is concerned with *what* is planned and its educational validity. All other steps are concerned with whether, when, how and if the plans will be selected as part of SUNYAB's offerings. Many decisions at this level are contingent on the fiscal situation and usually determined by it. The process is cyclical because it begins with the departmental initiation and returns to the department for implementation, and hierarchical since approval must be gained at each succeeding level before any additions or changes are made in the curricula at SUNYAB.

5. The Collegiate System

Since 1967 the University has been developing the Collegiate System as an additional dimension of its educational programme. The name 'Colleges' in some ways is misleading, since the term is commonly associated with some kind of residential setting. The colleges at SUNYAB were introduced primarily to enrich the students' educational experience; unfortunately, residential facilities have been largely unavailable. The present plans for the new north campus, however, do include a residential Collegiate educational programme.

The Collegiate System is composed of non-degree-granting units (colleges) offering courses that are outgrowths of the expressed concerns of its constituents. They are more temporary and flexible than most courses offered through the Faculty System. The colleges may offer either credit or credit-free programmes, some of which are on an experimental one-term basis. The emphasis in all cases is on developing programmes which are designed to meet individual student needs, with a focus on the *undergraduate* level.

The Collegiate System at present comprises 17 colleges, the Collegiate Assembly, the Director of the Collegiate System, and standing and *ad hoc* committees.

Significantly, the Director of the Collegiate Assembly has noted that:

> . . . the collegiate units are defined as *ad hoc* academic structures responding to the expressed needs of faculty, staff and student. This shift in definition has made the collegiate system quite unique in this country. While the creation of such flexible academic structures leading to a multitude of educational settings of varying sizes has often been advocated, we know of no other comparable institution which has made possible the creation of this kind of flexible, temporary structure.[1]

Organization of the colleges

A college may be proposed by any group of students, faculty, or staff at SUNYAB. The Collegiate Assembly then reviews the proposals with respect to educational objectives, feasibility of design, and resources needed to implement the programmes. The establishment of a new college depends upon the approval of the Assembly, in accordance with the regulations of the Vice-president for Academic Affairs. Each college is headed by a Master.

The Collegiate Assembly

The Collegiate Assembly, the policy-making body of the system of colleges, was established in April 1970. It has 26 voting members; one vote for each of the seven Faculties; one vote for the Dean of the Undergraduate Division and one for each division of the Student Association (i.e., Undergraduate, Graduate, and Continuing Education Divisions), and one for a representative of each College. The Collegiate Assembly is headed by a Director, who is elected by the Assembly; the nominee must be approved and the final appointment made by the University

---

1. Konrad Von Moltke, Director, Collegiate Assembly, *Annual Report*, SUNYAB, 1971.

President. All policy matters are subject to approval by the Assembly which is also responsible for the election and/or recall of the Director.

The Director is in charge of co-ordinating, on a day-to-day basis, policy matters determined by the Collegiate Assembly, and of all external information flow except that pertaining to a single college.

There are four standing committees (Planning, Resource, New Programme Development, and Programme Evaluation) and an information centre in the Collegiate System. Normally a committee has seven voting members, with at least one member of each committee being a faculty representative. Each College is represented on at least one committee.

6. The Division of Undergraduate Studies

The responsibilities of the Division of Undergraduate Studies are extraordinary since this Division must co-ordinate all undergraduate studies for more than 10,000 students in over 70 degree programmes. In addition, four academic departments are carried within the Division rather than within specific Faculties. These are: Aerospace Studies, Physical Education for Men, Physical Education for Women, and Secretarial Studies.

The faculty of the Division of Undergraduate Studies includes practically all teaching members of the University community. However, few of the University's 1,400 faculty members are actually working directly under the Division's auspices, even though approximately 70% of the student population is seeking a bachelor's degree. The faculty of this Division is empowered to recommend to the Faculty Senate requirements for admission, graduation, and conferral of degrees.

Actually, the faculty as a whole is ultimately responsible for all decisions within the Division, but for the most part this responsibility is delegated either to the Dean or to the standing committees. The Dean of the Undergraduate Division is mainly responsible for co-ordinating the types of instructional services to be offered.

In addition, the Dean and his staff maintain two important services through the Office of Advisement and the Office of Evaluation. The Office of Evaluation, established in 1969/70, is designed to apply psychometric[1] methods to the teaching-learning setting in order to assess the effectiveness of courses as well as student attitudes toward them. The Office of Advisement is designed to help undergraduate students clarify their educational objectives so they may best utilise available resources.

The two standing committees of this Division are the Policy Committee and the Curriculum Committee.

The *Policy Committee* consists of five faculty members selected by the Faculty Senate Executive Committee, with due regard to the respective undergraduate enrolments of the Faculties, and two students chosen by the Student Association.[2] As the major governing body of this Division the Policy Committee plays a crucial

1. See Glossary, p. 211.
2. Bylaws of the Division of Undergraduate Studies, SUNYAB.

role. Issues discussed by the group include criteria for promotion of faculty members, standards of academic honesty, and organization of athletic programmes.

The *Curriculum Committee* is composed of seventeen members. One representative from each Faculty, five other faculty members selected in proportion to undergraduate enrolments and five undergraduate students are responsible for the review and approval of any proposed departmental undergraduate course (see Figure 6).

7. The Division of Graduate Studies (Graduate School)[1]

The Division of Graduate Studies is authorised to offer programmes and recommend the granting of degrees at levels beyond the first degree, with the exception of professional degrees which are controlled by the respective schools and Faculties. Its prime responsibility is to assist the functioning of academic programmes, and to co-ordinate and standardise degree requirements and admissions procedures. The rôles of the departments and the Division regarding admissions are as follows: each department is responsible for admitting its graduate students within guidelines established by the graduate division according to criteria it develops. Normally, these include the possession of a bachelor's degree or its equivalent. Such criteria are considered a matter of record in the Office of the Dean of the Graduate Division and are subject to periodic review either by a Divisional Committee or the Division's Executive Committee.

Organization of the Division of Graduate Studies

The Division is organised around all graduate programmes. One type of basic unit in the Division of Graduate Studies is any department supervised by the Division which has an approved programme leading to an advanced degree. Secondly, circumstances associated with the nature of advanced studies may justify the existence of special aggregations such as interdivisional programmes, centres, or institutes. The third type of basic unit is a department organised by and within the Graduate Division itself (e.g., the Experimental Pathology Department of the Roswell Park Memorial Institute). There are 57 doctoral and 70 masters programmes. The Graduate Division is responsible for the evaluation and operation of these programmes as discussed in Section H of this Part.

Administratively, the Division of Graduate Studies is organised around the Dean and his staff, the Executive Committee, Divisional Committees, the Council of the Division of Graduate Studies and several other committees.

The Dean of the Graduate Division is appointed by the Trustees upon recommendation by the President and Chancellor. His responsibilities include the administration of policies determined by the Graduate Division and the Vice-president for Academic Affairs.

The Executive Committee is composed of the President, Dean of the Graduate Division, Chairmen and one elected member of each of the seven Divisional

---

1. The information given herein is based on the 1970/71 Graduate Division Bulletin, the Bylaws of the Division of Graduate Studies and an interview with the Dean of the Graduate Division.

Committees, plus three members appointed by the Dean. The Executive Committee gives counsel to the Dean regarding matters of policy, and exercises general supervision over standards and operation of graduate programmes.

Divisional Committees exist for each of the seven Faculties and are representative bodies having one member from each of the constituent units (e.g., the Classics Department). The responsibilities of the Divisional Committees include the review (with power to accept or reject) of all programmes for advanced degrees. The committees refer controversial cases to the Division's Executive Committee for final action.

The Graduate Council is composed of members of the Executive and Divisional Committees. The President of the University or, in his absence, the Dean of the Graduate Division acts as presiding officer. The Graduate Council executes and implements the policies of the division.

The Graduate Faculty are those formally appointed members of the teaching or research staff affiliated with graduate programmes. Appointments to the Graduate Faculty are made by the President upon recommendation of the Committee on Appointments, the appropriate academic department, and the Dean. Out of a total of 1,400 faculty members of SUNYAB, approximately 900 are members of the Graduate faculty.

8. The Division of Continuing Education

The character of the Division of Continuing Education is unique in relation to the rest of the University because it provides a different kind of educational service, involving a broader spectrum of both faculty and students.

Over the years this Division has served three different, though not mutually exclusive, populations:

1. Those seeking a degree (associate, bachelor or graduate) who are unable to do so on a full-time basis during the day;
2. Those desiring to learn new vocational skills or to up-date their knowledge of their present profession; and,
3. Those seeking to increase their knowledge and understanding of cultural matters and/or public affairs.

To serve these groups this Division has offered a variety of both semester-length degree-credit and shorter (one day to three weeks) non-credit courses. Many of the non-credit courses have been co-sponsored by community organizations.

Administration

The Division is headed by a University-wide Dean, with an associate dean, whose responsibilities are similar to those of the other Divisional Deans.

The Division's Credit Programmes are supervised by assistants to the deans and directors of advisement, registration, and admissions, while its Credit-Free Programmes are headed by programme directors, a programme co-ordinator, and a conference co-ordinator. Non-Programme activities are administered by the Director of the Adult Advisement Centre, the Director of Urban Extension and the Director and Chief Engineer for the campus radio station WBFO.

The Division's main policy body is the Executive Committee composed of the President of the University, the Dean, and two elected members from each of the Faculties participating in the Division's programmes. This committee gives counsel to the Dean regarding matters of policy and exercises general supervision over standards and operations.

In 1971 56% of the faculty consisted of staff affiliated with other Divisions on Campus, 28% were off-campus instructors (employed in business, industry, or other institutions), with the remaining 25% being teaching assistants.

Activity areas
The Adult Advisement Centre. This facility offers career, education, and University information to groups as well as to individuals. This counselling is based upon an interview and testing service conducted by the Centre to help adults evaluate their capabilities for college work.
Office for Urban Extension. The activities of this office are divided into three main areas, the largest being the implementation of credit programmes for adults. Supported by State University funds and administered by Millard Fillmore College, these programmes are recognised as valid toward a University degree, with classes offered in various locations on and off campus.

The second area is a workshop programme conducted to provide specialised educational experience in response to the needs of specific groups. Workshops include a variety of programmes for the Department of Inspection and Licenses of the City of Buffalo, orientation programmes for parents of in-coming freshmen at SUNYAB, and a community relations programme for the Buffalo Municipal Housing Authority.

The third area of activity of the Office of Urban Extension involves the campus radio station, WBFO. Licensed by the Federal Communications Commission, WBFO operates one studio at the University and another, known as the satellite studio, in the inner-city area. This satellite studio is designed to provide for communication between the University and the inner-city community.
Office for Credit Programmes: Millard Fillmore College (MFC). The teaching staff of Millard Fillmore College (MFC) is drawn from both intra- and extra-University sources. At present MFC operates with a relatively high student/faculty ratio as compared to the day division (approximately 26/1 versus 13.5/1).

The trend of increased enrolment noted for the Division of Undergraduate Studies is also a significant factor for MFC. It is hypothesised that the increase is due not only to a greater number of transfers from community colleges, but from an increase in returning Viet-Nam veterans and the expansion of programmes in the inner city. During MFC's 1970 autumn semester, the average student carried a two-course load worth 8.7 semester hours. Tuition assistance is provided to nearly a quarter of the students by their respective employers.
The Office of Credit-Free Programmes. This Office was originally established as a department of Millard Fillmore College in 1965. Its purpose was to plan and

implement credit-free educational programmes for an adult clientèle, primarily those who have earned a bachelor's degree. Since its inception approximately 10,000 persons per year have participated in its scheduled conferences, institutes and courses.

9. *Division of Summer Sessions*

Since 1965 the focus of the summer session at SUNYAB has been to facilitate and promote the year-round operation of the University. As a result of this new direction, the Division has experienced a 300% enrolment increase; on a credit-hour basis, the summer session now provides a total of one-sixth of all instruction in the University. Through concentrated study, students may now complete almost a full year of undergraduate requirements during the three full summer sessions. Registration for summer courses at SUNYAB is currently among the highest in the country.

B. Types of educational programmes offered

1. *Curricular rationale*

In 1967, University planners conceived of SUNYAB as a

> centre for education and research directed toward the study of man and his environment, from molecules to populations, from interstellar signals to political conflict, from extinct cultures to contemporary forms of art[1]

obligating the University to

> improve dramatically the processes of learning, to further scholarship, and through research and teaching to serve and aid in the solution of the problems of our society and in the achievement of its potentials. These problems include poverty in the midst of plenty; the relation of the individual to an institutionalised society; the development possibilities for minority groups; the technological and economic gulf between the rich nations and the poor; and the need to achieve peaceful solutions to international conflicts.[2]

To enable men and women to succeed at SUNYAB in this three-fold mission it was felt there must be:

> opportunities to understand the essential unity of the search for all knowledge, while mastering specialisations. To this end we will seek to provide broader avenues of interaction among the various academic programs and these disciplines, and between faculty and students.[3]

1. *State University of New York at Buffalo: Campus Academic and Development Plans,* SUNYAB, 1968.
2. Ibid.
3. Ibid.

On this premise the curricular character of SUNYAB was encouraged to develop. Since 1968 the increased size of the University has permitted students not only to choose from among varied options for educational programmes, but to explore knowledge across ever-broadening disciplinary lines.

2. The curriculum process

New programmes sponsored by the University are generally initiated at the departmental level by its teaching staff. Following approval by a Faculty Curriculum Committee, the suggested programme is discussed and voted upon by the entire Faculty teaching staff, and, if approved, is implemented. Officially, the Curriculum Committee of the Division (Graduate or Undergraduate) under whose auspices the course will be sponsored, gives it final approval. However, this committee merely reviews the courses for duplication or overlapping, rather than for educational validity; the latter decision is reserved for the Curriculum Committee of the individual Faculty.

Virtually no formal curricular planning occurs on a University-wide basis. The teaching staff is required to define programme objectives before their approval and inclusion in the University's Bulletin, but there is no pre-set University 'design' or 'curricular purpose' around which courses develop. The development of new courses and programmes according to departmental objectives is essentially the function of the instructors who decide to teach them. An exception is made when the State mandates SUNYAB to introduce a new programme such as architecture into its bulletin and the University complies accordingly (see Section C of Part I).

The Collegiate Assembly may disestablish a course or programme it finds lacking in relevance or which no longer meets the needs of its constituents; this is accomplished on the advice and review of its Programme Evaluation Committee.

3. Degrees offered at SUNYAB

The following degrees are offered by SUNYAB:

Associate in Arts[1]	Master of Fine Arts
Associate in Applied Sciences[1]	Master of Library Science
Bachelor of Architecture	Master of Science
Bachelor of Arts	Master of Social Work
Bachelor of Fine Arts	Doctor of Dental Surgery
Bachelor of Science	Doctor of Education
Master of Architecture	Doctor of Medicine
Master of Arts	Doctor of Philosophy
Master of Business Administration	Juris Doctor
Master of Education	

---

1. These degrees offered only at Millard Fillmore, Division of Continuing Education. See Glossary, p. 210.

4. Experimental and special programmes

The following paragraphs present a partial description of the University's experimental and special programmes. For the sake of brevity, only a sample of these programmes will be discussed. The Colleges, previously described in Section A of this Part, are included because their status in the University is basically experimental. Other programmes included in this chapter should be considered representational.

The Colleges

The seventeen Colleges, which collectively may be considered a programme of study, cover a wide spectrum of styles and themes. Together they are a means of providing both traditional and progressive forms of education without applying an absolute standard. One characteristic common to all the Colleges is the large degree of student participation in the decision-making process. The apparent differences between them derive from differences of style.

Courses offered through the Colleges are subject to greater fluctuation than departmental courses, since they tend to reflect more closely the immediate interests of those involved. Students may take four credits per term in experimental credit-bearing programmes and as many elective approved courses as their degree programme permits. A Collegiate unit may appoint non-tenured Fellows, establish its own form of internal governance, or disestablish itself after notifying the Assembly.

Experimental programme in independent studies (EPIS). This programme has been in existence since 1968, and its continuation has been recommended by the Faculty Senate; thus, it maintains more a permanent than an 'experimental' status in the University. The purpose of EPIS is to broaden educational opportunity, recruiting students on the basis of *potential,* rather than their academic ability as demonstrated in high school. In order to realise promised opportunity, the programme provides students with extra financial and educational assistance, while requiring that EPIS students complete their academic programmes as competently as the students recruited by conventional criteria. EPIS, however, is more than an admission procedure for minority groups (its main constituency): it serves to link SUNYAB with the local community.

Students are admitted into EPIS by an Admissions Committee or committee composed of representatives from the EPIS staff, the EPIS student association, Admissions and Records, the Faculty Senate and the communities from which the bulk of the student applicants come. Admission forms are the same as for other students, but extra questions are added.

All students admitted into EPIS must agree to attend the EPIS summer session courses which constitute an integral part of their programme. The summer workshops offer an intensive programme in reading and reading skills, individualised as much as possible. During the academic year supplementary courses in reading and other skills are required for students who continue to need help. Students are dropped from the University for academic reasons only if they have not performed adequately in the regular University offerings, not on the basis of tests in academic skills or on their performance in developmental courses.

Bulletin Board Courses
1. Twenty students can request the initiation of a Bulletin Board Course. Such courses are designed to allow students and faculty to initiate and participate in courses they would like to see offered which are not currently available in a Department, Division, or College.
2. The instructor of such a course must be a teaching member of the University Community. If a particular area of instruction can be covered only by a qualified person who is not a teaching member of the University Community, a regular faculty member of SUNYAB takes on the full responsibility for the academic supervision and procedures of such a course.
3. The proposal for a new Bulletin Board Course has to be cleared initially with the Assistant to the Dean of the Division of Undergraduate Studies. Subsequently, the course proposal will be processed, as any other course, through the office of the Assistant Dean for presentation to the Division of Undergraduate Studies Curriculum Committee.
4. Unless specifically requested and justified, a Bulletin Board Course is approved for one semester only. Subsequently, each course is evaluated by both the instructor and the students involved in the course. Any Department, Division, or College has the option to absorb an approved Bulletin Board Course as a regular course of their programme.

C. The teaching staff at SUNYAB

1. The Faculty Senate

The Faculty Senate of SUNYAB is considered a legislative body of the University with the voting faculty as its constituent members. Voting faculty are those who hold academic rank, i.e., assistant professors, associate professors and full professors. The President of the University, the vice-presidents and certain non-teaching professional staff members (e.g., from the Libraries) are also members of the Faculty Senate. The means by which this organization is established and its basic operations are outlined below:

> *Officers:* Elected by and from the Voting Faculty.
> *SUNY Senators:* Elected by and from the Voting Faculty and Professional Staff (one from Health Sciences, three from the other six Faculties).
> *Senators* (Faculty Representatives): Elected by and from the Voting Faculty and the Libraries.
> *Executive Committee Faculty Representatives:* Elected by and from the Senators of each Faculty and the Libraries.

Standing and Special Committees: Appointed by the Executive Committee: faculty, staff, students.

Legislation: By the Senate upon basis of committee reports; may be referred to the Voting Faculty for referendum—recommendations to the President.

Role of the Faculty Senate

The Faculty Senate is essentially an *advisory* body—all its powers lie in making recommendations to the President of the University, who has the ultimate responsibility for the management of the institution. The functions, powers and duties of the Senate are outlined below:

to advise the University President, the University Council, the Chancellor, the State University Board of Trustees, and the Governor with respect to all maters which may effect the general character of the University;

to initiate investigations affecting the educational efficiency or standards of the University with respect to

(i)   the establishment or dissolution of all academic and all research units;
(ii)   matters relating to student affairs;
(iii)   general University admissions policies;
(iv)   general University athletic policies;
(v)   general policies relating to University financial aids;
(vi)   general University publications and library policies;
(vii)   establishment of University Articles of Governance;
(viii) major reorganizations of existing Faculties, Schools, Colleges, Division, Departments and other academic units.

Relationship with the Faculty Senate of SUNY

The Faculty Senate at Buffalo has virtually no formal relationship with the State University Faculty Senate, the State-wide body. The SUNYAB campus sends four representatives to the SUNY Faculty Senate and these four representatives serve as an informal link with the State Senate. The Senate has no relationship with SUNY administration in Albany. The SUNY Senate has no authority to over-rule the SUNYAB Faculty Senate decisions.

Relationship with SUNYAB administration

Officially the SUNYAB Faculty Senate is considered an important component of the University administration and academic organization. With regard to the actual impact the Senate has on University management, an officer of the Senate stated that:

> Technically the administration can over-rule virtually any Senate decision. Actually, however, this is seldom if ever done. To do so would quickly erode the faculty's confidence in the administration. In some instances Senate

decisions may get modified somewhat by the administration in their implementation due to practical kinds of considerations which the Senate was not aware of.[1]

There is little doubt that the University administration and the Faculty Senate are closely tied. What may be questionable is the actual influence the Senate has on administrative decision-making. Recent events have shown that the administration has ignored many Senate recommendations, including several in regard to major academic appointments and governance policies. In addition, although the Senate has had practically no influence in regard to the fiscal policies of the University, recently the Senate was able to place two of its members on the SUNYAB budget committee, a move that holds some promise for creating more direct influence in these matters.

Also, as a result of Senate initiation and a series of referendums, the Articles of Governance for a University Assembly were ratified in December of 1972. The major purpose of the Assembly is to develop greater co-operation between the several current governance structures. Significantly, the voting members of the Assembly include not only faculty and professional staff, but also the Civil Service employees, the various student divisions (graduate, undergraduate, Millard Fillmore, professional students in medicine, law and dentistry) and even the alumni. Thus, with its university-wide representation, the SUNYAB Assembly's essential function will be advising all higher levels of State educational control on matters affecting more than one of its constituencies. While it is not the intention that the Assembly replace the primary jurisdictions already existing, the greater co-ordination of deliberations and recommendations on University policies will probably influence their formulation and enactment.

Just what actually is the relationship of the Senate to the administration and the rest of the University community is not completely clear. It is certain, however, that without the support of the faculty, no administration can expect to implement its policies either smoothly or efficiently. What the future holds for SUNYAB may be largely dependent upon the final settlement of this situation. From this point of view, it is important to mention the Senate Professional Association (SPA).

Unionism among university professors

The Senate Professional Association is a collective bargaining organization representing university professors, whose legal sponsorship falls within the construct of a public union. The fifteen-member executive board represents 15,000 heterogenous members ranging from technical assistants to M.D.s and Ph.D.s on twenty-eight different campuses across the State system.

The significance of the union is the fact that it is organised and sanctioned under law (Taylor Law) to bargain independently with the Governor of the State and the Office of Employee Relations, which means the teaching staff can collectively *challenge* those decisions in the system that affect them. The Senate Professional Association has gained salary increments and established grievance procedures.

---

1. The statements cited above are the responses of the Senate Secretary to a list of questions designed for this case study.

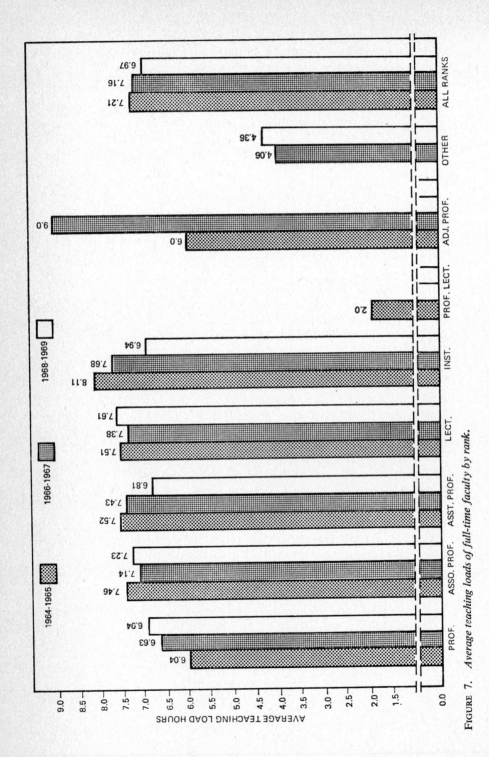

FIGURE 7. *Average teaching loads of full-time faculty by rank.*

2. Faculty teaching loads

Although the amount of time a faculty member spends in teaching is not strictly regulated, it is nevertheless a factor in determining promotion and tenure. The general University-wide policy with respect to this issue is based upon a 12-hour load as the normal expectation. Exceptions to this are made at departmental and divisional levels. A survey conducted in the autumn of 1969[1] revealed that professors of all ranks averaged 56.1 hours a week on the job. The survey showed that full professors worked an average of 57.8 hours a week; associate professors, 57.3; assistant professors, 54.9; lecturers, 56.2; and instructors, 51.6 (see Figure 7). It should be noted that these are the estimates of the faculty members themselves.

Classroom hours broke down to 6.94 for full professors, 7.23 for associate professors, 6.81 for assistant professors, 7.61 for lecturers, and 6.94 for instructors. Also shown was the fact that faculty members with substantial administrative responsibilities spent less time in the classroom than those with few or no administrative chores: 5.21 hours as compared to 7.25 hours. Comparatively, those who teach and engage in substantial research carry more teaching load hours than those who teach and discharge administrative responsibilities.

Classroom hours also fluctuated from one discipline to another. Engineering faculty members spent a significant part of their time in the laboratory and 6.48 hours a week in class, while education professors averaged 8.08 hours weekly in class, not counting laboratory work. All Faculty reported spending approximately 25% of their time in instruction and preparation, while junior faculty members used almost half their time in these pursuits. Personal or departmental research and writing account for 21% of their time. Administrative chores took 16.8%; sponsored writing and research, 6.9%; outside professional activities, 4.7%; other activities within the University, 3.2%; and 'other' activities, 2% (see Figure 8).

In 1971 a questionnaire designed for this case study asked department chairmen whether their departments specified the amount of time a faculty member must spend in teaching. The survey showed that 61.7% of the University departments actually do establish requirements in this area.

	% Yes	% No
University Total	61.7	37.0
Educational Studies	37.5	50.0[2]
Arts and Letters	100.0	0.0
Engineering and Applied Sciences	42.9	57.1
Social Sciences & Administration	86.7	13.3
Law & Jurisprudence	100.0	0.0
Health Sciences	50.0	50.0
Natural Sciences & Mathematics	66.7	33.3

Despite the workload actually carried by the teaching staff at the University, the State Legislature, in July 1971, passed a 'sense of body' resolution calling for

1. Report Faculty Load Survey, Fall Semester 1968-1969, *Research Reports,* Vol. III, Office of Institutional Research, SUNYAB, 1969, pp. 154-170.
2. Ten per cent or more of this faculty did not respond to this question.

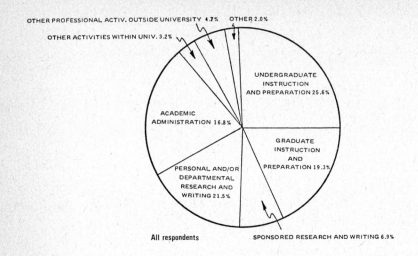

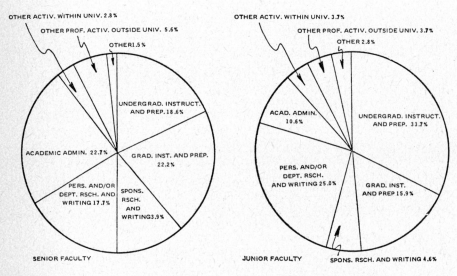

FIGURE 8. *Full-time faculty: average percentage times spent in various activities.*

the adoption of minimum classroom contact hour standards for State University faculty. The bill, vetoed by the Governor, was *not* implemented. The fact that the State government has begun to concern itself with regulating teaching hours at the university level, however, is significant.

3. Teaching load equivalences[1]

The following equivalences or 'ground rules' were applied in calculating the total instructional loads for members of the faculty in the several divisions:

A. Regular courses (undergraduate, graduate):
   1. Lecture, lecture-seminar, lecture and recitation, lecture and discussion, lecture and conference: one contact hour equals one hour for load purposes.
   2. Field instruction (social welfare): four contact hours per student per week—allow one hour for each student enrolled for load purposes.
   3. Laboratory: two or three contact hours equals one hour for load purposes
   4. Studio (Art): two contact hours equals one hour for load purposes.
   5. Seminar and individual supervision (Education): one contact hour per student per week plus three contact hours for seminar—allow one hour for each four students enrolled plus number of credit hours for load purposes.

B. For equivalency purposes, administrative and research work must be at least 50% or more before it is considered 'substantial'.

4. Evaluation of the teaching staff

Appointment, promotion and tenure

The process of appointment, promotion and tenure is an intrinsic part of the inter-action between any university and its faculty. Unlike the other SUNYAB employees whose positions and promotions are determined by New York State Civil Service rules and regulations, faculty appointments, promotion, and tenure are managed through mechanisms which operate at department, Faculty, and administrative levels.

New appointments to the University are not determined by need alone but are modified by the number of full-time equivalent students (FTE)[2] and the State budget. Once the availability of a position has been determined, the following requirements and procedures apply:

1. Three letters of support from people *outside* the University, from a department of equal university status, are solicited. The evaluations should give special attention to *teaching* capabilities, and *originality and reliability of research*. A short curriculum vitae is *required* from each outside reference.
2. *Current Curriculum Vitae* of applicant, employment, education, research, publications, membership in associations and professional organizations, references from authorities in the field.
3. *Letter from Chairman of the department* to which applicant would be appointed. Included in this letter should be the procedure initially used to arrive at the decision, the quantitative vote, and a short statement concerning the applicant *vis-a-vis* the Faculty and the department in the context of department planning.
4. *If the appointment is approved* by the Executive Committee of the Faculty,

1. See Glossary, page 210, under FTE (Full-Time Equivalent).
2. See Glossary, p. 210.

the Provost is authorized to send an acceptance letter to the candidate unless appointment carries tenure and/or the rank of Professor (including term appointments). In the latter case, the Provost forwards all gathered materials plus his recommendation to the President's Review Board (composed of six members of the University faculty at large appointed by the President). The main criteria used by the Board in the evaluation of appointments, re-appointments, promotions and tenure are:

a. relation of talents of the proposed candidate to plans for the development of the department and the University as a whole;

b. evaluation of the candidate's creative contributions, either scholarly or artistic;

c. documented evidence of teaching ability including contributions to educational innovations;

d. public and community service;

e. a tenure rank should not be granted if a better-qualified person is available elsewhere.

Upon review of the Board, *and* approval of the President, appropriate action may be taken by the Department.

The President's Review Board considers promotion to Full Professor and term appointments to the rank of Professor or Visiting Professor for more than one semester. It should be noted that it decides upon new appointments *only* when tenure is involved.

Promotion and tenure

Promotion and tenure are initiated through various departmental committee structures, on which a senior faculty member or chairman serves as a reviewing agent. Departmental policy determines whether or not students are represented; in most cases the students are included.

In line with the regulations of the SUNY Trustees, *tenure but not promotion* is programmed, i.e., a time comes when a decision *must* be made. However, early requests are often initiated. A recommendation to full professorship usually results from an annual review of the accomplishments of the associate professors by a department's senior professor. Promotions and tenure are based on the following:

1. *Two letters from within* the University supporting the request from faculty of equal or greater status.

2. *Three letters of support from outside* the University.

3. *Current curriculum vitae of applicant.*

4. Letter from the Department Chairman indicating procedure used to arrive at decision, vote (quantitative), and a short statement regarding individual's promotion.

The following information *must* be included in each recommendation for promotion or tenure: scholarly achievement; faculty member's performance in teaching, other department or faculty evaluation forms, or letters from graduates and/or undergraduate students, etc.; University service—Committee work, administrative posts held by the candidate, etc.; public service—civic offices, professional societies, etc.

The above information is sent to the Provost's Office. In cases of promotion with tenure, granting of tenure, or promotion to full professor, the Provost, after consultation with the Executive Committee, adds a letter of recommendation to the set of credentials and forwards the material to the Vice-president for Academic Affairs. After action is taken by the Vice-president for Academic Affairs, the President's Review Board and the President, the Provost's Office informs the Department of the resulting dicisions.

5. *In the event of a 'no' decision* at any level, the faculty member may appeal to a SUNYAB Faculty Senate subcommittee which may further appeal to the SUNY Senate group and the SUNY Chancellor.

Compensation

The ability to recruit faculty is related to the pay-scale as well as to the academic environment of a university. According to data compiled by the American Association of University Professors (AAUP), SUNYAB ranked 22nd in the United States in average compensation to full-time faculty members during the year 1970/71.

Reviews of teaching methods and courses

The Student Course and Teacher Evaluation (SCATE). The first attempts to standardise teaching evaluation were made by a student committee partially supported by the Student Association. During the autumn of 1967, with a staff of only two undergraduates, the committee conducted its first course survey and published the statistical results. Since then the Student Course and Teacher Evaluation (SCATE) has been published twice more, in 1968 and 1969. With an increased staff of 20 members, the committee has been in continuous operation.[1]

A course and teacher evaluation programme is a tool for measuring and improving the quality of education within the University. The SCATE project represents an attempt to make such a programme University-wide, by means of a standardised, computer-scored questionnaire distributed during final examination week.

Traditionally, the University has failed to recognise and reward good teaching. Promotion and tenure have too often been determined by the quality and quantity of publications. The goal of SCATE is to offer a measuring device of teaching quality. Department tenure committees might effectively apply SCATE evaluations to individual tenure cases. In this way students are able to voice their criticisms and affect a process which has long been closed to them. Additionally, the evaluation may be used by the individual professor to improve his own instruction and

---

1. The information used here concerning SCATE is based on the 1969 Summer Report. There was no 1970 survey—probably as a result of the fact that the 1969/70 academic year was so disrupted by campus disturbances. The 1970 spring semester, as at many other American Universities, was cut short in order to avoid actual physical conflict on the SUNYAB campus.

gauge the success of his teaching concepts. Besides using SCATE for tenure considerations, a department may find SCATE helpful in an examination of the relevancy and continuity of a course in terms of other courses and the needs of the students.

Unfortunately in 1969 the SCATE evaluations were limited to courses offered only in the Undergraduate Division of three Faculties (Arts and Letters; Natural Sciences and Mathematics; and Social Science and Administration). The primary reasons for this were lack of financial support, insufficient student and faculty participation, and poorly constructed questionnaires. Currently, the Office of Vice-president for Academic Affairs is implementing a similar, but improved, evaluation at both undergraduate and graduate levels.

The Faculty of Natural Sciences and Mathematics teaching review. Other mechanisms for evaluating teaching quality have been initiated by the individual 'Faculties'. For example, the Faculty of Natural Science and Mathematics began this work in the autumn of 1970 by attempting a rigorous examination of teaching methods. The Faculty quickly realised, however, that no 'correct' answer was readily available, and instead focused their energies toward the improvement of the quality of instruction within the Faculty.

Action within the Faculty was initiated by a sixteen-member committee consisting of both faculty and students appointed by the Provost. On the basis of two course questionnaires the committee was able to derive information which was then analysed and distributed to the faculty members. The two-page forms included questions about lectures, course content, examinations, grading and general matters. In addition, there were sections for data concerning the student. The student was asked to evaluate his instructor's knowledge and attitude toward the course, as well as his lecture and 'blackboard' technique. The evaluation forms were handed out to students during the final examination with addressed envelopes attached. The Committee put the data on computer cards and statistically analysed them. Individual faculty members were then informed as to their students' comments.

In reviewing the questionnaires, the committee has called for a firm commitment to excellence in teaching, making several recommendations:

That the summary reports be made a permanent part of each faculty member's dossier;

That evaluation of teaching ability become required as a formal and regular criterion;

That the Provost create 35 annual summer salary awards to full-time faculty and graduate teaching assistants who have shown excellence in teaching.

It recommended also:

a. a service for video-taping of lectures be made available upon request so that each faculty member could see himself as others see him,

b. speed experts be made available upon request,

c. programmes for the improvement of teaching by assistants be organized.

University Survey of Courses and Teaching (USOCT). The University Survey of Courses and Teaching was designed and developed for the Millard Fillmore College (MFC) Student Association (Division of Continuing Education) by the Office of Evaluation at SUNYAB. This survey is composed of a five-points ranking, ranging from strongly agree to strongly disagree on 45 items. The 45 items sample student reactions to course grading, content, instructor performance and delivery, relatedness of assignments, and general course organization. The first survey was conducted in 1971 and was limited to volunteer instructors having a class size of 20 or more students. The results of the survey are available to all students, instructional staff and administrators.

D. Students at SUNYAB

1. Student progress and participation

The framework of the basic undergraduate programme adheres to the philosophy that undergraduates should exercise considerable responsibility in structuring their academic programmes, particularly in choice of electives and in fulfilment of distribution requirements. The Division of Undergraduate Studies has generalised the requirements for attaining the bachelor's degree, according to the following structure:

1. A minimum of 32 hours of electives from the areas of:
   Humanities, Sciences and Technology, Educational Studies . . .
2. A coherent 'major' programme or an individual field of the students' own conception. The individual field allows limitless independence in programme design.

As an extension of this philosophy, student participation has been sought to a certain degree in areas directly affecting the student's progress through the University. In some departments students participate as members of curriculum committees; in others, they serve as advisory members to such committees; in yet other departments, there is no direct involvement as members of such committees. Students serve as full members of the Policy Committee of the Division of Undergraduate Studies, an advisory body to the Dean of the Division. Provision has also been made for one-third student representation on the Division of Undergraduate Studies Curriculum Committee, whose function is to review all credit-earning courses offered at the undergraduate level and to give final approval.

2. Admissions

Admissions standards at SUNYAB attempt to attract an entering student population with a median academic achievement of a 3.40 high-school Grade Point Average[1], 92 percentile rank in high-school graduation class, and 207 Regents Examination scores[1]. However, under the programme of special admissions,

1. See Glossary, p. 211.

marginal students are admitted via the Experimental Programme in Independent Studies (EPIS) and the Educational Opportunity Programme (EOP).

Application to SUNYAB is generally carried out during the first semester of the student's senior year in high school, thus admissions are partially based on grades from his junior high-school year. Application papers are sent directly to the student. He then gives part of these papers to his high-school guidance counsellor for affixation of grades and special test scores, to be forwarded to the central admission processing centre of SUNY in Albany. The remaining portion is sent to Albany by the student himself indicating his particular preference for one of the 65 SUNY units, along with all pertinent personal information. In Albany the application is matched with Regents Scholarship Examination scores (given once a year by the State), application fees are collected and reports are provided to the various State University units (when applications to more than one institution are involved). Those students who are unable to submit Regents Scholarship Examination scores may submit scores from the Scholastic Aptitude Test (SAT) or the American College Testing Service (ACT).

Actual admissions figures are determined by a committee serving under the Vice-president for Academic Affairs. The basic controlling factor in the number of admissions is the number of budgeted full-time equivalent students (FTE's) decided upon by the SUNY Central Administration in Albany.

In evaluating students, there are various separate applicant categories.

(a) Regular undergraduate freshmen admissions
This category is defined as *individuals applying directly from secondary schools* to the day-school undergraduate programme. Admissions decisions for this group are based upon the data received by the SUNY Central admissions-processing centre in Albany. These, when received at SUNYAB, are translated for computer use. Students are admitted on a predicted grade-point average, computed by a regression formula which takes into consideration high-school rank, class size, and Regents Scholarship or other previously mentioned examination scores. An arbitrary cut-off point is set to accommodate the number of full-time equivalent students budgeted.

In an attempt to allow the admission of more 'disadvantaged' students, the criteria for admission have been changed slightly by placing more emphasis on high-school *rank* rather than grade point average or examination scores. Such changes, plus the increasing numbers of all applicants, have made admissions decisions more difficult in recent years. In 1962 there were 5,416 freshmen applications, of which 2,280 were registered. For the 1970/71 academic year, out of 12,500 high school seniors who applied, only 1,890 freshmen were registered in the autumn of 1970.

In addition to the increased number of applicants, there has also been an increase in the academic level of those students. The 1970 freshman class has the largest number of students (56%) with high-school averages between 90 and 94 ever admitted. In 1968 this figure was 38% and in 1964 it was only 25%. A total of 61% of the 1970 class had high-school averages of 90 or higher, compared with

27% in 1964 and 41% in 1968. A comparable increase has occurred in mean Regents Scholarship Examination scores; the 1967 mean was 193 while the 1970 mean was 211 (out of a possible score of 300). The 1971 freshman class Regents Scholarship Examination scores average was even higher, with 90% of the students having scores above 207.

Of the students accepted for admission, usually 40% actually enrol; of those rejected, it is estimated that 80% of them could do passing work had they been accepted.

The composition of the 1971 freshman class was determined by a variation of the above criteria. Thirty-six percent of the students were chosen on their high-school rank *alone*; another 36% on the basis of their grade-point average and performance on the Regents Scholarship Examination; 20% were admitted through Educational Opportunity Programmes, and 8% were admitted mainly on the basis of their high-school aptitude and interest in the natural sciences and mathematics.

Local admissions. Students from the City of Buffalo and Western New York comprise 50% of the freshman class for the 1972-73 acamedic year. The majority of the remainder comes from New York State, and the rest come from other states and foreign countries.

An increase in the number of Buffalo area residents stems from a decision by the President of the University and approved by the Faculty Senate. The percentage of Western New York students (local) at this University has ranged between 48 and 54.

(b) Admissions of transfer students

The ability of the University to accept transfer students has been proportional to the number of applications received; they have steadily increased. Generally, applications are ranked on the basis of their college transfer average, with regard to the programmes to which they apply. *Students are accepted only to specific programmes.* Highest-ranking applicants are offered admission first. Students who have been dismissed from other colleges for academic reasons may apply for admission one year after the date of dismissal. They may, however, attend SUNYAB summer school to raise their academic standing. When an overall 'C' average has been attained, they are eligible for admission to the day division but must still compete for an opening.

(c) Special programmes admissions

The four undergraduate day-school programmes currently functioning are Experimental Programme in Independent Studies (EPIS); Search for Education, Evaluations and Knowledge (SEEK); Regular Admissions, Disadvantaged (RAD); and Student Tutorial.

The Experimental Programme in Independent Study (EPIS), a federally funded programme, is expressly designed for all applicants who are considered disadvantaged. So that the University may accommodate as many disadvantaged students as possible, academically qualified EPIS applications are currently referred

149

through the regular admissions procedures, but such students are also admitted upon recommendations by the local Community Action Organization (CAO), community leaders, and guidance cousellors.

The Regular Admissions Disadvantaged programme (RAD) involves students who apply for regular admissions but are accepted primarily on the basis of guidance counsellor's recommendations. They are given special priorities in counselling, financial aid and tutoring.

All the special programmes for disadvantaged students have presented a problem for the SUNYAB Admissions and Records Office in the establishment of valid criteria for acceptance. As yet, no parameters have been established which enable reliable prediction of success for these students in the University.

(d) Foreign students admission
Foreign students are admitted on the basis of their overall academic record, grades, class rank, English proficiency, and ability to finance their aducation.The criteria used are designed to adhere as closely as possible to American university standards. The SUNYAB Office of Admissions and Records has currently introduced a preliminary admissions screening form to reduce excessive time-consuming processing. It should be noted that the admission of foreign students to the graduate programmes is decentralised and carried out by each department (see below).

(e) Graduate admissions
The application for admission to the Division of Graduate Studies is handled by each department, which determines its own criteria. Such criteria are kept on record in the office of the Dean of the Graduate Division and are available for periodic review by a Divisional or the Executive Committee. For the academic programmes it is generally expected that an applicant will have completed all requirements for a bachelor's degree prior to his admission, and that he will have taken at least one of the various standardised examinations such as the Graduate Record Examination.

(f) Division of Continuing Education—Millard Fillmore College
Another area of admissions handled through the Office of Admissions and Records is that for Millard Fillmore College (MFC), a unit of the Division of Continuing Education. MFC primarily provides academic programmes for adult students in the Buffalo area. Adults receive initial priority in MFC. The qualifications for entrance to Millard Fillmore College vary from that of the day school, and in general are more liberal.

Qualifications to enter a credit programme: resident within the community area; high-school or Government Equivalence Diploma (GED) with no prior college work; married status or family responsibilities; full-time work; and, financial self-support.

Those applicants who fulfil the above requirements but who have had prior college work will be admitted (i) if their overall transfer average is 'C' or better, or (ii) in line with MFC retention standards if their overall average is below 'C'.

From time to time Millard Fillmore College offers enrolment to students who would not normally qualify under the above requirements. One such programme initiated in 1969/70 with 15 students is the Mature Adult Student Programme (MASP). This programme is one which supports part-time students in MFC (originally financed by the University at Buffalo Foundation) and allots up to eight hours of academic credit to qualified applicants. Qualifications are that the student meet regular admission requirements but may not have attended college within the past three years. Approximately 87 % of the students accepted eventually enrol.

3. Registration: a management system

The registration system obtains the major portion of student data necessary for instruction. Simultaneously, the system, computerised by the University's data processing centre, serves as the major source for such crucial information as statistical and grade reports, student accounts receivable, revenue distribution and mailing lists.

As an aftermath of chaotic registration procedures, a concept of integrated data processing has evolved in an attempt to improve registration and organise the scattered collection of information. At this point, the Student Academic Records Administration (SARA) system facilitates the total management operation of SUNYAB, by co-ordinating the collection, storage, processing, and distribution of information. This eliminates the duplication of data collection and ensures the availability of important information.

A University-wide computerised information system is a long-range goal that is currently being implemented in stages at SUNYAB. Computerised registration, considered the foundation of the SARA system and all future information systems, provides for the establishment of the University's student data bank. Future phases of SARA will expand this data bank and extend its other services to all authorised University users.

In order to register students on-line, utilising terminal devices, two basic data files, one for student data file and another for course offerings, are established. These files must be available (on-line) to both the computing system and the terminal.

As a result of these files, two other data files are generated. The first is an Enrolment Statistics File, including such information as enrolment by class level (freshman, sophomore, etc.) credit hours for class level, and instructors' and students' hours of instruction. The second file will be the current semester's registration file. Generally, it will store major student data items and all information for each course in which a student enrols.

For the student, SARA registration is a fairly simple process. The student fills out the blank student data form only once during his academic career; during each successive registration, Admissions and Records provides a data form completed by computer which needs only to be approved or corrected.

In order to register, the student consults a comprehensive course listing, published each semester, and prepares with his academic advisor a 'time conflict-free' schedule for himself. After filling out the class schedule (course request) form, he submits it to the Office of Admissions and Records which assigns him a time to report to the appropriate location, where the student submits his materials and after 24 hours reports to another area where he receives a print-out which serves as proof of registration and entitles him to receive a student identification card. If his selected first choice course is filled, the computer assigns him his listed second choice. Should the student be dissatisfied with his schedule, he may, during the first two weeks of the semester, submit a 'drop' or 'add' form to the computer; after this period, he must obtain faculty permission to add a course. A course may be dropped at any time prior to two weeks of the close of the semester. At intervals throughout each day of the registration period, the computer produces a class status list which gives the student an up-to-date choice of available course offerings. As the system is refined, the student will receive his schedule within three hours after submitting the course requests. Eventually, plans call for the installation of remote terminals allowing students to deal directly with the computer and to receive an immediate response.

The computer keeps track of the request and enrolment figures for all classes. In this way, academic divisions are better informed of class demand for any one course so that they could conceivably add extra sections.

4. Student governance

Student governance on the SUNYAB campus consists of six autonomous government organizations: The Student Association (SA), representing day undergraduate students; the Graduate Student Association (GSA); Millard Fillmore College Student Congress (MFCSC), representing students attending evening classes; the Dental Student Association (DSA); the Medical Student Assembly (MSA); and the Student Bar Association (SBA). These organizations present varying efforts to control matters which concern students.

At its highest level of operation, student government on the SUNYAB campus attends to:
1. The budgeting and administering of the Student Activity Fee providing for extra-curricular activities.
2. Supplying a judiciary to attend violation of University rules and regulations.
3. Influencing the determination of issues concerning academic matters.

5. Evaluation of student performance: the grading system

The means by which a university evaluates student performance is an important index of the institution's overall view of education. The following section presents a brief outline of the grading system currently employed at SUNYAB.

In 1968 SUNYAB established an evaluation system based upon three major assumptions:
1. The evaluation system is a determinant of student learning.

2. The effectiveness of any single evaluation system varies among different students, different instructors, different courses, and different disciplines.
3. Students can and should be given considerable responsibility in the design of their individual academic programmes.

These assumptions became the basis of a system for evaluation as outlined below:

1. Students should be advised of their progress and motivated to work toward these goals;
2. Faculty should be advised about the progress of individuals and of the class as a whole toward the goals of individual courses;
3. Administrators and faculty should be provided indicators of their role in offering advisement, allocating financial aid, recommending academic dismissal, recommending honours and awards, and recommending graduation;
4. Graduate schools should be provided indicators for their role in recommending acceptance or predicting probable success in graduate work, and allocating financial aid;
5. Employers should be given indicators for predicting the probable success of a graduate as an organizational member.

In 1968 it was the judgment of the special committee that no *single* evaluation system could meet all of these objectives effectively; a system which motivates some students may not motivate others, and a means of measuring progress in one course may not do so adequately in another.

For these reasons the system outlined below was established and is currently employed at SUNYAB:

1. The following three alternatives are the basis of the evaluation system
   a. Letter grading (A = outstanding, B = above average, C = average, D = below average or marginal, F = failure).
   b. Written descriptions of student performance.
   c. Satisfactory/Unsatisfactory grading (the grade of S would earn credit; a grade of U would not).
2. With the approval of the appropriate academic committees, any professor in any course in any semester may designate that course as having only *one* of the above alternative evaluation schemes
   a. provided that students are apprised of this fact at the time of registration for the course; and
   b. provided that, if it is a required course for any portion of the student body, and where staff is available, there exists at least one other section of the course evaluated on other schemes.
3. For all other courses where professors do not mandate the form of evaluation, the standard evaluation system should be letter grading.
4. In any course where an option is available and when agreed to by the professor, a student may choose to be evaluated in the written form.
   a. No limit is to be set on the number of courses to be taken with written evaluations for undergraduate or post-bachelor students.
   b. For written options, a letter 'W' shall appear on the transcript and the written evaluation shall be placed in the student's personal file at the end of

the semester. For student protection, a letter grade shall also be filed separately at the Office of Admissions and Records.
c. The written evaluation option may be elected at any time up to submitting the final grade.
d. The written evaluation, except under extreme circumstances, may not be converted to a letter grade.
5. In any course where such an option is available, a student may choose to be evaluated by the satisfactory/unsatisfactory option.
a. For undergraduate students total 'satisfactory' credit hours should not exceed 25% of the total credit hours taken towards the bachelor's degree. There should be no limit for post-bachelor students.
b. Notification of the student's choice is to be made to the Office of Admissions and Records before the beginning of the fourth week of the semester. Professors may request information on the proportion of a class on S/U grading but not the grading choice of individual students.
c. The letter 'U' shall be placed on the student's records for courses in which he received a letter grade of 'F': the letter 'S' shall be recorded for all grades A to D. The letter grades shall be kept on permanent file by Admissions and Records.
d. At any time, for valid reasons, a student may request his Division to release his letter grade in a S/U course to specific departments, other undergraduate schools, graduate schools or employers.
6. In cases where grade-point averages are required they shall be computed on letter-graded courses only, with note being taken of the number of credit hours represented. Users of grade-point average should be strongly urged to consult written evaluations where they exist.
7. No University-wide rankings of students should be computed.
8. University honours and prizes at SUNYAB should be based on both grade-point average (GPA) and written evaluations.
Having determined a grade for the student, the instructor submits it to the Office of Admissions and Records as prescribed. Currently, a mark-sense form is used to transport the grade from the instructor to the Office of Admissions and Records. If a student selects a written evaluation as the main part of the grade, that evaluation is attached to the form and the student will also receive a copy of the written evaluation.

6. Supportive non-instructional activities

The Office of Foreign Student Affairs
The Office of Foreign Student Affairs, a unit of the Division of Student Affairs, co-ordinates and administrates educational programmes and services for the approximately 1,000 foreign students attending SUNYAB, comprising 6.7% of SUNYAB's full-time enrolment of 17.2% of the graduate school population, who represent more than 80 countries. The Office attempts to assist foreign students in managing the transition to new situations, and conversely to make the University

aware of this dimension with its attendant concerns and problems. In doing so, the Office co-operates with other offices in the Division of Student Affairs, the Council on International Studies, community action organizations, and certain departments and Faculties.

Summer planning conferences—The Office for University Orientation
This Office was established in 1969 co-ordinate the resources of the academic community in developing orientation programmes. It is concerned with freshmen, special admission students, transfer students, graduate students, and faculty. Mainly supported by the Division of Student Affairs which supplies staff, and the Office of Academic Affairs, it operated in 1970/71 on a budget of approximately $70,000.

Traditionally, summer planning conferences were offered to first-time students in order to acquaint them with the SUNYAB facilities, and to help them plan their first semester schedules. For the past two summers experimental sessions offering innovative approaches have been conducted within the regular summer planning conferences, including experiments in group dynamics, the use of films, and encounters with important members of the University community.

E. Space utilisation

1. Planning the utilization of teaching and research space

The administration of space both for on- and off-campus facilities is the responsibility of the Office for Facilities Planning (OFP). Its main task involves the allocation, distribution, maintenance, rehabilitation and inventory of space. This Office not only translates needs to 'amounts' of space, but is also involved in planning for the new North Campus, together with the State University Construction Fund and the New York State Urban Development Corporation.

Upon receiving the stated needs of each of the seven Faculty and other University units, a programme is developed that translates those needs to specific spatial quantities. Large project approval decisions must be evaluated by the Vice-president for Academic Affairs, followed by the Executive Vice-president, the University President, and finally the SUNY Central Office for Facilities Planning in Albany. If new facilities are involved, the State Construction Fund reviews bids, selects contracts and supervises construction. Decision-making authority is a function of the amount of space and money involved: the greater the amount, the higher in the hierarchy of authority the decision must finally rest.

The Office for Facilities Planning at SUNYAB, headed by the Vice-president for Facilities Planning, is divided into the following departments: Architecture and planning, Construction and rehabilitation, Equipment, Leases and temporary Quarters, Scheduling and Inventory, Information systems support, and Logistics and occupancy phasing.

Teaching and research facilities

At SUNYAB the problems of space and facilities allotment are complicated as a result of the following factors: (a) a division of facilities on several campus sites; (b) a phasing stage as new facilities become available on the new North Campus; and (c) a general existing condition of over-occupancy.

At present, most teaching is done at two locations:

1. *The Main Street Campus*, (South Campus) which is the central campus site. Located in the City of Buffalo, it houses the administrative offices as well as most of the existing teaching space.
2. *The Ridge Lea Campus* (Interim Campus), located in Amherst, is a 15-minute drive from the South Campus and 10 minutes from the new North site. These facilities are all rented; the property is expected to be converted into a shopping centre by the owners after the North Campus is completed.

Other facilities that are at present used for teaching include the Law School, the Bell facility (formerly owned by Bell Aerosystems Corporation) or health facilities (Meyer Memorial Hospital, Buffalo General Hospital, the Veterans Administration Hospital and Roswell Park Memorial Institute). Figure 9 illustrates the temporal relationships of these facilities. (There are about 40 off-campus facilities in all.)

Indices and criteria for utilizing space

In 1969 the Office for Facilities Planning computerised physical space inventory data and applied a 'Net Area Study' to every academic department, for sixty-seven SUNYAB facilities, in order to compare actual space held with justified areas. Occupancy is the resultant percentage of a comparison between the amount of space justified by SUNY space standards (based upon FTE load) with the amount of space actually held.

During the fiscal year 1970 the Office for Facilities Planning (OFP), Logistics and Occupancy Phasing, successfully co-ordinated space re-allocations which reduced several of the severest over-occupancies to acceptable levels. It also developed a series of occupancy studies which have provided a predictive capability for class schedules, busing requirements and rental space flexibility.

In order to accomplish its tasks the Logistics and Occupancy Phasing of the OFP collects and analyses an enormous amount of computerised data, one aspect of which involves the proration of space.

Proration of space. There are three characteristics of any room (space) to be prorated: function, classification, and control. Since the former deals with physical characteristics of the space it does not normally change within a reasonable time-span unless substantial modifications are performed. When a room has two or more classifications, such as 'stockroom' and 'office', it is divided into *segments* and given a code room number.

Control and function are prorated by percentage based on area, time or both. For example, if a room is divided into two, and department A either controls half the room all the time or all the room half the time, it is then prorated at 50%

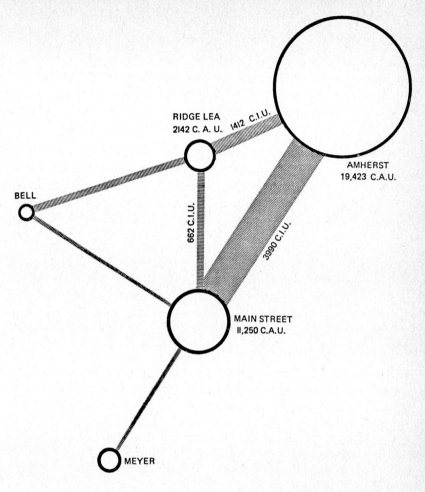

RIDGE LEA
2142 C. A. U.   1412 C.I.U.

AMHERST
19,423 C.A.U.

BELL

662 C.I.U.

3990 C.I.U.

MAIN STREET
11,250 C.A.U.

MEYER

C.A.U. = CAMPUS ACTION UNIT
C.I.U. = CAMPUS INTERACTION UNIT
(BASED ON FALL/70 DATA)

FIGURE 9. *Study B of the Phasing Model.*

control for A. Proration of function is determined in the same manner as control. Before any space can actually be prorated, however, inventories must be taken and the following questions asked: 1. Where is the space, how to identify it? 2. Who currently controls the space? 3. What is the physical space? 4. What function does the space currently serve?

The over-occupancy problem
No matter how sophisticated a computer programme may be, it cannot solve the basic problem of overcrowding. Over-occupancy is one of the major problems now

157

facing SUNYAB because of the enormous recent increase in students, faculty and staff without a corresponding growth in facilities. While the rented Interim Campus and other facilities have relieved some of the pressure, the demand for space still surpasses the supply.

2. *Planning for 1977*

On the basis of data now being collected, the Office for Facilities Planning is developing a plan for phasing into the new North Campus facilities as they become available.

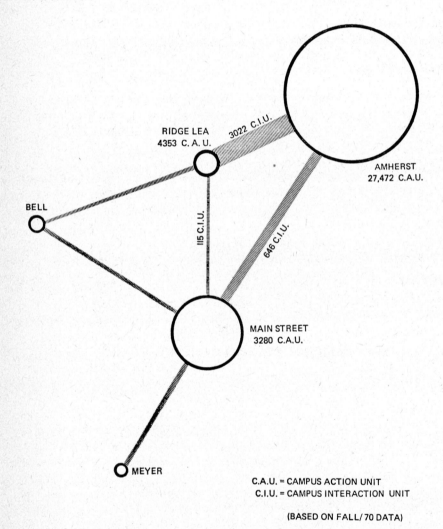

FIGURE 10. *Temporal relationships of SYNAB campus sites, 1977.*

Figure 10 shows the temporal relationships of the various campus sites as they will exist in 1977. This is not a simple problem and several approaches have been formulated using computer modelling.

Course file maintenance

Once the space inventory is made and facilities prorated, data are collected concerning the needs of the users. Just as data are developed for space, a corresponding Computerised Course Catalogue File is also maintained. For every course taught each semester a special data sheet is prepared which takes into consideration 29 points of information. When a *new* course is offered, the following information must be provided: Begin and end dates, Budget account number, Credit hours, Course number, Course section (where applicable), Course title, Course type, Days offered (or 'arr.' for 'to be arranged'), Division, Faculty unit code, Frequency, Fund code, Instructor's name, Instructor's social security number, Maximum enrolment, Related courses, Start and stop time ('arr.' for 'to be arranged'), Weeks. After this information is recorded, the appropriate space is allotted on the basis of the corresponding space inventory. Finally, a computer master tape is produced and all course listings with their room assignments are published for student registration.

Classificatory 'side-effects' of computerisation

Because computerised data collection requires clearly defined categories, several areas of classification have consequently been standardised. One of the standardisations relates directly to teaching—the definition of course types.

Definition of course types. The definition of course types has been developed in conjunction with the Office of the Vice-president for Academic affairs. On the Course file data Sheets, an entry must be selected from one of the following:

Type of Instruction	Definition
Lecture (LEC)	Classroom instruction, primarily through lecture presented by an instructor, with discussion not precluded but incidental to lecture. (Size of class is not a factor).
Discussion (DIS)	Classroom instruction carried on primarily through inter-action among students and instructor. In some cases, it may supplement a large lecture.
Recitation (REC)	Classroom instruction, carried on almost exclusively through inter-action between instructor and students, which is designed to supplement a large lecture.
Seminar (SEM)	Classroom instruction for a limited number of students who share with the instructor responsibility for preparation of material to be discussed in class.
Laboratory (LAB)	Individual or group work carried out by students under supervision of instructor, requiring special facilities (e.g., laboratory or studio) and equipment. In the sciences, it

	may be a supplement to lectures; in the arts, it may be a lesson or practice session.
	Field trips and courses providing supervised practice in a clinic (e.g., psychological or speech) or classroom (elementary, secondary school) which is usually not a campus facility, are included.
Tutorial (TUT)	Individual study and instruction, usually arranged by mutual agreement of instructor and student, not requiring classroom space.
Conference (CON)	Not a regularly scheduled class, but a special one-time meeting, lecture, or discussion or a series of them.
Programmed instruction (PGR)	Individual instruction which may require special equipment (machines, tapes, etc.) which often requires a specially equipped room, but in some cases may not require classroom space.

3. Ongoing and future development: new North Campus

As projected by the State University of New York, in 1975 the University at Buffalo is to provide facilities for a total of 36,700 full- and part-time students. To accomplish this the design and construction of more than 8.25 million net square feet of space on the 1,200-acre Amherst site is planned. This complex when completed will accommodate an on-site population of over 50,000 students, faculty, and staff.

The scale, complexity, and co-ordination of this project required the State University Construction Fund (SUCF) (a State agency) to create an organisational framework and develop new techniques to augment the traditional planning process. More than 20 planning firms are now working in a co-ordinated effort under the Fund's direction to ensure that the resultant facilities not only satisfy the University's programme, but also realize the full potential of the site. A portion of the planning is being done by the New York State Urban Development Corporation in the development of a new community adjacent to the campus. Within the University itself, the Architecture and Planning Division of the Office for Facilities Planning is the main co-ordinating unit.

The basic organisational planning pattern for projects such as this is detailed in the following paragraphs.

STEP NO. 1 — GENERATION OF THE ACADEMIC MASTER PLAN (AMP)
The SUNY Academic Master Plan (AMP) represents the long-range development goals of higher education within New York State. It presents, for SUNYAB, as an example, the number of full-time equivalent (FTE) students expected to be enrolled during projected five-year intervals.

STEP NO. 2 — DISTRIBUTION OF FTE WORKLOAD
Based on the FTE projections by instructional level contained in the Academic

Master Plan, resources are assigned to the various academic programme units within the Institution by its academic offices, in concert with policies established by SUNY.

STEP NO. 3 — JUSTIFICATION OF SPACE
The FTE workload distribution is used as base data in a mathematical model generated to determine quantities of net square feet required to support the functions of the University. Factors and formula variables are set for institution type by the SUNY Office of Campus Development (OCD) on a state-wide basis. When a total justified space quantity is derived, it is compared to the Existing Space Inventory, with the remainder forming the quantity of space allotted for new development.

STEP NO. 4 — GENERATION OF THE MASTER ACTION PROGRAMME (MAP)
SUNYAB Facilities Planning, SUNY Office of Campus Development (OCD) and the State University Construction Fund (SUCF) collectively generate the Master Academic Plan (MAP), as well as a phasing document for the development of facilities. Factors involved in this document consist of academic priorities, dollar flow projections, labour market capabilities, construction staging, etc.

STEP NO. 5 — PROGRAMME GENERATION
A facilities programme consisting of space definition and distribution as well as equipment requirements is generated for each functional University Unit.

There are an additional nine stages, composed of the more usual: approval, budget request, dollar appropriation, architect selection, design, final approval, dollar allocation, project construction and occupancy. Most of these later stages more directly involve central State facilities and personnel, although SUNYAB maintains its concern at appropriate levels.

F. Information and library resources and auxiliary academic units

In addition to the somewhat complex academic organization discussed in section A of this Part, there are a number of other academic units which are not incorporated in any of the faculties but report directly to the Vice-president for Academic affairs. These include:
1. Co-operative College Centre: A non-university unit financially administered by the Office of the Vice-president for Academic affairs and whose function is to offer educationally and economically deprived members of the Buffalo community remedial work in preparation for admission to four-year colleges and universities.
2. Council on International Studies: Co-ordinates overseas programme, lecture series by distinguished foreign visitors, some aspects of the Critical Languages

Programme, and those educational and scholarly activities that have international relevance.

3. Information and Library Resources: Originally consisted of the Computing Centre, the Libraries, the Instructional Communication Centre and the Division of Instructional Services. Currently, the Computer Centre has been transferred to the Office of the President. The Instructional Communication Centre and the Libraries report directly to the Vice-president for Academic affairs.

1. The University computer services

The Office of Computer Services (OCS) provides the entire SUNYAB community with academic, administrative and research computer services.

Through local and remote batch processing, OCS serves the basic computing needs of undergraduate and graduate students, faculty and staff. In the administrative areas, OCS is responsible for systems design and implementation, as well as processing and maintenance of all computerized administrative, accounting and student record systems. Its primary function is information processing and developing. The Director of OCS is administratively responsible to the Assistant Executive Vice-president (see Figure 2, page 00, SUNYAB Functional Organization). The Computer Services has two major facilities, a CDC 6400 and an IBM 360 model 40 computer.

Administrative functions

The administrative functions of the Office of Computer Services are organized under a University Information System consisting at this point of two major sub-systems:

1. Financial Administration,[1] under which is subsumed:
   a. budgetary planning and reporting, including projection of future budgets; and
   b. accounting affairs—payroll, health benefits, seniority rankings, hiring and retirement fund matters.
2. Student Academic Records Administration (SARA)[2] with responsibility for:
   a. student registration—a totally computerised system of student course registration was the subject of study and development within OCS for a period of more than two years. The first computerised registration occurred during the summer of 1970. Full implementation of the system was completed by the spring term of 1971.
   b. maintenance of a student cumulative grade file.[3]

All computerised administrative functions are the responsibility of Office of Computer Services and the Management Information Systems (MIS) Committee who advise the Assistant Executive Vice-president. SUNYAB is anticipating the eventual integration of management systems on common data base. Such integration

1. See Section G below.
2. See Section D above.
3. See Section E above.

would provide the ideal climate for the development of efficient and farsighted management systems development.

Whereas the Office of Computer Services (OCS) and Management Information Systems (MIS) have full responsibility for programme development and utilization for all administrative computing functions, a student or faculty member is responsible for his own programming. The Office of Computer Service (OCS) provides software support in the following forms:
1. Non-credit instruction in programming techniques.
2. Seminars dealing with different aspects of computer theory and technology.
3. The NYBLIB—a library of regularly used routines and documentation, maintained in the CDC 6400's memory bank.
4. Consultant services.

Since the central computing facility is located at the Interim Campus, physically isolated from the majority of potential users, OCS has developed a communications network of two major sub-systems:

Remote batch terminals—these terminals, with some small computing capacity of their own, are directly connected to the CDC 6400 over standard telephone lines. Five such terminals are in operation on the Main Campus with other terminals at the SUNY Colleges at Buffalo, Brockport, Fredonia and Geneseo.

Typewriter terminals—over 40 such terminals which permit job entry, editing and execution are located on the main campus. These terminals are connected to the IBM 360/40, and to the CDC 6400 via the Communications Channel Adapter.

Computer utilisation and service allocation

Increasing application of computer technology is reflected in the rapid growth of computer utilisation. During the 1970-71 fiscal year the CDC 6400 was operated 17 shifts per week, maintaining reasonably fast turn-around time for batch jobs, while the IBM 360/40 has already reached the saturation level. It is expected that CDC 6400 use would approach saturation during the current year.

There are three areas in which preparation for future service demands is seen as required:
1. Interactive computing—or conversational computing, provides the opportunity for an individual to sit at a terminal and edit and monitor an ongoing computer function. The Office of Computer Services (OCS) is involved in a feasibility study to determine precise needs and methods for meeting this need under existing budgetary constraints.
2. Management information system development—the University's management has a need for an integrated system for the provision of timely, accurate and readily available information.
3. Improved graphics capability—a heavily used OCS service is a plotting facility that employs seven-year-old equipment. This equipment needs upgrading to provide increased output as well as inter-active capability.

2. Libraries

The SUNYAB libraries consist of the Lockwood Memorial Library, housing the Social Sciences and Humanities collection, and several unit libraries, i.e., Health Sciences Library; the Science and Engineering Library, including the Physics and Chemistry units; the Law Library; the Music Library; the Art Library; the Interim Campus Library; and the Reserve Library.

All materials within the SUNYAB libraries are catalogued, shelved and circulated under the Library of Congress classification system.

In addition to holdings maintained directly by the on-campus system, the University Library participates in several co-operative programmes that make available additional information resources to the Library's patrons. Foremost among these is the Five Associated University Libraries, an association composed of SUNYAB, Syracuse, Rochester, Cornell, and Binghamton Universities.

The University Library also publishes a variety of reports, newsletters, handbooks and journals (a total of 22 publications during 1970) and has a prodigious collection of 20th century poetry, as well as a famous James Joyce collection.

Management of libraries

The Director of Libraries is a member of the Council of Provosts and University-wide Deans; he does not directly participate in curriculum planning, nor do any librarians, except through their discussions with the departmental library committees.

All librarians have faculty status and are represented in the Faculty Senate and all its bodies. The librarian participates in the budget planning process by working in sessions with the Academic Vice-president and in the discussions of the Council of Provosts.

The principal factor affecting the University Libraries' ability to support the instructional, research and public service activities of the University is the inadequacy of its space.[1]

Library strengths

Its strongest programmes have been its purchases of current monographs, monographic series and journals in bio-medical sciences, anthropology (Human Relations Area file), nineteenth- and twentieth-century English, American and French literature, including its distinguished collection of modern English poetry, mathematics, classics, art history, and philosophy.

Another strength is its microfilm collection of documents and rare texts; in number of units it is one of the ten largest in the country, although inadequacies of space and equipment and of cataloguing make it less accessible than it should be.

The professional staff of the libraries is considered competent, but not enough staff have been hired adequately to serve and support the existing programmes or fulfil plans to establish new services.

1. Most of the material in this section is adapted from a status report prepared by the Director of Libraries for the Middle States Accreditation Commission.

The libraries provide generally an adequate support to most aspects of existing educational programmes, although there are some difficult problems in matching collections and programmes, because of the very rapid changes in the character of the academic programmes.

These difficulties are noticeable at present in the programmes in History, Modern Languages, Law, Music, Education and Mathematics. Problems of this sort will increase in the future. The library system does not provide strong support to programmes under the general rubric of International Studies and World Affairs because of its very limited ability to buy materials in non-Western and Slavic languages. It also tends to be unsatisfactory in those areas requiring out-of-print material.

Major problems
The lack of an adequate planning process at the state-wide and local levels is one of the major problems.

Availability or accessibility is perhaps the most fundamental measure of the value of any library system. Ironically, as the collection grows, it is becoming less useful to the University it should serve. There is little information about the use of the library other than the conventional information about circulation and in-house use of materials; these figures indicate that it circulates between 500,000 and 750,000 items a year, for in-house use and for use outside the libraries. While this number has been increasing sharply in the past few years, it does not seem very high compared with other institutions of similar size which circulate more than a million volumes from one major library unit a year to a smaller student and faculty body.

The library has no real information about the areas of undergraduate instruction for which students draw heavily on the library. It does not pay sufficient attention to the needs of undergraduates, and to the necessity of providing access to current media and resources.

More recently, the library is attempting to deal with this problem by the creation of a specific undergraduate library. More than simply a place to study in the already crowded conditions, the library will be a duplicate collection of the main holdings in those areas considered to be basic to undergraduate studies, particularly in arts and letters. In addition to the readings from new courses, the lists from the reserve library, and the directions to be gained from academic planning sources, the main instrument for constructing such a core collection is the Stanford University Undergraduate Library model which lists approximately 100,000 volumes. Though it was hoped that such a collection could be purchased immediately, the limited funding has made this impossible. Only the first stage, a reading room facility and a limited number of books, is now available to students; the target date for the completed facility is September 1973.

The libraries are acquiring their resources at a decreasing rate, and at a rate which is not adequate to the needs of the University's academic programmes. In 1971/72 it added approximately 80,000 volumes, of which approximately 20,000 will be bound journals; five years ago it added over 120,000 volumes.

The basic equipment is described as adequate, but in need of repair. The proposed library buildings of the new campus will make a profound difference in the situation, for currently none of the major library units can house new materials without moving old materials to storage. Also, the dispersion of library resources into many different locations makes it difficult to provide access to materials. Many professors are forced to put large number of books on reserve. Although the library has tried to provide the materials most directly related to courses of instruction at the University, the lack of depth of the collection in main areas as well as the lack of multiple copies of essential material has forced the overloading of the Reserve Library, and probably worse, has stripped the open stacks of relevant resources in a number of areas.

The library budget for 1971/72 represents 5.5% of the total University budget. In submitting a budget request, the library is required to indicate which portion of the funds would be intended for maintenance of present programmes and which portion would go toward improvement, innovation and expansion. For 1971/72, all the monies requested were intended solely for maintenance of already existing services. The effect of such an austerity budget is most noticeable in the area of new acquisitions. Not only has the University budget been pared, but Federal sources of money for acquisitions have also been reduced.

Planning for the new library
Circumstances dictate that the present library, under tremendous daily pressure to meet user needs, be operated on a contingency basis which leaves little room for University-wide participation in the planning process. However, the impending move to the new North Campus has afforded the opportunity for planning that can be relatively long-range in nature.

The planning involves systematic information-gathering, consulting, reviewing, designing and approving by many agencies functioning at SUNYAB, both at local and state levels, as described in Section E above, in the discussion of planning for the new campus. The building of the libraries will coincide with the construction of the academic units.

3. The Instructional Communication Centre

The Instructional Communication Centre's (ICC) primary purpose is to provide educational communication services and programmes, organized around three main functions; 1) instructional communication services, 2) instructional communications research and development, and 3) information dissemination concerning media services.

The instructional communications services are carried out by five divisions within the ICC: Campus service, Media library, Graphic production, Motion picture production, and Instructional television. Essentially, these divisions acquire, co-ordinate, operate and maintain facilities and equipment for use in the teaching-learning process.

4. Division of Instructional Services

An increasingly vital component of the University's information/decision-making sub-system is the Division of Instructional Services. This office defines its objectives as the application of psychometric methods[1] in the classroom, and the extension of psychometric theory to administrative decisions.

Operationally, Instructional Services has three sub-departments (University research, Student testing and Programming and scoring) which have distinct functions, but operate as a unified force in the University's attempts to improve instruction.

University research

The department of University Research:
1. Provides information to administration, faculty, and students about the non-academic characteristics of the freshman class.
2. Adds to the existing substantive and methodological knowledge in the social sciences, especially with respect to higher education and to the development of the late adolescent/early adulthood period.
3. Trains personnel, including graduate students, in the research techniques of the social sciences.
4. Provides consulting services to other departments.

The Division's recent activities have included the production and publication of the Biography of a Class (BOAC), reports on freshman classes (which analyse and compare data going back to 1964), 'student experience', and numerous consultant tasks involving summer session planning, orientation and admissions decisions.

Student testing

The principal purpose of the testing office is to provide the entire community with professional assistance in all stages of testing and evaluation. The testing section has facilities for individual and group administrations, and also aids in the construction, interpretation, selection and utilisation of tests and other evaluative instruments.

Programming and scoring

The objectives of the Programming and scoring unit of the Division of Instructional Services are in a large part defined externally with respect to the operation itself. *Scoring service* exists to provide the faculty with timely and meaningful processing of machine scorable examinations.

The programming group provides data processing services to various units of the Division of Student Affairs. At present, its prime responsibility is to the Division of Instructional Services in support of Scoring service and University research. It also provides significant service to the Financial aid office and to University placement. Programming also operates two systems for the School

---

1. See Glossary, p. 211.

of Medicine and from time to time aids other University organizations with data processing needs.

In support of University research the programming staff, together with the scoring staff, provide aid in the collection, reduction, analysis, presentation and preservation of the data used for report publishing. It was for these purposes that the unit was originally formed.

G. The budget system

The common denominator that mediates decisions regarding the academic and physical plan and facilities sub-systems of SUNYAB is the financial sub-system. Its philosophic intention is to be 'the plan of expenditures that reflects educational process in fiscal terms'; however, under the present system, there seems to be a trend towards the budget leading rather than reflecting the direction of academic decision-making. Budgetary decisions are made on the basis of staff and physical resource needs with little input from the teaching and research components of SUNYAB.

The interchange between these sub-systems is loosely defined; as a result, those officers in charge of budgetary allocation often define SUNYAB directions. This is apparent to the budgetary officers as well as to the administration, who agree that protection against budgetary leadership should be a function of a strong academic element of SUNYAB. This academic element should endeavour to ensure its own directions by making internal decisions based on the evaluation of the success of its programmes and then aligning budgetary allocations accordingly.

In an effort to encourage this approach, SUNYAB officials have initiated a number of procedures that have facilitated decision-making from an academic point of view. An example is the priority programmes analysis of the Division of Graduate Studies, which attempts to determine which programmes should be allowed to expand, remain constant, or be phased out. Through focusing on the strengths and needs of the University, rather than using an across the board cutback when allocating funds for departmental use, it is hoped that the funds will be used in a more productive way.

A system to collect needed information could link SUNYAB's sub-systems for more effectively balanced decision-making. Aware of this, SUNYAB is currently engaged in planning for a 'Management information system' that will be designed for the specific needs of this campus.

1. Budget system process

The SUNYAB budgetary sub-system is the University's most complex component. It is also its most dynamic system, being continually assessed, projected and adjusted in light of new information and events. It is a system both rigid and flexible. Its rigidity lies in the limitations of the legislature's appropriations. Its flexibility is largely a function of necessity: available funds must be programmed and dispersed to the satisfaction of both decision-makers and recipient programmes.

2. Relationship with the SUNY system[1]

The SUNY system, as it now operates, presumes centralised budgetary management and is designed to gather and assess data for higher education units. Computer operations, however, fail to provide for decentralised internal management or to adequately analyse basic data. The automated services in Albany are simply not designed to process required information for internal budgetary administration at Buffalo.

In response to this operation gap, SUNYAB designed and implemented its own Programme Planning and Budgetary System (PPBS). In 1965 PPBS operations were parallel to those of SUNY, yet more capable at internal management needs.

3. Management of the SUNYAB budget system

The central administrative component of the SUNYAB budget system is the University Budget Office which designed the present system, handles all pertinent data and prepares the budget. The Budget Office is part of the Office of the Vice-president for Operations and Systems and is directly responsible to the Assistant Vice-president and Controller. Figure 11 describes the relationship and details of the office operation.

The University Budget Office promotes decentralised budgeting and recognises the School or Division as the basic fundable unit. The Division reports to a University Vice-president who assumes budgetary responsibility in his area. Each School or Division represents an autonomous 'budgeted entity' with its own programme, budget, and accounting identity.

Departments, Centres and other offices derive their funds from the total appropriation of the organisational unit to which they belong. For example, each academic department in the Faculty of Arts and Letters works under an overall budget which it shares with all other departments in the Faculty. There are 21 major Operating Divisions set up for the budget system; these are:

Seven faculties

Arts & Letters	Law & Jurisprudence
Educational Studies	Natural Science & Mathematics
Engineering & Applied Sciences	Social Science & Administration
	Health Sciences

Thirteen other Divisions

Division of Undergraduate Studies	Summer Sessions
The Graduate School	Residence Halls

1. Based on the December 1970 SUNYAB Operating Budget Report and the SUNYAB Budget Projection Cycle Sequence-Reports (March 1971).

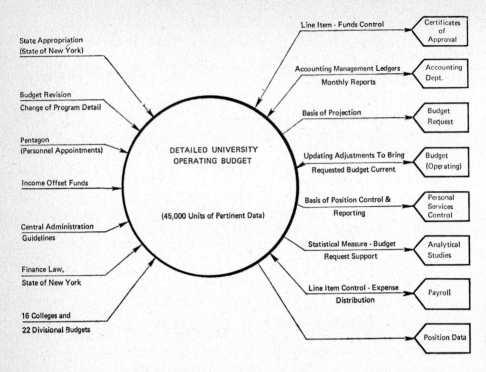

FIGURE 11. *University operating budget: co-ordinative functions*

Office of the President
Vice-president Academic Affairs
Vice-president Facilities Planning
Vice-president University Relations
Vice-president Student Affairs
Vice-president for Research
Vice-president Operations & Systems
Millard Fillmore College,
    Evening Division

Co-ordinator for Information Services
Libraries
Computing and Data Processing
Faculty Senate
Storehouse
Instructional Communications Centre

One general Division including
Insurance, Membership Fees, Western New York Nuclear Research Centre.

Within these divisions are 382 Departments or 'budgeted entities', of which 143 are instructional.

The budget process
The level of the budgeted entity—each budgeted entity within each budget division prepares an annual budget request. In the case of academic programmes/departments the request must be justified in terms of long-range goals as expressed in the Academic Plan. All budgeted entities, however, must justify their budget

requests in terms of four specific areas which are totalled, correlated and adjusted for each Major Operating Division and for the University as a whole. These four areas are:

1. Workload (Ongoing and Increased).
2. Improvement.
3. New Programmes.
4. Development.

Each of these areas is used to determine the needs of the budgeted entity in terms of instructional and non-instructional staffing requirements, temporary services, supplies and expenses, equipment related to new instructional positions and equipment in general. It should be made clear that each request, integrated with items such as FTE's and workload statistics, is partially pre-determined by the limitation of the operating budget approved by the State.

Since State Finance Laws provide the Department of Audit and Control with the legal right to expend public funds, all operations must be certified and segregated by 'funds' established by that office. These 'funds' are divided into six major areas at the State level:

1. State Purpose Funds.
2. Income Funds.
3. Income Funds (Reimbursable Income Offset).
4. Restricted Endowment Funds.
5. Student Loan Funds.
6. Dormitory Income Funds.

Every appointment must be approved and certified within one of these funds as well as along subdivisionary lines or 'accounts'. Figure 12 is a graphic representation of the SUNYAB budget projection cycle which is used to calculate a projected budget programme in terms of these funds, by department, and by function.

The level of the budget operating division—each Faculty is a separate budget operating division. The Provost of the Faculty is charged with the responsibility of preparing his divisional budget request and of administering funds appropriated under the current budget. Each faculty is budgeted a certain amount for resources, faculty positions, etc., according to decisions made by the Vice-president for Academic affairs. The Provost then works and consults with each department chairman to determine the needs of the department and the details of resource allocation. The completed Faculty budget, prepared to the guidelines of the Vice-presidents, is forwarded to the Budget Office which acts as the co-ordinating agency for the Vice-presidents.

Co-ordinating function of the university budget office—the budget office must prepare and disseminate vice-presidential guidelines. In addition, it is charged with the supervision of Operating Divisions and subsidiary budgeted entities in preparing their budget requests. As co-ordinating agency of the Vice-presidents, the Budget Office must consolidate the entire institutional budget. Figure 11 illustrated the co-ordinative functions of the Budget Office in terms of pertinent data variables.

171

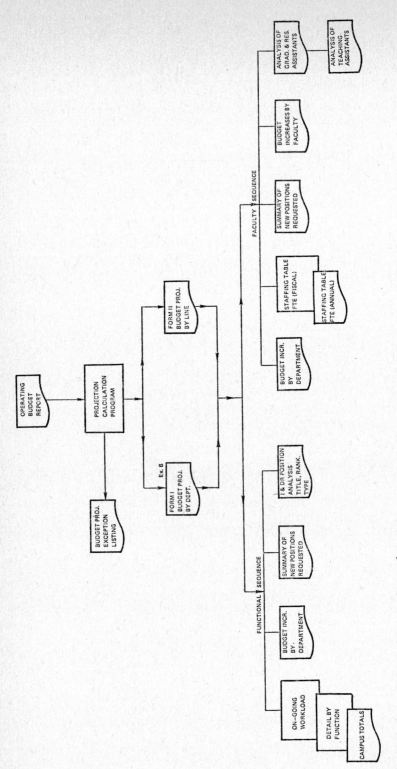

FIGURE 12. *SUNYAB budget projection cycle*

Eventually the data are summarised into the four budget request areas, i.e., ongoing workload, etc. The statement below summarised the 1971/72 Budget Request.[1]

General Dimensions of the 1971/72 Budget Proposal
The 1971/72 budget proposal calls for a State operating budget of $72,935,560 constituting an increase over the 1970/71 base budget of $8,892,391. Of the total increase, $3,989,244 is required for ongoing workload; $2,915,815 is dedicated to increased workload and $1,854,732 for improvement of programmes and $42,600 for new programmes. As in previous years a significant distortion of the budget is produced by the need to provide almost $4 million for the rental of facilities.[2]

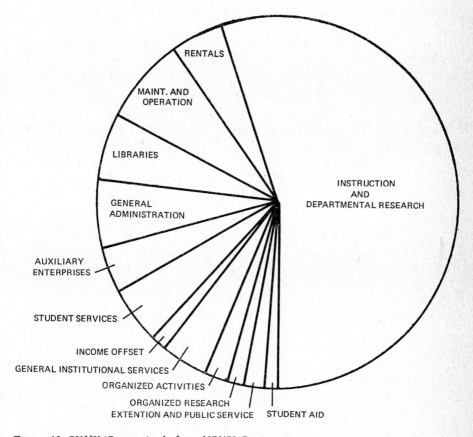

FIGURE 13. *SUNYAB operating budget: 1971/72 Request*

1. SUNYAB 1971-72 Budget Request, SUNYAB 1970, p. 3.
2. The Ridge Lea Campus facilities are entirely rented from a private concern (see also Section E of Part II).

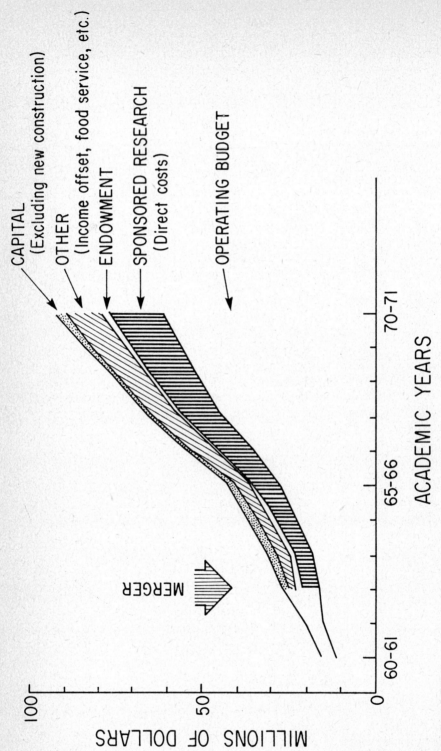

FIGURE 14. *SUNYAB total budget operating revenues, 1961-71*

174

Figure 13 is another type of summary statement from the same budget request; this graphic summary presents the operating budget in terms of various institutional operations.

Figure 14, which traces the growth of the University's total budget from 1960/61 to 1970/71 (requested), separates operating revenues and expenses into general operating budget, capital budget, sponsored research funds, endowment income and other non-appropriated dollars.

An additional explanation is needed here to clarify the difference between the University's *proposed* budget and its *actual* operating budget. The gross budget is what the University projects for fulfilment of all programmes. The operating budget, of course, is that amount which the University actually expends. Since the State Budget is partially based on previous budget requests/expenditures, a 'savings factor' is figured in. This savings factor is based on the impossibility of any large, dynamic institution completing all of its planned programmes. Such reasons as personnel turnover and priority shifts often make programme completion impossible. The savings factor, usually figured at around 2.7% of the proposed budget, is automatically subtracted from the budget request, leaving a 'net operating budget'. The State (i.e., either the Legislature or the Division of the Budget) places an additional constraint on the University by mandating an 'expenditure ceiling'—the University is told to suppress programme expansion to prevent overspending. The result of this policy is that the University's actual operating budget may be as much as $3 million less than its justified requests.

Both verbal and graphic statements are, by nature, very general and cannot indicate the full extent of data-gathering and co-ordinating requisite to the institutional budget. Essentially, however, the bulk of the data inputs consists of facilities-planning information,[1] enrolment figures and position (faculty/staff) correlations.

Tables 1 to 4 are examples of the kinds of of data tabulations and correlations made for budget purposes.[2] The tables all list data comparatively for fiscal years 1968-69, 1969-70, 1970-71 and 1971-72. Several other tables, although developed for budget purposes, are not given in this section, but can be found in Section H below, where they are relevant to the discussion of teaching.[3]

Budget review phase within the University—once the University budget office has completed its analyses and has prepared the total institutional budget according to the guidelines of the Vice-presidents, the Vice-presidents review their respective concerns and make necessary adjustments. The adjusted and consolidated budget is then sent to the Office of the President who reviews it and may adjust or approve it as he sees fit.

1. See Section E above.
2. From the SUNYAB Comparative Statistical Summary by Major Division—September 1970 (revised January 1971).
3. In Section G the pertinent tables are: Table 5, Student/faculty ratios; Table 6, Ratio of teaching to non-teaching personnel.

TABLE 1.   Average support cost per instructional FTE

	Fiscal Years			
Instruction and department research	1968/69 Actual	1969/70 Actual	1970/71 Budgeted	1971/72 Projected
Faculty of				
Arts and Letters	2.71:1	2.95:1	2.97:1	2.95:1
Educational Studies	2.70:1	2.79:1	2.82:1	2.82:1
Engineering and Applied Sciences	1.87:1	1.91:1	1.95:1	1.95:1
Health Sciences	1.60:1	1.60:1	1.64:1	1.67:1
Law & Jurisprudence	1.55:1	1.52:1	1.40:1	1.40:1
Natural Sciences & Mathematics	1.47:1	1.47:1	1.53:1	1.53:1
Social Sciences & Administration	2.25:1	2.19:1	2.31:1	2.31:1
Division of Undergraduate Studies	n.a.	n.a.	n.a.	n.a.
Millard Fillmore College[1]	5.88:1	5.78:1	5.26:1	4.57:1
Summer Sessions[1]	13.22:1	23.77:1	23.77:1	23.77:1
University-wide summary				
Regular Sessions	1.78:1	1.80:1	1.93:1	1.94:1
Evening Division[1]	5.88:1	5.78:1	5.26:1	4.57:1
Health Sciences	1.60:1	1.60:1	1.64:1	1.67:1

1. Teaching FTEs are statistically equated; the ratios reported are subject to distortion as part-time, hourly, and salaried non-teaching positions are also paid via Temporary Service Funds.
n.a.   Not applicable.   Non-teaching FTEs greater than teaching FTEs, resulting in a negative ratio.

The final internal action on the budget request is its preparation for *informal* presentation to the SUNY Central Administration.

SUNY central administration review—the presentation to the SUNY central administration is actually a Preliminary budget request. This request, which is usually in great detail, is reviewed by the Chancellor of the State University in a session with the President of the University Centre (i.e., Buffalo). The SUNY central administration develops its overall SUNY budget after such reviews with each State University unit of the system. The completed formal budget request is then forwarded to the State's Division of the budget.

The Division of the budget—the Division of the Budget is an administrative office of the Governor of the State and is charged with the responsibility of overseeing and reviewing the formal budget requests of all State institutions, departments, etc.[1] The University of Buffalo's budget request, as part of the total SUNY budget request, is forwarded to the Division of the budget. The President of

1. In 1969-70 New York State appropriated $625,341,000 for higher education. That was 45% more than the State's 1967-68 appropriation and almost 700% more than the sum provided a decade earlier, 1959-60 ($78,546,000). The 1969-70 figure represents $34.20 *per capita*, which placed New York only 21st among the 50 States, but despite the 'poor' showing at that level, the total appropriation of $625.3 millions ranked second only to California's $749.2 millions.

TABLE 2. FTE enrolment distribution by level as a percentage of total enrolment

All functions	Teach., Grad. & Res. Asst's. (head count)	Percent of total	Graduate[2] enrolments (head count)	Grad. enrol. as percent of total (head count)	Ratio Teach., Grad. & Res. Assistants to Graduate enrolment
Total	*1 013*	*100.0*	*5 727*	*100.0*	*1:5.7*
Teaching Assistants	597	100.0			
Graduate Assistants[1]	416	100.0			
Faculty of Arts and Letters	*226*	*22.3*	*640*	*11.2*	*1:2.8*
Teaching Assistants	141	23.6			
Graduate Assistants	85	20.4			
Faculty of Educ. Studies	*83*	*8.2*	*2.148*	*37.5*	*1:25.9*
Teaching Assistants	71	11.9			
Graduate Assistants	12	2.9			
Faculty of Engr. & Appl. Sci.	*87*	*8.6*	*699*	*12.2*	*1:8.0*
Teaching Assistants	50	8.4			
Graduate Assistants	37	8.9			
Faculty of Law & Jurisprudence	*3*	*0.3*	*530*	*9.3*	*—*
Teaching Assistants	—	—			
Graduate Assistants	3	0.7			
Faculty of Nat. Sci. & Math.	*223*	*22.0*	*453*	*7.9*	*1:2.0*
Teaching Assistants	134	22.5			
Graduate Assistants	89	21.4			
Faculty of Social Sci. & Admin.	*276*	*27.3*	*1 257*	*21.9*	*1:4.6*
Teaching Assistants	153	25.6			
Graduate Assistants	123	29.6			
Div. of Undergraduate Studies	*50*	*4.9*			
Teaching Assistants	48	8.0			
Graduate Assistants	2	0.5			
V.P. Academic Development	*17*	*1.7*			
Teaching Assistants	—	—			
Graduate Assistants	17	4.1			
Graduate School	*47*	*4.6*			
Teaching Assistants	—	—			
Graduate Assistants	47	11.3			
President's Office	*1*	*0.1*			
Teaching Assistants	—	—			
Graduate Assistants	1	0.2			
Faculty of Health Sciences	*61*	*100.0*	*1 191*		*1:19.5*
Teaching Assistants	26	42.6			
Graduate Assistants	35	57.4			

1. Includes Research Assistants.
2. Includes Graduate Masters and Graduate Doctoral, adjusted for actual Fall, 1970/71 enrolment.

TABLE 3. Budgeted direct costs per FTE student (in dollars)

	Fiscal Years			
Instruction & Departmental Research	1968/69 Budgeted	1969/70 Budgeted	1970/71 Budgeted	1971/72 Requested
Faculty of				
Arts and Letters	1 233	1 304	1 328	1 503
Educational Studies	1 142	1 186	1 246	1 368
Engineering & Applied Sciences	2 501	2 330	2 608	2 634
Health Sciences	5 470	6 149	6 464	6 798
Law & Jurisprudence	1 238	1 400	1 300	1 142
Natural Sciences & Mathematics	1 923	2 403	2 483	2 493
Social Sciences & Administration	1 093	1 044	1 222	1 285
Division of Undergraduate Studies	1 201	802	852	1 448
Millard Fillmore College	480	477	440	590
Summer Sessions	413	400	450	412
University-Wide Costs (Budgeted I & DR)				
Regular and Evening Divisions	1 299	1 286	1 362	1 548
Regular Sessions	1 415	1 622	1 522	1 680
Millard Fillmore College	480	477	440	590
Summer Sessions	413	400	450	412
Health Sciences	5 470	6 149	6 464	6 798

SUNYAB is called to a special hearing to answer questions and offer further justification as needed. When the budget request is finally approved it becomes an official part of the Governor's Executive budget, which in turn is sent to the State Legislature.

Legislature approval—The State Legislature reviews the SUNYAB request as part of the Executive Budget and also as a separate entity. Special education committees with considerable expertise in the financial aspects of higher education review the request and may call upon the SUNYAB President to report to them. In every year since 1962 these Committees have in some way acted upon the request before recommending its approval. Once the Legislature approves the budget (the Executive budget) the SUNYAB budget becomes operational.

The budget cycle timetable
Figure 15 is a graphic presentation of the calendar of budgetary events as outlined above. The complete cycle has actually taken as much as eighteen months to complete; and, it is not unusual for the University to be operating for several months without knowing whether its current budget has been *officially* approved.

The following statement is taken from a 1970 'memorandum' prepared by the University Office of institutional research:

> The difficulties which derive from formula budgeting are numerous and do not warrant reciting in detail, but they fall within two categories: 1) there are

TABLE 4. Degrees granted and costs per degree (in dollars)

Instruction and Departmental Res.	1968/69			1969/70		
	FTE enrolment	Degrees granted	Instr. cost per degree	FTE enrolment	Degrees granted	Instr. cost per degree
Faculty of						
Arts & Letters	*2 825*	*486*	*5 402*	*3 249*	*472*	*6 477*
Baccalaureates	2 381	424		2 739	412	
Masters	259	54		302	38	
Doctorates	185	8		208	22	
Educational Studies	*1 430*	*507*	*2 470*	*1 605*	*583*	*2 423*
Baccalaureates	476	25		543	160	
Masters	457	318		608	336	
Doctorates	497	64		454	87	
Engr. & Applied Sciences	*926*	*339*	*4 001*	*1 101*	*444*	*3 578*
Baccalaureates	611	210		676	271	
Masters	212	113		312	160	
Doctorates	103	16		113	13	
Law & Jurisprudence	*523*	*111*	*4 400*	*528*	*109*	*5 081*
Doctoral of Law	523	111		528	109	
Nat. Science & Math.	*2 255*	*305*	*8 168*	*1 952*	*311*	*8 950*
Baccalaureates	1 823	193		1 580	204	
Masters	214	75		163	64	
Doctorates	218	37		209	43	
Soc. Sciences & Admin.	*5 280*	*1 611*	*2 580*	*6 128*	*1 667*	*2 764*
Baccalaureates	4 152	1 247		4 970	1 311	
Masters	772	305		782	305	
Doctorates	356	59		376	61	
Div. of Undergraduate Studies	*578*	*69*	*3 537*	*903*	*65*	*3 758*
Associate in Arts	145	17		226	23	
Associate in Applied Science	433	52		677	42	
Health Sciences	*1 600*	*281*	*20 586*	*1 534*	*332*	*19 202*
Baccalaureates	582	217		469	253	
Masters	173	30		890	47	
Doctorates	845	34		175	32	
University Wide Summary						
Regular Session	*13 817*	*3 428*	*3 682*	*15 466*	*3 651*	*3 907*
Associate in Arts	145	17		226	23	
Associate in Applied Science	433	52		677	42	
Baccalaureates	9 443	2 199		10 508	2 358	
Masters	1 914	865		2 167	903	
Doctorates	1 882	295		1 888	325	
Health Sciences	*1 600*	*281*	*20 586*	*1 534*	*332*	*19 202*
Baccalaureates	582	217		469	253	
Masters	173	30		890	47	
Doctorates	845	34		175	32	

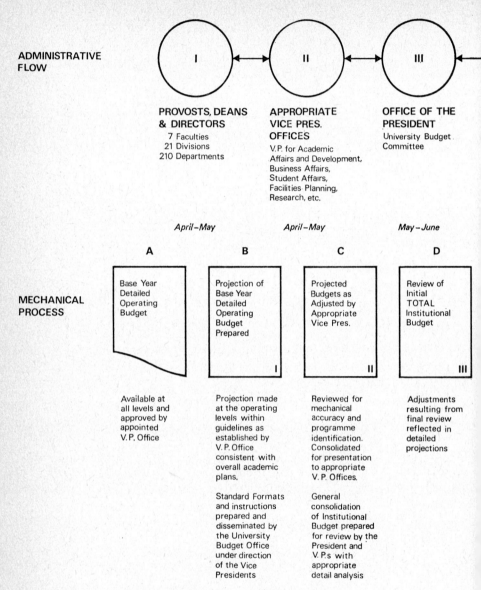

FIGURE 15. *Calendar of budgetary events.*

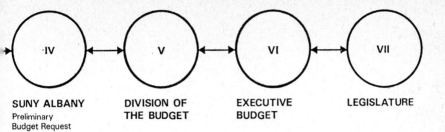

IV	V	VI	VII
SUNY ALBANY Preliminary Budget Request	**DIVISION OF THE BUDGET**	**EXECUTIVE BUDGET**	**LEGISLATURE**

June – July	*September*	*January*		*March*
E	**F**	**G**	**H**	**I**
Review of Budget Request with Appropriate Analysis III	Budget Request Presented to Central Administration IV	Formal Budgetary Presentation prepared and submitted IV	Hearings by the Division of the Budget V	Legislative Action Appropriate Bill Acted upon VII

Final posture
of the
Institutional
Budget agreed
upon internally
by all
Administrative
Officers
 	
Informal
presentation
prepared for
submission to
SUNY Central
Administration
	State University
	reacts to the
	proposals and
	mutual agreements
	are reached
	between Campus
	and Central
	Administration
	
	Budget requests
	adjusted and
	reconsolidated
	and reported
	out reflecting:
	1. Institutional
	   request
	2. V. P. area of
	   responsibility
		Copies to:
		Central
		Administration
		Division of
		the Budget
			Additional
			analytical
			material
			developed
			as required
			
			Copies of the
			Budget Requests
			available to
			Legislative
			Committees
				Appropriate
				adjustments are
				made in the detail
				budgets as
				directed by the
				V.P. Offices
				
				Adjusted Budget
				becomes
				operational
				
				Cycle repeats

those which arise because certain educational presumptions are inextricably 'locked into' the system, defying reconsideration. For example, . . . teacher-directed classes in classrooms, and resources accordingly are committed to such ends. . . 2) Other problems arise because decisions which are essentially educational in nature fall by virtue of the formula budgetary system to non-educational personnel: special dispensation is required to violate a formula. Academic administrators, for example, who attempt to change the composition of their budget . . . but who, unfortunately, have only an educational judgment on which to base their proposals, face a maddening experience. Budget personnel, . . . frequently are disposed to accept only non-educational 'justifications' for such changes, e.g., economic efficiency or statutory requirement.

In short, the formula approach to resource allocation in higher education suffers two intrinsic defects: it inhibits (perhaps it prevents) needed educational change and it too *frequently fails to reserve educational decisions to educators*.

. . . Despite the defects of the formula approach, budgeting in general is clearly not a demon to be exorcised from the body academic. . . There is a rationale which animates it in part, . . . a rationale expressed most succinctly in the phrase 'fiscal accountability'. A fiscal *carte blanche* to educators, given solely on the basis that non-educators are unqualified to pass competently on educational matters, is no more wise than it is feasible. For educators are not gods. The interest which states maintain in the fiscal accountability of the recipients of their tax monies, including educators, is wholly legitimate.

. . . What is needed instead is a fiscal system which holds educators accountable but which permits them a wide latitude of discretion in educational concerns.[1]

H. Evaluation: an objective overview

At present, there exists no integrated means of evaluating the University. The current system of evaluation is relatively unco-ordinated and, thus, the carefully planned University budget must be considered as the only evaluative mechanism.

Tables 5 and 6, excerpted from the 1970 Report of the University budget office and the University's budget request, present basic information concerning ratios and distribution figures of students, faculty, graduate research and teaching assistants, and various non-teaching personnel. These are included here as an indicator of the evaluation processes. In this case, financial support is a function of evaluation.

Despite the fact there is no integrated means of evaluating the University as a whole, there do exist various mechanisms both external and internal to the University that evaluate particular aspects of institutional growth, excellence and comparative standing. The following paragraphs discuss those mechanisms.

1. Walter C. Hobbs, "The Trouble with the Budget", Office of Institutional Research, SUNYAB, January 1970.

TABLE 5.   Student-faculty ratios

Instruction & Departmental Research	Fiscal Years			
	1968/69 Actual	1969/70 Actual	1970/71 Budgeted	1971/72 Requested
Faculty of				
Arts and Letters	12.91	14.48	14.85	13.55
Educational Studies	14.25	15.28	15.73	14.58
Engineering & Applied Sciences	8.58	10.15	9.48	9.81
Health Sciences	4.25	3.96	4.05	3.97
Law & Jurisprudence	18.31	17.98	21.17	23.31
Natural Sciences & Mathematics	12.24	10.55	10.64	10.91
Social Sciences & Administration	16.80	20.19	17.48	16.86
Division of Undergraduate Studies	22.09	38.25	30.36	23.96
Millard Fillmore College	18.46	23.34	26.42	21.07
Summer Sessions	21.80	24.57	24.51	31.02
University-wide averages				
Regular Session-Evening Division	14.51	16.04	16.08	14.91
Regular Sessions Only	14.09	15.29	15.06	14.32
Evening Division Only	18.46	23.34	26.42	21.07
Health Sciences	4.25	3.96	4.05	4.97

TABLE 6.   Ratio of teaching to non-teaching personnel

Instruction & Departmental Research	Fiscal Years			
	1968/69 Actual	1969/70 Actual	1970/71 Budgeted	1971/72 Projected
Faculty of				
Arts and Letters	2.71:1	2.95:1	2.97:1	2.95:1
Educational Studies	2.70:1	2.79:1	2.82:1	2.82:1
Engineering & Applied Sciences	1.87:1	1.91:1	1.95:1	1.95:1
Health Sciences	1.60:1	1.60:1	1.64:1	1.67:1
Law and Jurisprudence	1.55:1	1.52:1	1.40:1	1.40:1
Natural Sciences & Mathematics	1.47:1	1.47:1	1.53:1	1.53:1
Social Sciences & Administration	2.25:1	2.19:1	2.31:1	2.31:1
Division of Undergraduate Studies	n.a.	n.a.	n.a.	n.a.
Millard Fillmore College	5.88:1	5.78:1	5.26:1	4.57:1
Summer Sessions	13.22:1	23.77:1	23.77:1	23.77:1
University-wide summary				
Regular Sessions	1.78:1	1.80:1	1.93:1	1.94:1
Evening Division	5.88:1	5.78:1	5.26:1	4.57:1
Health Sciences	1.60:1	1.60:1	1.64:1	1.67:1

n.a.   Not applicable.

1. External processes: accreditation

The State University of New York at Buffalo, as a member institution of the State University of New York, subject to the rules, regulations, and policies of that system, is accredited by the Board of Regents. The entire State University system and all individual member institutions are accredited by the Middle States Association of Colleges and Secondary Schools.

The Middle States Association of Colleges and Secondary Schools

The Middle States Association of Colleges and Secondary Schools is an independent organization established in 1887 for the improvement of educational institutions and for the development of better working relations among secondary schools, institutions of higher education, and other educational agencies in the Middle States. Membership follows accreditation by either the Commission on Higher Education or the Commission on Secondary Schools.

The Federation of Regional Accrediting Commissions of Higher Education (FRACHE)

The activities of the Commission on Higher Education are co-ordinated with those of similar commissions in the other five regions of the country through the Federation of Regional Accrediting Commissions of Higher Education.

As the agent of the constituent commissions, the Federation develops and codifies general principles and procedures for institutional evaluation and accreditation. It seeks generally to strengthen and increase the effectiveness of higher education in all appropriate ways. The Federation's general aim is to establish a national consensus on accrediting in higher education for regional application. Institutions of higher education are accredited by the six regional accrediting agencies and are provided with consultative and other services through the commissions which constitute the Federation.

The nature of Middle States Accreditation

While Middle States accreditation is unconditional, it must be re-affirmed at approximately ten-year intervals. Accreditation action concerns the whole institution and is based on an institution's own objectives for its students. Obviously it does not reflect standardisation. Its meaning has to be interpreted in relation to each institution's goals. It does not imply similarity of aims, uniformity of process, or comparability of institutions. *The most significant aspect of Middle States accreditation is its effect upon the institution itself. The evaluation process requires that each member institution periodically review its own concepts, goals, and operations, supported by the expert professional criticism of a visiting team which reports to the institution and to the Commission.*

Action by the Commission

After the visiting team, drawn from accredited institutions, primarily in the Middle

States area, has made its report, the Commission determines appropriate action. Committee recommendations require ratification by the full Commission, which may recommend accreditation, a deferred decision, pending reports, or denial of accreditation. Striving for a charter of excellence, the university under scrutiny seeks prestige and the recognition of other member institutions; thus, in accordance with its own goals, the applicant attempts to fulfil the following standards as stated by the Commission: clearly stated purposes and objectives; a responsible board of trustees; a general education curriculum; programmes emphasising theory and skills; an intellectual atmosphere of growth; a persistent concern for objectives; emphasis on continuous intellectual and professional development of the faculty; clear definitions of responsibility; physical facilities proportional to the requirements of the educational programme; stability of resources. As of this writing, the State University of New York is preparing for a Middle States Evaluation. To this end all member University Centres are required to prepare evaluations for the University central office. This is the fourth time the University at Buffalo has been evaluated since 1921.

The American Council on Education rating of graduate programmes (ACE)
Because each graduate programme is unique, qualitative comparisons are rendered extremely difficult, if not impossible. On the other hand, given an acceptable set of measurement criteria, a means of rating programmes of the same discipline in different universities might be established. Unfortunately, no such criteria have as yet been formulated and consequently the only available inter-university comparison is one based upon *reputations* of graduate departments. The American Council on Education's (ACE) 1970 Rating of Graduate programmes was published as a follow-up study to a similar "reputation-based" survey conducted in 1964. Three disciplines at SUNY at Buffalo were listed among the top-ranked departments: English, Pharmacology, and Physiology.

Physiology at SUNYAB ranks seventh in the nation in the report, up from 17th in 1964. English, rated 'less than adequate' in 1964, now ranks 17th. The English programme was the only discipline at any school in the nation to show such a great improvement during the five-year period. In Pharmacology, SUNYAB ranked 20th in the nation.

2. Internal processes: Graduate School evaluation

Since October 1969 the Graduate Division has been in the process of evaluating existing higher degree programmes,[1] the main evaluative instrument being a committee of recognised scholars and faculty not associated with the SUNY system or the particular programme. Final approval rests with the New York State Department of Education.

1. 'Higher degree' here only refers to the M.S., M.A., M.F.A., Ph.D.

Preparation for evaluation
The Office of the Dean of the Graduate Division initiates the evaluation by appointing a committee of scholars in the appropriate field. The evaluation of each programme is expected to have unique characteristics and emphases. For both proposed and existing programmes, the Executive Committee of the Graduate Division recommends general guidelines for a formal statement that is submitted to the State for approval. The responsible administrative officer of the Faculty (or School) certifies that the programme described will be part of the educational mission of that unit, and that the unit is prepared to commit the necessary resources.

Preliminary review
The statement for the proposed or existing graduate degree programme is then (a) submitted directly to the Office of the Dean of the Graduate Division for initiation of evaluation without prior review by the appropriate Divisional Commitee or (b) reviewed by the appropriate Divisional Committee and then submitted to the Office of the Dean for initiation of evaluation.

Initiation of evaluation
Following the preliminary review stage, the Dean of the Graduate Division appoints a committee of scholars from within and outside the University to review, evaluate and make recommendations concerning the programme.

Evaluation by the Committee
Using guidelines provided by the Graduate Division, the Evaluation Committee develops appropriate criteria and procedures, conducts its evaluations, and reports its findings and recommendations.

Each evaluation team and the related personnel may develop sets of questions such as the following, which deal with issues suggested by the Graduate Division: the goal of the programme, the need for the programme, its present directions, the quality of its offerings and scholarship, its resources and evaluative mechanisms.

Actual evaluation, which continues for several months or a year, involves a series of committee meetings with the Dean of the Graduate Division, departmental faculty members, students in the programme, and any others deemed necessary.

At the end of these meetings the Committee prepares a first draft and a final report of its evaluation, both of which are submitted to the Dean of the Graduate Division. The report should include the Committee's recommendation to give full or provisional approval, or rejection of the programme. The Evaluation Committee identifies the strengths and weaknesses and may provide recommendations for further development of the programme.

Follow-up to the evaluation
After the Dean of the Graduate Division receives the final report of the Evaluation Committee he transmits it to the concerned department or faculty group. The department then responds to the report: if the recommendations of the Com-

mittee fall short of faculty expectations, opportunity is provided for open discussion.

Actions

The Divisional Committee either approves or rejects the report and so notifies the Dean; likewise, the Dean receives the recommendations of the Executive Committee. He makes appropriate recommendations to the Vice-president for Academic Affairs, who reports to the President; the President transmits the recommendations to the SUNY Central Administration, which in turn reports to the State Education Department, where the final decision is made. Approval returns the programme to the involved faculty; sometimes a provisional approval for three years with subsequent review is rendered. Programmes which are not approved may be submitted for review or simply phased out.

The Undergraduate Office of Evaluation

The Undergraduate Office of Evaluation, established in June 1970, is responsible for improving the learning climate at SUNYAB on the basis of the following objectives: a need to increase instructional quality; a need for a system to demonstrate accountability in relation to the quality of instruction; and a need for a system by which the full resources of the University can be used in nonpolitical ways.

Toward these ends, the Office of Evaluation has:
1. Generated a 'Proposal to Improve the Climate of Learning within SUNY', August 1970. This proposal was submitted to the Chancellor and to all institutions within SUNY with a request for evaluation and feedback.
2. Distributed a 'Content Analysis . . .' of the foregoing proposal based on feedback from responding institutions.
3. Assisted in planning and implementation of a four-day 'Institute on Behavioural Objectives' held by the School of Nursing as an initial step to implement the foregoing 'Proposal'.
4. Developed the University Survey of Courses and Teaching (USOCAT), a survey instrument designed to evaluate instruction.
5. Entered 159 classrooms by invitation to administer USOCAT.

Although the above accomplishments indicate that the Office of Undergraduate Evaluation has been active since its inception, it must still be considered an undeveloped component of the total University system. The Office has been restricted in its operation by a lack of personnel and resources; thus, it has had little or no impact on the ongoing academic operations of SUNYAB.

III. Research

A. The research environment

Although no formal mechanism for long-term research planning currently exists at SUNYAB, the State University of New York, in a document released in November, 1971, has attempted to design one for the entire SUNY system. This document, although not at present operative, suggests the direction which may be taken in the future as a result of the discussions evolving from the Master Planning Symposia.

Individual research originates on the basis of the researcher's field of interest, as well as by precedent. Although the individual researcher is free to initiate his own proposals, he is always limited by the amount of financial support available.

The following discussion describes the research environment, those loosely defined environmental indicators which often direct trends of current research, and the requirements of various disciplines as perceived by key faculty administrators.

1. Funding: perspectives and perceptions

During the last decade health and health-related science research has repeatedly been the most heavily supported. Figure 16 graphically illustrates the increases in SUNYAB-sponsored research expenditures for the years 1956-1970. This increase is partly due to the large numbers of federally funded health-related grants. Although the percentage of federal funds varies from year to year, the Government remains the primary source for SUNYAB research funds.

The 1969/70 fund sources divided by sponsor categories are as follows:

Federal governments	93%
Other governments	1%
Private non-profit organizations	5%
Private industries	1%

Table 7 further indicates the degree of federal involvement during the past few years.

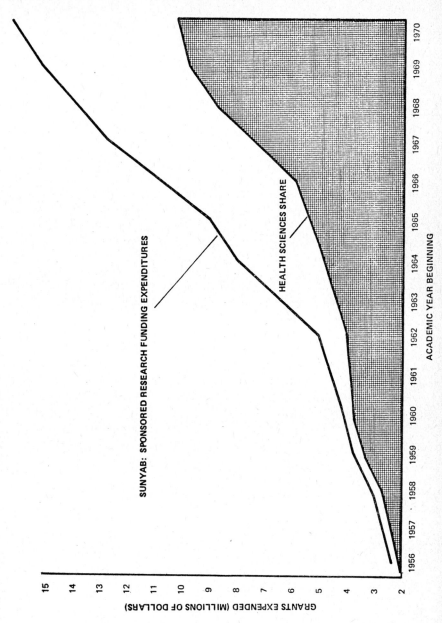

FIGURE 16. *SUNYAB sponsored research funding expenditures, 1956-70.*

TABLE 7.   SUNYAB sources of research funding, 1967-70

Sources of funds	1967/68	1968/69	1969/70
Federal Government	$12 111 957	$13 126 206	$14 099 093
Other Governments	228 514	174 107	146 323
Private non-profit organizations	310 269	501 260	815 462
Private industries	35 411	100 214	93 686
Total	$12 686 151	$13 901 787	$15 154 564
Percentage Federal Government	96 %	95%	93%

SOURCE   Annual Report, Vice-president for Research, SUNYAB, 1970.

Table 8 lists Faculty/Department research expenditures for the same 1967-70 period in terms of Faculties and Departments.

For each of the three academic years listed above the Faculty of Health Sciences alone was responsible for more than 60% of all sponsored research expenditures. In contrast, the entire Faculty of Arts and Letters spent less than 1% of the total University research expenditures in 1969/70.[1] As indicated by Table 8, research expenditures of this Faculty have actually decreased 62%, although the actual dollar amount for 1969/70 was still appreciably higher than that of 1967/68.

Although the Faculty of Health Sciences was awarded the largest share of funds, its expenditures increased only 12% in 1969/70 compared to 39% for the Faculty of Engineering and Applied Sciences and 20% for the Faculty of Social Sciences and Administration, with a net gain of 9% for the entire University.

There is a trend showing that both government and private funding agencies are now turning their interest toward research related to social and environmental problems such as urban development, racial tensions, pollution and mass transportation.

On another perspective, the former Provost of the Faculty of Health Sciences has described the paucity of knowledge about research funding and the deceptiveness of statistics. In his view, many young faculty members are being rejected in their grant applications during these times of record fundings for research. Inadequate information does not reveal the effects of few but very large grants which hide the more general cutbacks. Nor does it show the swing away from grants to contracts with governmental agencies which take from one sector of the University to give to another. And finally,

> Without doubt, the most serious problem we have in responding to these changes in federal funding of educational and research programs is our inability to document the profound effects which they are having upon our University. At the present time, we are forced to an anecdotal type of response primarily because we are not prepared to tell what is happening to us at the institutional level at any given moment in time.[2]

1. The 1970/71 figure, just released at the time of this writing was 65% for Health Sciences.
2. *Reporter,* SUNYAB, Vol. 2, No. 2, 1971.

TABLE 8. Expenditures on sponsored research and training programmes by Faculties and Departments (1967-70)

Faculty or Department	1967/68	1968/69	1969/70
Faculty of Arts & Letters			
Architecture, School of	—	—	12 821
American Studies	—	—	3 184
Art	611	880	4 468
Classics	7 516	5 382	3 694
Drama	—	1 846	500
English	3 953	46 033	33 971
Modern Languages (3 departments)	48 753	189 986	14 179
Music	1 951	9 849	18 475
Other programmes	—	—	4 851
Total	62 784	253 976	96 143
Faculty of Engineering & Applied Sciences			
School of Engineering	430 104	441 828	517 874
School of Information & Library Studies	—	—	67 851
Department of Computer Science	—	—	23 608
Other programmes	—	—	3 279
Total	430 104	441 828	612 612
Faculty of Natural Sciences & Mathematics			
Biology	703 770	593 030	600 537
Chemistry	524 252	537 093	526 106
Geological Sciences	13 886	4 874	9 520
Mathematics	135 636	164 302	100 538
Physics & Astronomy	163 800	195 367	248 894
Statistics	46 652	106 597	137 149
Other programmes	—	—	6 239
Total	1 587 996	1 601 263	1 628 983
Faculty of Social Sciences & Administration			
Management, School of	61 080	176 810	251 363
Social Welfare, School of	379 750	249 024	335 867
Anthropology	50 809	22 264	85 668
Economics	18 214	30 375	52 703
Geography	2 431	5 963	3 826
History	3 907	14 021	26 798
Linguistics	—	—	16 592

Table continued overleaf

NOTES
1. Data in this table are actual expenditures under grants and contracts during the fiscal year (July 1-June 30), including direct costs and accrued overhead. Expenditures during a given year have no necessary relationship to new grants received during the year nor to the backlog of unspent grant funds on the books.
2. This table includes only grants and contracts administered by the Research Foundation of SUNY. Other grants are administered by the University at Buffalo Foundation, Inc., and grants and contracts from New York State agencies are administered directly through State University. Grant expenditures in these latter two categories amount to approximately 6.5% of expenditures in the above table, i.e. approximately $900 000 in 1968-69 and $1 000 000 in 1969-70.
3. There are a number of blanks and apparent inconsistencies in this table because of a change in accounting procedures in 1969-70 compared to 1968-69.
4. "Faculty of Educational Studies" includes the Educational Development Project in Paraguay.
5. Funds indicated for the Graduate School are various types of pre-doctoral fellowships and traineeships and the educational allowances accompanying such fellowships and traineeships. These funds are allocated to and expended by various departments in the University.

TABLE 8 (continued).

Faculty or Department	1967/68	1968/69	1969/70
Philosophy	12 727	21 964	4 757
Policy Sciences	—	—	76 569
Political Science	136 187	222 144	106 930
Psychology	354 548	335 205	372 271
Sociology	53 346	83 985	68 120
Speech Communication	37 731	52 086	57 181
Other programmes	—	—	4 509
Total	1 110 730	1 213 841	1 463 154
Faculty of Educational Studies	530 854	740 001	722 275
Faculty of Law & Jurisprudence	61 436	64 261	8 552
Graduate School	502 320	620 268	607 633
Division of Continuing Education	59 829	112 869	76 230
Division of Undergraduate Studies	—	—	1 354
Computing Centre	478 151	166 383	165 502
Library	—	—	73 816
Total, Other than Health Sciences	4 824 204	5 214 690	5 456 254
Percent, Other than Health Sciences	38%	38%	36%
Faculty of Health Sciences			
Basic Health Science Departments			
Anatomy	70 755	79 089	60 342
Biochemistry	463 639	512 998	564 298
Biophysical Sciences	234 987	222 242	224 120
Microbiology	741 070	714 433	684 989
Pathology	287 486	352 733	486 201
Pharmacology	256 295	292 729	325 300
Physiology	397 556	677 146	755 112
Total	2 451 788	2 851 370	3 100 362
Medicine, School of—Clinical Departments			
Gynecology-Obstetrics	128 517	129 852	129 630
Medicine	1 177 859	1 400 390	1 767 514
Neurology	27 952	32 281	25 493
Pediatrics	867 372	803 820	599 344
Psychiatry	200 653	234 258	217 717
Social & Preventive Medicine	443 740	423 688	443 568
Surgery	216 189	221 856	310 868
Regional Medical Programme	232 876	501 491	877 992
Other departments & programmes	18 060	20 782	29 871
Total	3 313 218	3 768 418	4 401 997
Dentistry, School of—Clinical Departments	607 789	742 507	682 800
Health Related Professions, School of	110 113	178 590	201 554
Nursing, School of	207 791	157 779	283 596
Pharmacy, School of	971 828	722 133	885 994
Center for Theoretical Biology	112 656	212 724	136 640
Paraguay project (Medical/Nursing)	86 764	53 576	5 367
Total, Health Sciences	7 861 947	8 687 097	9 698 310
Percent, Health Sciences	62%	62%	64%
UNIVERSITY TOTAL	$12 686 151	$13 901 787	$15 154 564

2. Department of Defense research

Governmental influence upon nature of the research conducted on most American university campuses, although widely accepted, has recently come under attack; the area most violently criticised is the U.S. Department of Defense (DOD). Opponents object to the classified nature of most DOD-sponsored research, and the resulting restriction of publications, as contrary to the principles of a free and open university and to the needed intercourse of ideas. Some oppose conducting of any DOD-funded research on campus, regardless of the classification of the material.

3. Special research sources

Those agencies listed in Table 9 (and other similar private agencies) are the main sources of research funds for the State University of New York at Buffalo. Researchers may obtain additional support from other agencies in the form of special grants-in-aid or university research fellowships. Two of these sources, the Research Foundation of the State of New York Foundation and the University at Buffalo Foundation, discussed in a subsequent chapter, primarily administer research funds. A third source is the SUNY Committee for the Distribution of institutional funds.

University Committee for the Distribution of institutional funds
The SUNYAB Committee for the Distribution of institutional funds was established in 1965, to distribute funds derived in lieu of tuition for certain fellowships and from general institutional support grants for faculty members, graduate and undergraduate students.

Typical sources of such funds are the National Science Foundation and the National Institutes of Health. The Committee working under the direction of the Vice-president for Academic Development (from 1965-68, under the direction of the Dean of the Graduate Division) distributes the funds.

The SUNYAB Committee awards grants to each of the seven Faculties to support research and creative activity. Each Faculty establishes its own procedures and criteria for evaluating proposals.

The SUNYAB Committee for the Distribution of Institutional Funds also considers inter- and extra-faculty proposals. The following guidelines are suggested by the Committee for the preparation of proposals. Grants should ordinarily:
1. Initiate some new activity, rather than supplement inadequate budgets of projects supported from other sources.
2. Support research or creative activity rather than solely provide a service to the SUNYAB community or to the community at large.
3. Support projects that will either terminate when grant funds are exhausted or will attract support from other sources.
4. Be smaller since limited funds prevent the awarding of very many large grants.
The Committee consists of members from each of the Faculties, several University Administrators and two student representatives.

TABLE 9.   Sources of funds by individual sponsors, lised in order of magnitude in 1969/70

Source	1967/68	1968/69	1969/70
Public Health Service	8 347 075	8 972 063	10 146 071
National Institutes of Health[1]	(6 844 901)	(7 247 344)	(7 238 627)
Health Serv. & Mental			(2 743 692)
Health Adm.[2,3]	(1 502 174)	(1 724 719)	
Consumer Protection & Environ.			(163 752)
Health Serv.[2]			
National Science Foundation	1 382 707	1 062 711	1 228 976
U. S. Office of Education	401 515	594 588	842 612
Department of Defense	469 408	618 149	608 114
Social & Rehabilitation Service[4]	411 829	447 467	471 086
Atomic Energy Commission	96 325	229 286	229 938
National Aeronautics & Space Administration	217 085	209 979	185 227
American Cancer Society	78 717	148 192	136 915
Office of Economic Opportunity	229 210	294 012	104 392
Ford Foundation	21 602	16 782	86 178
Office of Saline Water	60 981	65 175	74 144
Agency for International Development	142 503	132 741	74 365
Control Data Corporation	0	68 375	73 204
U. S. Department of Labor	0	48 350	65 039
Federal Water Quality Administration	47 891	37 653	52 606
N. Y. State Department of Education	45 732	60 998	51 635
American Chemical Society (PRF)	27 957	54 407	47 399
American Heart Association	10 951	18 877	41 436
National University of Asuncion	38 662	24 474	39 817
N. Y. State Science & Technology Foundation	83 940	41 504	28 268
Erie County Health Department	51 918	47 131	23 963
Corporation for Public Broadcasting	0	0	22 300
Life Insurance Medical Research Fund	4 031	15 576	20 613
Lever Brothers	11 195	14 141	18 099
Arthritis & Rheumatism Foundation	8 707	248	14 836
Damon Runyon Memorial Fund	8 076	17 508	10 137
W. K. Kellogg Foundation	44 376	45 248	5 753
All other sponsors	443 758	619 152	451 441
UNIVERSITY TOTAL	12 686 151	13 901 787	15 154 564

NOTES
1. "National Institutes of Health" includes the nine National Institutes of Health, National Library of Medicine, Fogarty International Center, and other units.
2. "Health Services & Mental Health Administration" includes National Institute of Mental Health, Regional Medical Programs,Community Health Service, National Communicable Disease Center, Maternal & Child Health Service (formerly Children's Bureau) and other units.
3. "Consumer Protection and Environmental Health Services" includes Food & Drug Administration, Environmental Control Administration and National Air Pollution Control Administration.
4. "Social & Rehabilitation Service" formerly called Vocational Rehabilitation Administration.

B. Research organization: the research proposal selection process

Once a research area is decided upon, a faculty member presents his proposal to his department chairman. In many cases the researcher's colleagues will assist him in the initial preparation, although faculty competition for grants often precludes such co-operation. The department chairman then reviews the proposal for scientific content and overall value in relation to departmental and university commitment of resources. The next review, by a Faculty Provost, examines budgetary aspects and space or facilities requirements of the proposal. According to the nature of the research project, however, departmental and faculty reviews are sometimes bypassed. The proposal is then submitted to the Office of the Vice-president for Research, where improvement of the presentation may be suggested in light of policies and procedures of the funding agencies and of SUNY and SUNYAB. At this level the procedure is often informal; the Vice-president or other pertinent officers may exert personal efforts to help the project director prepare the formal proposal. Once the proposal is completed, appropriate funding agencies are selected to receive the proposal for consideration; at this point, a proposal may be fully approved as it stands, revised by mutual agreement, or rejected. If approved, its resources are fiscally administered by the institution in accord with funding agency regulations, and the laws or bylaws of appropriate university institutions. Figure 17 illustrates the flow of research proposals and the administration's action on them.

Research projects are not imposed upon universities, research institutes or individual researchers. It is often known by the individual researcher and the office providing research management what federal and private funds have been earmarked for particular areas (i.e., education, health science, etc.).

The future of the research situation naturally hinges on government and private foundation funding, and this is indeed difficult to assess. Thus, reliable predictions concerning traditional and private funding agencies can be of enormous assistance to an individual researcher and to the University as a whole. Also implicit in the funding process are factors of quality evaluation, resource requirements, and proper funding agency selection for each submitted proposal.

Variables and constraints affecting 'capture ratios'

The following list enumerates the two essential kinds of variables, controllable and uncontrollable:

Controllable:
1. number of proposals with probability of success,
2. equivalent cost of researcher incentives for each proposal,
3. equivalent cost of review effort for each proposal,
4. equivalent cost of research project operation for each proposal,
5. equivalent cost of error in agency selection for each proposal,

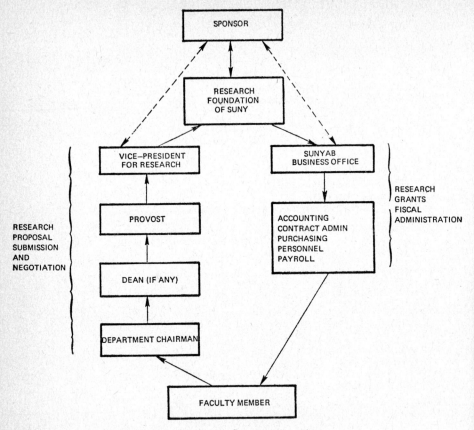

FIGURE 17. *Flow of research proposals and administrative actions.*

6. support level requested of the funding agency for each proposal,
7. total equivalent cost of available researcher incentives in the University,
8. quality rating for each proposal, and
9. proposal conformity to policies.

Uncontrollable:
1. number of proposals submitted for consideration, and
2. dollars available from the funding agency for research in the area of each proposal,
3. competing proposals for any particular programme,
4. bias or knowledge of reviewing panel.

The conditional probability of funding of a submitted proposal depends upon the quality of the proposal, the support level requested and the proposal's conformity to institutional and agency policy.

The probability of a proposal submission by a researcher is based on the amount of research incentives provided by the University and the availability of research money associated with the particular discipline of study or project area of the proposal. Within the University, there are finite resources which can be provided as researcher incentives; such limitations are factors which lead to further variables. The resources must be free resources, i.e., clearly unallocated, in order to be considered and reduced to equivalent costs.

The present process of proposal selection involves all the above indicated variables, but as yet no attempt has been made to improve the process except through increased communications between the administration and faculty researchers. Even if a model-based process (i.e., one that would involve computing the relationship of variables for each proposal) were attempted, many difficulties would arise: primarily, much of the necessary data does not exist and, therefore, a rather lengthy process of data acquisition and model verification would need to be performed either on proposals submitted in past years or through informal implementation of the process in the immediate future. At present, there are no plans to collect these data or to make such an analysis.

C. Research resource funds management

The management of research resource funds includes not only the administration of funds, but the raising of funds as well. Of the three administrative mechanisms for these purposes, only two have direct ties with SUNYAB: the Research Foundation and the University of Buffalo Foundation.

1. The Research Foundation
of the State University of New York

The Research Foundation, chartered by the Board of Regents in 1951, a private, non-profit corporation and not an agency of the State of New York, is more important than the UB Foundation. While it operates closely with the State University, it is essentially a private and independent foundation.

The Foundation's main purpose is to provide and administer *funds other than State appropriations* for university research on all SUNY campuses.

Since 1951 the State University has benefited from outside support by well over $100,000,000 in grants made to the Foundation. When a grant is approved, the money is forwarded to and administered by the Foundation under co-operative procedures approved by the Boards and administration of both SUNY and the Foundation.

Essentially the Foundation's relationship to individual researchers takes one of the two forms, as illustrated in Figure 18, a highly simplified model which elimitates many intermediate steps.

Awards are allocated in funding blocks of one-year periods, thus placing a substantial premium on rapid and effective recruiting and supply techniques. Under such conditions, delays in obtaining equipment and supplies can be ex-

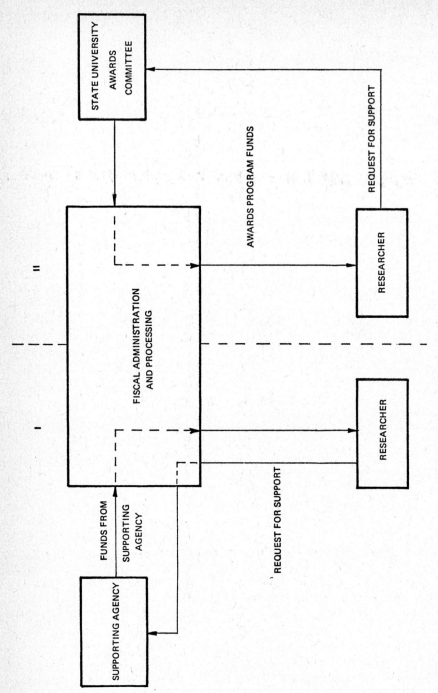

FIGURE 18. *Relationship of the Research Foundation to the individual researcher.*

tremely costly in time and personnel; therefore, the administrative system of the Research Foundation of SUNY is oriented toward the needs of the laboratory and the project with full recognition that a high order of uncertainty as to resources, outcome and strategy is associated with any research programme.

Organization

The organizational relationship between the State University and the Research Foundation emphasizes decision-participation functions.

The Albany office of the Research Foundation is basically an administrative group which provides banking and accounting services, general record maintenance, and an application submission service.

The Research Foundation is also involved in (a) providing ongoing advisory and application processing services, (b) maintaining the accounting systems and procedures, (c) servicing the personnel records, (d) reporting in appropriate and various ways to all sponsors and to State University officials, (e) maintaining and designing administrative systems, and (f) providing administrative guidelines and training.

The Research Foundation does not undertake fund-raising in the traditional sense and employs no persons for this purpose.

'Overhead' funds are provided by sponsors at an average rate of about 58% of salaries and wages of any research proposal. Local campus administrative activities on behalf of the Research Foundation have cost about 4% of expenditures since 1966.

The fiscal designee system

By definition, the State University is decentralised to campus levels of activity except for various central processes such as budgeting.

The Research Foundation parallels this decentralisation through its fiscal designee system, which established a fiscal accounting system with each particular campus. Under this system the local campus head official chooses a fiscal designee, who together with the university president, is the responsible agent for Research Foundation affairs on campus. This jurisdiction includes the means and details of purchasing and employment procedures, but does not include the choice of supplies or equipment, which is the responsibility of the research project director. While local campus authority is preserved, key data and supporting records are available to, and form a part of, the State University's basic recording and administrative system. This is an important consideration, as sponsored funds form a sizable portion of its operating budget.

It is the Research Foundation's responsibility to assure that funds are properly utilised. Expenditures may be incurred only against active grant funds or for the liquidation of encumbrances incurred while such accounts were active. Any transaction certified for payment by the local fiscal designee for disbursements must include, but is not limited to, assurances that (a) value is received from all funds spent; (b) its procedures provide for decision-making at the point of competence; (c) funds are available to meet all commitments; (d) on the face of the transaction the purposes appear to be sound and related to the programme which the grant is supporting; and (e) all transactions generate reviewable and auditable records.

Computer development in the Research Foundation. The administrative operations in Albany are increasingly being computerised. Direct access terminals in the Research Foundation's offices and on major campuses will eventually be linked to the IBM computer centre in the Research Foundation in Albany. This tele-processing network will ultimately serve SUNY and provide crucial information for each project director.

Computer expansion plans. The expansion of State University-sponsored activities places new and increasing demands upon the Research Foundation and its data-processing section. For example, the formation of campus field offices dictates that information be readily available at remote points. A hierarchy of capabilities is planned to provide service to both Campus and Central Office staffs in order to attain optimum fiscal administration.

The proposed areas regarding application processing fall into two broad cate-gories. The first, the expansion and refinement of the applications that are at present processed by the data-processing system. Secondly, a series of new applica-tion areas will be implemented to utilise the wealth of information stored as a result of the present processing. The ability to generate special reports upon demand and to 'inquire' of this data base is a key factor in the application devel-opment.

Research Foundation awards programme. The Research Foundation and State University of New York seek to encourage scholarly and creative activities, through seven programmes of awards available exclusively to members of the faculty of State University of New York. These programmes provide project funds, through grants-in-aid and living support through the Faculty Research Fellowship and University Research Fellowship programmes. Descriptions of the programmes to be directly funded under their supervision are outlined below.

For review purposes, all awards are classified under the following as *Social Sciences Humanities*, *Natural Sciences*, or *Arts* (including creative work and critical studies). All applications are evaluated by the University Awards Committee under procedures and guidelines established by the Committee and approved by the Joint Awards Council. Final recommendations are made to the Chancellor of the University who bestows the awards on behalf of the Foundation and the University.

The overall programme format offers either *small* awards ranging from $100 to $3200, or *larger* awards up to $11,600.

For the larger awards, the Committee requires that applications be made to other agencies for financial support and discourages complete dependence upon its programmes for project funding. The Committee in its determinations takes into account the possibility that substantial support for the applicant or the project may be available from other sources. However, the Committee recognizes the necessity for supporting the younger faculty member until he can seek other funding.

The principal investigator is responsible for submitting a final report summarising the activities pursued and results achieved at the completion of the project.

The State University Press may assist a member of the faculty in the publication of book-length research.

Criteria for evaluation of awards. In evaluating applications the Committee considers capability and seriousness of the applicant and the value of the proposed project. The criteria are: educational background, experience, honours, publications, works completed (including exhibitions and performances), and evaluation by colleagues. Seriousness of purpose is also judged by the extent to which the project has been developed at the time of the application and the reputation of the applicant for dedication to such activities. Evaluation of the merit of the project itself is largely a matter of judgement by the Committee but this may be influenced by statements made in the application or in supporting letters of recommendation. Recommendations of senior scholars concerning the above criteria are weighed heavily. The manner in which the application is proposed is often significant. None of the above should be construed as favouring only the mature scholar. In its judgements, the Committee fully recognizes that the younger scholar has not had time for full professional growth.

Unacceptable projects. The following are considered unacceptable projects in regard to Research Foundation Awards:
1. Those activities which are aimed primarily toward personal gain rather than professional contributions.
2. The evaluation of a course or a study of how a subject is taught elsewhere; applications concerned only with instructional materials or techniques.
3. Textbook preparation.
4. Activities which ordinarily pay their own way or from which income is derived.
5. Studies restricted to local problems in the administration or operation of an institution.
6. Studies to be used for a thesis or doctoral dissertation.
7. Applications seeking capital construction, major rehabilitation and support of conference-type meetings.

Figure 19 shows for each year from 1954 to 1969 the funds distributed through the Research Foundation Awards programme.

2. The University of Buffalo Foundation

The University at Buffalo Foundation, Inc., a private non-profit corporation with an accumulated endowment of approximately $35 million, was formed ten years ago at the time of merger with the State University to provide private resources for enrichment of academic programmes and services at State University of New York at Buffalo.

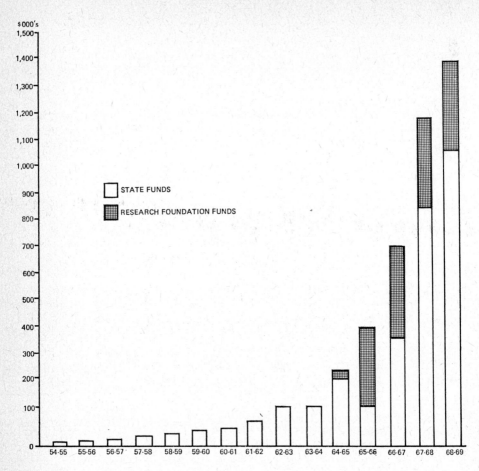

FIGURE 19. *Funds distributed through the Research Foundation Awards Programme (1954-69).*

The intent of the U/B Foundation is to help complete the financial require-ments of the programming of SUNYAB. The ten strongest public institutions of higher education in this country all have achieved their excellence by counting on approximately one-third of their support from non-public sources. While SUNYAB does not envision that level of private support, it is acutely aware that the full realisation of its future plans depends upon adequate funding from the private as well as the public sector. It is clear that SUNYAB cannot exist solely on what dollars the State will supply in the next few years.

One of the most valuable contributions of the U/B Foundation to SUNYAB is the provision of approximately $45,000 each year in supplemental expense funds for administrative officers. This includes deans, department chairmen and provosts as well as the president and vice-presidents. The fund is made available to the president, who allocates it to various officers in accordance with priorities and needs. The monies are used for a variety of purposes which the State cannot necessarily be expected to finance: scholarships and fellowships; special research and teaching equipment; experimental educational programmes; support for distinguished scholars; specialised library acquisitions; student loans; grants for research projects; support for conferences and seminars; support for community projects such as dental and medical clinics; payment for unexpected costs in recruiting faculty; costs for visiting faculty, etc.

The following 1969/70 figures reflect the nature of the breakdown of research spendings. The total expenditures on sponsored programmes including research grants, training grants and several types of pre-doctoral and post-doctoral fellowships and traineeships was $16,150,000.[1] The 1969/70 total was divided among the various categories of activities as follows:

Research	67%
Training	29%
Conferences/public service	2%
Facilities	2%

The 1969/70 total was divided among the several administrative mechanisms as follows:

Administered by SUNY Research Foundation	$15,150,000
Administered by University at Buffalo Foundation	850,000
Administered by N. Y. State (grants from N. Y. State agencies)	150,000
Total	$16,150,000

D. Research facilities

Specific structures designed to fulfil faculty research needs have been established within the basic SUNYAB academic system. Known generally as 'research centre', they generally operate within the discipline of the established faculties, using pre-existing physical facilities. In this sense, then, the centres do not operate independently.

Centre for Information Research

The Centre for Information Research was formed in 1969 to investigate and implement new methods of organising and dealing with the accelerated growth of scientific and technical information. Located within the Faculty of Engineering

1. At the time of writing the 1970/71 figures were released by the University, but the breakdown was not as complete as the 1969/70 figures. Consequently, it was decided to utilise the previous year's figures. As a matter of note, however, the total expenditure on sponsored programmes in 1970/71 was $17,202,022, an increase of 6.5% over 1969/70.

and Applied Sciences, it involves interdisciplinary participation of researchers from many areas of the University.

The Centre consists of three separate but inter-related branches:

1. The Technical Information Dissemination Bureau (TIDB) provides experimental computer-based scientific and technical information services for its clients, mainly local business and industrial firms.
2. A library and information systems research and development branch.
3. A branch for basic research on information transfer methodologies deals with such topics as the study of language structures and artificial languages, theories on information organization, and the development of multi-access computer networks.

2. Social Sciences Measurement Centre

In 1970 the University established its Social Sciences Measurement Centre, to focus on improved development, standardization and evaluation of research instruments.

3. University Centre for Scientific Measurement and Instrumentation

The University Centre for Scientific Measurement and Instrumentation, established in 1970, exists to develop a sophisticated resource for instrumentation and measurement and to provide an interdisciplinary research programme in this area of the physical and biomedical sciences. The Centre, at present, attempts to pay special attention to the practical utilisation of new techniques in humanitarian and social areas. Examples of such studies include the detection and control of environmental pollutants, clinical monitoring, and the measurement of oceanographic and atmospheric characteristics.

4. Roswell Park Memorial Institute

The Roswell Park Memorial Institute, a branch of the State Department of Health, located in the downtown area of Buffalo, is one of the best-equipped centres in the world for the study of malignant diseases. The Institute's staff (including many University scientists) engages in fundamental research in the fields of biochemistry, biology, biophysics, chemistry, microbiology, pharmacology and physiology. Many speciality programmes are offered at the graduate level, in co-operation with the University Departments of Medicine, Surgery, and subspecialities. Roswell Park Memorial Institute thus supplements the scientific facilities of the University in staff, equipment and breadth of research.

5. Centre for Theoretical Biology

This Centre provides a locus for the interdisciplinary research of the Departments of Biophysical Sciences, Biochemistry, Biochemical Pharmacology, Biology,

Chemistry, Mathematics, Statistics, Geology, and various Engineering Departments, as well as the Roswell Park Memorial Institute. The Centre's main function lies in identifying the general conceptual bases underlying experimental biology, as well as examining special concerns such as the Mars programme of National Aeronautic and Space Administration (NASA) and the Saline Water Programme of the Department of the Interior. Special funds are available for sponsorship of independent study by undergraduates.

6. Survey Research Centre

Newly established in the Faculty of Social Sciences and Administration, the Survey Research Centre serves as a teaching and research facility for faculty members of SUNYAB as well as for other units of the State University system. In addition to offering instruction in undergraduate and graduate survey research methods, the Centre provides consulting services concerning research design and data-processing and analysis.

7. Western New York Nuclear Research Centre

The Western New York Nuclear Research Centre, located on the main campus, is a non-profit corporation owned by the State University of New York and operated by a separate Board of Trustees. Founded in 1961 for the purposes of education, training and research in the field of nuclear energy and health-related sciences, the Centre is designed to meet the needs of industry, the fundamental scientist, and the medical profession. The heart of the Nuclear Centre is an advanced-type pool reactor which operates at 2 million watts steady state and is licensed to pulse at 2,000 megawatts peak power. Present equipment includes instruments for the detection and analysis of radiation, a 400 KEV proton accelerator, a high-current 1.5 MEV electron-accelerator, and a sub-critical training reactor. A hot cell and special laboratories are available for radiation experiments.

8. The Centre for Immunology

The Centre for Immunology (established 1969) is an integral part of the School of Medicine and the Health Sciences Faculty, with an interdisciplinary science orientation.

The purpose of the Centre is to assure the integration of immunological research and teaching in SUNYAB. Extensive collaboration with the Health Sciences Faculty, affiliated hospitals, and national and international institutions is also under way.

SUNYAB was selected as the site for such a centre, because it is one of the few institutions in the world which includes the five most important fields of human immunology: (1) microbial immunology, (2) immunogenetics, (3) immunopathology, (4) immunological analysis of tissues, (5) immunodiagnosis.

E. The students' rôle in research

Although there are no university-wide policies regarding activities of students in research, there has been much participation both at the undergraduate and graduate levels. In many cases graduate students are selected for admission because their academic interests are similar to those of department members.

Students in research: Faculty perceptions

The following information concerning students and research was obtained by surveying the various Faculties. With regard to the encouragement of student research participation, 82.7% of those questioned answered yes, with only a 16.0% negative. As for graduate student participation solely in research, 40.7% affirmative and 56.8% negative responses were obtained. When asked what level of students participate in research the following was found:

University, all levels	7.4%
Seniors only	1.2%
Graduate students, all levels	74.1%
Doctoral students only	13.6%
Research assistants only	0.0%

48.9% of all graduate students involved in research were given financial assistance by the department.

IV. Final comments

SUNYAB experienced enormous growth over a relatively short period of time with the additional support received as a result of the merger with SUNY.

During the expansion period SUNYAB increased its budget, staff, enrolment, buildings, and library holdings in geometric proportions. The relative national position of its graduate programmes, according to the study made by the American Council on Education in 1970, went from 65th in the nation to 41st with high ratings in the areas of Physiology, Pharmacology, Bacteriology, Psychology and English.

In describing the decade from 1962 to 1972, a former Dean and current professor of Education expressed the following opinion:

> We at SUNYAB have been and are in a state of flux. It startled me to reflect that in the past six years I have known three presidents (at SUNYAB). They have been men with different values, styles, energy components and potentials. During this period I've seen morale go to heights and depths. I have seen a high level of productivity shattered and essentially stopped for a period of months;[1] I have seen years of general well-being and times when anxieties were expressed in all kinds of counter-productive matters.
>
> Within SUNY I have seen a radical change in the Governor's attitude towards education and the State University. I've seen the Legislature begin to exert itself in different directions. I've seen the power of the Trustees and the Chancellor diminish, so that now both are weaker, at least with reference to effectiveness.
>
> I've seen students change rapidly, too.
>
> We have had anything but constancy. . . People have said, 'We've got to have some leveling off. We've got to have something we can count on.'[2]

The challenge of the 70s

Constancy, levelling-off, and stability also seem to be in the minds of both university planners and managers. They recognize that the decade of the 70s will

1. Statement refers to period of campus unrest, academic year 1969/70.
2. SUNYAB *Reporter*, April 29, 1972, Vol. 3, No. 28.

be one of change, so their plans will not be merely a substitute for change, but will enable them to manage it. In anticipating these changes, accessible channels have been provided for the process to occur. It is apparent that SUNYAB must deliberately define ways of designing and maintaining stability, yet at the same time provide flexible mechanisms for change.

The economic strain which has limited the growth SUNYAB expected in programmes, building, salaries, etc. has had a reflective effect. Departments have been scrutinised and only the most worth-while programmes will be supported (selective growth). The Master Plan preparations, together with the visitation of the Middle States Commission for Accreditation, are forcing SUNYAB even further to reflect and examine its objectives and their implementation. This self-examination can also serve to re-stabilise the University so that it may emerge with directions set for the 70s.

While stability is paramount, paradoxically, flexibility shares the same priority. The SUNYAB administration considers the faculty to be inflexible when it refuses to agree to eliminate a certain programme, even when the indices for its phasing out are apparent. Teaching is almost sacrosanct, from the standpoint of University managers, who view the faculty as obstructionists to the goals of the University.

The faculty, on the other hand, feel manipulated and unable to influence the decisions that will affect them most. This lack of autonomy is both disconcerting and confining to a group that has traditionally been a forerunner of faculty involvement, even though the local campus administration consults with the faculty on institutional issues. As part of a politically-based State system, SUNYAB must respond according to the requests and regulations of the SUNY Central Administrative Offices. Plans designed at the local campus can be altered or altogether discarded by cutbacks from the State Legislature, or a denial of funds. The budget directors, in the final analysis, dictate what *will* be done. However, the newly created Senate Professional Association may be a decisive factor in shifting the present state of affairs. For the first time in the State's history of higher education, representatives of the faculty and professional staff collectively bargain with the Governor and the Office of Employee Relations rather than with the local campus president and the local board of trustees. The effect of these negotiations should alter university relations with the administration and its governance mechanisms.

Among the most important aspects of any system is a communications network with free flow and interdependence among its components. Each component of the system need not equally perform every function of a university, if all functions can be fulfilled by a system as a whole. For this reason, it is important to view SUNYAB as a dynamic system co-operating regionally with the other institutions of higher learning. By implementing the concept of 'Regionalism', component members of the higher learning institutional complex can be strengthened and made distinctive through co-operative exchange, rather than weakened through competition and diffusion.

Another challenge the University must face is that of community accountability. A recent study analysed the effect and impact of the University on the incomes of the population in the Buffalo area. SUNYAB, its faculty, staff and students generated a total local income of $91,563,000 in Buffalo and Erie County during 1970. This 'Economic Impact Study', according to a SUNY director, "is the first in what will be a series of special studies to gather information about unexplored but significant aspects of the University." The intentions of this study are improved community communications as well as accountability.

Glossary

Ad hoc Committee: terminates with completion of mission.

AMP: Academic master plan.

Assistantship: graduate student with assigned duties; teaching, research or what professor assesses necessary, with stipend.

Associate degree: a two-year programme of study with the completion of sixty-four hours in a specialized area, i.e., Secretarial Studies, Sciences and Liberal Arts.

Bachelor's degree programme (B.A.): usually a four-year undergraduate degree-granting programme.

Commencement: the ceremony in which degrees are conferred on graduating students.

Credit for educational programme: an arrangement of courses which do not acknowledge units of academic work contributing to a degree.

Consortia: an agreement among institutions for mutual exchange.

D.O.B.: the State Division of the Budget.

Ed.D.: Doctor of Education.

Ed.M.: Master of Education.

E. O. P.: Educational Opportunity Programme.

E. P. I. S.: Experimental Programme in Independent Studies.

Faculty: with capital 'F'—a teaching and research unit of the Faculty System, composed of Schools or/and Departments.

faculty: with small 'f'—instructional staff in general.

Four-Course Norm: four courses per semester, each course four credit hours.

Freshmen: first-year student in bachelor's degree programme: completed fewer than 28 hours.

FTE: FTE Types: 1. Non-instructional: all positions not directly engaged in instructional process; includes Provosts, Department Chairmen, up to and including the President.

2. Instructional: those positions engaged in instructional process; (budget purpose restricted to functional groups reported in Instruction and Departmental research. Faculty can be non-instructional or instructional).

3. Student FTE: statistical abstraction designed to relate the instructional process to the instructional units and to provide for mathematical summation of full-time and part-time indicators by level of instruction through agreed-upon weighting formulas. It is mathematically derived by dividing credit-hours generated by

> level of instruction by agreed-upon definition of full-time student.
> (i.e. 15 credit-hours = 1 FTE student lower division
>   15 credit-hours = 1 FTE student upper division
> If a student is taking 18 credit-hours and another student is taking
> 18 credit-hours = 36 credit-hours = 2.40 FTE's.
> The 15 credit-hour may change from year to year as the state
> decides.

Grade-point average: quotient of the sum of the grade quality points multiplied by the number of credit hours taken. Used as an index of quality of performance.

Graduate: one who has completed the undergraduate programme.

Interim campus: (Ridge Lea), rented facility used temporarily until the new North Campus is ready; a ten-minute bus ride from main campus.

Junior year: third year in a course of study at higher levels of education.

Main Street Campus: established location at which most of instruction is located.

New Amherst Campus: North Campus development under construction at a separate site.

Non-instructional staff: clerical staff.

M. A.: Master of Arts.

M. A. S. P.: Mature Adult Student Programme (in Millard Fillmore College, division of continuing education).

M. E. D.: Master of Education.

M. F. A.: Master of Fine Arts.

M. S.: Master of Sciences.

M. S. W.: Master of Social Welfare.

One credit-hour course: a course which grants a single unit of academic work (unit of academic work = credit-hour).

OCD: Office of Campus Development, a central office located in Albany to co-ordinate the development of all SUNY campuses on a statewide basis.

Ph.D.: Doctor of Philosophy.

Psychometric method: the method of measuring mental states, mental processes and their relationships.

Proration of space: the division and distribution of space proportionately.

RAD: Regular Admission Disadvantaged.

Recitation: usually an aspect of the lecture-method where student responds with answer when questioned by professor.

Regents score: score as a result of taking state-wide examination testing academic excellence.

Reserve library: A library in which books can be read *only* in the library; usually books requested by a professor are held in reserve for his students to refer.

Ridge Lea Campus: see Interim Campus.

Roswell Park Memorial Institute: SUNYAB affiliated medical and research treatment centre (cancer).

SARA: Student Academic Records Administration.

SEEK: Search for Education, Evaluation and Knowledge programme.

Senior year: last year of a four-year study in an aspect of higher education. (undergraduate).

Student FTE: see FTE.

Sophomore: second-year student in a programme in higher education (undergraduate).

South Campus: see Main campus.

Standing committee: Committee whose mission is continuing and is written in as part of the by-laws of the organization.

SUCF: State University Construction Fund.

SUNY: State University of New York.

SUNYAB: State University of New York at Buffalo.

Total free elective system: a programme of study in which courses are selected by the student rather than prescribed by the department, division or adviser.

System of indicators and criteria for planning and management at the Western Australian Institute of Technology

H. W. Peters
Assistant Director (Administration and Finance),
Western Australian Institute of Technology

Contents

I. The economic development of Australia, and the system of higher education within which the Western Australian Institute of Technology functions . . 215

II. Integration of Western Australian Institute of Technology development planning into the economic and social development of Western Australia and Australia 229

III. The Western Australian Institute of Technology system of decision-making and planning, indicators and criteria 242

IV. Flow of information at the Western Australian Institute of Technology . . 270

V. The Western Australian Institute of Technology system, foreseeable developments and applicability to other institutions. 278

Glossary 283

Appendixes 285

Note

This case study has benefited greatly from the assistance and information given by many government departments, institutions and individuals. Colleagues at the Western Australian Institute of Technology have been most co-operative in providing data and advice.

The author is grateful to all those organisations and individuals who have helped in the preparation of the case study. Opinions expressed and any errors in fact or figure are solely the author's responsibility.

I. The economic development of Australia, and the system of higher education within which the Western Australian Institute of Technology functions

A. Demographic data on Australia and Western Australia

Australia is an island continent of nearly three million square miles in which about 12.8 million people live. About 56 per cent of the population live in the five mainland capital cities; the most recently available figures show that 62 per cent of the people live in cities of 100,000 and over, with a further 7 per cent living in towns of between 50,000 and 100,000; the remaining 31 per cent live in small towns or in rural areas. As far as Western Australia is concerned, out of a population of 1.0 million, 67.7 per cent live in the capital city of Perth. About 7.0 per cent live in towns of 10,000 and over, with the remaining 25.3 per cent residing in small communities or in rural areas.

The pattern of age distribution is shown in Table 1.

TABLE 1.   Age distribution

	Australia	%	Western Australia	%
16 years and under	4 067 501	32.41	334 712	34.15
17—23 years	1 551 150	12.36	128 143	13.08
24—65 years	5 969 820	47.56	449 946	45.91
Over 65 years	963 236	7.67	67 247	6.86
	12 551 707	100.00	980 048	100.00

SOURCE   Commonwealth Bureau of Census and Statistics

B. Social, economic and administrative structure of Australia, including Western Australia

In 1901, the then British colonies formed a federation of States[1], becoming the Commonwealth of Australia, as a dominion of the then British Empire. A constitution was framed and, remarkably, has only been changed in minor degree since that time.

Australia remains part of the British Commonwealth, but has long since achieved full independence. In many matters, the six States are regarded as being sovereign, and indeed they strongly resist any diminution of their own decision-making powers exercised through State legislatures.

In general terms, the States have the main responsibility in such fields as hospitals, education, industrial development, roads, water and electricity supplies. The Commonwealth has power in, for example, foreign affairs, defence, income tax, social services (such as pensions and unemployment benefits) and civil aviation. However, even if some aspects of the nation's life are *de jure* the responsibility of the States, the Commonwealth exercises great *de facto* influence, through its possessing the bulk of taxation powers. Since 1942 the power to impose income tax and other major revenue-producing taxes has belonged exclusively to the seat of Federal power, i.e. the Commonwealth Parliament. Taxation power has inevitably led the Commonwealth into assuming more and more responsibility and influence in many key fields. Most objective observers would agree that for the last few years, one of the major political and economic problems of Australia has been (and continues to be) the dichotomy caused by the Commonwealth largely controlling the finances in many activities for which the States are politically, socially and legislatively responsible. The States have consistently sought a growth tax, and in June 1971 achieved the transfer of payroll tax (a levy on salaries and wages paid by employers) from the Commonwealth to themselves. Current opinion seems to be that this is only a partial solution, and further negotiations between the Commonwealth and the States are bound to occur.

Economically, Australia is a capitalist or private enterprise society. Immediately before the Second World War primary industry was an important sector of the economy, but Table 2 illustrates the changes which have occurred in the last three decades or so.

Whilst remaining a private enterprise society, Australia has seen in recent years, in common with other capitalist countries, the emergence of government as the major controlling influence in the economy, and the introduction of legislation to control private enterprise in areas in which conflict with public interest was observed or envisaged. Examples of the latter have included legislation to restrict unfair trading practices, and laws on environmental controls and regional planning. Most public utilities and services are owned by the Commonwealth or State

---

1. In addition to the six States there is the Australian Capital Territory, which is the seat of the Federal Government, and the Northern Territory, which is administered by the Commonwealth.

TABLE 2. Australian production (net) and employment

	Primary		Manufacturing		Mining & quarrying			Total
	$M	%	$M	%	$M	%	$M	%
Production								
1939	415.2	37.2	633.0	56.8	66.8	6.0	1 115.0	100
1949	1 053.5	46.1	1 137.5	49.7	96.7	4.2	2 287.7	100
1959	2 030.8	34.1	3 685.2	61.9	236.7	4.0	5 952.7	100
1969	3 035.4	26.8	7 589.0	67.0	700.8	6.2	11 325.2	100
	('000)	%	('000)	%	('000)	%	Total	%
Employment								
1939	423.9	38.0	625.1	56.0	65.8	6.0	1 114.8	100
1949	400.8	29.8	890.0	66.2	53.0	4.0	1 343.8	100
1959	393.8	25.7	1 088.0	71.0	50.2	3.3	1 532.0	100
1969	442.0	23.5	1 384.0	73.3	60.5	3.2	1 886.5	100

SOURCES Commonwealth Bureau of Census and Statistics

Governments: examples are electricity and water supplies, telephone and tele-graphic services, railways and metropolitan omnibus systems.

Australia is a comparatively egalitarian society, with a salary and wage structure which is largely determined by an arbitration and conciliation system. Table 3 adequately illustrates this facet of society.

TABLE 3. Income distribution

Grade of actual income	Number of taxpayers	%	Total actual income ($000)	%
Below $1000	488 821	9.8	327 198	2.7
1000 — 1999	1 214 733	24.3	1 634 054	13.6
2000 — 2999	1 319 534	26.4	2 680 744	22.3
3000 — 3999	1 004 324	20.1	2 681 341	22.4
4000 — 5999	684 994	13.7	2 485 690	20.7
6000 — 7999	160 057	3.2	847 367	7.1
8000 — 9999	56 320	1.1	400 273	3.3
10000 — 19999	60 388	1.2	659 484	5.5
20000 and over	10 252	.2	283 814	2.4
TOTAL	4 999 423	100	11 999 965	100

SOURCE Commonwealth Bureau of Census and Statistics, *Taxation Statistics 1968-69.*

Trade unions occupy a significant position in Australia, and total union membership appears to be about 2,314,000, which is approximately 50% of wage and salary earners[1]. Many industrial awards contain compulsory unionism clauses. The employers combine in many different types of association, but in general are more fragmented than the unions. Australia's arbitration and conciliation system is well developed and brings employers and employees into a legal structure, which determines salaries, wages and working conditions. In recent years there have been some signs of direct bargaining between unions and groups of employers, but as yet the arbitration and conciliation system remains the dominant factor in industrial relations.

To a large extent, Western Australia is representative of the whole nation. It has a State Parliament comprising an upper and a lower house. Elections for the lower house are held every three years, with universal suffrage for all persons over 18 years of age. In common with Australian tradition, the electoral boundaries give rural and non-metropolitan areas a weighting, i.e. the number of electors for such parliamentary seats is far less than in the urban areas.

C. Overall economic and manpower planning

Ultimate decision-making power in Australia is vested in governments. (The ministerial groups are termed 'Cabinets'). As a result of the bulk of financial authority being vested in the Commonwealth, the Federal Cabinet is the senior body. It receives advice and recommendations from the public service, organised in functional departments, and, when framing a Federal budget, receives submissions from and holds discussion with groups such as the Associated Chambers of Manufacturers, the Associated Chambers of Commerce Australia, and the Australian Council of Trade Unions. Nevertheless, the decisions are made by the Government, taking into account political and economic considerations.

A major Commonwealth department involved in overall economic and manpower planning is the Department of Labour and National Service. It advises that although no formal manpower planning is undertaken in Australia at present, manpower and training matters form an integral part of the nation's overall economic objectives, which include the attainment of the maximum possible rate of economic growth compatible with the maintenance of full employment and internal and external stability.

At a National Conference of Training for Industry and Commerce held in May 1971 the Minister for Labour and National Service stressed the need to base effective training programmes on investigations of projected national needs. He undertook to review existing manpower data available in the country, and in particular emphasised the need for improved collection, compilation and presentation of statistical information and for detailed surveys of future manpower

---

1. As indicated to the writer in correspondence with officers of the Department of Labour and National Service.

requirements in order to provide a sound basis for developing planned training programmes.

The relationship between economic planning and higher education is at present fairly remote. While manpower needs are taken into account, as far as possible, in planning the development of universities and other institutions of higher education, detailed forecasts of needs for highly trained people are not yet available to guide the development of higher education.

D. Gross national product and education

From the statistical data available, it would appear that for 1970 the gross national product (GNP) per head of population was of the order of $A2,500. The GNP figure for rural output has been declining for several years, offset, however, by the rise in the non-farm output of goods and services. Measured over the six years up to and including 1970, the non-farm sector is responsible for between 90 and 93 per cent of all production of goods and services.[1]

A document issued by the Commonwealth Statistician in March 1971 on 'Expenditure in Education' estimates that 4.3 per cent of GNP was being spent on education in the financial year 1969/70. For the previous year the estimate was 4.1 per cent. And in 1970 the then Western Australian Minister for industrial development, Mr. C. W. Carr, said that in the previous five years expenditure on education in Australia had increased by nearly 70 per cent, compared with an increase of only 37 per cent for the GNP. He expressed his belief that "all agree that education is inseparable from higher productivity, economic advancement and personal betterment".

E. The structure of the Australian higher-education system

The main streams of higher education are the universities, the colleges of advanced education (to which category the Western Australian Institute of Technology belongs) and the teachers' colleges. All major higher-educational institutions are government owned, although in the case of all the universities and many of the colleges of advanced education they operate under parliamentary legislation which gives them a large degree of autonomy and designates them as separate corporate and legal entities.

The main distinction between universities and colleges of advanced education is that the former are oriented towards academic studies, while the colleges are primarily concerned with applied studies involving direct links with industry. Thus in the colleges there is a greater concentration on part-time studies associated with employment, and far less on graduate training and research. And at the same time there is, in the colleges, a primary emphasis on teaching.

1. *The Australian Economy 1971*, Canberra, The Treasury, July 1971.

Teacher education has traditionally been carried out in teachers' colleges operated by the State departments of education. However, significant changes are occurring, with some of the colleges of advanced education now entering the field of teacher education[1]. It may be reasonably postulated that, progressively, teacher education will be located in universities, colleges of advanced education and some teachers' colleges (probably linked through co-ordinating agencies) in an endeavour to diversify the philosophical approach and skills of graduate teachers. Many educationists are advocating an end to teacher education being carried out in isolation from other disciplines. Recent reports to the South Australian and Queensland Governments point in this direction.

The financing of universities and colleges of advanced education operates on the following formula:

	State	Commonwealth
Recurrent expenditure	$1.85 (including student fees)	$1.00
Capital expenditure	$1.00	$1.00

In addition, the Commonwealth makes some limited unmatched grants, of which an example is $250,000 per triennium to the colleges of advanced education (in total) to improve library collections. There are also a number of Commonwealth educational research granting bodies. The Australian Government has additionally made significant direct-aid capital grants for teacher and technical education institutions. It also operates significant scholarship schemes, although as yet it has not used the system to attract students into employment fields in which there are shortages of graduates. The sources and totals of recurrent finance for higher education in Western Australia are given in Table 4.

The Commonwealth Government has two advisory bodies which recommend the level of support desired from the Commonwealth. These are called the Australian Universities Commission and the Australian Commission on Advanced Education,[2] and their recommendations are made on a triennial basis. (The role of these advisory bodies will be examined further in Section II, when consideration is being given to the links between higher education and central government.)

Membership is decided by the Commonwealth Government. Whilst universities have obtained a number of appointees on both bodies, the colleges of advanced education have been less fortunate. This anomaly has been a subject of considerable criticism and no logical explanation has yet been offered. Students have not obtained representation and the Australian Union of Students is campaigning actively on the matter. Members are said to be mainly selected on a basis of community representation, and whilst services given have been time-consuming and arduous, many educationists are critical of the apparent randomness of selection.

1. The Western Australian Institute of Technology has submitted a proposal for a considerable expansion of its work in teacher education in the next Triennium 1973-1975.
2. Founded in 1965 as the Commonwealth Advisory Committee on Advanced Education, and in late 1971 made a statutory body known as the Australian Commission on Advanced Education.

TABLE 4. Sources of recurrent finance for higher education (Western Australia) in Australian dollars

	1966/67		1967/68		1968/69		1969/70		1970/71 (estimate)	
	Commonwealth	State	Commonwealth	State	Commonwealth	State	Commonwealth	State	Commonwealth	State
University of Western Australia	2 306 000	3 200 000	2 652 000	3 778 775	2 833 000	4 094 962	3 281 000	5 064 861	3 824 000	5 446 135
Western Australian Institute of Technology	363 000	1 111 589	776 000	1 383 232	912 000	1 844 164	1 929 000	2 962 348	2 303 000	3 741 000
Teachers' colleges		2 506 144		2 901 121		3 564 995		4 698 062		5 653 000
Kindergarten Association		178 700		251 800		278 000		319 000		484 283[1]

1. Actual

NOTE Separate figures are not available in respect of the proposed new Murdoch University, recurrent expenditure for which is included in the University of Western Australia figures.

SOURCES Western Australian State Treasury

It is important to realise that, notwithstanding the considerable influence of the statutory bodies, the decisions on resource allocations to higher education institutions in the final analysis are dependent on negotiations which take place between them and the Commonwealth Treasury, and even more importantly on the discussions which occur between the Commonwealth Treasury and the various State Treasuries. However, the Commonwealth Government is essentially reliant on its two advisory bodies, i.e. the Australian Universities Commission and the Australian Commission on Advanced Education, as far as planning and management in higher education are concerned.

Table 5 gives relevant financial data for the current triennium 1970-1972.

TABLE 5. Funds for universities and colleges of advanced education, Triennium 1970-1972 (in thousands of $A)

	Universities	Colleges of advanced education
Recurrent (operating) funds All States plus Australian Capital Territory	523 920	128 000
Capital funds All States plus Australian Capital Territory	106 787.6	102 943

NOTE The figures quoted are those appearing in the relevant Commonwealth Acts of Parliament. They exclude supplementary grants made for increases in academic salaries, which are approved by the Commonwealth and State Governments, and a decision, without creating a precedent, to grant supplementaries for increases in non-academic salaries over and above those estimated.

Another important link between the Commonwealth and the States is the Australian Education Council. The Council consists of the Ministers for Education from the six Australian States, and its meetings are also attended by the States' Directors-General. The Directors-General may speak freely in the Council meetings but if any issue is put to a vote only the Ministers are entitled to vote.

There are no formal terms of reference for the Council's activities. Issues of mutual education interest are discussed with a view to obtaining a uniform approach on matters that are common to all Departments. The Council is used as the means of making a united approach to the Federal Government on educational issues. It is not uncommon for the Council to invite the Commonwealth Minister for Education and Science to attend a part of its meeting set aside for discussion of matters relating to Commonwealth-State interests.

The role of Education Departments in State planning and management in higher education is not significant, if measured in a formal sense, apart from the area of teacher education and sub-tertiary work in some of the technical colleges. In some instances, such as Western Australia, a proportion of adult education is the responsibility of the Education Department. However, the departments do play a significant role through having members on the governing councils of universities and colleges of advanced education, and also on the higher education co-ordinating authorities. Furthermore, close links are maintained between the departments and the various organs of higher education in respect of such matters as (a) demographic data, (b) secondary system enrolments and input into the tertiary system, (c) foreseen needs in some aspects of education as e.g. special studies in art and music, and (d) teacher education in those instances where trainees are being educated either fully or partly by universities or colleges of advanced education.

Of particular significance in Western Australia is the recently created Tertiary Education Commission, which has the responsibility of co-ordinating and rationalising all higher education in the State. (Its role and functions are examined further in Section II, in relation to the links between higher education and central economic and social planning.)

It is, as yet, to early to assess the performance of the Tertiary Education Commission. It has assumed the responsibilities for State accreditation of degrees and other awards for the Western Australian Institute of Technology, although the awards are made in the name of the latter. In addition, the Commission has played a significant rôle in the acquisition of sites for foreseen higher educational institutions, and in recommendations to government on such major issues as teacher education. The degree of success which it will achieve in the rôle of rationalising and co-ordinating higher education in Western Australia is difficult to predict, for a great deal depends on the manner in which it will exercise its autonomy, particularly in its relationship with the State Treasury.

F. The place and role of the Western Australian Institute of Technology in the system of higher education in Western Australia

There are three elements of higher education in Western Australia, namely the University of Western Australia, the Western Australian Institute of Technology and the teachers' colleges. In addition, there is sub-tertiary work carried out by the Technical Education Division of the Education Department.

Planning has now commenced for a second University (Murdoch), as a result of a government decision taken because the physical and other facilities of the University of Western Australia are likely to reach saturation-point in the middle 1970s. An Act to establish the Murdoch University Planning Board was promulgated in 1970. Whilst official statements set 1975 as the year of first student intake, there are currently some doubts on the viability of such an institution by that year. The Murdoch University concept was strongly motivated by the need for another veterinary science faculty in Australia, but this need is lessening as a result of the economic difficulties being encountered in rural industry. The new university envisaged entering into teacher education, but this will now need to be reconsidered in view of the Western Australian Institute of Technology's proposal to set up a major teacher education faculty in 1975. The Murdoch University will almost certainly be founded, but the year of its first intake of students deserves to receive critical analysis by both the Australian Universities Commission and the Tertiary Education Commission, as well as the Commonwealth and State Governments.

The University of Western Australia Act does not specify role, functions or objectives. The main disciplines of study with which the University is concerned are: Agricultural Science, *Architecture*, Arts, Dental Science, *Economics & Commerce*, Education, *Engineering*, Law, Medicine, Psychology, Science, *Social Work*.[1] Its entrance requirements are matriculation, although there is a limited intake through a Mature-age Examination system.

In the next Triennium 1973-1975 the University, subject to discussions with the Tertiary Education Commission and the Australian Universities Commission, and to the governmental decisions on financial grants, wishes to enter e.g. computer science, fisheries science, electronics, geochemistry and geophysics. It has expressed interest in chemical and metallurgical engineering and in a master's degree in business administration. Present indications are that a pilot scheme in chemical engineering, as a post-graduate course, is more likely to be introduced at the Western Australian Institute of Technology. The introduction of a higher degree in business administration is likely to be the subject of debate not only in Western Australia but throughout the nation. (Many colleges of advanced education already are substantially involved in studies in administration and regard such courses as essentially more fitting to their vocational philosophies than to the research-oriented basis of the universities.)

The range of studies currently available at the Western Australian Institute of Technology is: Agriculture (especially farm management), Applied Science, *Architecture*, Art & Design, Asian Languages & Studies, *Commerce & Administration*, Computing, Earth Sciences, *Engineering*, Home Economics, Library Studies, Medical Therapies, Social Sciences, Surveying.[1]

The major plans of the Western Australian Institute of Technology for 1973-75 include building technology, teacher education, the extension of paramedical studies and masters' degree qualifications in such areas as social sciences, engineering and the applied sciences.

The functions of the Western Australian Institute of Technology have been clearly enunciated in the appropriate Act.[2] Section 7 of the Act in part reads as follows:

"7. The functions of the Institute shall include the following:
   (a) to provide facilities for higher specialised instruction and to advance training in the various branches of technology and science;

---

1. The disciplines in *italic* are those in which both institutions, the University and the Western Australian Institute of Technology, are involved. The University is primarily concerned with the study of a discipline as such: the Institute of Technology is more concerned with the application of knowledge.
2. The Western Australian Institute of Technology Act No. 94 of 1966.

(b) to aid the advancement, development and practical application to industry of science or any techniques;

(c) to encourage and provide facilities for the development and improvement of tertiary education whether on a full- or part-time basis to meet the needs of the community in the State."

In 1963, when Dr. H. S. Williams, then Director of Technical Education in Western Australia and now Director of the Western Australian Institute of Technology, submitted a case[1] for financial assistance on behalf of the Institute to the Martin Committee, he stressed that work at the Institute should complement rather than compete with the work of the University. Thus, in comparison with courses at the University, professional courses at the Institute, in his view, should be related to the more immediate and changing needs of the local commercial and industrial community. Running through the submission, however, was the assumption—already queried with respect to ideas about the future pattern of the university education in Western Australia—that whereas work at the Institute of Technology should largely be concerned with the teaching and practical application of the knowledge needed for various professional occupations and qualifications, work at the University should mainly be related to the theoretical development of subject disciplines and professional knowledge and the discovery or extension of knowledge.

The scale of the two institutions can be seen from Table 6.

TABLE 6. Student and staff numbers in the University of Western Australia and the Western Australian Institute of Technology

	1967		1969		1971		1975 (projected)	
	U OF WA	WAIT	U OF WA	WAIT	U OF WA	WAIT	U OF WA	WAIT
Students full-time	3 796	1 060	4 410	1 547	5 295	2 280	6 240	6 282
Students part-time	1 893	1 810	2 332	2 639	2 704	3 347	3 596	6 809
Students external	305	—	358	334	375	563	352	1 427
TOTAL	5 994	2 870	7 100	4 520	8 374	6 190	10 188	14518[1]
Academic Staff	414	158	452	250	499.5	319	702.5	600
Other Staff	891	96	933	281	1 015	483	1 381	939

1. Or 8,275 full-time-equivalent students.

1. Submission on Technical Education to the Committee of the Australian Universities Commission on the Future of Tertiary Education, 1963.

G. Basic information on the Western Australian Institute of Technology

In the early 1960s industrial development in Western Australia began to accelerate, partly on account of a series of major mineral discoveries. The number of students in professional level courses at Perth Technical College (which has a long history in the State) began to increase substantially. The State Government decided to establish a technological institute, and so the Western Australian Institute of Technology was formed, but as part of the Technical Education Division of the Education Department. An announcement to this effect was made by the State Government in 1962, and on a major site of 240 acres at Bentley, a suburb of Perth about six miles from the city centre, building began in late 1963. This is the main campus, but as of 1971 four teaching departments remain in central city premises, which are overcrowded and inadequate and shared with the Perth Technical College. The current plan is for the Western Australian Institute of Technology to house these departments at Bentley by 1976.

The Martin Report[1] to the Commonwealth Government in 1965 endorsed the concept of the Institute and in 1966 an interim grant was made to the Institute by the Commonwealth. The State Government formed a committee to examine the future needs of tertiary education.

In an interim report the Jackson Committee[2], as it became known, recommended autonomy for the Institute. Legislation to this effect was passed in December 1966 and an Interim Governing Council was set up in February 1967. (The full Council was appointed in March 1969.) The Jackson Committee, in a later report, recommended the incorporation into the Institute of other colleges of advanced education. In 1969 the Institute incorporated the Schools of Occupational Therapy and Physiotherapy and the Muresk Agricultural College as departments, and the W. A. School of Mines at Kalgoorlie as a branch. (The latter was originally to be made an autonomous body, but as a result of representations made by the mining industry the State Government decided to make it a branch of the Western Australian Institute of Technology, in order to give it greater strength in such matters as library resources, educational research, staffing and administration, i.e. those areas in which it is difficult for a small institution to be adequately serviced.)

Since these events, two other Commonwealth Committees have had significant influence on the Western Australian Institute of Technology, as part of the Australian system of colleges of avanced education.

The Inquiry into Salaries in Colleges of Advanced Education (the Sweeney Report) in May 1969 led in 1970 to university salary scales being applicable to the Western Australian Institute of Technology, with some minor differences and without the sabbatical leave provisions applicable to University academic staff. The Western Australian Institute of Technology does provide some degree of

1. *Tertiary Education in Australia,* Report of the Committee on the Future of Tertiary Education in Australia to the Australian Universities Commission, Vol. III.
2. *Tertiary Education in Western Australia,* Report of the Committee appointed by the Premier of Western Australia under the Chairmanship of Sir Lawrence Jackson, Perth, September 1967.

study leave to staff and has a three-month service leave provision after every seven years' service, as compared to one year of study leave after six years' service at the University. (The latter condition of service is now being treated as a privilege rather than a right, and is by no means generally applicable to all Australian universities.)

The Committee of Inquiry into Awards in Colleges of Advanced Education (the Wiltshire Report) in June 1969 recommended degree-granting status to colleges of advanced education and by May 1971 the national and state accrediting systems had been reasonably well defined. The Commonwealth and the States agreed to set up national machinery for accreditation of degrees at colleges of advanced education. An Australian Council on awards in advanced education has been established by a joint action of the States and the Commonwealth.

In Western Australia the Tertiary Education Commission will be the accrediting authority and detailed procedures have been agreed between the Commission and the Western Australian Institute of Technology. In 1970 the Western Australian Institute of Technology Act was amended to allow it to award degrees, and the first are likely to be conferred for students completing their studies in 1971. All awards are to be made by the Western Australian Institute of Technology in its own right and name. The question of retrospectivity remains to be resolved. For the next few years, it is likely that the Institute will be confined to bachelors' and masters' degrees, although in time it is likely that doctorates will be introduced.

This appears to be an appropriate moment at which to comment on the degree of autonomy enjoyed by the Western Australian Institute of Technology, both in theory and in practice. It will have been seen previously that Western Australia has a Tertiary Education Commission with overall co-ordinating and rationalising powers. This gives the Commission the central policy rôle in tertiary education in Western Australia, but as yet it is difficult to predict the extent of the effect on the autonomy of both the University of Western Australia, and the Western Australian Institute of Technology. Certainly, the Commission is likely to be predominant in policy determinations in (a) the level of tuition fees, (b) the introduction of new courses, (c) new institutions, and (d) such major matters as teacher education.

The Tertiary Education Commission has the responsibility of advising the State Government on the level of financial support it should give the Western Australian Institute of Technology for triennia, in the same way as the Australian Commission on Advanced Education advises the Commonwealth Government. However, both bodies are advisory and not decision-making. The latter remains in governmental hands, with a major responsibility being vested in the respective Treasuries. It is axiomatic that the Commonwealth and State Treasuries exercise very great influence on the decisions of governments, but nevertheless there remains the element of political decision, i.e. the degree of emphasis to be given to competing demands, governed at least in part by public opinion and the strength of arguments produced by pressure groups.

As far as academic policies are concerned, higher educational institutions have a great degree of autonomy. British and Australian tradition has been such that examinations, assessments, curricula structure and kindred matters are the responsibility of the institutions. In the case of the Western Australian Institute of Technology, in particular, a great deal of regard has to be paid to the viewpoints of professional associations and organisations. Western Australian Institute of Technology awards lead, in almost all instances, to full membership of the professional associations (after, in some instances, practical experience), but the latter from time to time carry out their own investigations, with a view to re-endorsing accreditations. Until the advent of the Tertiary Education Commission the Western Australian Institute of Technology had a large degree of autonomy in deciding between competing demands, e.g., whether to introduce quotas in some courses, or the relative priorities to be given to growth in existing courses as against the introduction of new courses. In *de jure* terms this power seems to have been significantly reduced through the creation of the Tertiary Education Commission, but in *de facto* terms this may not prove to be the case. The Western Australian Institute of Technology will have far greater resources than the Tertiary Education Committee for investigating problems and working out policy recommendations, unless the latter is to develop its own research and planning teams on a large scale. It may prove to be more efficient and effective for the Tertiary Education Commission to have a small specialist staff, and to augment its resources by making research and development grants to institutions and individuals, in possession of the appropriate resources and abilities. In the long term, if the Western Australian Institute of Technology has been thorough enough in its own investigations, both academically and financially, most of its recommendations on new courses and similar matters are likely to be endorsed by the Commission.

II. Integration of Western Australian Institute of Technology planning into the economic and social development of Western Australia and Australia

A. Federal and State mechanisms for links between higher education and planning

As has been seen, the principal bodies responsible for the links between higher education and central economic and social planning in Australia at the Commonwealth level are the Australian Universities Commission and the Australian Commission on Advanced Education. Both are advisory to the Commonwealth Government. Final decisions on the level of financial support are made by the Commonwealth Government after consultation with the States, with legislation subsequently being enacted through the Federal Parliament.

The Australian Universities Commission was formed in 1958 to advise the Commonwealth Government on financial needs of the universities at three-year intervals (triennia) and to continuously review university development. This had been one of the principal recommendations of the Murray Report[1].

The Commonwealth Advisory Committee on Advanced Education was formed in 1965, and in 1971 was made a statutory body known as the Australian Commission on Advanced Education. Its role is, for the colleges of advanced education, analogous to that of the Australian Universities Commission for universities.

At the State level various mechanisms exist, but to date there is only one instance of a single co-ordinating body for all forms of higher education: this is the Tertiary Education Commission of Western Australia, which was first formed in 1969, and made a statutory body in 1971. Its function is best understood by reference to the parliamentary Act[2] which made it a body corporate.

Under the Act, the functions of the Commission include the promotion, development and co-ordination of tertiary education, having regard to the needs of the State and financial and other resources available to it; the review of submissions of tertiary educational institutions relating to triennial programmes and the making of recommendations to the State Government on the levels of financial support requested in the submissions; the making of recommendations to the governing bodies of the Institutions on the terms and conditions of appointment

1. Report of the Committee on Australian Universities 1957.
2. Western Australian Tertiary Education Commission, Act No. 84 of 1970.

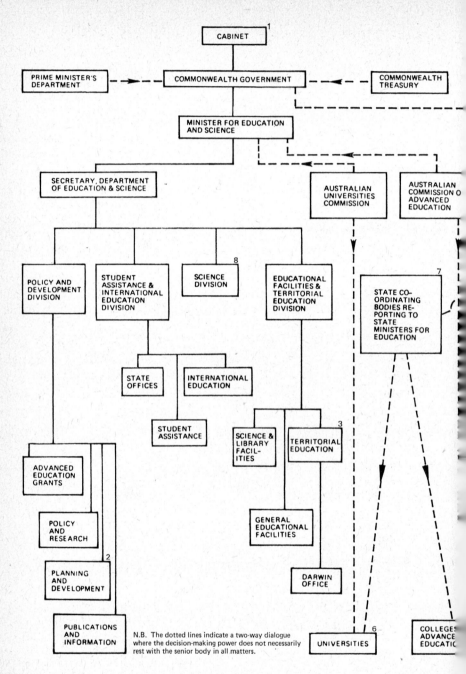

FIGURE 1. *The education system in Australia, December 1971.*

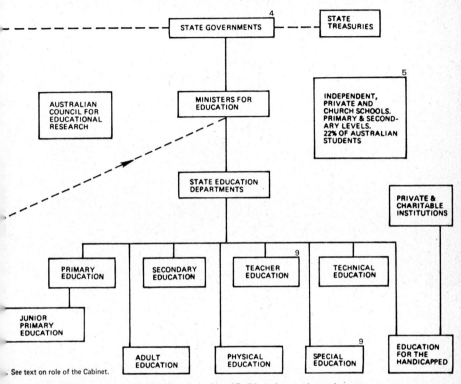

See text on role of the Cabinet.

Controls curriculum development, aboriginal education, the teaching of English to migrants and per capita grants to independent schools.

The Commonwealth Department of Education & Science administers all government education in the Australian Capital Territory and Northern Territory.

All State finance is allocated among the States at an annual Premiers' conference from Commonwealth funds realised by taxation etc. It is then re-allocated within the State according to priorities.

The independent schools have private sources of finance but also receive a per capita grant from the Commonwealth, as well as some State support.

The universities and CAEs are autonomous in themselves but derive finance from both State and Commonwealth sources. Both operate under the auspices of the two national co-ordinating bodies the AUC and ACAE, as well as any State bodies that may exist.

Such bodies include
The WA Tertiary Education Commission   Queensland Advanced Education Board (CAEs only)
The Victorian Institute of Colleges (CAEs only)   The NSW Higher Education Authority.

Studies scientific research in Australia and overseas, and provides grants for research in Australia.

Responsibility for many spheres of education such as teacher training, the arts, agricultural, technical education etc. is often shared between the State education departments and tertiary education institutions.

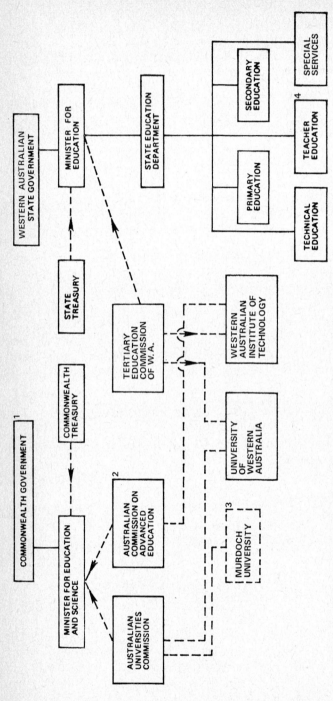

1. Commonwealth Finance is provided in matched grants of $1 Commonwealth to $1 State for Capital Expenditure, and $1 Commonwealth to $1.85 State for Recurrent Expenditure. The Commonwealth also provides unmatched grants in certain specific areas viz. Education Research and Libraries. The State contribution includes student fees.

2. Formerly the Commonwealth Advisory Committee on Advanced Education (C.A.C.A.E.).

3. The Murdoch University is still at the planning stage. See text.

4. See text on changes likely in Teacher Education.

FIGURE 2. *The Western Australian education system in 1971.*

and employment, including salaries for staff, whether academic or otherwise; the consideration of proposals for new courses of study, with particular reference to the achievement of rationalisation of resources and the avoidance of unnecessary duplication; the co-ordination of criteria for entrants to tertiary educational institutions; and the promotion and undertaking of research into the needs and problems of tertiary aducation.

As with the Commonwealth higher education bodies, the Tertiary Education Commission is advisory to the State Government, and it is by a process of consultation with the Commonwealth Government that ultimate financial decisions are made. In due course, the decisions are enacted by the State Parliament through annual budget legislation introduced by the Government. The financial legislation is in conformity with that passed by the Federal Parliament for the triennia.

Figures 1 and 2 are a diagrammatic representation of the Australian and Western Australian systems of higher education.

B. Federal and State evaluation system

The universities and the colleges of advanced education make submissions to the Federal and State Governments, and their advisory bodies, on a triennial basis. To illustrate the system, by 1971 the submissions will have been made for the period 1973-75. Whilst each institution has variations in its approach and its techniques, the following summary of the Western Australian Institute of Technology submission for 1973-75, which runs to over 340 foolscap pages, will be broadly representative:

General Review and Commentary on the 1970-72 Advanced Education Programme
Overall Pattern of Development 1973-81
Major Objectives for the Third Triennium, 1973-75
Master Site Development Programmes
Capital Works Programme
Staff, Student and Library Projections
Present Courses and Proposed New Courses (1973-75)
Computer Development in the Institute
Recurrent Expenditure 1973-75
Organisational Structure
Reviews and Forecasts—Teaching Departments
Reviews and Forecasts—Central Service Facilities and New Developments
Basic Triennium Planning System
Supporting Schedules Capital Works Programme 1973-75

Visits are made by the relevant government authorities and discussions held with each institution. In addition, consultation takes place between the Australian Universities Commission and the Australian Commission on Advanced Education; between the latter and the respective treasuries; and in Western Australia between the Tertiary Education Commission and the higher educational institutions. The data submitted are most comprehensive but apart from consideration of major new developments (such as the establishment of a new institution or the introduction of a major new course of study), there is little evidence as yet to suggest any high degree of sophistication in the evaluation procedures. By and large, political and economic decisions, i.e. the level of financial support, are predominant and are made by governments in consultation, with advice from relevant government departments.

The triennial submissions are essentially quantitative, in that information on student and staff numbers, equipment, capital works, library stocks, operating costs, courses and new developments, is given in exhaustive detail. Nevertheless, some institutions such as the Western Australian Institute of Technology often take a qualitative approach by defining broad objectives for the years ahead. The following extract from the Western Australian Institute of Technology's submission for 1973-75 is illustrative: "... to make significant advances in the implementation of certain major educational policies, primarily (a) the clarification of the award structure of the Institute with particular reference to the granting of degrees for appropriate courses; (b) liberal education; (c) the extension of interdisciplinary activity and teaching; and (d) staff development." The Submission deals with those matters and items such as educational media and continuing education in considerable detail.

With the rapid expansion of expenditure on higher education, there is at least some likelihood of change towards more systematic investigation, inclusive of comparative date and computer simulation of alternative policy decisions. As with every human enterprise, size brings complexity, inevitably involving the development of more sophisticated criteria for decision-making. However, at present methods are random and they are influenced more by political considerations than by economic or social planning.

The triennial reports of the Australian Universities Commission and the Australian Commission on Advanced Education are a significant element in the evaluative system. These are generally published about six months prior to the commencement of a new triennium.

C. Feasibility testing of the higher education plan and its consistency with overall planning

The above concept has been interpreted as requiring information on (a) the testing of the higher education plan in relation to e.g. finance, community needs, national resources, management ability and design and building capacity; and (b) the relationships between the input from the secondary education system, the pool of students in the working population and the output from higher education being in step with the foreseen needs of the community. Government authorities have been consulted, and the general view is that feasibility testing of the above nature is not consistent with the existing method of operation in Australia.

Most higher educational institutions are autonomous and each embarks upon a programme of course development based on its assessment of the needs of an ambient community. As an example, if a college of advanced education in an industrial area assesses that there would be a demand for a course in industrial design, then it would be likely to introduce such a course on a comparatively small scale and if the course proves to be popular, to progressively expand the facilities. The advisory committees to governments appear to take the view that the idea of feasibility testing implies that a national scheme would be instituted as the result of a pilot study. This does not, in fact, occur in Australia.

The advisory bodies to governments are concerned with such factors as finance, community needs, human resources and design and building capacity, and seek to obtain sufficient data from the institutions covering these aspects before recommendations are made to Government on financial allocations. Their recommendations on new courses are generally based on a subjective judgement that the courses are viable. The advisory bodies have said that they are most concerned with the availability of statistical data regarding output of matriculated students, the number of students in the work force and the nature of student intake into higher educational institutions. However, there seems to be an opinion that data at the moment is not sufficiently sophisticated to enable the conclusions to be as valid and effective as is necessary.

Considerable information has been given on manpower planning earlier in this report, but it should be added that the most commonly held view among educational administrators in Australia is that, where temporary imbalances occur between the output of academic institutions and the needs of industry, commerce and government, the operation of the laws of the market-place ultimately results in the situation being corrected. Recent economic difficulties, resulting in an increasing time-lag in securing employment, are throwing doubts on this somewhat complacent view.

Many of the institutions of higher education in Australia do carry out some elements of feasibility testing within the limits of their resources. It may be postulated that both the institutions and the governmental authorities are beginning to show greater interest in feasibility testing and a number of theories and models are now under discussion.

D. Higher education and manpower planning

The principal government agencies are the Department of Labour and National Service and the Department of Education and Science, with a high degree of co-operation existing between them. The Minister of Labour and National Service recently said the urgency of national education policies was increasing because of: "...the growing demand for complex skills and technical knowledge in the labour force to match the sophisticated systems and equipment now used in industry and commerce; the increasing exposure of Australian industry and commerce to international standards of technical competence, performance capability and product quality; the rapidity of technical innovation in individual industries calling as it does for continual training over the period of a working life." The context of the Minister's statement was related more to technical training than to higher education, but it may well prove to be a forerunner of greater national efforts to relate manpower planning and higher education.

By and large, Australia has tended to adopt an approach to manpower planning which has broad policy objectives and then to endeavour to influence the market mechanism where necessary so that its operation will produce the required result.

In a single institution, such as the Western Australian Institute ot Technology, a high degree of contact is maintained between the teaching departments, the professional organisations and the employers. The majority of academic staff are members of their professional organisations, many holding executive office. Programmes of visits to employing organisations by staff and students are a regular part of many courses. Whenever professional accreditation bodies visit, the opportunity is taken to discuss graduate output and market demand. Many of the professional bodies conduct market assessments and discuss these with the teaching departments, whilst the Institute itself has carried out a number of surveys on the employment of graduates. Already, however, every new course is subjected to a detailed market survey, which is cross-checked by research and planning staff and, where appropriate, with relevant external bodies. As a single illustration, the procedure in the Institute's Department of Accounting and Business Studies has established links with manpower planning through contact with the Commonwealth and State Public Services and by direct contact with professional institutions, including the Australian Society of Accountants and the Chartered Institute of Secretaries, the Institute of Chartered Accountants in Australia, and the Commonwealth Institute of Valuers. The Department also looks at the incorporation of businesses and the registration of public companies on the basis that all businesses registered require accounting services of some type.

Preliminary discussions have been held between the Institute and the Department of Industrial Development and Decentralisation on the need for a long-term survey of the relationships between the economy ot the State and the developmental programmes of the Institute. However, progress has been slow because the value of long-term planning is still being argued in Australia.

E. Students and graduates: demands and needs

The Western Australian Institute of Technology carries out its own market surveys when considering proposals for new courses. A course proposal is required to include information on such matters as: (a) the purpose of the course; (b) evidence of need, including the results of questionnaire surveys, supporting statements from employers or professional bodies; (c) degree of availability of the course in its initial stages; (d) structure of the course; (e) an estimate of student numbers for five years ahead as supported by accumulative evidence and argument; and (f) estimate of new resources involved, inclusive of staff, equipment, accommodation, consumables and library materials.

At the time of enrolment, academic staff endeavour to counsel students on their choice of disciplines. However, it is becoming increasingly apparent that the procedure needs considerable strengthening, inclusive of more vocational guidance in the secondary education system. A proposal to have specialist counsellors attached to academic divisions is gaining favour.

Entrance qualifications vary from course to course, with higher academic abilities (as demonstrated by examinations) generally applying in courses where quotas are set and/or student demand is greater. Scholarships and similar means are used in minor degree to attract students to courses where numbers are insufficient for economy of operation. But this causes some misgivings, because whilst increased numbers may aid the Institute, job opportunities are often doubtful. An interesting recent development is the greater concentration on two-year courses for those students who upon enrolment or during their studies would be better serviced by less demanding courses than the three-year degree course.

The Institute has a flexible entrance policy and in general tends to support moves for the replacement of matriculation type examinations by a continuous assessment system in secondary schools. Such an assessment system is under consideration by the State Department of Education.

The Counselling Service at the Institute was created in 1970 and is in the process of being built into a major element in its operations. The provision of adequate and up-to-date information on occupations and career prospects is regarded as a necessary adjunct to the vocational counselling process and a Careers Information Centre is being developed. Information files are available for student perusal, grouped into two segments—by occupation and by employer. For graduate employment a successful programme of campus visits by employers has been established which brings together employers and students during the final year so that the vocational counselling process culminates in the graduate obtaining a satisfactory professional appointment with a minimum of delay.

The student body has its own independent organisation in the Student Guild, which has representatives on the governing Council and the majority of the significant internal boards, including the Boards of Study which are concerned with curricula development. Every endeavour is made by the Institute to obtain student opinion on all matters of significance, inclusive of educational content and method.

For a period of three days prior to the commencement of the teaching year an orientation programme is carried out. This generally includes such activities as addresses by senior academics, information on the Student Guild and its affiliated associations, the showing of an Institute film and guided tours of the campus. In addition, short addresses are given on counselling and on the use of the library facilities, and arrangements are made for new students to meet the Heads of Departments. Each student is issued with a manual which is a guide to the Institute and its policies.

The composition of the student body in the University of Western Australia and the Western Australian Institute of Technology in 1971 is summarised in Table 7. Quotas were minimal and related to particular courses where there were

TABLE 7. Enrolments in the Western Australian Institute of Technology and the University of Western Australia, 1971

	Western Australian Institute of Technology				University of Western Australia			
	FT	PT	Ext	Total	FT	PT	Ext	Total
(a) Courses common to both institutions								
Agriculture	60	—	—	60	175	18	14	207
Architecture	193	177	1	371	101	11	—	112
Arts	171	358	127	656	1 488	1 376	221	3 085
Commerce	379	1 198	258	1 835	589	469	31	1 089
Dental Science	15	—	—	15	125	9	—	134
Education	—	72	73	145	302	419	88	809
Engineering	527	637	8	1 172	670	27	—	697
Science	301	503	48	852	1 102	299	20	1 421
Social Work	71	—	1	72	31	13	—	44
Sub-total:	*1 717*	*2 945*	*516*	*5 178*	*4 583*	*2 641*	*374*	*7 598*
(b) Other courses								
Applied Medicine	318	40	—	358	—	—	—	—
Art & Design	159	223	27	409	—	—	—	—
Asian Languages	21	31	5	57	—	—	—	—
Home Economics	36	61	9	106	—	—	—	—
Law	—	—	—	—	192	61	1	254
Library Studies	29	47	6	82	—	—	—	—
Medicine	—	—	—	—	520	2	—	522
Sub-total	*563*	*402*	*47*	*1 012*	*712*	*63*	*1*	*776*
GRAND TOTAL	2 280	3 347	563	6 190	5 295	2 704	375	8 374

FT = Full-time; PT = Part-time; Ext = External.
SOURCE Research & Planning Branch, Western Australian Institute of Technology.

limitations in physical resources, but present evidence suggests a greater imposition of selective quotas in 1972.

In the majority of instances the existence of similar courses in both institutions is justified by the difference in approach, the University being more concerned with the body of knowledge within a discipline and the Institute adopting a more practical or vocational approach. However, in some instances (such as social work) there is little justification for both institutions running parallel courses. Until the advent of the colleges of advanced education, many universities including the Western Australian University ran vocationally-oriented courses. It would be in the long-term interests of both types of institutions for an assessment to be made wherever there is evidence of some duplication, and decisions made to rationalise the situation by transferring courses from one to the other. However, the difficulties of carrying out such a programme of rationalisation are immense, because of the vested interest of both parties and of the professions concerned. Such a programme could be successful only if the governments concerned used their finance-granting powers forcefully and in strict accord with a clear-cut national policy.

F. Curricula and socio-economic plans

The relationship between the development and review of curricula and the country's socio-economic plans is probably the most significant element in an institution of higher learning—certainly in an institute of technology. There is a tendency for all educational programmes to lag behind needs.

Education is essentially concerned with tomorrow. The student's working life is years ahead. He will perform in a different society from the one in which he is receiving his education. By necessity, if not by choice, he is being educated in the world of now for the world to be. It thus seems as though higher education has to grapple with the extremely difficult problem of the development of a higher-education system which is relevant to tomorrow's needs and yet serviced by today's inadequacy of both resources and knowledge. No matter how visionary and imaginative may be the approach of educationists, most courses of study inevitably are trailing the advent of new knowledge. The Western Australian Institute of Technology is showing an increasing awareness that continuing education may provide part of the answer to this problem.

There is also a growing area of opinion which supports the thesis that curriculum development is likely to move towards basic common courses in the first year, some specialisation in the second year and a high degree of specialisation in the third and subsequent years. If such a policy is developed the students specialised work in his final years may be more relevant to his needs and the advent of new knowledge.

The Institute has several major bodies which inter-link on the development of curricula in relation to the needs of the community. The organisational and decision-making structure of the Institute is shown in Figure 3 and is described in detail in Section IV.

The core of the structure is known as a Board of Study, the function of which is to ensure that all courses for which it is responsible are educationally sound and attuned to the needs of the profession and/or the community. It concerns itself with such matters as: course objectives, curriculum structure, teaching/learning situation, specific entrance requirements, advanced standing, and rationalisation of units with other courses. The Boards of Study are widely representative and inter-disciplinary, with counsellors and education development officers being involved for their specialist knowledge.

Reporting into the Boards of Study are Subject Committees, of which there is one for each subject taught in the Institute, the membership comprising all the staff teaching the subject from time to time. The Subject Committees are respon-

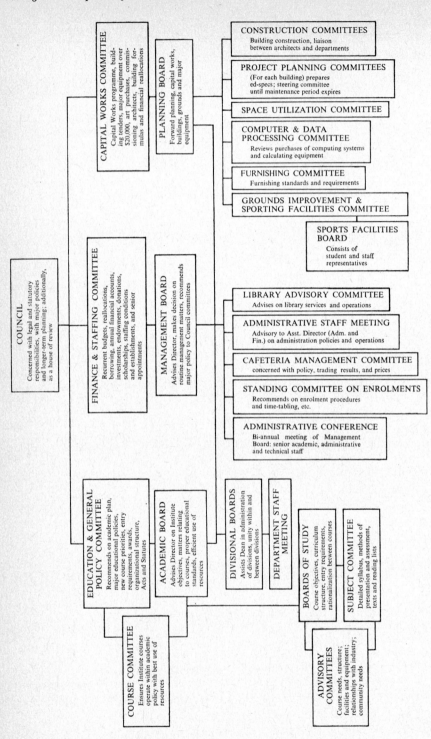

FIGURE 3. *Western Australian Institute of Technology: organisational and decision-making structure*

sible for: the detailed syllabus for the particular subject, the methods used in presenting the unit, the method of assessment and decisions on texts and reading lists.

An important adjunct to these academic bodies are advisory committees; (a) these provide a channel of communication and advice between the Institute and the segment of industry, business and the community services relevant to the particular course or group of courses concerned; (b) in particular, the committees advise the Institute on: (i) course needs, (ii) the structure and general content of courses, (iii) facilities and equipment, (iv) development of relationships between the Institute and industry, and (v) such other matters as are relevant to assist the Institute to be aware of and cater for community needs in the particular fields concerned. The composition of advisory committees ensures that there is strong representation from relevant employing organisations, professional bodies and related educational institutions.

Broad academic policies are set by the Academic Board, which recommends and/or reports to the Education and General Policy Committee. A Standing Committee of the Academic Board is that known as the Courses Committee, the function of which is to ensure that all courses operate within academic policy and make effective use of Institute resources. In order to do this, it will consider overall aspects of courses such as: total student contact hours, teaching methods, viability in terms of student numbers, specialist units required, curriculum structure and liberal studies content.

In recent months, the Institute has been deliberating on the necessity for developing a long-range educational plan looking forward for about a decade. The idea has recently been endorsed in principle by the Academic Board and may be summarised as: (a) a comprehensive plan, embracing all aspects of the educational process and reflecting the overall educational objectives of the Institute; (b) a plan which is integrated into the economic and social development of society and of the nation; (c) a context which shall encourage and enable change, and which is primarily concerned with the qualitative aspects of educational growth; and (d) a description of the intentions of the Institute over a specified time period, and of alternative ways and means of achieving the expressed intentions.

III. The Western Australian Institute of Technology system of decision-making and planning: indicators and criteria

A. Introduction

An essential factor in effective decision-making and planning in a higher educational institution is adaptability to change. The Western Australian Institute of Technology system is evolutionary and endeavours to maintain a high degree of flexibility, in order to be able readily to accommodate changing economic and social circumstances, with particular emphasis on (a) the level of financial allocations from Governments, which is determined by the state of the economy and social attitudes to higher education, (b) fluctuating and changing demands for graduates in different disciplines, (c) the variations in first-year intake, which is often influenced by student perception of career opportunities, and (d) changes in knowledge which have an impact on curricula and thus on resource decision-making.

The Institute, indeed, operates in accord with a philosophy that the only constant is change. Thus it keeps under constant and critical review its organisational structure, its decision-making system, its planning methodology, and detailed educational plans for varying periods of time ahead. Inevitably, there are constraints on the extent of change and the speed with which changes in policy are implemented; such constraints include the physical and financial resources, the need for detailed research and development programmes on current and foreseen problems, and the involvement of its staff, particularly academic, in consideration of contemplated major educational decisions, such as the reorganisation of the academic year. In addition to the internal, there are external restraints, such as the attitudes of professional associations and the decisions of such bodies as the Tertiary Education Commission and the Australian Commission on Advanced Education.

As an illustration of the philosophy of adaptability and constant surveillance, in 1971 a complete review of all aspects of the Institute was undertaken. Senior management held meetings with the teaching and senior support staff of all departments, to discuss and investigate such matters as long-term educational plans, teaching loads, departmental organisation, budgetary problems, relationships with the community and the organisational structure of the Institute. The meetings were condected on an open-forum basis.

Similar techniques were employed for the Educational Services (such as the Library Counselling, External Studies and Educational Development) and the Administrative and Finance Division. In some instances organisation and methods investigations were initiated, examples being library systems and organisation, accounting systems and reporting methods, and the purchasing system.

B. The basic triennial planning system

By August 1971 the Western Australian Institute of Technology had submitted to State and Commonwealth Governments its submission (i.e. educational plans and financial requests) for the triennium 1973-75, together with indications of foreseen developments for the period 1976-78. A general description of the system as applied to the Triennium, developed by the Research and Planning Branch under the general direction of the Planning Board, is set out in this section, followed by a discussion and evaluation of the system of indicators in use. (The role of the Planning Board is shown in figure 3 in Section II.)

The programme was conducted in accordance with Institute policy that estimates were to be based on projected educational and employment demand for courses. No restrictions were to be placed on student intake other than those which might be indicated by employment demand. Preliminary planning indicated that accurate estimates of demand would best be achieved by building up the requirements on the basis of resource demands for individual classes. In order to cope with this on a wide scale, it was necessary to devise a planning system beginning with student projections for the period 1971-76. These projections were converted to subject enrolments and finally to class enrolments. Resulting hours of class contact and distributions of class-size provided the bases for estimation of teaching staff and salaries, classrooms of various types and staff offices.

Techniques were developed which enabled the derivation of a variety of growth indexes for student numbers, student-hours, full-time-equivalent students and class-contact-hours. These were used to project car parking and cafeteria demands, and various budgetary items. Requirements for other resources, such as laboratory equipment, non-teaching space, administrative and wages staff, all bore varying relationships to the above parameters. The end result, therefore, was one of strong compatibility between capital and recurrent budgets and student enrolments.

1. Student enrolments

A consideration of the wide range of courses offered by the Institute brought early recognition that a first planning requirement would be a projection of the total enrolment based on demographic principles. This would provide a guideline for the projections of individual course enrolments (see below) and hence for the remainder of the programme.

The guideline projection was completed during 1970 and upgraded in accordance with the 1971 enrolment as at 31 March. The projection of individual courses was finalised in May 1971; these were aggregated and compared against the guideline projection. The comparison is presented below.

Year	1971	1972	1973	1974	1975
a. Individual courses	6 170	7 330	9 030	10 870	12 840
b. Guideline	6 170	7 270	8 640	10 230	12 130
c. Difference $(a-b)$	0	60	390	640	710
d. Percentage $\dfrac{c}{b}$	0	0.8	4.5	6.2	5.8

The differences were considered not to be significant and the reasons behind this decision will be evident from the following commentary on assumptions underlying the guideline projection, and other significant potential growth factors, no account of which could be taken in the guideline projection.

The basis of the projection was State population growth[1] (including migration) in selected age groupings with allowances for an increasing percentage of secondary-school students attaining the Leaving Certificate and an increasing percentage of successful Leaving Candidates enrolling at the Institute. The latter two trends show accelerated increases over the last two or three years. The accelerations were ignored in favour of conservative average linear trends based on a longer period. Had the more recent trend been fully accepted this alone would have eliminated the differences shown above.

Listed below are other factors which are difficult to quantify but which, if they materialise, may boost the Institute intake:

1. The introduction of two-year sub-professional courses, which could have a dual effect of attracting students, who otherwise would not have entered a tertiary Institution, and of decreasing drop-out rates by providing a more appropriate objective for many students who currently enrol in degree or equivalent courses.
2. As from 1972 the granting of degrees will make the Institute courses more attractive.
3. Recent indications are that during the next few years the mature-age element of annual first admissions to tertiary education is likely to grow at a more rapid rate than the Leaving-Certificate-pool element. No allowance has been made for this possibility in the guideline proecjtion, which assumed that the above two elements are in constant ratio.
4. The Institute is committed to increasing the provision of continuing-education courses. Present indications are that demands for these courses will grow significantly.

Two assumptions of the guideline projection, one in respect of overseas students and the other in respect of migrant intake, may to some degree offset the conservatism of the projection. An annual rate of increase of 5 per cent was chosen for overseas students. Although this may prove to be high the numbers involved constitute only 1 per cent of total annual increase. Migrant intakes may be reduced in future years, but to what degree the net intake may be affected is debatable.

---

1. From estimates published by the Commonwealth Bureau of Census and Statistics.

Again, the effect on the growth indexes derived for the projection would probably not be significant.

Clearly, the factors which may cause the guideline projection to be an underestimate far outweigh those which might tend to produce the reverse effect. It was decided, therefore, to proceed with the detailed planning of resource requirements on the basis of the projection of individual course enrolments.

2. Estimation of resource requirements

Enrolments in individual courses were projected as a first step in obtaining class projections. Annual new enrolments were estimated in consultation with the teaching departments on the basis of former trends and estimated industrial demand for course graduates. Total annual enrolments in each course were calculated for each academic level, taking into account previous student drop-out and pass rates. In a number of cases drop-out rates were modestly reduced on the assumption that exclusion policies introduced in 1970 had resulted in an abnormal number of dropouts.

A matrix of transition probabilities representing student flow from academic level within course to subject was constructed from 1971 data for individual teaching Departments. The set of probability matrices thus formed provided a means of analysing departmental interdependencies and of projecting subject enrolments. These were converted to class enrolments using specifications of class size, type, etc., recorded on Institute Space Planning and Staff Establishment forms. In a number of instances the specifications were modified in accordance with intended changes in tuition patterns. In this area the centrally controlled programme of annual room allocations was an invaluable source of information on tuition patterns.

The resulting estimates of student-hours, class-contact-hours and class-size frequency distributions, formed the basis for the projection of resource requirements. Requirements for proposed courses were estimated separately, using average class-size and class-contact-hours per student in individual courses.

3. Teaching staff

Excluding estimates for a likely pilot study in a country town, 100 miles from the main campus, the projections of full-time equivalent students for 1975 are 6,917 for existing courses and 1,282 for proposed courses. The total figure of 8,199 represents an increase of 4,409 or 116 per cent on the 1971 figure of 3,790. Full-time-equivalent teaching staff projected for 1975 are 584, which represents an increase of 92 per cent on the 1971 figure of 304. Of the 1975 figure 472 are for existing courses and 112 for proposed courses. Full-time-equivalent student/ staff ratios resulting from the projections are:

1971	1972	1973	1974	1975
12.5	13.2	13.9	14.0	14.0

showing an increase of 12.5 per cent in the ratio over a four-year period. This increase is a matter of policy arising from a decision to make greater use of technological and teaching aids.

An examination of differing student/staff ratios in similar institutions, and of their degree of effectiveness, has produced no conclusive evidence of a 'correct' ratio. The opinion is offered here that raising the student/staff ratio, within reason, will not lower educational quality, provided that (a) comprehensive planning is given to introducing new teaching methods and aids, and (b) greater emphasis is given to the lecturer becoming more of a counsellor for the solution of student problems and thus to replacing the traditional lecture as the core of the teaching/learning process.

4. Space requirements

Estimates of space demand were based on projections for 1976. Increases in general classroom space, over and above additional classrooms to become available during the current triennium, amounted to 93 rooms including 4 lecture theatres. This represents an increase of 2,622 student-stations to be provided during the third triennium.

In estimating general classroom supplies it was assumed that, on the average a room would be utilised for 60 per cent of the time available each week, namely, 9 a.m. to 9.30 p.m., Monday to Friday. Even though current utilisation is higher, at 69 per cent, the lower figure of 60 per cent was considered to be a more desirable basis in view of the length and scope of the projection. Present policies with respect to general classroom allocation were also assumed for the project. These state that no teaching department has exclusive ownership of rooms. As much priority as possible is given to each department regarding the use of rooms in its own building, but all departments are entitled to use any room wherever this is feasible.

Room-mixes were estimated for each of five separate acedemic sectors. The mixes are optimum in the sense that they will closely approximate class-size frequency distributions and will permit maximum off-loading of classes between departments and divisions. For example, because of day-night imbalances in room utilisation in various areas, it was possible to allocate approximately 70 per cent of the room-hour demand for new courses (excluding the proposed major entry into teacher education) to rooms estimated for existing courses. The utilisation of student-stations should thus be of a reasonably high order.

Practical classrooms (including drawing rooms) specified for proposed buildings have been justified on the basis of investigations conducted by the Research and Planning Branch. These include laboratory facilities for various disciplines of study. Existing laboratory facilities at the main campus, matched against class demands in 1976, indicated that present supplies would be adequate with the exception of a requirement for another Science laboratory

Car parking estimates indicated a total demand in 1976 for 3,744 car bays. Of these approximately 720 or 19 per cent would be assignable to new course demand. An attempt was made to build up a picture of peak traffic flow on the campus surrounds and at assumed access points. The rationale indicated likely 15-minute peak morning flows on the main entrance road ranging from 190 to 1,030 vehicles, and likely access flows totalling 2,570 vehicles. These flows are considerable, with access flows in particular indicating a probable need for six or more campus entries.

5. Review of the planning process

The extraction of 1971 course and subject enrolment projections was a fully computer-assisted operation. The remainder of the programme was carried out manually but with considerable assistance from a desk type computer. The exercise, although time-consuming, has provided a strong statistical basis for the triennial submission and moreover has enabled the Institute to gain a deeper insight into the problems, limitations and solutions associated with resource planning. This has resulted in the formulation of a comprehensive computerised planning system which, it is hoped, will be in operation when planning the fourth triennium. In addition to what has been accomplished for the third triennium, the system will take into account average and marginal unit costs per student, thus allowing exploration of the financial implications of sets of alternative management policies and assumed or estimated social and industrial demands.

An information base for the programme was established during the years 1968 to 1971 inclusive, using three basic data collection forms: (a) the Statistical Enrolment form, (b) the Student Study Programme, and (c) the Space Planning and Staff Establishment form. Figure 4 overleaf is a flow-diagram indicating the logical sequence of operations comprising the research and planning triennial planning programme.

6. Enrolment projections

The full planning system has been briefly described. By way of illustration, it is amplified in relation to enrolment projections in Appendix A (page 285).

New enrolments depend upon (a) the size of the new student-population pool, (b) the proportion of that pool obtaining a tertiary qualification, (c) the proportion of (b) who enrol at the Institute in the following year, and (d) who also re-enrol subsequently. It is also necessary to calculate subject enrolments.

The model proved to be accurate within limits of 3 to 4 per cent per annum, as far as total student numbers are concerned, but the variation between projected and actual has in some instances been of the magnitude of 100 per cent in individual courses. This has not presented significant difficulties for the institution, mainly due to its policies of centralised room-loading and retaining budgetary reserves to accommodate unforeseen eventualities. However, the discrepancies have highlighted the need for more systematic investigations of professional manpower needs. The difficulties involved in such investigations are immense in an economy in which national planning is politically suspect. They would be compounded by the self-protective devices of many professional bodies (licensing), which aim to restrict numbers not on grounds of need but in order to improve incomes and status.

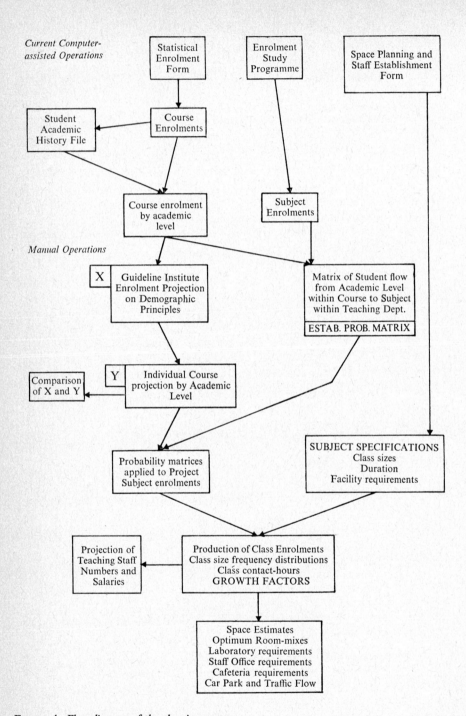

FIGURE 4. *Flow diagram of the planning process*

C. Ratio of acceptances to applications

Up to and including 1971 there were only three restraints exercised by the Western Australian Institute of Technology in the enrolling of qualified applicants. The first was a limit to the numbers which could be accommodated by specialised physical facilities (examples include laboratories in para-medical fields of study where close supervision and safety elements are involved, and a course such as social work which involves field work and is thus dependent on the availability of supervision in e.g. hospitals and child welfare centres). Another limitation was in those courses in which career opportunities can be measured with a high degree of accuracy. These are generally courses which involve cadetships from a limited number of employing agencies, although there are a few courses in which the profession has conducted major investigations into foreseen needs.

The remaining restraint was all-embracing and related to the physical capacity of the campus, availability of teaching staff and the extent of monetary resources. All teaching periods are pre-scheduled prior to enrolment and, without central approval, no further teaching periods may be allotted. This is a general policy which to date has not required any rigid implementation.

Up to and including 1971 the number of qualified applicants not accepted was extremely limited, when measured on an Institute-wide basis. However, there is abundant evidence of socio-economic factors preventing many qualified applicants from applying for admission. Tertiary education in Australia is heavily weighted in favour of upper- and middle-income families. This is likely to become a major political and social issue and the writer whole-heartedly supports the policy of the Australian Union of Students, which is for means-tested scholarships, based on need, and the abolition of tuition fees. There is a case for the scholarships to be far more generous for living costs than is the case at present.

In those courses where quotas are applied some qualified applicants have failed to gain admittance, although it should be emphasised that, in such courses, selection processes go beyond certificated proof of meeting the academic requirements by including interviews and specially designed tests for aptitude and attitudes. A similar pattern is expected for 1972 but beyond that year it is as yet impossible to predict whether or not there will be a rising number of qualified applicants failing to obtain admittance. This will be determined by the availability of recurrent finance and capital works approvals, as decided by the State and Commonwealth Governments.

D. Number of graduates in relation to demand

As has been said in Section II, Australia has not as yet adopted a manpower planning system and in higher education relies on the operation of the market-place to correct any temporary imbalances between graduate out-put and the demands of the economic society. In general terms, as far as the Institute is concerned, no evidence has yet emerged to show that graduate output has been in excess of demand. In this connexion there is a need to differentiate between different disciplines of study. Many undergraduates hold cadetships from government departments and instrumentalities, and private employers, and hence upon graduation are guaranteed employment.

Schoolteachers are a large group falling into this category, whilst courses which have similar guarantees of employment include physiotherapy, occupational therapy and social work. In some courses there is mounting evidence that graduates move into different, although allied, fields of employment relatively soon after obtaining their qualifications. Examples include accountants who transfer into management and marketing, and linguists who enter commerce.

There is, however, some evidence that the output in some fields is not sufficient to meet demand. Such a situation is almost inevitable in a developing economy. Examples include engineers (civil, mechanical, electrical and electronic) and specialists in computing science and information processing. The most positive proof of these shortages is the continual efforts of the Commonwealth Department of Immigration to attract migrants with the required qualifications. (This is further illustrated by the need of the Institute itself to advertise overseas for academics and professional staff in such disciplines as engineering, librarianship and Asian languages.)

On this question of graduates in relation to demand it is important to realise that the Institute has a special responsibility for part-time and external students, who are already in employment, and are generally seeking additional qualifications to progress in their chosen careers. The 1971 enrolment figures amply illustrate this facet of the Institute's role in higher education in Western Australia:-

	%
Full-time students	37
Part-time students	54
External students	9
	___
	100

E. Proportion of graduates in student body

In 1971, of fifty-seven courses in the Institute, all but five were at undergraduate level. A reasonably significant shift into post-graduate work is foreshadowed for 1973-75, as will be indicated later in this section. There are, however, a considerable number of graduates taking horizontal studies. In first-year intake in 1971 the relevant percentages of students with graduate qualifications in other disciplines were approximately as follows:

	%
Full-time students	5.4
Part-time students	42.0

The term 'graduate qualifications' has been defined as possession of a university degree or a diploma of a technical institute. The latter would be the greater by a ratio of approximately 3:1.

F. Student/teaching staff ratio

The institute method for calculating the number of full-time-equivalent students taught by a department is a theoretical measure of weekly workload on the department according to enrolment records. It is obtained by dividing the number of weekly student-hours generated from each course to the teaching department by the prescribed weekly hours of class attendance corresponding to each course. The same method is used in the conversion of external students to full-time-equivalent students. All such full-time-equivalent student values are then aggregated to obtain the total full-time-equivalent student load on the department. It will be observed that student-hours may be generated to a given teaching department from courses administered either by the teaching department itself or by any other department.

The number of full-time-equivalent teaching staff required by a department is obtained by dividing the number of class-hours taught by the department by the accepted full-time lecturer workload of 16 hours per week.

Determination of weekly class-hours

The number of class-hours associated with lectures is obtained from time-tables. Class-hours associated with tutorial or practical classes are obtained by dividing the number of student-hours assignable to such classes by accepted average class size. The staff workload associated with external students is calculated on the basis of 1 full-time-equivalent staff member to 12 full-time-equivalent external students. Time allowances for higher studies and new staff orientation are expressed as Class-Hours.

The student/staff ratio is based on theoretical full-time-equivalent measures rather than student numbers because the former method takes far more accurate account of the time spent by students in class, and hence of the actual workload imposed, than does the latter method. For example, it is possible for Departments A and B to have the same workload in terms of student-hours and class-hours and hence (but not necessarily) to require equal numbers of staff, whilst A's student enrolment may be considerably greater than B's due to A's enrolment containing a greater percentage of part-time enrolments. (For a more detailed analysis of the student/staff ratio see Appendix B, page 291.)

For a great many subjects at the Institute the tuition patterns consist of a combination of large lecture classes of varying maximum size ranging from 60 to 200 supported by small tutorials, seminars, workshops or laboratory classes for which an average class size of 12 to 15 is set, and is achieved within each division or, as is often the case, within the departments. Hence annual departmental class-size distributions contain a constant small class-size element which significantly affects the behaviour of the overall mean class-size.

In fact, lecture classes cannot exceed 200 in size since this is the largest-sized lecture theatre planned for the campus. A graph depicting the above function would be subject to sudden downward shifts as lecture class-sizes reached the 200 mark. The percentage of lecture classes which are estimated to exceed 200 during the next four years is not relatively large. In the years immediately subsequent to this period, however, reductions in average lecture class-size could be expected. The problem therefore further reduces to one of estimating the mean size of future lecture classes.

The Institute educational system is not one which has operated in a reasonably steady state over a number of years. Consequently there is a lack of accurate trend data for class size, and it becomes necessary to estimate the behaviour of mean lecture size by projecting in turn, subject enrolments, class-contact-hours, and class-size distributions over the short term.

In summary, the systems developed at the Institute for middle-term planning enable the establishment of full-time-equivalent student/staff ratio trends which may, with suitable interpretation, be applied in the long-term projection of teaching staff. Table 8 shows values of the ratio resulting from a recent planning exercise for the 1973-75 triennium. It will be noted that with two exceptions, namely Div. 1, 1973 and Div. 3, 1972, the series are monotonically increasing and appear to be approaching maximum values by 1975. This of course is in keeping with the approach of mean class-sizes to their limiting values. However, as mentioned earlier, downward fluctuations are likely subsequent to 1975 due to the arrival of numerous lecture class-sizes at the 200 mark.

TABLE 8. Student/staff ratio

	Actual			Projected		
	1970	1971	1972	1973	1974	1975
Div. 1	9.9	9.7	11.6	11.2	11.6	11.8
Div. 2	9.6	10.7	11.0	12.2	12.3	12.3
Div. 3	16.2	17.4	17.2	18.1	18.2	18.5
Institute	11.4	12.5	13.5	14.1	14.4	14.7

In the engineering and scientific disciplines the ratio is considerably lower than in the arts and humanities, as is normal in most institutions. However, the validity of the extent of the difference may be questionable, for whilst laboratories and workshops require low student/staff ratios, the marking load, assignments and personal tuition (i.e. outside prescribed contact hours) are often of greater magnitude in the arts and humanities than in the more technological disciplines. The use of a simple ratio has limitations and it may well be that weighting factors should be brought into use to allow for different gradings of staff. In technological disciplines, far more use should be made of junior academic staff and of technicians.

G. Rate of drop-out: student wastage

In the majority of institutions of higher learning in Australia, student wastage (i.e. through drop-out or failure in assessment and/or examination) is of such magnitude as to present a major problem. It is generally accepted that, as an average for Australian institutions, only about 60 per cent of students succeed in graduating. Many explanations have been put forward for the high incidence of drop-out and failure, including the attraction of high wages in semi-skilled occupations available to younger people and the diversions of a society which is affluent and accords ample opportunities for leisure-time pursuits. Many studies have attempted to correlate success in tertiary education with results in matriculation and leaving-certificate examinations. However, the correlations have been negative to such an extent that many educationists are firmly of the opinion there are no proven pre-determinants for success in higher education.

At a productivity seminar conducted by the Institute in June 1970 a detailed analysis of the 1969 results was presented. This is briefly summarised below:

Subjects enrolments	20,124 =	100%
Examined or assessed	15,927	
Drop-out	4,197 =	20.855%
Examined or Assessed	15,927	
Passed	13,576	
Failure	2,351 =	11.683%
Subject enrolments	20,124	
Dropped out or failed	6,548 =	32.5%

In 1970, the Research and Planning Branch estimated, on the basis of student numbers, that the drop-out rate in course enrolments was 10.6 per cent for full-time students and 22.3 per cent for part-time students. (These figures exclude enrolments in miscellaneous units, generally taken for interest only, in which the drop-out rate was remarkably high at 57.9 per cent.) The overall drop-out rate was 20.7 per cent, with by far the highest incidence occuring with part-time and external students.

In its submission for 1973-75 the Institute has said there is 'a pressing need for more planning, research and development in higher education.' A case has been presented for the inclusion within its operating funds of a significant sum for special research projects including the following:

Educational wastage. A study of the reasons for withdrawal and failure by full-time and part-time students (particularly the latter), and the development of educational procedures to counteract these.

Selection of students. Particular reference is made to external and part-time students; students who do not enter the Institute directly from secondary school; and the use of secondary school results and recommendations for selection purposes.

Student Progress. Development of the most effective methods of counselling, and monitoring of student progress.

The educational needs of part-time students. Ascertaining to what extent these are different from those of full-time students, and to what extent modified or different educational programmes and organisational systems are required to cater for the needs of part-time students. If appropriate, the development of new programmes and organisational systems.

H. Proportion of new subjects in the curricula per year

In the terminology normally used in Australia, a course is a field of study leading to a degree or other academic award and in many instances subsequently to membership of a professional association. A subject is a unit within a course. Courses and subjects are kept under constant review by the Boards of Study and the Subject Committees. Modification in subject material is dealt with in depth by a Subject Committee, reporting to a Board of Study. An analysis for 1970 indicated that in more than of 20 per cent of subjects, material had been significantly amended (mainly to accommodate new knowledge and emerging new needs), whilst a larger percentage had been modified in slighter degree.

As to the reshaping of courses, since the advent of the Courses Committee in November 1970 up to the end of August 1971, significant changes had been made to 12 courses out of a total of 57. A number of minor changes had been made to a large number of other courses. As an illustration of course review, the case of the award in Asian Studies is a good example. As from 1972, a mandatory requirement for completion of the award is an academic year spent in the appropriate country (such as Malaysia, Indonesia or Japan), in order to absorb attitudes, cultures and background. The time may be spent in e.g. work in industry or study at a university. This new policy has been accepted as a principle and will apply to all foreign languages taught by the Institute.

Turning now to the introduction of new courses (fields of study), in 1971 the number of courses being conducted amounted to 57, of which 17 were introduced in 1970 and 1971 and of which 5 are in the process of being phased out. Three new courses were scheduled for introduction in 1972.

As far as the Triennium 1973-75 is concerned, the Institute has submitted to the State and Commonwealth preliminary information on the new courses which may be introduced. It has said that only early demand surveys have been undertaken but they will be subjected to very close scrutiny by established market investigations before formal approval is sought from the Tertiary Education Commission and the Australian Commission on Advanced Education for their introduction. Many of the proposed new courses employ existing units (subjects) and facilities, thus making only limited demands for additional resources. The preliminary list of new courses for 1973-75 amounts to 44: 10 two-year undergraduate diploma; 9 three-year degree or equivalent; 17 one-year post-graduate; and 8 master's degree or equivalent.

In budgetary terms for the Triennium the Institute has estimated that, for recurrent expenditure, $M40.7 (88 per cent) is for growth in existing courses and $M5.5 (12 per cent) for new courses and developments. (These figures exclude $M4.1 requested for total library expenditure, in which the percentage allocation would tend to favour new courses and developments.)

I. Ratio of available books per student

Table 9 gives details of library stocks (main campus plus subsidiary campuses) as existing in 1970, estimated accurately for 1971, and foreseen for 1972-75.

TABLE 9.   Libraries: stocks, 1970-75

Stocks	1970 (actual)	1971	1972	1973	1974	1975
Total number[1] of volumes	50 000	62 000	76 000	105 520	135 700	167 000
Total number of units of microfilm	20	100	200	300	400	500
Total number of non-book materials	5 794	8 304	13 200	19 200	23 800	28 600
Total number of periodical titles	1 687	1 870	2 020	2 150	2 500	3 000

1. The number of titles is estimated at about 90 per cent, the remainder being multiple copies. Expenditure on the latter is increasing, reaching 26 per cent of total purchases in 1971.

In October 1971 the main library moved from temporary accommodation into a major new building. Floor space for collections, services and working activities increased from 25,000 square feet (2,323 square metres) to 70,000 square feet (6,503 square metres); shelf capacity in linear feet increased from 8,000 feet (2,438 metres) to 25,000 feet (7,620 metres). Hours of opening increased from 60 to 90 per week.

The Principal Librarian holds the view that the most reliable measure of resources is the monetary expenditure per full-time-equivalent student. Table 10 illustrates the achieved and foreseen growth rate.

TABLE 10. Library expenditure: growth rate

	Full-time-equivalent students	Total library expenditure in $	$ rate per full-time-equivalent student	$ rate per full-time-equivalent student at 1969 price levels (est.)
Actual 1969	2 714	165 885	61.12	61.12
Actual 1971	3 790	437 550	115.45	103.91
Projected 1975	8 275	1 628 000	196.74	159.37

The difficulty with this measure is that it does not reflect the viability of the collection, either in terms of relevance of library materials to students and staff or in the degree of use made of the materials. Utilisation statistics are a vital ingredient in developing a more rational measurement technique, but as yet the Library has not been able to produce sufficiently detailed data. Computerisation is the likely answer to this problem, but in the meantime the whole policy of acquisitions needs review. At present, the teaching departments dominate selection, but a more rational system might well be subject budgeting as against departmental, allied to the staffing of the Library with bibliographical experts in the various disciplines of study. Such experts would work with the subject committees, which would become the acquisition decision-making bodies. Utilisation data would be supplied to the committees. It would seem likely that in the longer term measurement techniques will be developed which will relate materials available to student numbers, and evaluate them by reference to utilisation factors. At the same time, it is hoped that courses of instruction in library use and literature sources will be introduced; and that, in general, the Library will be increasingly integrated into the educational life of the Institute.

J. Availability of teaching and research equipment

Table 11 gives details of the progressive build-up of equipment in teaching departments. It is to be remembered that the Institute is primarily a teaching institu-

TABLE 11. Teaching equipment expenditure (in $ to nearest $ 1 000)

1967-69 (actual)	1970-72 (estimated)	1973-75 (requested)
1 489 000	1 511 000	4 732 000[1]

1. This projection allows for a major new computer installation and the re-equipping of the Engineering departments, which are scheduled to be transferred to the main campus from the obsolete accommodation temporarily occupied in the central city.

tion with research (of an applied nature) being of secondary consideration. This situation may change in the coming year through the recent establishment of a research, development and consulting company (a separate legal entity, owned by the Institute, called WAIT-AID Ltd.), on which more will be said later in this chapter.

The teaching departments, in the main, are well equipped for the primary purpose of student instruction. A requirement of the Commonwealth Government is that major equipment is to be primarily for teaching purposes. This is interpreted as meaning at least 50 per cent of utilisation being for teaching. However, it would be idle to pretend that in some fields of study there are not significant deficiencies. In most instances the main cause (aside from financial limitations) is the lack of adequate buildings on those sites which are temporarily being occupied pending the erection of new and more adequate facilities on the main campus. Two other factors which impinge on teaching equipment are (a) a general policy of giving the greatest priority, where necessary, to additional teaching and support staff and (b) some caution in acceding to all teaching department requests for equipment due to an awareness of technological change and the growing importance of teaching aids which may make possible more tuition by illustration rather than by access to an actual piece of machinery. A matter which deserves greater consideration than it has hitherto received is the joint financing and use of equipment between industry and higher education, especially in testing and research fields.

When requesting items of major equipment (defined as costing over $A2,000) the information required from departments includes details of the item, ancillary equipment, estimated maintenance costs, estimated yearly utilisation, relevance to teaching and utility for other purposes. Decisions on broad allocations are made by the Planning Board and the Capital Works Committee, but decisions on individual items are made by academic divisions in accordance with a general policy that detailed decisions should be made as close as possible to the working level.

The present computing facility, although performing valuable work in student instruction, administrative data-processing and test marking, will soon be inadequate, and a case has been submitted to the State and Commonwealth Governments for a much larger-scale time-saving computer with a remote batch and remote consoles, to cover foreseen needs to 1976. Such an installation would handle student batch processing: remote console usage: administrative data-processing: document reading and machine scoring of tests: library processing: staff and student research projects and computer centre housekeeping.

K. Availability of instructional space

As at 30 September 1971, the instructional space available was as shown in Table 12.

By the end of 1972 the following is expected to have been added to the main campus: 8,000 square feet (743 square metres) laboratories and workshops,

TABLE 12.   Instructional space (in square metres)

	Laboratories & workshops	Class-rooms etc.	Other	Total
Main Campus (Bentley)	1 672	4 645	186	6 503
Other sites	557	1 115	279	1 951
Per student	1.87	3.75	.94	6.57

6,000 square feet (557 square metres) class-rooms, etc., 4,000 square feet (372 square metres) other, i.e. a total of 18,000 square feet (1,672 square metres).

The capital works programme for 1973-75 submitted to the State and Commonwealth Government calls for the net addition of 290,000 square feet (26,942 square metres) of instructional space. The main *per capita* improvements would be in laboratories and workshops, recreational and private reading areas.

The Institute employs a centralised space control system which, in 1971, achieved a 69 per cent general class-room utilisation based on a $62\frac{1}{2}$-hour week. (A similarly high utilisation factor has been obtained for laboratories and workshops, which are regarded as having a maximum weekly usage of 45 hours.) The system has to date been largely manual but computerisation is now under careful scrutiny and is likely to be introduced by 1973. The three years in which the centralised space control system has been in operation have demonstrated the feasibility of achieving: (a) maximum economic effectiveness of room-period utilisation; (b) major reorganisations and consequent spread of time-tabling patterns in a system incorporating a considerable number of inter-departmental and inter-divisional servicing activities; (c) a general awareness of and increased consideration for the problems and requirements of other departments with respect to physical resources (i.e. a change in attitude of departments whose buildings are formally designated as related to specific disciplines); and (d) computerisation of the manual approach to room allocation.

L. Availability of other space

As at 30 September 1971 other space available, measured in square metres, was as shown in Table 13.

TABLE 13.   Other space available

	Staff offices	Recreation and similar	Total
Total area	4 831	1 486	6 317
Per staff member	13.4	3.7	18.1

By 1972 the total space is expected to have increased by 35 per cent. The capital works programme for 1973-75, as submitted to governments, if fully accepted, would add 143,000 square feet (13,285 square metres.) (It is to be noted that these figures exclude libraries, for which details appear on page 000 above.)

Staff offices are virtually fully occupied and in general the building programme succeeds only in keeping pace with increases in staff. Some instances of overcrowding have occurred, particularly at the city campus, which is in the process of being transferred to the main campus (a major undertaking involving a capital works programme of approximately $M12.5, of which 20 per cent has to date been spent) and in the central administration building.

A firm decision has been taken to maintain about 130 acres of the 280 acres main campus for sporting and recreational facilities. A valid criticism of the present facilities on the main campus is the limited space available for informal discussions and mixing amongst students. The intention is to rectify this situation over the next few years. Some progress has been made by the newly completed stage 1 of the Student Guild building, which is planned to be extended about 1974; however, the present limited number of foyers, small study and reading rooms, and conversation areas, is evoking a substantial degree of student criticism.

M. Unit costs per graduating student

Development of a mathematical model for the analysis of historical costs is at a preliminary stage. The model requires the allocation of costs to departments on a teaching basis and the subsequent distribution of these costs to courses. A manual application has been made to 1969 cost data and the generalised computerisation of the basic framework of the model is proceeding.

In the formulation of a method for projection it is necessary to establish functional relationships between classified departmental costs and combinations of planning parameters, e.g., student-hours, full-time-equivalent students and/or staff, student and/or staff numbers and class-contact hours. Research into these relationships at the Institute is at a preliminary stage. However, it is considered that the approach is probably feasible and will at least enable the projection of departmental recurrent costs in accordance with projected planning parameters Projected costs would then be distributed to courses in the same manner as were historic costs but in accordance with a projected tuition pattern. Computerisation of the model in conjunction with computerised subject enrolment projections will permit considerable refinement in the methods of departmental cost allocation being described. These methods are discussed in some detail in Appendix C (page 293).

N. Research of professional calibre

As has been said previously, research is secondary to teaching in the Western Australian Institute of Technology, and in some disciplines, such as accounting and business studies, research is negligible. The approach in the engineering departments is piecemeal, although some interesting work has been done on projects such as the atmospheric pollution problems which might arise from a projected extension of a power station in a major industrial complex near Perth.

In the applied sciences, however, a large number of highly professional research projects are constantly in hand. As an example of this situation the Department of Chemistry carried out, or was continuing with, 34 significant research projects in 1970, whilst in the current year the Department of Physics has completed, or is continuing with, 39 projects of some considerable magnitude. Evaluation of research work is the responsibility of Heads of Departments.

In August 1971 the Institute established a company limited by guarantee, called WAIT-AID Ltd. A brief description of the foreseen role of this new venture is that it will provide applied research and consulting to industry, commerce and government. It will endeavour to aid the advancement, development and application of science and technology in the interests of Western Australia. The company will operate on a commercial basis through the negotiation of contracts and the obtaining of patent and other rights for new inventions, designs and processes. The development of the company is likely to accentuate the degree of applied research within the Institute, maintaining however, to a large extent, a direct relevance between research and the teaching programmes. WAIT-AID Ltd. is likely to appoint a Research Committee in 1972 and this will be concerned with evaluation of executed and projected work.

O. Distribution of staff time between teaching, research and other activities

Since the Institute's primary objective is teaching, the major proportion of academic staff time is devoted to the teaching function, i.e. direct staff/student contact (through lectures, tutorials, laboratory and workshop sessions, seminars, etc.) and the allied requirements of preparation, assessment and examinations. A lecturer, on average, has a direct teaching commitment of sixteen hours per week, whilst a senior lecturer averages ten hours per week. These averages exclude reduced teaching loads which are granted for higher degree studies, in-service teacher education programmes and special assignments. The extent of the allied requirements varies from discipline to discipline. The teaching year is normally thirty-five weeks, with an additional five weeks for enrolments and examinations.

The degree of time devoted to applied research varies significantly between different fields of study. A subjective opinion would indicate a considerable time involvement in the applied sciences and far less in other disciplines. By the terms of contract, an academic is entitled to earn up to 25 per cent of the maximum of his career range through private and consultative work, where it is relevant to the teaching process and in the interests of the longer-term objectives of the Institute. Records of such earnings for a twelve-month period ending 30 June 1971 indicate that 40 per cent of academic staff were engaged in such activities, and that they were earning, on average, about one-third of the amount permissible.

In some ways, the Institue has a degree of ambivalence in its attitudes to and policies for research. The general policy is to accentuate the importance of teaching, yet exhorting staff to engage in applied research, either through WAIT-AID Ltd. or on private and consultative work. The latter is not part of any official staff time-table and indeed the contract does not specify any time requirement other than for teaching. Staff are regarded as responsible professionals required to execute their various duties with competence, without being bound down by too many bureaucratic rules. But there is little doubt that applied research is often neglected, because of the extent of teaching and allied requirements. The more dedicated staff persist with research work, but recognition of this extra effort is often minimal. This unsatisfactory state of affairs has resulted from governmental and institutional wishes to avoid strict emulation of universities, but it has a logical inconsistency, for the colleges ot advanced education are directly concerned with industry, commerce and the professions. The latter need applied research and there is at least some evidence to suggest that teaching ability is enhanced by reasearch work.

Undoubtedly, teaching staff have a variety of other commitments, such as curricula development, private counselling of students, liaison with industry, commerce, government and professional associations, and membership of standing and *ad-hoc* Institute Committees. As is true of any large organisation, the extent of such activities, the amount of effort and time devoted to personal development and keeping up with new knowledge, varies from individual to individual. Without being able to give objective evidence, the general opinion within the Institute is that the majority of academic staff accept their professional responsibility as outlined above. The organisation itself has reiterated on numerous occasions a belief that its academic staff is the most significant of its resources.

As an aid to enabling academic staff to concentrate on those activities, for which their knowledge is most suitable, the Institute pursues a policy of strong support. Table 14 illustrates this policy.

TABLE 14.   Teaching staff/support staff ratios

Ratio to:	1970 (actual)	1971 (actual)	1973 (projected)
Technical	1:0.39	1:0.39	1:0.38
Administrative and clerical	1:0.55	1:0.61	1:0.68
Library	1:0.19	1:0.21	1:0.26
TOTAL	1:1.15	1:1.23	1:1.33

Realising that it needs to have more adequate knowledge of time utilisation, the Institute has decided to conduct an enquiry in 1972, along similar lines to those employed by the enquiry of the Committee of Vice-Chancellors and Principals of the Universities of the United Kingdom in 1969/70. The enquiry may lead to clearer definitions on work load distribution, i.e. between teaching, allied responsibilities and applied research.

P. System of indicators in decision-making

1. *Staff, teaching and research*

In the previous pages considerable detail has been given on specific indicators. It is necessary now to evaluate the indicators and to comment on their interactions on one another in the significant decision-making processes of the Institute.

Many of the indicators appear on the surface to be of a quantitative nature, but a deeper insight will reveal that many express in quantitative terms decisions and judgments which have been made from a qualitative viewpoint. An apt illustration is the pass/fail rate in assessments and examinations, which are qualitative decisions, made by the academic staff directly concerned with the subjects and courses. The Institute holds the view that examiners and co-examiners have the essential responsibility for the assessment of students. Nevertheless, a number of safeguards are built into the system, including methods of resolving differences of opinion between examiners, the ability of failed candidates to obtain re-marks, availability of deferred and supplementary examinations in certain circumstances, and an appeal system for students who have been excluded or placed on restricted study programmes because of unsatisfactory academic results.

A significant quantitative check on qualitative judgments is a policy of the Academic Board that where the success rate in a subject is below a set percentage, the teaching department, in conjunction with a central review board, shall thoroughly investigate the reasons. The main purpose of this technique is to safeguard against some element of inequity having distorted the results: an example would be an examination question being obscure or involving material not adequately handled in the teaching year.

The programming of teaching work is the responsibility of a head of department, assisted by his senior lecturers who normally are appointed to exercise academic leadership in specific fields of study. Contracts require lecturers to teach 12-20 hours per week and senior lecturers 8-12 hours per week. In addition, a head of department is expected to teach 5-6 hours per week, and to the extent that it is practicable, the deans of academic divisions are enjoined to give at least a weekly lecture in their particular field of excellence. Academic staffing establishments are set on a divisional basis, using a combination of an average of 16 hours per lecturer, 10 hours per senior lecturer for classes and lectures, and a staff/student ratio for all other teaching activities, such as laboratories, tutorials and seminars. The dean, as head of the academic division, allocates positions to departments, and thereafter the full responsibility rests with the heads of departments to set the teaching loads and responsibilities of each member of his staff.

The qualitative judgment which is used includes the imperatives of creating a teaching team (i.e. the compounding of strength by the combination of abilities) and of obtaining staff who have had a significant degree of practical experience in addition to possessing the required academic qualifications. Where newly appointed staff have not had previous teaching experience, the teaching load for the first year is reduced and the staff member participates in an in-service teacher-training programme. Latterly, the Institute has been conducting more such programmes for all staff, with particular reference to the application of the new media to teaching.

A staff review scheme has been accepted in principle by the governing Council and the Academic Staff Association, with the details now being negotiated by a working party formed from the two groups. It is likely to be introduced in 1972, and essentially will be a system of evaluation of the performance of staff. The scheme will provide for acceleration within the salary scales and the withholding of an increment. Undoubtedly, self-development will be reflected in the operation of the scheme, but philosophically this aspect of an individual's career is regarded as his professional responsibility, not as a measurable factor in assessing performance.

The development of WAIT-AID Ltd., described earlier, is likely to accentuate the degree of applied research and consultative work carried out for industry, commerce and the community services. The general manager is an academic with management and consulting experience, combined with the ability to communicate effectively with scientists and technologists. As the company develops it is probable that committees to deal with detailed policies for research and education will be created, and it may be reasonably expected that academic staff will have majority representation on such committees. It is to be understood that the contractual work to be undertaken by the company is primarily to be related to utility value for the education programmes of the Institute. A possible difficulty is conflict between teaching commitments and potential contracts; and a realistic attitude may be to lessen teaching loads when research contracts are clearly in the interests of the State's economy. Indeed, it could well be that WAIT-AID Ltd. has the potential to become an integral part of overall State planning, providing its role is not hampered by governmental indecisiveness and self-interested opposition from government departments and private organisations.

2. Physical planning

Considerable detail has been given of the quantitative approach to building and equipment programmes. However, qualitative influences are significant. The Institute has developed a code of building planning formulae (the word 'standards' being deliberately avoided to emphasise flexibility of decision-making). The code is a comprehensive document covering, e.g. space requirements, functions and special considerations for all types of accommodation including furnishings[1].

1. The document runs to thirty-two pages and those interested may obtain a copy by writing to the Institute Architect's Office, Western Australian Institute of Technology, Hayman Road, South Bentley, Western Australia 6102

The aesthetic and physical planning of any building project takes cognizance of many fundamentals, none of which should be regarded as having priority over the others. Foremost in the thinking is an analysis of requirements, but with new educational institutions and the need to avoid built-in obsolescence, this is often one of the last factors that should be considered in detail. Because of this, forward planning becomes a matter of intuition and is translated into flexibility of planning to allow extensions and modifications to early-stage buildings on the presumption that education is a changing process and that what is adequate now will assuredly be less than adequate, or completely out-moded, in a few years' time. Buildings must be maintained and serviced. This factor creates equations of high initial cost and low maintenance cost materials *versus* low capital cost and high maintenance cost in the planning submissions. In addition, there is the high capital cost and high maintenance cost solution, which must be avoided. Resources generally are limited, and this creates the need to achieve economical design solutions. For an account of the planning processes currently in use at the Institute see Appendix E (page 307).

In summarising Institute policy for design and construction of buildings, the vital element is a complete critical analysis at all stages of planning. Any scheme worthy of serious consideration must be capable of withstanding such analysis and criticism; however, it is to be realised that criticism should be staged—criticism in concept and factors concerned with the total analysis of a scheme should occur in the early submissions at a feasibility study stage—criticism relating to detailed considerations should occur at the later stages. Encouragement must be given to induce broad criticism at the early stages and to minimise such criticism once a total concept has been considered and approved. Criticism in detail would be looked for at the final design stage and during documentation of working drawings. Reassessment of detail, leading towards revisions during the contract phase, should be avoided as far as possible as variations during the contract phase inevitably lead to extended contract time and escalation of cost.

It should be the aim of any design and planning team to reduce built-in obsolescence to a minimum—this is approached by delaying as long as possible finalisation of the education specification and by shortening as far as possible the time spent in documentation. A broad variation to this is a concept of setting a building form and building the shell of a project in advance of letting contracts for fitting out and equipping such buildings. This process can be applied to a lesser extent in an orthodox building-contract arrangement by leaving a particular area void, subject to a sub-contract to be let at the latter stage of the building programme. This is pertinent where the type and physical characteristics of equipment may not be known at the time the initial contract is scheduled for commencement.

The most significant attitude which has developed progressively in the Institute is the imperative of flexibility in buildings, because of the inevitability of change in higher education.

3. Financial resources: operating costs

The institute operates on triennia, but nevertheless constructs annual budgets which, in total, agree with parliamentary legislation, but may vary significantly in allocations to different functions. These result from changing policies, methods of teaching, and the shifting of emphases on resource centres (e.g. a subjective judgement to increase library expenditure to encourage more private study is an endeavour to improve the pass rate). Table 15 illustrates the effect of changing policies.

TABLE 15.   Operating costs by percentage

	1967-69 Actual	1970-72 Budgeted	1973-75 Projected
Teaching staff	49.50	45.61	40.97
Teaching support staff	9.78	12.08	14.29
Other direct teaching costs	10.50	6.62	6.39
Administrative staff	6.59	7.34	6.60
General overheads	5.23	5.30	5.28
Libraries	4.35	5.92	7.47
Buildings, premises and grounds	9.86	11.60	12.50
Other	4.19	5.53	6.50
	100.0	100.0	100.0

In the next section a flow chart will give the full details of the preparation of an annual budget.

In the meantime, the general policy of budget preparation is (a) all measurements are made in physical terms, then translated into monetary; (b) where physical (and thus monetary) demands exceed resources available, subjective judgements are made; and (c) budgets reflect policies of the Institute in a very large degree, although on occasions a subjective judgement made under (b) in fact influences policy. The actual room for decision-making is restricted, as is illustrated by Figure 5.

4. An overview

The Institute is still a young institution, being now in its seventh year of autonomy. Its decision-making processes have been evolutionary and will continue to change: this has been a deliberate act of policy, reinforced by the rapid growth achieved. Student numbers have been increasing at about an average of 20 per cent per annum.

Certainly, some successes have been achieved and some strengths demonstrated. There has been an acute awareness of the need to respond to change. Some ob-

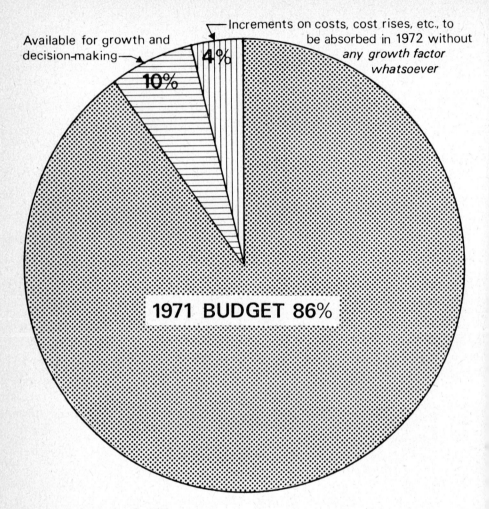

Available for growth and
decision-making

Increments on costs, cost rises, etc., to
be absorbed in 1972 without
*any growth factor
whatsoever*

10%

4%

1971 BUDGET 86%

FIGURE 5. *The budget for 1972.*

servers have regarded this facet of the organisation as due in large part to its
youth, and its being part of a new system of higher education in Australia, i.e.
the colleges of advanced education. However, experience in other countries partly
belies this opinion, for many new institutions tend to ape the older in the mistaken
belief that this would bring status and reputation. Generally the reverse happens,
for trying to resemble one's elders often leads to a public image of being second-
class. The Western Australian Institute of Technology has avoided this pitfall
by deliberately seeking to be different in educational policies and in its management
structure. Educationally, it has striven to develop and maintain a high regard for
vocational utility of course structure and additionally to be responsive to emergent

new fields of social need. The latter has been evident in paramedical studies and computing science.

In management, it has tended to be closer to industrial and commercial ideas rather than to those of traditional academia. The latter has been particularly evident in the development of strong sections dealing with (a) educational research and development and (b) research and planning in quantitative terms. It has been demonstrated in developing useful and relatively sophisticated techniques in cost analysis and basic planning systems. Nevertheless, the general concept of more scientific management has had substantial opposition from within the Institute. Many academics have regarded senior management as being over-concerned with resource decisions and thus under-concerned with educational philosophies and policies. The criticism has some validity, for on occasions emergency resource decisions have been made with detrimental effect on the teaching/learning processes. Too often, however, the difficulty has been the placing of the senior management in a position with little ground for manœuvre. This has been caused by governmental decisions to restrict funds in the somewhat devious way of requiring the institution to absorb cost increases without sufficient supplementary finance. (It is a matter of some cynicism within the Institute that governments who are charged with responsibility for incomes and prices penalise autonomous institutions when governmental policies fail, but do not treat their own departmental structures in the same way.)

Despite the strong management bias of the Institute, it has been little more successful than traditional universities on many major educational issues. The semester system took over three years to gain agreement in principle, and although now scheduled for 1973 may still encounter substantial internal opposition. Many academics seem to require consensus of opinion, which is impossible, and are unwilling to accept majority decisions. A remarkable skill is shown in protracting debates and discussions.

The strong data-based triennial submissions are a credit to the Western Australian Institute of Technology, but there is a significant weakness in that other institutions do not provide similar data to governments. The latter tend to praise the Institute's detailed investigations and data, and then proceed to ignore them in reaching financial grant decisions. This increasingly apparent attitude is causing many senior staff, including the writer, to consider whether the Institute should concentrate less on the data-and-investigation approach and more on the political. A by-product of this growing attitude is criticism of the way in which many governmental decisions are made: behind closed doors, in so-called confidential discussions, and without any real public knowledge of the issues at stake. A glaring example of this situation is that the triennial reports of the Australian Universities Commission and the Australian Commission on Advanced Education reveal only the financial allocations agreed between the Commonwealth Government and the State Governments, and do not reveal either differences between governments, or those between governments and institutions.

It is a personal opinion that the lack of definitive policies of governments has been and remains one of the greatest barriers to higher education in Australia.

267

However much time and effort is expended by a single institution in developing indicators and criteria for internal decision-making, it is largely aborted if governments fail to develop long-term plans and thus a real commitment to the financial implications. This too often leads to 'stop-go' policies, with an organisation in a growth situation and encouraged to develop by government suddenly finding that funds are restricted, and thus that developmental policies must be abruptly reversed.

Much of the difficulty lies in the uneasy and inadequate financial relations between the Commonwealth and State Governments. In too many fields the former has the financial resources and the latter have the responsibilities. This situation is adversely affecting Australian development in many fields, including higher education. Doubtless, the problem could be solved (as e.g. by the Commonwealth assuming full financial responsibility for higher education), but other problems would remain. These include an antipathy in the Australian community towards planning of a long-term nature, and to the application of adequate resources to research and development. Nowhere is the latter more apparent than in higher education. Expenditure on research and development in higher education has been estimated at 0.1 per cent of the annual costs of the system. This is clearly insufficient, and would never be tolerated in any other industry of equivalent size. No national co-ordinating body or system exists, thus leading to further inefficiencies through duplication of efforts.

The Western Australian Institute of Technology management structure operates within the constraints of its environment, of which some criticism has been made. Yet it would be quite wrong to ignore the fact that governments have grounds on which to criticise higher educational institutions, including the Western Australian Institute of Technology. In common with its sister institutions, the latter has not yet accepted in any depth the idea of public accountability. It has continued to procrastinate in many policies which would reduce costs without impairing quality. These include the continuance of too many optional subjects in which the variation in content is insignificant; failure to seriously consider granting academic credit for work performed outside the institution; and stubborness in continuing courses for which the demand is small, despite knowledge of the high costs thus incurred.

A significant weakness of the Institute organisation is the limited number of senior men in the top administration. The management group of six individuals is far too small to handle the range of problems in a growing and complex organisation: and the results of understaffing at this level have included (a) a growing remoteness from the body of the organisation, despite every endeavour to avoid isolation, (b) an over-burdening of the individuals with both too much pressure and too wide a field of decision-making, and (c) a feeling amongst staff that the group is exercising too much influence and power. Recent organisational discussions have opposed any effective strengthening of the group, mainly on the grounds of preferring a small group, which has at least the virtue of being cohesive, to an enlarged group, which may suffer from communication breakdowns. The matter is debatable, and probably the answer for the Institute, in the current climate of opinion, is greater decentralisation of decision-making, with the management group gradually moving to a position of dealing mainly with middle- and long-range planning and decisions.

Another acute weakness has been a lack of coherence in the policy role of the Academic Board, which has tended to procrastinate on big issues and to devote too much time to trivia. This is probably endemic to academic institutions, but it is disappointing that even a new institution has failed to create an effective educational-policy instrument. The difficulty lies in trying to get decisions on a participatory basis and yet within a time-scale in which decisions are likely to be effective. There is no easy answer in a knowledge-oriented organisation, but perhaps the creation of a centralised office of academic policy might assist. Part of the trouble has been inadequate documentation, and thus could be overcome by the employment of more specialists. A move in this direction would seem to be inevitable.

In summary, despite the trouble areas, there is cause for optimism for the future. The organisation recognises its weaknesses and that is very much a step in the right direction. The Institute, in 1971, made a number of significant decisions which will markedly shape its future. These included decisions on the review of all aspects of the organisation; the foreseen educational resource needs to 1975; the reassessment of the latter in detail over the next few months; the preparation of an academic plan to 1981, to be kept continually under review; and the intention to consider and debate throughout all strata of the institution its present organisational structure and to amend it in the light of the dialogue.

However, the shape of the future is largely dependent on governmental policies, both Federal and State, and it is at this level that the greatest reforms are necessary. The reforms needed include more systematised planning and policy-making, a commitment to the financial consequences, and more public discussion of the issues involved. The latter would require both governments and institutions to disseminate information more widely, and more fully, than is the current practice.

269

IV. Flow of information at the Western Australian Institute of Technology

A. Information flow system

The Institute has several formalised communication systems. A weekly bulletin is issued to all members of staff, giving details of decisions and events, and this is indexed at four-monthly intervals. A guide to procedures is in operation and includes information on organisation and general features, academic policies, administrative matters, financial systems, staff policies, student affairs, enrolments and examinations, library procedures, buildings development and maintenance, and general information and emergency services. Minutes of boards and committees are widely circulated, and this policy includes the governing Council and its committees, with the exception of special appendixes dealing with matters of a confidential nature. (The majority of such appendixes involve staff appointments and accordingly are not distributed, in the interest of the staff concerned.)

The official organ of the Institute is the *Gazette*, but although used for internal communications its primary concern is external, for it is widely distributed throughout Australia to sister institutions, government departments, industry, commerce and the professions. The Academic Staff Association has introduced recently its own *Staff News*, and it would appear probable that this journal will become an open forum for the debate of conflicting ideas. The Student Guild, since its inception, has had its own publication *Aspect*, which is published fortnightly throughout the academic year. The Institute administration contributes a regular column, dealing with policies and events, but specifically avoiding any comment on student affairs or opinions.

An annual report is made to Parliament and is widely distributed. Its contents include an overall report by the Council on the government and progress of the Institute, the capital works programme, the auditors' report and financial balance sheets.

Of more importance to the Institute itself, as far as the communications system is concerned, are the internal annual reports of the teaching departments and other elements of the Institute. The teaching departments report on such matters as staff, students, courses, teaching methods and projects, activities of both staff and students, community relationships and liaison with industry and the professions.

Every institution of higher learning is complex in its operations and so, necessarily, is its communication network and the kinds of information which it uses for decision-making. Any attempt to fully describe the system would be self-defeating; the amount of detail would confuse rather than inform It therefore seems more appropriate to concentrate on a representative group of boards and committees, setting out their functions and responsibilities, and the information which is used in reaching decisions and/or recommendations to other bodies, whether internal or external (see Figure 3, page 240).

1. Council and its committees

The governing *Council* at a special meeting in April 1971, declared its rôle to be akin to that of a policy-determining Board of Directors. To fulfil this role, it decided:

1. To give more power to committees and the management to carry out policy.
2. To rationalise efforts and time involvements.
3. To introduce the concept of longer-term thinking by all committees, but with emphasis on one committee (the Education and General Policy Committee), and to bring ideas to the Council, which will lead to longer-term decision-making.
4. To provide Council with more time to concentrate on major issues, such as negotiations with Governments and the Tertiary Education Commission.

The policy document then proceeded to enunciate the type of issues with which the Council would have the most concern as being:

1. A conscious exercise of its autonomy.
2. The academic, physical and financial plans for triennia in two phases, (a) submission, (b) reconsideration in preparation for, and then in the final knowledge of, the financial decisions made by the State and the Commonwealth governments.
3. The academic, physical, organisational and financial plans for, say, the next decade.
4. The degree of permanence of teaching buildings and ways and means of (a) cost savings, (b) allowing for technological changes.
5. The further improvement of relationships with industry, commerce and the professions.
6. The growing importance of continuous education, and modern methods which may be relevant thereto.
7. The economic needs and related educational needs of the State.
8. The development of mutual aid programmes with State instrumentalities, Commonwealth organisations and overseas bodies.
9. The priority ranking of educational investigation and research projects and their financing.

The Council has three committees: *Finance and Staffing*, *Capital Works*, and *Education and General Policy*, each of which has specific powers in decision-making and the making of recommendations. All documentation which comes

271

before Council has emerged from internal bodies, such as the Management Board, the Planning Board and the Academic Board.

After the experience of over six years, it can be said that the structure of the Council and its committees has been largely effective and efficient. Probably the major weaknesses have been (a) a reluctance, with a few notable exceptions, to debate publicly, as distinct from privately, major differences of opinions between the Council and governments, and (b) the relative failure of the Council to be seen as an integral part of the body corporate; the latter in spite of the most strenuous effort by the Council to achieve dialogue with the staff of the Institute. The failure is seen as more the fault of the staff, which by and large tend to view the Council as paternalistic and yet remain unwilling to put forward constructive alternatives to the present system.

An alternative which is personally favoured is the reduction of the number of ex-officio and government appointees and an increase in the number of staff and student representatives. Modern business corporations, of similar magnitude, would not tolerate a governing body in which external members predominated.

2. *Major control boards*

The functions of the *Management Board* and the *Planning Board* may be summarised as advising and assisting the Director in regard to:
- (a) the efficient administration and utilisation of resources of the Institute;
- (b) forward planning;
- (c) preparation of policy recommendations for Council and its Committees;
- (d) the progress of capital works programmes;
- (e) co-ordination of the activities of the Institute.

The Management Board is primarily concerned with day-to-day activities and resource decisions on an annual basis. The Planning Board concentrates its attention on the building programme and long-term planning, with particular responsibility in regard to the submissions for triennia.

The Management Board consists of the Director, Deans of Academic Divisions and Assistant Directors, in charge of central functions. The same group forms the Planning Board, with the addition of specialists, e.g. the Institute Architect and the Research and Planning Officer.

In many instances, the Boards seek the advice of the Divisional Boards or of specialist units. Meetings are fully documented, although conducted in a relatively informal manner. On occasions, *ad hoc* working parties are set up to investigate specific problems and to make recommendations. Such working parties are often multi-disciplinary and include academic and support staff.

The Management Board visits each teaching department annually, although in 1971 face-to-face communication was even more intensive because of the open forum nature of the Year of Review meetings.

The Management and Planning Boards are hard-working and effective instruments but, as with most groups, are often prone to inter-personal disputes, largely because most of the members experience conflict between protection of vested interest in the part as against the well-being of the whole.

The functions of the Academic Board are to advise the Director in regard to policy on:

    (a) the nature and objectives of the Institute;

    (b) courses and all matters pertaining thereto;

    (c) the achievement of proper education standards;

    (d) the efficient use of Institute resources.

The Board is broadly representative of the academic body, with some elected members. On major issues it tends to create working parties, and these initiate Institute-wide discussion prior to making recommendations to the Board.

It will be noted that the major Boards are advisory to the Director, but it is rarely that he exercises his right of veto and/or ultimate decision. Imposed decisions are regarded as unsatisfactory in most circumstances.

To date, the Academic Board is not seen as satisfactory in operation, as distinct from theory, either by its participants or by those affected by its deliberations. The reasons are manifold and include:

1. An unwillingness, natural to many academics, to be concerned with the efficient use of resources.

2. The tendency to avoid deadlock by the device of appointing a sub-committee, although aware that this is often only procrastination, a delaying tactic.

3. The ability of a vociferous minority to block change, on the grounds of academic freedom and thus the need for further debate and/or research. (A Working Party took three years to make recommendations, only to have them emasculated by the full Board.)

4. Inadequate documentation, largely as a result of not having a senior academic with the responsibility and the time to ensure it.

3. Divisional Boards

The functions of a Divisional Board are:

    (a) the efficient administration of the Division in conformity with Institute policy;

    (b) forward planning;

    (c) preparing policy recommendations for the Management Board;

    (d) the achievement of co-operation and unity within the Division, with other Divisions and with the Central Administration of the Institute.

The Boards are chaired by Deans, and comprise Heads of Departments and elected staff members.

B. Specific illustrations of information flow and decision-making

To illustrate the Institute system, four specific areas have been investigated and described in flow charts (see Appendix F, page 309). This technique appears to be more descriptive and understandable than any textual approach. The areas illustrated are courses, staff establishments, annual budget construction, and major educational policies or plans.

C. Management criteria

In 1969 the Council adopted a series of control criteria for management purposes. Part of the document is given in Appendix G (page 000). In the years since the Council decision many of the criteria are fully in operation, whilst others are still being processed. At the present time the Academic Divisions are undertaking investigations into criteria to be used for the control of their own operations.

Budgetary and cost analyses have reached a substantial degree of sophistication, as have many of the supplementary criteria. A significant failure has been in the area of subject proliferation. Each specialist wants his own specially designed option, and as with most similar institutions, most academics have a desire to add to course content but never to reduce it. The Institute teaches over 800 subjects and the number increases each year. A thoroughgoing and even ruthless examination of subject proliferation should be made, but the pre-requisite is the development of the objectives of courses, in the knowledge that degrees and diplomas are foundation stones for continuing education.

D. Development and productivity

As has been said, the Institute clearly appreciates the need for the achievement of greater productivity and has developed many criteria of measurement and methods by which to accomplish it. A major objective for the triennium 1973-75 has been stated as the use of new techniques in management and planning. The submission continues:

> *Management and planning techniques*
> Appropriate management data for decision-making is of increasing importance with the greater scale of the organisation. A number of major techniques have been developed within the Institute and these are likely to be accelerated in their application through computerisation. Examples are techniques related to,
>
> > central scheduling of teaching space
> >
> > cost analyses per equivalent graduate
> >
> > analysis of student wastage, including drop-outs and examination failures
> >
> > manpower demand surveys
> >
> > revised budget methods with emphasis on planning and programming
> >
> > control criteria for various facets of administrative and educational organisation

      costing of projected building projects

      utilisation of equipment procedures and controls

      analysis of effectiveness of purchasing policies

      computerisation of planning for future triennium submissions

The main emphasis will be on the improvement of planning and management in order to achieve maximum utilisation of resources whilst ensuring improving quality in education.

A technique which has been endorsed in principle is that known as "Delphi", for the systematic solution and evaluation of expert opinions. The "Delphi" technique is likely to be used for some aspects of the middle- and long-term education plans to 1981.

As far as resources are concerned, the Institute is planning not only for the computerisation of historical cost analyses, but also towards the computerisation of forward planning simulations. Preliminary work is in progress between the Department of Computing and Data Processing, and the Research and Planning Branch of the Administration.

The criteria which can be used to evaluate the Institute's development plan, with particular reference to the ability to meet socio-economic needs, have been examined at various stages in this case study. The criteria used are multiple. Yet, despite all the efforts which have been made to use quantitative and qualitative criteria and to relate one to the other, and despite the magnitude of some of the Institute's plans and methods for measuring effectiveness and efficiency and for projecting the future through simulations, there remains a missing link. This may be defined as a total systems approach. As yet, the Institute has not developed an integrated systems approach; and indeed many staff members of the Institute doubt the feasibility of its achievement.

In late 1971 there was some evidence to suggest that governments might diminish the growth rate of higher education in Australia by reducing the financial grants for the triennium 1973-75, if calculated on a percentage of Gross National Product basis. In these circumstances, the writer strongly advocated a procedure of:

    (a) a long-term education plan, flexible in design and kept under review;

    (b) a process of selection from the above into time periods, i.e. triennia;

    (c) the costing of (a) and (b) in detail and for each course, new or projected, on a per-equivalent-graduate basis;

    (d) the relating of (c) to the element of social need and demand, through a process of judgment, after obtaining as much data as is possible from government, industry, commerce and the professions;

    (e) the postulation of financial, economic and social consequences of alternative plans prepared on the basis of the above information.

That the process is difficult is undeniable, but it would be preferable to the current position in Australia whereby decision-making is *ad hoc* in nature, and judgements are budget-dominated and related in a small degree only to social and economic consequences.

E. Evolution of current system

In 1967 the Institute became an autonomous body. For about eighteen months of operation the majority of decisions, aside from those involved in day-to-day management, were made by the governing Council. In many instances the decisions arose from the recommendations of the Director, who had consulted with senior academic and administrative staff. During this period, however, the internal decision-making structure was being created, for the Council had early made clear its intention to delegate responsibilities to the greatest extent possible, as soon as machinery and staff were available. In retrospect, the Council made a large number of decisions which have stood the test of time. However, it would be idle to pretend that some errors in judgement did not occur; in most instances these resulted from inadequate consultation with staff, particularly academic.

By 1969 the Council had delegated many of its responsibilities and powers. The internal management structure had been established with a fair degree of success, particularly in resources decisions, relationships with the student body, and the development of curricula in relation to socio-economic needs. During that year the Institute made a significant step by fully taking over the responsibility for its building programme, which previously had been shared with the State Department of Public Works.

In 1970 the present system was largely in operation, although a weakness remained in that the Academic Board's rôle had not been debated clearly. (At present the rôle is better understood but, in the view of many academics, remains too passive in operation.) On the other hand, the Academic Staff Association was beginning to emerge as a strong body on the negotiations of salaries and conditions. The Administrative and Finance Division had been established successfully, by a policy of blending personnel from different backgrounds and of achieving a significant rôle in resource decision-making.

The concept of decentralisation of decision-making was initiated by the Administration and has gradually gathered momentum. Productivity became a significant issue in 1970. The Institute, as a corporate body, and its staff, came to realise that resources were becoming inadequate in relation to demand, at the current level of productivity in higher education. A seminar on productivity was conducted and described by the Director as "...a unique exercise in a tertiary educational institution in Australia—namely a self-examination with a view to increasing productivity." It led to 1971 being declared a Year of Review and to the adoption of many of the criteria enunciated in this study.

1972 brought further changes. The process of self-examination was accentuated. The Academic Staff Association became involved in educational issues, no longer restricting itself to industrial-type matters. The Council continued the process of delegation and reshaped its role towards major problems and longer-term thinking and planning. The proposals for an education plan to 1981 and for a total review of the Institute's organisational structure were accepted. Moves towards decentralisation were continued, with the objective of decentralised operation within policy and budget being achieved by January, 1973.

1972 saw the achievement of more consultative processes between the different components of the Institute. Some criticism was made by academics of an allegedly excessive influence being exercised by the Administration and Finance Division. However, the Division continued to reiterate the viewpoint that, if its influence had been disproportionate, the responsibility rested with the academic body for not exercising its counter-influence.

F. Effectiveness and defects
of the communication system

This is an appropriate stage at which to comment upon the effectiveness of the communication system within the Institute, including the feedback mechanism.

Theoretically, the system is open in nature, designed to transmit information speedily and effectively, yet with ample feedback channels. Each segment of the Institute is in communication with all other relevant segments, whilst Institute-wide matters are extensively debated and recorded, with decisions fed through a whole network of channels. Objections to either policies or projected policies can be raised at virtually any level of the organisation; and on many occasions senior management has reversed decisions, as a result of feedback uncovering previously unknown factors.

Yet, the system has major defects in operation. This is inevitable in a complex and large organisation, for all the communication theories break down, to some extent, because people react differently to information. It is interesting to note how even a simple statement is often subjected to entirely different interpretations. Both the spoken and written word are influenced by the perceptions and preconceptions of the receiver.

The causes of the defects include: the dissemination of too much information, resulting in the blocking of the communication channels; failure to keep to terms of reference by some boards and committees; and many staff being so preoccupied with their own field of activity that Institute-wide information is disregarded. The Management Services Branch of the central administration answers literally thousands of questions a year on policy matters; the vast majority of these answers have been published and are on indexed files in all sub-units of the organisation.

Whilst the opinion is held that communication systems can never be better than the participants, it may well be that the Institute should devise ways and means of a more selective distribution of material and, alongside this, a more positive direction of material to those sub-units to which the information is vital. Another development, which was planned for 1972, is a more comprehensive central control board system for deadlines, taking into account the interlocking nature of many decisions.

A final observation on feedback is that the senior management group, in particular, needs to be strengthened in numbers so that its members may maintain a greater range of informal contacts. Evidence abounds to show that informal communication channels are a necessary adjunct to the best of formal communication systems.

V. The Western Australian Institute of Technology system: foreseeable developments and applicability to other institutions

A. Evaluation

The Western Australian Institute of Technology's system of indicators and criteria for planning and management has shown a particular strength in its adaptability to change. In the period of just over six years' existence as an autonomous institution it has improved, changed and modified indicators and criteria, organisational structure and communication methods in ready response to changing conditions and circumstances. Some of the changes have resulted from experience gained; others have been direct innovative measures.

The general attitude of flexibility of approach to decision-making remains a cornerstone. There is little doubt that the Institute was able to accommodate change because it was a new institution, untrammelled by tradition, and operating in a new and important segment of the system of higher education in Australia. However, many other new institutions have patterned themselves on the old and, accordingly, it needed a conscious decision by the governing Council, management and staff of the Western Australian Institute of Technology for the opportunity to be seized. In retrospect, it would appear that the major strengths of the Institute system, aside from responsiveness to change, have included:

1. A firm decision by the Council to delegate responsibilities, and thus to concentrate on the broad policy issues, with particular emphasis on the longer term.
2. A relatively sophisticated system of financial management, supported by thorough investigation of the consequences of varying resource allocation decisions.
3. The establishment of an Educational Development Unit in 1970, as the first of its kind in a college of advanced education in Australia, to provide dissemination of information on new educational developments, advise staff on solving problems in teaching and learning, the evaluation of new educational procedures, staff education programmes and research into current and foreseen educational practices.
4. The announced intention to make the development of educational media a major objective for the next few years.

5. The achievement of a strong research and planning branch to carry out a systematic analysis of current results and to develop a triennial planning system of far greater depth and sophistication than is the Australian norm: the prog-ramme for 1972 included the computerisation of the Cost Analysis Model and the establishment of a more comprehensive planning system capable of rapid implementation, yet generalised in its construction so as to permit the variation of input parameters.

6. The making of every endeavour by management to improve the communications system, with particular emphasis on more and more open forums to discuss and recommend on major education and resource decision-making policies.

7. The introduction of a highly systemised, yet flexible, policy for the design and construction of buildings, with a strong cost control element; and the develop-ment of procedures for educational specifications/architectural briefs which al-low for interdisciplinary approaches, allied to every endeavour to rationalise and co-ordinate physical resources.

8. The opening-up of channels of communication between the Institute and the community for the more effective curricula development in relation to socio-economic needs; particularly through the establishment of advisory committees and relating these to the more academic thinking of Boards of Study; and the linking-in of applied research and consulting to the relevance of teaching content and methods.

9. Pioneering work in historical cost records and forward simulations of the impact of alternative and varying resource allocation decisions[1]: and the devel-opment and use of a whole series of management criteria, essentially concerned with economy of operation.

10. The recent decision to give higher priority to middle- and long-term educa-tional plans, through widespread discussion and debate through the academic body, and the examination of resource implications by central administrative and financial branches.

11. Serious endeavours to achieve a reasonable balance between, e.g. (a) the legiti-mate right of academics to exercise leadership in the teaching/learning processes, and the rationalisation of resources, and (b) the achieving of Institute-wide policies and budgets, yet with as much encouragement as possible for academic divisions and departments to make detailed decisions, through a policy of a substantial degree of decentralised decision-making.

12. Finally, such unique experiments as self-examination of the productivity of the Institute, and the conduct of open forum discussions between management and staff to isolate and then resolve both current and foreseen problems.

On the other hand, there are a number of weaknesses in the present management and planning system; the only hopeful aspect of this situation is that at least the Institute management and many staff not only recognise the weaknesses, but are

1. The costing systems as outlined in Section III are under serious consideration for adoption in some aspects of higher education in the Province of Ontario, Canada. Several Australian co-ordinating bodies and institutions are beginning to show interest, after a rather apathetic reaction when the systems were foreshadowed in 1970.

intent on obtaining solutions, which will be modified and improved in recognition of the fact that education is being subjected continuously to the forces of change. Internally, the significant weaknesses are seen as including:

1. The relative failure of the Academic Board, as the main academic policy-making body, to exercise greater leadership, thus allowing other elements of the Institute to be either exercising or to be considered as exercising too much influence in policy-making; on far too many occasions the Board has demonstrated strength only in negative terms, by blocking change, and even the most ardent supporter of the Board would find it hard to point to a major constructive policy having emerged from it. The causes are manifold and include a desire by some senior academics for the Board to be ineffective, thus protecting their vested interest, the lack of a specialised secretariat to ensure adequate documentation of major proposals, and an attitude of mind amongst its members that the Board's task is protection of the *status quo* rather than concern for change.

2. The failure to achieve an effective and representative educational policy authority has led inevitably either to an usurping of power by other organs, such as the Management Board, the Planning Board and the Courses Committee, whenever circumstances have demanded decisions within fixed time-scales, or to the submergence of a proposal for change in a morass of protracted and acrimonious debate.

3. An under-staffing in the senior management structure of the Institute, which has led to some errors in judgement because the demands of growth and innovation have at times been greater than the resources available for adequate investigation and consideration; there have been instances of the group over-riding a sub-committee to which it has granted decision-making power, causing deep resentment and a loss of morale.

4. A too heavy concentration on quantitative measurement to the partial neglect of qualitative criteria; an illustration would be preoccupation with close examination of class contact hours per week, but little consideration being given to the objectives of the course itself.

5. A tendency on occasions to tackle too many significant problems simultaneously, without adequate investigation of priority rankings, resource commitments and the techniques to be used; in part, this is a by-product of the over-burdening of senior management, some members of which do not themselves help, as a result of tending to want even the most trivial items discussed by central boards. (An examination is currently in hand on the agenda items considered in 1971 by central boards, with a view to analysing time wasted on trivia.)

6. An over-burdening of many academic staff in committee and similar work, to the disadvantage of their self-development and thus limiting their degree of contribution to the longer-term goals of the organisation; as is so often the case, the more able and willing staff are those most often asked to undertake committee or special assignment work. It has been estimated, as a result of a number of small-scale studies, that the heads of teaching departments spend 25 per cent of their time at meetings. The problem is common to higher educational in-

stitutions, where ample discussion and decision by consensus are expected; a partial solution lies in improvement in secretariat service and perhaps more importantly in the quality of chairmanship.

7. A failure to properly evaluate the communication network, resulting in an over-burdening of the system, and a consequential growing inability to distinguish between the significant and the insignificant; the system has been characterised by a desire for all decisions and the details of most discussions to be as widely circulated as possible, and no endeavour has yet been made to find out whether this is desirable or even wanted. (This would appear to be a legitimate matter for an Organisation and Methods investigation, for an inefficient communication network is both time-wasting and costly.)

On the external aspect, there are a number of weaknesses which bear upon the Institute, the most important of which include:

1. A present lack of clarity on the respective roles of governmental agencies (such as the Tertiary Education Commission) and the autonomous institutions of higher education; a prime example is the Institute requesting a Tertiary Education Commission policy on non-academic salaries in April 1971 and not yet having received a coherent reply.
2. A perceived dominance of the Tertiary Education Commission by the State Treasury, whose policies inevitably are budget-conscious and not necessarily concerned with socio-economic and political considerations.
3. An absence of clearly defined national objectives in socio-economic terms; there are no national guidelines as to the proportion of the nation's wealth which is to be used for higher education.
4. The absence within Australia of sufficient allocation of funds for research and development in education, and the lack of an integrating system for research activities.

B. Foreseeable developments

It has been observed correctly that a still photograph is inadequate as compared to a moving picture of development. The major foreseeable developments for the Institute would seem to include:

1. An educational plan for a decade ahead, kept constantly under review and responsive to changes in political and socio-economic events and forecasts.
2. The achievement of more participatory decision-making, i.e. of a community which has understood and accepted primary organisational goals, supplemented by secondary and tertiary objectives for students, staff and society as a whole.
3. The ultimate organisational structure being collegial in concept, with decisions being made closer to the sources of real knowledge, and with ample opportunity for deviations in detail, whilst retaining fundamental principles and goals of the whole organisation.
4. Computerisation of data for decision-making, in relation to educational policies and resource decision-making, and with a particular emphasis on

simulations of possible results of alternative policies, and ways and means of achievement.

5. Methods of improving the productivity of the educational processes, with the parallel development of more qualitative criteria for comparison with the many existing quantitative criteria, which in themselves will tend to become more refined and inclusive of qualitative problem areas.

6. The introduction of new techniques of financial resource decision-making systems, such as the Programme Planning Budgeting System, or alternatively a new system, along similar lines, but specifically geared to education.

7. The ultimate emergence of more sophisticated socio-economic planning on a national basis, thus facilitating institutional decisions being taken within a wider context.

C. Applicability to other institutions

Systems and indicators developed for a particular institution, operating in a specific socio-economic and political environment, can rarely be transplanted in their entirety, and without modification, to other institutions. Due allowance has to be made for a different locale, differences in history and rôle, the internal and external societies, and even indeed the personalities which will be concerned. In addition to these factors, a difference in approach is involved, depending on whether one is dealing with institutions in the process of founding or alternatively with institutions which are seeking to change their own systems and indicators in planning and management.

The author has an impression that many problems are common to many countries and societies, and that these include: rapid growth in higher education outpacing available resources, both human and monetary; the need to improve productivity in education without jeopardising quality; the challenge of continuing or recurrent education, in order to cope with new knowledge and the increasing aspirations of adults; experimental work in the learning/teaching process; the relevance of curricula as perceived by students in relation to the realities of life; and the undoubted need to improve methodology and judgement in management and planning.

Staff appraisal schemes in different institutions may agree in principle, i.e. on objectives, but the methods used are likely to vary. This case study has been concerned with an Australian institution. In higher education, however, the greater the degree of dialogue, communication and exchange across national boundaries, the more likely it is that improvements will be achieved. The world is changing; and education not only has to adapt to change, but in part to anticipate it. That is the task of today and tomorrow for all those involved in planning and management of higher education.

Glossary

Cadetship. An award offering a salaried career within government service, commerce or industry. In addition to professional training, it provides the opportunity for subsidised tertiary study.

Class contact hour. One hour of confrontation between instructor and student group.

Education specification. A detailed schedule of the specific physical requirements together with a statement of educational philosophy. It defines the total client requirement from which an architect designs the building.

External studies. A means of providing off-campus educational opportunities at the tertiary level for people who wish to undertake a study programme leading to an academic award but who cannot attend a campus regularly for instruction. It involves the use of a variety of educational techniques including printed study guides and resource materials, audio-visual materials such as audio and video-tapes, radio broadcasts and television programmes, telephone tutorials, special learning kits and a limited amount of face-to-face instruction.

Equivalent graduate. Student-hours due to subjects passed at or exempted from annual final or supplementary examinations, divided by the total hours of class tuition set for the course.

Leaving certificate. An award gained after five years of secondary schooling and an external examination conducted by a Public Examinations Board. A certificate is granted to each candidate who passes in any subject at the Leaving Examination; the certificate specifies the subject or subjects in which the candidate has passed.

For entry to tertiary institutions various subject passes from specified groups of subjects or combined aggregates of marks are required. (As well, for entry to the University of Western Australia higher pass levels on three additional examination papers are required.)

Quantity surveyor. A professional who specialises in the measurement and valuation of building work, and the cost control of building projects.

Recurrent expenditure. Includes all expenses that may be incurred for the daily operating costs of the Institute that are not associated with the initial cost of building or setting-up of amenities for use.

Space envelope. Space enclosed within imaginary vertical planes, bounding a building site, extending to a predetermined height above natural ground, street, or other predetermined datum level.

Tertiary education. The highest phase of the established education system, which generally requires the equivalent of a full secondary-school experience as a prerequisite to entry. Many institutions such as Universities, Vocational Colleges and Institutes of Technology provide the tertiary-education courses.

APPENDIX A

Amplification of enrolment projections

The full planning system has been briefly described in Section II. By way of illustration, it is amplified here in relation to enrolment projections.

Stage 1

In each year the number of new enrolments at the Institute depends upon the following factors:

(a) The size of the new student-population pool;

(b) The proportion of that pool obtaining a tertiary-entrance qualification;

(c) The proportion of those obtaining a tertiary-entrance qualification in the year n and who enrol at the Institute in the year $n + 1$. It is assumed that the proportion of the total who did not gain their tertiary-entrance qualification in the previous year will remain constant for each year of the projection.

Accordingly, annual new enrolments were projected by application to the 1970 new-enrolment figure of a combined index series consisting of:

(i) a *population index*, representing growth in selected age groups of the Western Australian population;

(ii) a *first propensity to enrol index*, representing annual growth in the population of the selected population pool gaining a tertiary-entrance qualification;

(iii) a *second propensity to enrol index*, representing annual growth in the proportion of students gaining a tertiary-entrance qualification in the year n and enrolling at the Institute in the year $n + 1$. The combined index was formed from the product of (i), (ii) and (iii).

Stage 2

A persistence equation was developed whose coefficient specified the proportion of students newly enrolled x years prior to the base year of the projection and who re-enrolled in the base year:

$$T_t = bN_t + cN_{t-1} + dN_{t-2} + eN_{t-3} + a,$$

where T_t = total enrolment in year t,

N_{t-x} = new enrolment in year $t-x$, $x = 0, 1, 2, 3$

a, b, c, d, e are constants, each less than unity, derived from 1970 enrolment data, and a is a residual factor.

The total projection in each year was obtained by application of the above equation to the results of Stage 1.

As far as *subject enrolments* are concerned the process of projection is briefly described hereunder.

A three-dimensional matrix (F) of student flow from three academic levels within course to subject within teaching department in the base year of the projection (namely 1970) was established. One such matrix was required for each department.

Column vectors of student flows were converted to probability vectors thus establishing a new matrix (P) in which each element specified the probability that a student in a given academic level in a given course would enrol in a given subject taught by a given department.

Diagrams depicting the flow and probability matrices are presented on pages 287-288. Notational descriptions of matrix operations follow on page 289.

MATRIX F : $f_{i,j}^{k}$, $i = 1,..,I$ the No. of subjects taught by a given Department.

$j = 1,..,J$ the No. of courses generating students to a given Department.

$k = 1,..,K$ the No. of academic levels in each Course j.

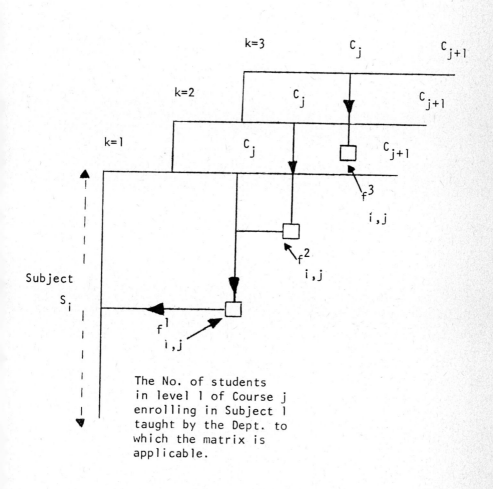

The No. of students in level 1 of Course j enrolling in Subject 1 taught by the Dept. to which the matrix is applicable.

MATRIX P : $\left[p^k_{i,j} \right]$, where $p^k_{i,j}$ is the probability that a
student enrolled in academic level k
in course j will enrol in subject i
taught by the Department to which the
matrix is applicable.

$$\sum_{i=1}^{l} p^k_{i,j} = 1$$

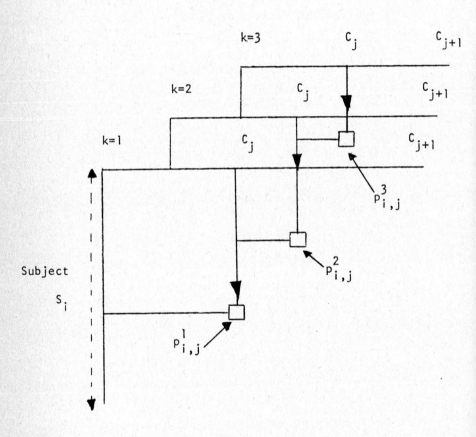

Notational descriptions of matrix operations

Flow Matrix (F)

Using the following notation:
For Teaching Department X

$F = \left| f_{i,j}^{k} \right|$ an $i \times j \times k$ dimensional matrix

$\quad i = 1, ..., I$ the number of subjects taught by Department X
$\quad j = 1, ..., J$ the number of courses generating to Department X
$\quad k = 1, ..., K$ the number of academic levels in Course j

$f_{i,j}^{k} =$ Number of students in academic level k of course j who enrol in subject i taught by Department X.

$S_i =$ total enrolment in subject i in base year

then

$$S_i = \sum_{j=1}^{J} \sum_{k=1}^{K} f_{i,j}^{k}$$

Probability Matrix (P)

Using the following notation:
For Department X

$p = \left| p_{i,j}^{k} \right|$ i, j and k as before (see para 1 above)

$p_{i,j}^{k} =$ probability that a student in academic level k in course j will enrol in subject i taught by Department X.

$$p_{i,j}^{k} = \frac{f_{i,j}^{k}}{\sum_{i=1}^{I} f_{i,j}^{k}} \qquad \text{so that} \quad \sum_{i=1}^{I} p_{i,j}^{k} = 1$$

Derivation of Projected Subject Enrolments from Projected Course Enrolments by Academic Level

Let $E_j = \left| e^k \right|$ be a k dimensional row vector of enrolments in each level k of a selected course in year n.

$Q_j = \left| p_i^{k} \right|$ be an $i \times k$ dimensional matrix of k, i dimensional probability column vectors for a selected course

then the student contributors from the selected course to each subject taught by Department X is given by the matrix product

$\qquad\qquad$ an i dimensional row vector

$U_j = E_j Q_j^{T}$ where Q^T is the transpose of Q matrix and has dimensions $k \times i$.

The aggregate of enrolments from all courses to each subject taught by Department **X** in the year n is given by

$$V = \sum_{j=1}^{J} U_j$$ the sum of all such row vectors U where V has dimensions $1 \times i$.

APPENDIX B

Student/staff ratio and class sizes

Taking the simple case where a course is taught entirely by one department, the ratio relating to students and staff associated with that course may be expressed as:

$$\frac{\text{Student-hours}}{\text{Prescribed weekly attendance hours}} \div \frac{\text{Student-hours}}{\text{Average class size X weekly teacher class-hour load}}$$

That is, given constant weekly prescribed hours of class attendance for courses and constant weekly class-contact-hour loads for teachers then, clearly, the full-time-equivalent student/staff ratio is a function of the mean class-size value. The base value of this latter variable is governed by educational policies and specified student groupings relating to individual subjects.

The ratio has the limitation for the Institute that it cannot validly be employed as a basis for inter-departmental or even inter-divisional comparison. A unique combination of all the controlling variables, including prescribed course hours, exists for each department. This is evidenced by the wide range of ratio values extracted from 1971 Institute enrolment data:

Departmental range:	6.3—17.3
Divisional range:	9.7—16.2
Institute ratio:	12.5

The ratio may prove to be an appropriate tool for the long-term projection of departmental teaching staff on the basis of projected full-time-equivalent students. The establishment of it as a predictor for a given department requires the derivation of a function which adequately describes the growth of mean class-size and hence growth in the ratio.

For many subjects there are large lecture classes supported by small tutorials, seminars, workshop or laboratory classes. In theory, under these conditions, the average class-size for each subject approaches a maximum limiting value which may be expressed mathematically as follows,

Let X = lecture class-size.

$\bar{a}$ = constant average small class-size.

k = ratio[1] of prescribed weekly lecture hours to those prescribed for classes in the constant small-size category.

---

1. This ratio refers to curricula specifications as laid down in the Institute Handbook and NOT to actual hours of class contact.

The following frequency distribution may be constructed:

Class-size (x)	Frequency of occurrence in hours (f)	f . x
X	k	k X
ā	X/a	X

then the mean-class size u is given by

$$1) \quad u = \frac{\Sigma f x}{\Sigma f} = \frac{\bar{a} \, X (1 + k)}{\bar{a} \, k + X}$$

As a numerical example, the mean class size u for the Department of General Studies is approximated by substituting current values of $\overline{X}$, ā and k into the right-hand side of equation 1), where $\overline{X}$ replaces X and is the average lecture class-size weighted by class durations.

$$\bar{a} = 14.5 \, . \, \overline{X} = 43.7 \, . \, k = 0.875$$

$$u \doteqdot \frac{14.5 \times 43.7 \times 1.875}{(14.5 \times 0.875) + 43.7} = 21$$

Assuming a *statistical* idealistic case:

where $\overline{X}$ may tend to infinity,

$$\lim_{\overline{X} \to \infty} = \bar{a} \, (1 + k)$$

That is, the greatest value of the overall mean class-size would approximate to ā $(1 + k)$. However, this is merely a theoretical consideration which illustrates the fundamental structure of the system.

A model for the analysis of historical costs

The model provides four basic facilities:

    (a) A synthesis of expenditures, by selected classifications, assignable to each course of study;

    (b) A perspective of the interdependencies between teaching departments, and their implications regarding costs and resource requirements

    (c) An analysis of wasted expenditure due to sub-optimised supply and demand conditions of physical resources, student withdrawal and failure rates;

    (d) A frame for the projection of cost patterns.

The basis of the model is the LEONTIEF type input/output matrix which distributes departmental teaching costs among courses in proportion as student-hours are generated from courses to departments.

The Institute uses the following notation:

D_i, $i = 1, 2 ..., m$: the set of departments administering Institute courses.

T_i, etc: the set of total costs incurred by departments in teaching.

C_j, $j = 1, 2 ..., n$: the set of courses offered by the Institute.

TCC_j, etc: the set of total costs assignable to courses.

K_j, etc: the average number of class-hours per week prescribed for Course j.

Y_j, etc: the number of years of study specified for Course j.

A: the $m \times n$ matrix of student-hour flows from courses to departments.

    (a_{ij}): elements of A whose values are the number of student-hours generated from Course j to Department i. That is,

$$a_{ij} = \sum_{p=1}^{p} n_p \, d_p$$

    where, n_p is the number of students generated from Course j to subject p taught by Department i and d_p is the duration in hours of subject p

        $p = 1, ..., P$

A schematic representation of Matrix A appears overleaf. It is to be noted that reference numbers, 1), 2), etc., identify items listed under Row and Column Sums with following paragraphs bearing the same reference number.

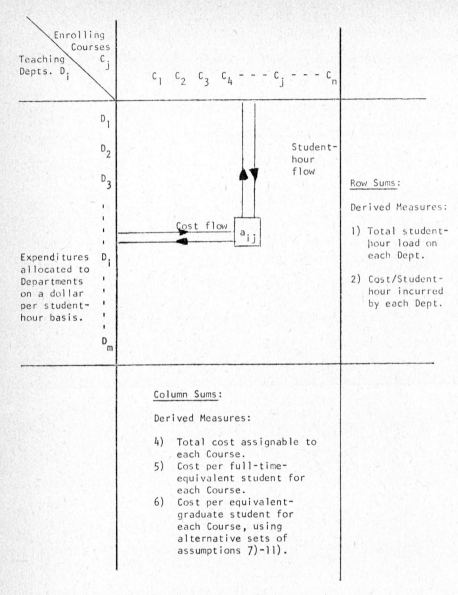

The following measures are derived by matrix operations:

1) The total student-hour load (L_i) generated to D_i from C_j is,

$$L_i = \sum_{j=1}^{n} a_{ij}$$

2) The cost per student-hour CSH_i incurred by D_i is,

$$CSH_i = T_i/L_i$$

3) The reverse flow of costs from D_i to C_j is,

$$CC_{ij} = T_i \cdot \dfrac{a_{ij}}{\displaystyle\sum_{j=1}^{n} a_{ij}}$$

4) The total cost assignable to C_j is,

$$TCC_j = \left[\sum_{i=1}^{m} T_i \cdot \dfrac{a_{ij}}{\displaystyle\sum_{j=1}^{n} a_{ij}} \right] = \sum_{i=1}^{m} (CSH_i \cdot a_{ij})$$

As far as unit costs are concerned, the model is developed below:

Definition 1. Full-time-Equivalent Student
A theoretical measure of the number of full-time students enrolled in a given Course, given by the total number of student-hours enrolled in the Course divided by the average prescribed weekly class-hour load for the Course:
For Course j:

$$FTE_j = \sum_{i=1}^{m} a_{ij}/K_j$$

Comment: In the case of a part-time course, K_j is set equal to the average of all K_j for full-time courses administered by the Department administering the part-time course.

5) The cost per full-time-equivalent for Course j is:

$$COST_j \ PER \ FTE = TCC_j \ / \ FTE_j$$

Definition 2. Equivalent Graduate
A theoretical measure of the number of graduates in a given Course and year.
For Course j:

$$EG_j = \sum_{i=1}^{m} a_{ij}/Y_j \ K_j = FTE_j/Y_j$$

Comment: In the case of a part-time course, K_j is set as before (see comment Definition 1); Y_j is set at the average value for full-time courses administered by the same Department.

6) The cost per Equivalent Graduate in Course j is:

$$COST_j \ PER \ EG = TCC_j/EG_j = Y_j \ (COST_j/FTE)$$

Alternative Costs Per Equivalent Graduate
7) OPTIMUM COST$_j$ PER EQUIVALENT GRADUATE:

The total number of student-hours $\displaystyle\sum_{i=1}^{m} a_{ij}$

(denoted Z_j) generated by Course j, and the total costs D_i incurred by Departments correspond to the assumptions of:

(i) Optimum utilisation of resources, namely space-time, staff and equipment associated with Course j.

Comment: The complications involved in such an assessment are extensive. This type of exercise has been studied only in broad outline at the Institute. It is regarded as a worthwhile study which should be conducted in proper detail.

(ii) No subject withdrawals subsequent to the finalisation of enrolments in Course j.

(iii) No examination failures in Course j.

8) Potential $Cost_j$ Per Equivalent Graduate:
Z_j is the total number of student-hours enrolled for in Course j under assumptions (ii) and (iii) of paragraph 7).

9) Pre-Examination $Cost_j$ Per Equivalent Graduate:
Z_j is the total number of student-hours corresponding to subjects examined for students enrolled in Course j under assumption (iii) of paragraph 7).

Comment: A distinction is made between students sitting for annual and deferred examinations and is applied where appropriate in the measurement of wastage (see paragraph 12)).

10) Post Annual Examination $Cost_j$ Per Equivalent Graduate:
Z_j is the total number of student-hours deriving from subjects passed at annual and supplementary examinations by students enrolled in Course j.

11) Actual $Cost_j$ Per Equivalent Graduate:
Z_j is the total number of student-hours deriving from subjects passed at both annual and supplementary examinations by students enrolled in Course j.

12) Measurement of Wastage:
Costs 7) through 11) provide measures of the component parts of total wastage in terms of costs per Equivalent Graduate.
For example:

8) $-$ 7), wastage due to sub-optimisation of physical resources.

9) $-$ 8), wastage due to withdrawals.

11) $-$ 10) $-$ 9): wastage due to annual examination failure rate.

9) $-$ 10), the value of the remedial effect of supplementary examinations. The reduction in cost per equivalent graduate may be compared against costs associated with the remedial sector of summer school activity.

11) $-$ 7), total wastage.

Wastage sources may be identified by a more detailed examination of the model at the course to subject level of disaggregation within teaching departments.

To date, an explanation has been given of the model as an instrument for the distribution of costs to courses once the expenditure incurred by departments has been established. A series of methods have been devised to allocate all expenditure to student hours.

Summary
Since full-time-equivalent course enrolment figures, in contrast to headcounts, are independent of full-time/part-time student ratios, it is clear that costs expressed in terms of full-time-equivalent afford a more valid basis for comparison of course costs. Further-

more, the full-time-equivalent figure *per se* is a more accurate measure of the workload imposed on resources according to the weekly class-hour load prescribed for the course.

"Equivalent Graduate" values are derived from full-time-equivalent course enrolments by dividing the full-time-equivalent values by the duration in years of the course. Both equivalent graduate and full-time-equivalent values therefore possess the same desirable characteristics.

The chief merit of the equivalent graduate concept is that it provides a means of measuring annual production in individual courses and observing the economic effects of the various causes of production wastage. The model then provides the means of tracing and examining sources of wastage at the subject level.

Finally, the model possesses three useful features which should receive special mention; computer programming of the model could be suitably generalised so as to permit:
 (i) easy updating of the model for the inclusion of new courses;
 (ii) effective functioning of the model throughout changes in the academic year structure;
(iii) it is possible that consequent upon policies of course liberalisation, demands for elective subjects may increase from year to year. The model would afford a means of observing the inter-departmental implications of such demands.

Further work is in process on the simulation of costs for a variety of policy-decisions, change in tuition patterns or physical resources, etc. The advent of a large-scale computer and ancillary equipment would materially assist in the development of both historical cost records and simulated cost patterns.

Historical cost model, applied to 1969 data

In general accord with the information given in Appendix C, the costs per full-time-equivalent student and per equivalent graduate have been determined for 1969. The methodologies are set out below, and the results obtained are given in Tables D.1 to D.7.

1. Methodology for Departmental Unit Costs per Student-hour for 1969

Unit teaching salaries

$$\frac{\text{Total teaching salary for department}}{\text{Number of student-hours taught by department}}$$

Note: This includes part-time costs and allowances for superannuation

Unit technicians' salaries

$$\frac{\text{Total technicians' salary for department}}{\text{Number of student-hours taught in laboratories by department}}$$

Note: This does not include salaries paid to typists and other clerical staff

Unit consumable cost

$$\frac{\text{Total consumables vote for department}}{\text{Number of student-hours taught by department}}$$

Unit cost of library acquisitions

$$\frac{\text{Total cost of library acquisitions for department}}{\text{Number of student-hours taught by department}}$$

Unit allowance for depreciation of minor equipment

$$\frac{10\% \text{ of value of minor equipment obtained by the department during 1966-69}}{\text{Number of student-hours taught by department}}$$

2. Methodology for Cost per Equivalent Graduate for each course in 1969

Number of F.T.E's

$$\frac{\text{Total student-hours enrolled in the course}}{\text{Average hours prescribed for each year of the course}}$$

> *Note: In the case of miscellaneous enrolments and short courses, the divisor used is the average prescribed hours per year of all full-time courses conducted by the department*

Number of E.G's

$$\frac{\text{Total student-hours enrolled in the course}}{\text{Total hours prescribed for the course}}$$

Teaching cost per F.T.E.

$$\frac{\text{Total teaching cost assignable to the course}}{\text{Number of F.T.E's in the course}}$$

Total cost per F.T.E.

$$\frac{\text{Total cost assignable to the course}}{\text{Number of F.T.E's in the course}}$$

Total cost per E.G.

$$\frac{\text{Total cost assignable to the course}}{\text{Number of E.G's in the course}}$$

TABLE D.1. Departmental Unit Costs per Student-hour for 1969

Item	Chem.	Maths.	Pharm.	Phys.	Arch.	Art & D.	C.Eng.	E.Eng.	M.Eng.	A. & B.S.	Admin. Stds.	Gen. Stds.	H.Ec.	Therapy	W.A. S.M.	Muresk
Unit Teaching Salaries	37.30	25.52	40.91	32.42	23.24	28.20	20.00	26.16	33.05	21.64	33.01	24.59	31.87	27.61	24.68	14.91
Unit Technician's Salaries	16.30	—	24.16	34.68	1.64	2.92	3.13	48.79	20.83	0.39	—	2.90	19.31	5.47	45.96	209.70
Unit Consumables Cost	7.59	0.52	9.64	4.55	0.37	4.06	0.95	4.23	1.63	0.31	1.10	0.34	8.29	2.09	4.16	25.12
Unit Cost of Library Acquisitions	0.60	0.63	0.64	0.80	0.31	1.05	0.33	0.51	0.77	0.39	2.77	1.14	1.71	3.22[1]	4.16[1]	—
Unit Allowance for Depreciation of Minor Equipment	0.50	0.09	0.22	0.33	0.10	0.53	1.34	2.72	1.40	0.12	0.21	0.15	2.13	0.53	3.28	3.11

1. This includes a special grant from the Commonwealth Government.

TABLE D.2. Divisional Unit Costs per Student-hour for 1969

Item and methodology	A. S. (including Muresk but excluding Halls of Residence)	A. A. E.	C. S. S.	W. A. S. M.
Unit Administration Cost				
Total Administration plus Clerical Salaries for Division	7.92	6.35	7.61	30.62
Number of Student-Hours Taught by the Division				
Unit Allowance for Depreciation of Major Equipment				
10% of Major Equipment in the Division	3.04	0.78	0.23	4.79
Number of Student-Hours Taught by the Division				

TABLE D.3. Institute Unit Costs per Student-hour for 1969

Item	Methodology	Unit cost
Unit Salaries for Central Administration	Total Salaries of Central Administration Number of Student-Hours Taught by the Institute	6.03
Unit Overheads for Central Administration	Total Cost of Overheads for Central Administration Number of Student-Hours Taught by the Institute	7.47
Unit Building Maintenance	Total Cost of Building Maintenance Number of Student-Hours Taught by the Institute	5.26
Unit Allowance for Building Depreciation	Total Cost of Building Maintenance Number of Student-Hours Taught by the Institute	5.26
Unit Allowance for Depreciation of Major Equipment	10% of Value of Major Equip. in Central Admin. Number of Student-Hours Taught by the Institute	0.91
Unit Salaries of Library	Total Salary for Library Number of Student-Hours Taught by the Institute	1.87
Unit General Library Acquisitions	Total Cost of General Acquisitions for Library Number of Student-Hours Taught by the Institute	0.25
Unit Overheads for Library	Total Cost of Overheads for the Library Number of Student-Hours Taught by the Institute	0.11
Unit Special Commonwealth Grant for Bentley Campus Library	Value of Commonwealth Grant Number of Student-Hours Taught on Campuses in the Metropolitan Area	0.04

TABLE D.4. Muresk Unit Costs per Student-hour for 1969

Item	Methodology	Unit cost
Unit Administration Cost (academic)	Total Administration plus Clerical Salaries for Academic Section at Muresk / Number of Student-Hours Taught at Muresk	5.54
Unit Administration Cost (residential)	Total Administration Salaries for Residential Sector at Muresk / Number of Student-Hours Taught at Muresk	21.05
Unit Consumables Cost (residential)	Total Cost of Consumables for Residential Sector at Muresk / Number of Student-Hours Taught at Muresk	15.32
Unit Allowance for Depreciation of Minor Equipment (residential)	10% of Value of Minor Equipment obtained during 1969 / Number of Student-Hours Taught at Muresk	0.44

NOTE Muresk is an agricultural residential college, a development of the Western Australian Institute of Technology.

TABLE D.5. Cost per Equivalent Graduate for Each Course in 1969

Course No.	Course by Department	Number of FTEs	Number of EGs	Teaching Cost per FTE	Total Cost per FTE	Total Cost per EG
	Chemistry					
631	Assoc. in Analytical Chemistry	9.83	3.28	874	2 260	6 780
632	Assoc. in Applied Chemistry	61.70	20.57	802	2 067	6 201
634	Assoc. in Engineering Chemistry	0.17	0.06	878	2 244	6 732
637	Assoc. in Pure Chemistry	7.63	2.54	770	1 973	5 919
638	Assoc. in Applied Geology	25.68	8.56	734	1 922	5 766
630	Miscellaneous	4.81	1.60	838	2 141	6 423
	Mathematics					
701	Assoc. in Mathematics	30.92	10.31	421	1 093	3 279
700	Miscellaneous	25.18	8.39	463	1 178	3 534
	Pharmacy					
731/2	Assoc. in Med. Lab. Tech.	76.78	25.59	979	2 504	7 512
733	Assoc. in Pharmacy	120.81	40.27	1 038	2 663	7 989
730	Miscellaneous	1.93	0.64	962	2 452	7 356
	Physics					
721	Assoc. in Applied Physics	76.93	2 564	658	1 799	5 397
722	Assoc. in Geophysics	10.31	3.44	739	1 964	5 892
723	Assoc. in Applied Sc. (Physics)	24.47	8.16	760	2 023	6 069
921[1]	P.G.D. in Applied Physics	4.87	4.87	719	2 054	2 054
720	Miscellaneous	4.79	1.60	717	2 049	6 147
	Muresk					
521[1]	Diploma in Agriculture	57.00	28.50	478	3 708	7 416
	Architecture					
611[2]	Assoc. in Architecture	222.17	55.54	673	1 732	6 928
612	Assoc. in Town & Regnl. Plng.	38.85	12.95	481	1 247	3 741
593[1]	Dip. in Quantity Surveying	6.68	4.92	567	1 480	2 013
811[1]	Dip. in Town & Regnl. Plng.	0.54	0.39	558	1 438	1 984
610	Miscellaneous	2.94	0.98	538	1 459	4 377
	Art					
621	Assoc. in Art Teaching	40.08	13.36	607	1 527	4 581
623	Assoc. in Design	40.62	13.54	733	1 846	5 538
624	Assoc. in Fine Art	29.81	9.94	733	1 846	5 538
625	Assoc. in Art	9.58	3.19	465	1 171	3 513
626	Assoc. in Industrial Arts	23.70	7.90	485	1 219	3 657
620	Miscellaneous	0.65	0.22	607	1 529	4 587
	Civil Engineering					
641	Assoc. in Civil Engineering	183.84	61.28	606	1 660	4 980
642	Assoc. in Highway Engineering	12.44	4.15	520	1 430	4 290
643	Assoc. in Surveying	84.57	28.19	650	1 815	5 445
640	Miscellaneous	1.85	0.62	465	1 350	4 050

1. Short course.
2. Four-year course.

[*continued*

TABLE D.5.   Cost per Equivalent Graduate for Each Course in 1969 *(continued)*

Course No.	Course by Department	Number of FTEs	Number of EGs	Teaching Cost per FTE	Total Cost per FTE	Total Cost per EG
	Electrical Engineering					
661	Assoc. in Communication Eng.	39.50	13.17	645	1 943	5 829
662	Assoc. in Electrical Engineering	41.62	13.87	652	1 900	5 700
663	Assoc. in Electronic Engineering	91.87	30.62	657	1 935	5 805
660	Miscellaneous	0.57	0.19	597	1 949	5 847
	Mechanical Engineering					
711	Assoc. in Mechanical Engineering	98.41	32.80	735	1 831	5 493
712	Assoc. in Metallurgy	17.19	5.73	750	1 874	5 622
713	Assoc. in Production Engineering	15.39	5.13	749	1 884	5 652
710	Miscellaneous	0.38	0.13	783	1 851	5 553
	Accounting & Business Studies					
651	Assoc. in Accounting	277.79	92.60	350	927	2 781
652	Assoc. in Commerce	59.10	19.70	359	953	2 859
653	Assoc. in Management Accounting	0.43	0.14	352	938	2 814
013[1]	Institute of Chart'd Accountants	32.19	17.35	350	932	1 734
014[1]	Institute of Chart'd Secretaries	7.32	9.47	349	929	718
650	Miscellaneous	4.46	1.49	349	930	2 790
	Administrative Studies					
691	Assoc. in Business Administration	0.67	0.22	493	1 077	3 231
692	Assoc. in Production Management	0.06	0.02	550	1 202	3 606
693	Assoc. in Public Administration	6.16	2.05	474	1 043	3 129
694	Assoc. in Administration	56.40	18.80	357	891	2 673
891[1]	P.G.D. in Administration	18.24	6.08	476	1 042	1 221
892[1]	Dip. in Educ. Administration	32.25	10.75	455	1 017	1 122
690	Miscellaneous	0.32	0.11	516	1 127	3 381
	General Studies					
671	Assoc. in Social Science	139.23	46.41	359	897	2 691
672	Assoc. in Social Work	63.17	21.06	425	1 065	3 195
673	Assoc. in Asian Studies	24.81	8.27	369	922	2 766
597[1]	Dip. in Applied Linguistics	6.99	4.56	369	924	1 416
670	Miscellaneous	16.31	5.44	369	924	2 772
	Home Economics					
592[1]	Dip. for Home Science Teachers	23.99	12.00	776	2 207	4 412
598[1]	Dip. in Home Economics	20.55	10.27	778	2 204	4 410
681	Assoc. in Home Science Teachers	0.20	0.07	797	2 303	6 909
682	Assoc. in Nutrition	1.85	0.62	716	2 002	6 006
684	Assoc. in Home Economics	3.28	1.09	756	2 157	6 471

1. Short course.

TABLE D.6. Total Costs assigned on a Departmental Basis in 1969

Department	Administration $	Teaching $	Clerical $	Technicians $	Consumables $	Allowance for Depreciation of Minor Equip. $	Library Acquisitions $	Student-hours spent in department Total	Student-hours spent in department Laboratory
Chemistry	16 726	148 755	2 432	44 716	30 266	1 980.1	2 408	3 988	2 743
Maths. (& C. & D.P.)	16 620	89 544	7 056	—	1 819	333.2	2 198	3 509	—
Muresk	12 643	27 245	15 338	62 911	45 892	5 679.0	—	1 827	300
Pharmacy	16 324	151 352	2 874	54 545	35 656	802.6	2 383	3 700	2 258
Physics	19 064	112 981	2 462	56 984	15 849	1 141.4	2 803	3 485	1 643
							Divisional Total	*16 509*	
Architecture	17 383	144 390	2 505	6 635	2 294	632.0	1 909	6 213	4 035
Art & Design	18 474	91 684	2 304	9 175	13 195	1 710.7	3 400	3 251	3 140
Civil Engineering	27 551	94 242	2 428	5 220	4 473	6 308.4	1 554	4 713	1 667
Elect. Engineering	16 648	82 095	2 561	54 933	13 271	8 519.9	1 596	3 138	1 126
Mech. Engineering	20 219	118 943	2 481	25 063	5 855	5 025.7	2 780	3 599	1 203
							Divisional Total	*20 914*	
Acctg. & Bus. Studies	16 729	137 844	2 254	716	2 004	757.0	2 463	6 370	1 822
Admin. Studies	18 435	31 693	2 340	—	1 059	204.8	2 659	960	—
General Studies	16 483	140 189	4 723	1 391	1 935	851.3	6 513	5 700	480
Home Economics	12 394	30 336	2 373	12 456	7 890	2 023.9	1 631	952	645
Therapy	15 171	30 370	4 054	3 120	2 303	581.1	960	1 100	570
							Divisional Total	*15 082*	
Kalgoorlie	38 861	57 528	—	35 800	9 698	7 634.4	4 277	2 331	779
							Grand Total	*54 836*	

TABLE D.7.   Total Costs, 1969

1. Total costs assigned on a divisional basis

Divisions	Administration: (Departments plus Deputy Director's Office) $	Allowance for Depreciation of Major Equipment $
Applied Science	130 786	50 186
Architecture, Art & Engineering	132 873	16 367
Commerce & Social Sciences	114 785	3 459
W.A. School of Mines	71 369	11 170

2. Total costs assigned across the Institute

	$
Central Administration Salaries	330 450
Central Admin. Overheads (including depreciation of Minor Equipment)	409 476
Building maintenance	288 625
Allowance for depreciation of Buildings	288 625
Allowance for depreciation of Major Equipment	497 909
Library Salaries	102 746
Library Overheads	6 179
General Library Acquisitions	13 704
Special Commonwealth Grant for Bentley Campus Library	2 100

3. Total costs assigned to Muresk residential sector

	$
Administration	38 463
Consumables	10 125
Allowance for depreciation on Minor Equipment	810

APPENDIX E

Physical planning processes

The processes currently in use at the Institute are discussed in chronological order, rather than in the order of importance of the various planning steps.

(a) The initial design concept must appreciate the fact that a major educational institution becomes a city in itself, with several types of traffic, servicing needs, parking problems, electrical, sewerage, storm-water, water, service layouts, as well as space envelope considerations to achieve an aesthetic design in sympathy with the surrounding terrain, and at the same time creating an environment conducive to the educational needs of the student.

(b) Functional planning must be directed to serve the need of the student, and this should be apparent in any design solution. Student circulation is paramount; nevertheless, all buildings require service and maintenance access. Campus roadways must be designed to minimise traffic and this is best achieved by using the surrounding street system as distribution roads and bringing traffic onto the campus into cul-de-sac type parking areas.

(c) The aesthetic needs of a campus may be met by the establishment of basic materials or colours or by the introduction of a modular basis architecture which could be repeated throughout the campus. A well-designed campus must show a flexibility of design approach within an overall design control.

(d) The analysis of requirement, which results in defining the educational need, is a long and detailed process which can be considered as several steps. The first step is the establishment of capital funds. This is done by assessing the demand for a particular course, or the demand by the community for a particular qualification, and translating this into a building requirement. The building requirement would be related to a description of the type of facility, the area per student of each type of facility, and an assessment based on this information of the probable cost to build and equip facilities to service such a course of study. Previous experience has shown that in educational type buildings, one can expect to achieve a net to gross relationship of between 65 and 70 per cent. Thus, the net area requirement may be grossed to make provision for corridors, wall thicknesses, toilets, other service facilities, etc. and the gross figure thus arrived at may be translated into dollars by a straight cost assessment based on the known cost of other similar buildings and known and forecast cost increases to project the budget figure to the date the new building may be erected. Once the budget has been approved and capital funds reserved, the academics who are involved prepare the basis of the education specification. By means of data collection forms, each room or facility in the building is described in full detail and information from the data collection forms is then edited into the education specification. The education specification is a document which describes in detail and lists, or otherwise specifies, all the requirements for the building. In parallel with this document, which relates primarily to the educational requirement, a technical brief is prepared that describes and specifies the architectural and technical standards required in the building. This is particularly necessary where more than one firm of architects or consultants is employed on the same campus. The compilation of an education specification is a function of working parties and committees. The data collection forms for any particular area may be the subject of detailed discussions by working parties of the academics involved with the particular area. The final assessment of all the data collection forms is the responsibility of the Project Planning Committee and the editing of these papers into an education specification is an administrative/technical function carried out by the Institute Architect's Office. This provides a safeguard to ensure an equitable and consistent standard across the campus. The education specification must be approved by the management of the Institute through the established communication channels.

(e) At all stages of planning, from the initial investigations to establish a budget for a proposal till the builder leaves the site, accent is given to cost control. The initial budget is based on the analysis by the Quantity Surveyor of previous projects, which is used as a basis for the triennial submission. At each stage of documentation, the feasibility design stage, the final design stage and pre-tender documentation stage, the Quantity Surveyor prepares detailed estimates. Initially the estimates are on a broad building-space basis; at the final design stage, estimating is done on a building-element basis and at the pre-tender stage, the Quantity Surveyor estimates from the measurements made in compiling his Bill of Quantities. During the construction phase, the Quantity Surveyor continues to advise on budgetary control, assesses value of work for progress payments, checks claims for variations, and administers the rise and fall price adjustment provisions of the Contract.

APPENDIX F

Examples of information flows and decision-making

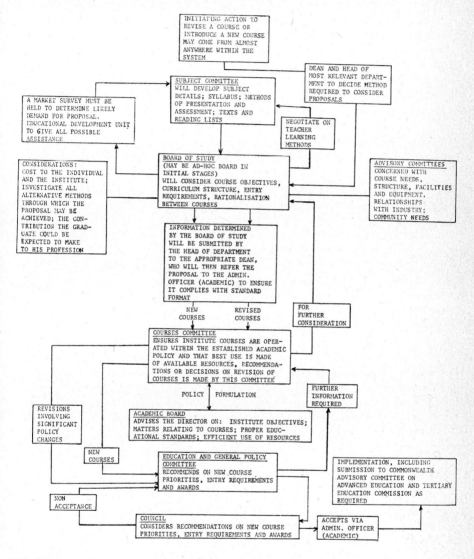

F.1.   *Revision of courses — introduction of a new course.*

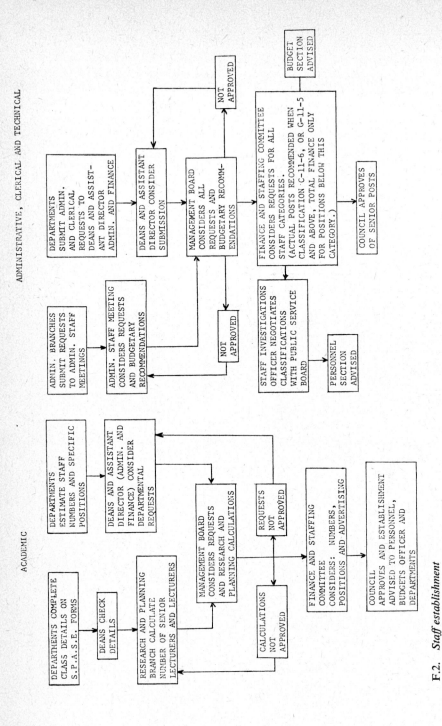

F.2. *Staff establishment*

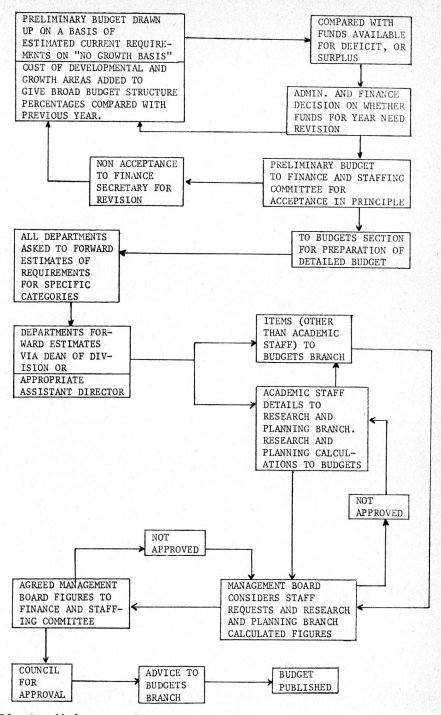

F.3. *Annual budget construction*

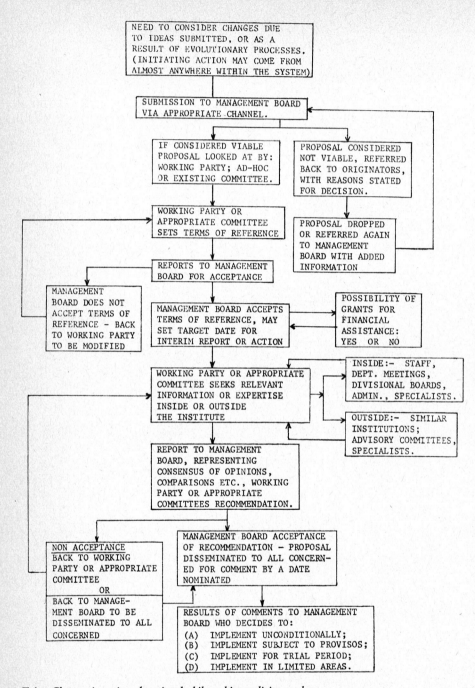

F.4. *Changes in major educational philosophies, policies or plans*

APPENDIX G

Control criteria for management purposes

In 1969 the Council adopted the following series of control criteria:

The first set of control criteria which would be relevant and helpful in improving efficiency is best related to the annual budget. In presenting an annual budget for the following year, each item is normally compared with the expenditure in the previous year: this time-honoured technique, applied to various percentage and ratio methods, serves a useful function, but it has a built-in weakness, namely that an item of expenditure, which is not fully justifiable, tends to become self-perpetuating. The relative misuse of funds becomes obscured by the force of habit. To illustrate what can happen, let us assume that an annual budget contains an item on publications, which for some years has been 1 per cent of total expenditure. As long as the 1 per cent remains, even if the actual monetary allocation has been doubled in company with the total budget, it is unlikely that any critical analysis will be made of, e.g., (a) the efficiency of standard annual publications; (b) the desirability or otherwise of new publications; (c) the numbers being printed; and (d) the justification of doubling the amount of money to be spent.

An investigation into the budgets of many education bodies and departments might well reveal that the following rule-of-thumb method is used:

(A) *Total Budget*

$$\frac{\text{No. of students estimated Year 2}}{\text{No. of students actual Year 1}} \times \text{Budget Year 1} = \frac{\text{Budget}}{\text{Year 2}}$$

(B) *Items in Budget*

$$\text{Item Year 1} \times \frac{\text{Budget Year 2}}{\text{Budget Year 1}} = \text{Item Year 2}$$

In contrast to this technique, which inevitably transfers inefficiency from year to year, the more appropriate method is to consider each item of expenditure, in detail and in isolation, and to thus construct a physical budget, from which ultimately is produced a fiscal budget. By this method, each item of expenditure must come under critical scrutiny, and at least once a year the efficiency of each aspect of the organisation would be tested.

A number of criteria can be used in the annual review, and some of these are set out below, divided into different categories.

Cost Analyses (Actual for year ended: estimated for year about to begin)

1. For each teaching department and/or course, the cost per equivalent graduate

and per full-time equivalent student should be known, and in sufficient detail to permit effective comparisons.

2. An assessment, arising from the above data, should be made of the amount of resources wasted on
   (a) drop-outs
   (b) failures.

3. Each department, under such a system, would be required to explain the wastage element and to justify the cost (at constant prices) per equivalent graduate and per full-time equivalent student.

4. An analysis per teaching department of average salaries for
   (a) academic staff
   (b) technical and other support staff
   would be made, in order to assess the effect of annual increments, and the commencing salaries of new staff, on the cost of running the department. (The need for such an analysis is easily seen when it is realised that annual increments and a rising average starting salary can erode the capacity of an organisation to expand, and will automatically cause a rising cost per graduate or per student. Knowledge of the facts may reveal a necessity to change recruitment policy and/or the ratio of full-time to part-time staff.)

Supplementary Analyses

1. A report from each department on the annual utilisation expressed in hours for each major item of equipment (costing say over $2,000). Such a report would be used to assess
   (a) the relative value of requests for new equipment
   (b) the desirability or otherwise of retaining existing equipment.
   (Such a technique does not preclude the possibility of purchasing or retaining equipment with a small degree of utilisation, but would ensure justification on demonstrable educational grounds.)

2. A report on the supply of stock items, including the value of stock-holdings at the end of the financial year, to enable calculation of the stock turnover rate; the number of transactions and the average value, in order to assess the degree of forward thinking and the success or otherwise in using the purchasing power of the organisation to obtain quantity discounts.

3. Statistical data is needed on the Library, including stockholdings, number of borrowings, number of readers, and if possible, a report on any volume which had not been borrowed for say six months. Such a review would not only be a commentary on the purchasing policy, but also an indicator on the success of efforts to promote individual study.

4. Teaching hours for each department, accompanied by a report from each head of department on work-loads, other than class-contact, which he considers his staff undertake. The latter would be subjective, but valuable in assessing the department's contribution to solving its own problems. (There is no logical reason why the industrial technique of necessity being the mother of invention should not apply to education.)

5. Staff-student ratios per department, set out under three categories:
   (a) academic
   (b) technical
   (c) other support.
   Academic staff establishments are likely to be set by formulae, which are outside

the scope of this article. As far as technical support staff are concerned, any major tertiary institution should have an organisation and methods officer, well qualified in work study, and he should investigate every laboratory and workshop at least once a year.

6. Maintenance costs of buildings and grounds should be reported in detail and with clear distinction between normal maintenance and minor new works. Each building should be the subject of a separate report, on a per-square basis, under major trade headings, e.g. electrical, mechanical, carpentry and plumbing. As far as ground are concerned, it would appear logical to divide these into recreational and other, and to give costs on a per-acre basis, with the separation of the significant elements, e.g. labour, water and new and up-keep purchases.

7. Administration costs are likely to involve a large number of items. As far as staff establishments are concerned, the organisation and methods experts should review each administrative section at least once a year. In the changing pattern of today, there is good reason to believe that the computer may be the best tool by which to reduce adminstrative costs, whilst simultaneously increasing the possibilities of obtaining significant data when it is required (and not too late, as is so often the case with clerical systems). Each item of expenditure should be the subject of a separate investigation and report, i.e. the physical budget should precede the fiscal.

The free exchange of data between institutions, and between the different parts of the whole system of education, should be achieved, if all are to benefit from each other's knowledge and systems. A few illustrations may reinforce the point.

On building costs, institutions should exchange data on each project, including the cost per square, gross-net ratios, materials used, design concepts. It seems truly incredible that each institution works in isolation, and that there is no national clearing-house for plans and costs of educational buildings.

As far as supplies are concerned, it would seem desirable for the tertiary institutions to supply each other with unit prices on all items of consumables and furniture etc. on which, say, more than $1,000 is spent per annum. It would seem high time that the big tertiary institutions used their purchasing power as efficiently as possible.

Let us turn to other control criteria, which may aid in achieving greater efficiency in education. A number are listed below:

1. Space utilisation analysis per unit of accommodation, on a student-station basis. (This would aid in ensuing the proper relationship of capital works to recurrent expenditure.)

2. Staff turnover rates and reports thereon, including comparative data from e.g. research organisations, and public service, selected major industries, and sister institutions. (Such information may assist in ensuring adequate personnel policies.)

3. A monthly general-purpose report on e.g. accidents, equipment breakdowns, reasons why offers of appointments were not accepted, number of computer runs and average times, and number of sheets run through offset and duplicating machines and the number of photo-copies made.

4. In commercial undertakings, such as a cafeteria and a bookshop, normal business methods should be employed, i.e. monthly trading accounts and profit and loss statements. Certain statistical data should be made available simultaneously, as e.g. number of meals, number of sales, average value of sales, and detail of peak load periods.

5. A report on the cost and results of each advertisement, to enable continuing review of the efficacy of the methods being used.
6. An annual report on the structure of curricula, with particular attention to
   (a) the class-contact hours
   (b) the staff contact hours (i.e. allowing for more than one staff member in laboratories and workshops)
   (c) the number of options available.
   (In the case of the latter, there is a high proliferation of options in the vocationally-oriented institutions, and justification should be rigorously enforced.)
7. Detailed annual reports on enrolments and examinations, which give the input and output data, and the raw material by which to compute the costs per equivalent graduate and per full-time equivalent student.

A university information system: case study carried out at the Catholic University of Louvain

Lucien Boxus, Armand Dodet,
Albert Gysels *and* Paul Walckiers

Contents

Introduction 319
I.   Concept of an information system 325
II.   The U.C.L. information system 335
III. The 'structure' file 351
IV.   The 'activities' file 354
V.   'Students' information sub-system 361
VI.   The financial sub-system 383
VII. The buildings and equipment sub-system 411
VIII. The personnel sub-system 413
IX.   Projects 415
Conclusion 425
Appendixes 427

Note

The opinions expressed in this study represent the personal views of the authors, and in no way involve the University's responsibility.

Introduction

A. Modern management techniques in the university

Modern society is increasingly dependent on the capacity for innovation of its various components, and the role of the universities is particularly important here. They are responsible for training the majority of highly qualified personnel and also contribute, through their research activities, to the advancement of knowledge and the evolution of society. The communication and extension of knowledge implies the development of a system of knowledge, which in turn shapes the cultural pattern of a society increasingly based on scientific research and its utilization. The strong influence of creative activity on the economy further aggravates the conflicts arising as to the purposes which such activity is to serve. The university will either relinquish one of its essential functions to other institutions, or having surmounted these difficulties, will assume constantly greater importance as a motive force.[1]

The university's vital role in society would alone justify the present concern for its efficient management. In addition, the scale of the resources invested in its operation, and the complexity of the decision-making procedures, mean that effective management is essential. The numerous and, only too often, contradictory aims assigned to the university add to the difficulties of directing it, so that new management techniques are clearly called for.

An information system forms the basis and the pre-requisite for the application of modern management methods, but very few universities have so far set about introducing one. Although the university encourages a strictly scientific approach in all fields of study, the academic world has always been somewhat hostile to any systematization of the universe in which students, researchers and teachers move and work. It is only in the course of the last ten years that the universities have found themselves obliged to apply the principles of modern management.

A first condition of rational management is the definition of the aims to be pursued by the institution concerned. The decision-making and executive structures are adapted to those aims, and their efficient functioning depends on the

1. A. Touraine, *A quoi sert l'université?*, cahiers n° 4 de l'Association des Universités Partiellement ou Entièrement de Langue Française, 1970, pp. 17-29.

communication of information. Some of the data supplied will respond to the administrative requirements; other more refined data will provide a basis for the decision-making process and for the supervision of the measures decided upon. The supply of data should be organized according to defined aims and the administrative and decision-making structures and requirements in such a way as to constitute a methodical information system.

There may be wide divergences both as to background and objectives in different higher educational institutions; the problems confronting the university and the aims it adopts depend on the economic, social and cultural environment, which determines the decisions to be taken and therefore the information required. As a result, the environment indirectly influences the coverage of the information system. In some countries, for instance, the quality of secondary education is very unequal; the information system will therefore be required to collect data illustrating existing disparities so as to enable them to be corrected. In other countries, a selection procedure may have been instituted for admission to the university; the information system will therefore have to provide data indicating the efficiency of such selection, and establishing correlations between the entrance-examination results and subsequent student performance. The capacity for data analysis also sets a limit to the degree of perfection to which the system is carried, as it would be useless to work out highly sophisticated statistics which are never analysed or used as a basis for decision.

Tradition, as well as the available human, material and financial resources, thus exerts a powerful influence on the choice of working methods. There can be no question of proposing a uniform system for all universities, since the environment conditions to a certain extent the coverage and operation of the information system. The responsible parties will therefore base any decision in the matter on a study setting forth the alternative methods of achieving an information system, comparing the advantages and drawbacks of traditional and automated methods of handling data, and taking into account the administrative operations and the data essential for management, the resources and constraints, the time required for application and the disturbances which any administrative reform may involve. The decision will be based on these qualitative and quantitative data, and once it is taken, the administration of the university will be set on a course which can be reversed only with some difficulty.

Our study will deal with the administrative reform initiated at U.C.L. (the Catholic University of Louvain). It is not put forward as an example to be followed, as every university has its distinctive characteristics. The authors nevertheless hope that the Louvain experiment will provide university authorities who have similar problems with some useful ideas.

B. Metamorphosis of the Catholic University of Louvain

The Catholic University of Louvain did not appear the most likely place for the early adoption of modern management methods. Its location in a small provincial town, its denominational character, the uniform socio-professional background of its students, and its long unbroken tradition, seemed to be factors adding up to conservatism. Yet this institution was to be troubled by successive upheavals which compelled it, as early as 1964, to opt for a new system of management.

Firstly, as a result of the growth in student numbers, the academic and departmental authorities found themselves heading a large and highly complex organization.

The administration of staff, buildings, finance, and so on, raised serious problems, and at the same time Louvain, which contains about half the total number of Belgian university students, felt the impact of the mounting political tension in the country. The demands of the Flemish deputies, representing the majority of the population, were inspired by the fear that the Louvain area, located in Flanders, would be gallicized by the numbers of French-speaking students and teachers. Matters came to a head in 1968, when U.C.L. was obliged to remove from Louvain.

The speedy separation of the ancient foundation into two universities, one French-speaking, the other Flemish-speaking, was matched by a corresponding division of the central and departmental administrative services. The first step was to constitute monolingual Faculties and appoint Deans and Rectors for the two linguistic segments; the second was to appoint two General Secretaries, one French-speaking and the other Flemish-speaking. These two executives drawn from the academic world took on the French or Flemish-speaking staff they needed as occasion arose.

The constitution of a completely new administrative set-up allowed the authorities to appoint staff of university level to handle the running of the Departments. This greatly improved the efficiency of the services concerned, which were traditionally manned by subordinate staff. In addition, the authorities encouraged the further training of executive staff by authorizing them to take leave of absence to follow a course of study abroad, or by enabling them to participate in the numerous Belgian or international commissions formed to investigate university matters. This proved extremely productive as a long-term investment.

The division of the universities was completed in July 1970. The *Université Catholique de Louvain* and the *Katholieke Universiteit te Leuven* acquired legal status under Belgian law, and became from then on independent for both academic and administrative purposes. A third legal body manages property jointly owned by the two universities and will ensure a smooth transition from the former situation. All matters relating to the university buildings are handled by this third corporate body, which has no competence on the academic side.

C. Limits of the study

This study undertaken at the request of the International Institute for Educational Planning will be restricted to an analysis of the U.C.L. information system, and gives a broad description of its nature, and a short account of how it was set up.

The work undertaken by the U.C.L. Analytical Unit deals strictly with university administration, and is not concerned with the reorganization of university hospitals and libraries.

Glossary

Batch processing. The operations are grouped together and processed as a single unit. The messages received by the computer are stored until the actual processing can be carried out.

Cathode screen terminal. Unit distinct from the computer, consisting of a typewriter-type keyboard and a screen on which all the conventional alphanumeric characters can be displayed.

Conversion table. Expression of the dual one-to-one relationship linking the elements of two information systems.

Data bank. Collection of information on a certain subject for the users' benefit. The term does not imply any specific organization of the contents of the bank.

Data base. A data base consists of magnetic files so organized as to permit multiple logical relationships between information belonging to different systems.

Datum-Information. These two concepts are treated as synonymous in the text. They are the coded representation or value of an elementary variable.

File. Series of data of the same kind, organized on the same lines, concerning a specific population.

Flow chart. Diagram of a logical sequence of operations included in a programme and represented by symbols.

Information. See datum.

Information system. See page 325.

Information sub-system. Sub-assembly of an information system.

Integrated information system. 'Integrated' indicates that several sectors of activity have been organized in the same system, and that the relationships between the corresponding data are ensured by a set of codes or machine pointers.

Job. Sequence of computer runs.

Management Information System (MIS). An MIS consists of four parts:
    1. A data base (DB);
    2. A DB control programme-retrieval and up-dating of the data it contains;

3. Programmes of specific application for users;
4. A message control programme from and to terminals.
It may also include:
DB safeguard programmes;
Creation and storage routines;
Statistical routines;
An inquiry language.
This system permits information to be handled at two levels:
basic level: elementary data;
management level: data classified according to variable criteria which are *a priori* unforeseeable.

Pointer. Address of an item of information in store. The pointers enable links to be established between data located in non-contiguous positions, both in the central store and on the mass magnetic medium.

Real time processing. The physical action and its recording by the computer are simultaneous. Communication between the computer and the source of action is by terminal.

Study-year. Curriculum or part-curriculum organized under Belgian Law or by the university, consisting of a set of courses followed by the students for one year. The U.C.L. offers 690 study-years, combining the 3,300 courses, and leading up to about 150 degrees or diplomas.

I. Concept of an information system

A. Definition

An information system may be seen as a balanced structure of individuals, machinery and procedures designed to produce a flow of relevant data collected both inside and outside the organization concerned. These data will constitute the raw material for decisions to be taken at every level of responsibility.[1]

Most authors emphasize the importance of the following elements: the integration of the data obtained and the ensuing operations, the breaking-down of barriers in the organization concerned, intensive use of electronic data-processing methods, and the automation of some decision-making. Hence an integrated system is the result of the organization of data collection, manual or automated processing, and the circulation of data in accordance with the needs of the authorities and of each separate unit of the whole structure. The co-ordinating equipment and procedures offer the exceptional advantage of enabling management to be based on information which is easily accessible and regularly up-dated.

B. Aims

Companies and administrative departments may be moved by various considerations when they decide to invest time and money in an information system. For example, a recent survey by the Diebold Institute (Federal Republic of Germany) identified the objectives shown in the table overleaf.[2]

While 70 per cent of those replying stressed the saving achieved by the use of data-processing equipment, the enquiry nevertheless revealed that 80 per cent of them referred to the speed and detail of the information obtained. In comparison with previous years, the number of users who considered automatic data-processing equipment to be a valuable aid to decision-making has sharply increased.

1. R. H. Brien: 'The Managerialization of Higher Education', *Educational Record*, Summer 1970, pp. 273-280.
2. Niederhoff R. P., *Decision-making and Management System*. Siemens Data Report, 5 (1970), No. 2, p.14.

Replies in order of numbers received	Reasons for introducing the system	Replies received (percentage figures)
1	Speedier information about the company's position	63
2	Saving in staff costs	51
3	More detailed information about the company's position	50
4	Necessity of using a computer because of the quality and volume of work required	43
5	Improvement of after-sales service	33
6	Shortage of manpower	32
7	Saving in cost of equipment	30
8	Release of capital (by stock reduction, for example)	23
9	More efficient use of capital committed	11
10	For publicity purposes	9
11	Others	5
		over 100[1]

1. Owing to multiple replies.

C. Necessity for a university information system

1. Functioning of the institution

If one considers the number of staff employed and students enrolled, the diversity of the activities pursued, and the scale of the financial and material resources deployed, it can be seen that the universities rank among the major enterprises in their respective countries. The rationalization of data-processing is a necessary condition for the proper functioning of their administrative and logistic services. Indeed, in many cases, considerations of economy and efficiency make the stream-lining of the payment of staff salaries, accounting operations, registration of students, and other such administrative tasks essential.

The speed and accuracy of the administrative work is an element which contributes to the confidence accorded to an institution by teachers, researchers and students. The satisfactory functioning of the administrative side is not merely an end in itself; it is of fundamental importance since any deficiency in the administrative machine impairs the institution's image in the eyes of its members. The streamlining of administrative tasks also lightens the burden of work on those in charge of research and educational units, and allows them to devote more time to their own special fields.

The improved quality of the information made available to the various responsible parties ensures a firmer foundation for the decision-making process. The data produced by the system serve the needs of planning; they are equally essential for the purposes of systems analysis, and for the construction of models to test alternative solutions to university problems. Furthermore, the availability of information about the activities of the numerous educational and research units allows a check to be kept on the extent to which targets have been achieved, and this is essential to the successful pursuit of a given university policy.

The information system permits some saving of manpower through the rationalization of the administrative tasks, but the numbers employed by the university administration will not be reduced as a result, since the utilization and interpretation of the data produced by the system require the employment of several analysts. The benefits to be obtained from a data system are not to be found in the level of employment. They derive from the knowledge about the institution which is made available, new means of supplying the management with relevant information to guide its action, and studies carried out on a more reliable basis.

Efficiency of administrative work, a good image of the institution, some lightening of the tasks falling to the senior staff, and added assistance in the taking of decisions—these are by no means negligible advantages. The diffusion of relevant information is also an important factor in the development of good relations between the members of the university community, and it may also be said that the participation of members of the university in its management is illusory in the absence of information about the problems involved. The regular production of such information is thus a pre-requisite for participation. The information system not only serves the purposes of administrative efficiency and internal relations, but also furthers a policy aim: the development of a dialogue between members of the university community.

2. Relations with the outside world

Decisions concerning the universities are often taken at national level, and the authorities therefore require information at that level in order to take these decisions. They can obtain this in useful form only if the data supplied by the various universities are compatible. Such uniformity presupposes the adoption of definitions accepted by all the institutions concerned, and identical procedures. The constitution of an information system is thus equally necessary at national and at institutional level.

D. Dynamic concept of an information system

An information system has to be introduced by progressive stages, each stage responding to different needs and corresponding to a specific level of organization and integration. It is therefore dangerous to forge ahead and aim straight for the most sophisticated level; in fact, it is only when the elementary needs of administrative operation have been satisfied that the subsequent stages can be worked out. Nevertheless, the success of the undertaking will depend on the general approach governing the first applications.

1. Improving administrative efficiency

The volume of administrative operations carried out in a large institution raises certain problems of organization, which are often solved through mechanization. This is commonly the case with the payment of staff salaries, accounting operations and student registrations. Similar reforms are sometimes introduced in other fields, such as drawing up timetables of courses, recording book loans or preparing the budget.

These innovations respond to a pressing need for administrative reform, and frequently result from a series of complaints from teachers, researchers or students. If carried out piecemeal, they may lead to worse confusion. A specific service should therefore be made responsible for the co-ordination of administrative reforms. This will avoid any duplication of staff and equipment, while the service will be responsible for identifying the data required for decision-making in the sectors of each activity concerned.

2. Data base

The recording of information on cards, tapes, discs or drums speeds up the processing and links up the various components of the system. The recording should therefore be planned so as to facilitate the inter-relations between the various files containing data on the human, financial and material potential, and the activities performed by the different departments and services.

The establishment of a data base poses certain technical problems, but the difficulties are to be found more in the use of the data than in their production. The abundance of information can be a serious drawback, as the relevant data may be swamped in a sea of paper. As an example, the general ledger of U.C.L. alone takes up three kilometres of paper annually! There can therefore be no question of extracting from it the pre-digested information required as a guide to decision-making in financial matters. The data base thus constitutes a first step towards an integrated information system. It enables the operation of the various services to be improved and accelerated, thanks to the information available and its computer processing; but it is not suitable for the production of succinct data such as is needed as a basis for decision.

3. Information system

The concept of an information system is more refined than that of a data base. Like the latter, the functioning of the system depends on the information produced by the administrative services, and enables the different types of information contained in the files to be linked up. The information system has three specific characteristics.

(a) Identification of relevant information

The formulation of a system must be preceded by the enumeration of the information required by the management of the institution, and this is determined by sifting the documentation contained in the various files. Periodic reports can then be produced manually or by automated equipment. For example, the financial information will show day by day the balance available in cash and in the bank, week by week the organization's commitments to third parties, and month by month the accounting balance and the proportion of the budget used. The regular production of detailed statements facilitates the marshalling of information for decision-making purposes. The differing degrees of aggregation of the basic data will thus correspond to the levels of decision; the statements will allow stock to be taken of the resources employed, and will also enable the relationships between the combinations of resources invested in the organization's activities and the standards of performance to be studied. Such information constitutes the essential material for subsequent systems analysis.

(b) Reorganization of services
An information system implies not only the marshalling of information for decision-making purposes, but also the reorganization of the operational services. At this stage, the system will take decisions automatically in spheres where human intervention is not necessarily required. The system thus releases human resources which can be more effectively redeployed. Examples are the automatic ordering of supplies when stocks fall to a certain level, the sending of reminders when the payment of registration fees is behind-hand, or checking the necessary formalities for registration. It is at this stage that the re-ordering of the information procedures to eliminate human intervention at certain points takes place.

(c) Supervision of performance
The third feature of the information system is the possibility of supervision offered to the authorities. Periodically, the various units of an organization may be asked to specify not only the volume of resources they require, but also the level of activity they wish to attain. The latter information has to be communicated in concrete terms, stating for example the number of degrees to be awarded, number of doctorates, or number of completed publications. It provides useful points of reference which enable the authorities to verify the performance of the different units, and give a considered opinion based on specific data. The information system enlightens the authorities on these points, and gives them the opportunity of reorienting their approach according to the results achieved.

4. Management system

The data base and the information system deal only with existing situations, leaving it to the responsible parties to decide whether changes are necessary. The object of the management system is to enable them to test the consequences of their decisions.

Linear projections or more sophisticated models consisting of a set of mathematical expressions describing analytically the relationships between the many factors of each component of the institution may be used for this purpose. The formulation of a simulation model demands:

1. Determination of the main dimensions of the universe to be described (e.g., teaching and support activities; research, support activities; administration of social services; buildings and maintenance).
2. For each dimension, definition of the parameters and the mode of expression of their relationships (financial terms, full- or part-time jobs, units of area, etc.), using linear or possibly curvilinear mathematical formulae.
3. Time weighting (rate of inflation, rate of discount on investment expenditure, spread of investment expenditure over the study, planning, construction and equipment phases, for example).
4. Determination of criteria of statistical acceptability.

The simulation model allows the incidence of a decision to be calculated for a series of assumptions. The model translates the short- and long-term effects into material or financial terms. For instance, on the basis of a projection of student numbers, the requirements for academic and scientific staff appointments can be estimated for several alternative teaching-staff structures; subsequently, using a system of norms, the consequences can be assessed in respect of utilisation and possibly construction of buildings, appointment of administrative staff, operating costs, etc.

The object of the management system is to maximise the use of resources for the achievement of the aims of the institution. The constituent data enable operational research techniques to be applied. The decision-maker, at this stage, has at his disposal relevant information, and also quantitative analyses which provide a firm basis for his reasoning. This is, of course, the ideal stage to which the systems analysts aspire. In practice, however, the system is found to be made up of different elements which will always prevent the most refined techniques from being applied to all the data.

In the first place, the constitution of a system is an exceedingly long business, an iterative process of trials, errors and part successes. As the enterprise is a living reality, it is bound to change, and data will alter. The system has to be adjusted accordingly, and can therefore never be regarded as completed. In the second place, the optimization of the use of resources can be considered only in a context of clearly defined objectives. The university differs from most other organizations in the complexity of its structure and the diffuse nature of the decision-making process. It is difficult to use operations research techniques in this context. To begin with, the calculation of an objective function becomes a very difficult matter; at the same time, the pursuit of different and often competing objectives by a large number of units obliges the analyst to apply difficult sub-optimizations when there are a great many interactions between the various elements of the structure. The activities of a major institution turn on a series of objectives some of which may appear to be contradictory; the optimum allocation of resources among those activities must then proceed from a higher objective, of such a general character that it becomes illusory to attempt to define it, still less to quantify it. This does not mean that systematic studies should not be undertaken since, failing the possibility of mathematical exactitude, they may draw upon expert opinion and considered value judgements, by applying the Delphi technique for example.

E. Sources of information

An information system consists of data drawn both from the institution and from its environment. Examples of the second category are as follows:
  (a) changes in Government resources and in the proportion allocated to higher education;
  (b) statistics on the employment market;
  (c) legislation concerning the statutes of universities, the conferring of degrees, etc.;
  (d) syllabuses of other universities;
  (e) recruitment of university staff in the country as a whole;
  (f) grading and remuneration of academic and scientific staff in one's own and other countries;
  (g) forecasting studies, etc.
By no means all of these can data be fed into a computer; the latter is indeed only one instrument, among many, in the constitution of an information system.

The data drawn from outside should enable the responsible parties to study their university's role in relation to the environment, and to draw the necessary conclusions for the management of the institution. Although neither the volume nor the technical level of processing of such data are comparable with those obtained from the university, their strategic value is obviously just as great.

F. Conditions of success

1. A political decision

The setting-up of an information system is not merely a matter of the successive reform of various procedures. It must, indeed, have the effect of improving not only the administrative operation of the institution but also the decision-making process.

In the long run, all the procedures will have to be integrated within the information system. Its progressive implementation is thus irreversible, if all or part of the capital invested is not to be lost. The decision to embark upon the introduction of an information system is thus binding upon the authorities themselves, the administrative services and the education and research units. This decision should originate at the highest level, and serve as a basis for the work of the analysts and heads of administrative services over a period of many years.

2. Overall plan

No set theory governs the progressive stages of setting up an information system, but experience shows that the first steps in mechanization hold some danger for the organization concerned.

At this stage, each administrative service is analyzed in turn. If the analysts do not work to an overall plan, there is no hope of building up a real system; furthermore, if the analysts cannot go against the wishes of those in charge of the various services (accountants, treasurer, etc.), the procedures will be mechanized without altering their bureaucratic character. The resulting system will be cumbersome and without effect on the decision-making process.

From the technical standpoint, analysis must be done before programming, or it will simply produce chains of bulky programmes, very difficult to handle. Any alteration in the chains will entail a considerable amount of work, so that analysts and programmers will spend most of their time adapting the existing programmes to new requirements, without inventing new applications, while the users will be obliged to work with obsolete data. The administrative services, which have to deal with urgent, practical day-to-day problems, will lose confidence, and will set up parallel manual files of their own. The final absurdity will be a doubling of the volume of work with no improvement in performance.

3. Flexibility and future prospects

The constitution of an information system rests on certain assumptions, especially as far as the aims to be achieved by the institution are concerned. If the system is not extremely flexible it can become a factor of resistance to change. After some time, the aims will tend to alter, and the answers supplied by the system will be less apposite; in certain cases, the information provided may even hide the real nature of the problems.

The time has come to provide information which can keep step with the evolution of the university. In preference to a figure for the number of students, for instance, one representing the number of hours' attendance at courses may be adopted. Even this, however, indicates only official performance, and can be used only as a basis for calculating remuneration and floor space. The 'management' figure might be the number of hours of actual contact, which would be obtained only upon enquiry. All such data should be incorporated in a satisfactory system, to meet all conjectures about the future of the institution and its component units.

University authorities who wish to rationalize the decision-making process will therefore take care not to leave the constitution of an information system simply to a team of technicians, as the results might, in the long run, be disappointing or even negative. The information system should enable them to measure the extent to which their aims are being achieved, and only if it does so can it be something more than a means of maximizing the use of resources in the service of objectives which may already be out of date.

4. Choice of methods

The setting-up of an information system is, in a sense, independent of the technical processes employed. Before the computer age, private or public entities recorded information in account books or on card indexes. This material met to some extent at least the requirements of the management. Nowadays, the volume of data needed and the growing complexity of universities argue in favour of the adoption of automated data-processing.

A uniform solution is, however, out of the question. On the contrary, the administrative heads will base any decision on this matter on a cost-benefit analysis comparing the advantages and drawbacks of the traditional methods and of automated data-processing. Such an analysis will take into account the material, human and financial resources which the institution can afford to devote to a data-processing service, the period required for the introduction of the reforms, and the perturbation they will inevitably cause in the functioning of the institution. The decision will have to be based on quantitative and qualitative data. Once taken, it will launch the university administration on a course which can be reversed only with great difficulty.

Section V.2 briefly compares the batch-processing and real-time-processing methods. It describes a method of analysis which takes a number of quantitative factors into account. The reader will note that, in spite of the slightly higher cost, U.C.L. chose the real-time-processing method. Time will show that this choice was justified by qualitative considerations of speed and sureness.

5. Timetable

Each university has different characteristics, and therefore different priorities.

The first step is to appoint a person responsible for the whole operation, constitute an analytical service, decide to allot machine time to the administration, and engage the first members of the staff required to work out the system.

The second step is to consider the required links with the sub-systems and decide on the coding principles and the timetable. The choice of data-processing will be made during this phase, which will also include intensive training of the analysts.

Next, the various sub-systems will be dealt with one by one, according to the university's order of priorities. Section II.4 describes, purely as an illustration, the various stages gone through at U.C.L.

6. Human resources

The formulation of an information system requires good leadership in the administration itself. One person must be invested with the responsibility for co-ordinating the procedures at the systems and methods level.

A variety of talents are needed in the setting-up of an information system. In a first phase, the accent will be on the rationalization of administrative procedures and on data-processing. Those responsible for these operations must have considerable organizing ability, and must be able to secure the assistance of a staff fully qualified in financial, accounting, statistical and computer techniques.

Later on, the application of the first data combinations will require the appointment of one or more psychologists, sociologists and economists. At the management-system stage, operations research techniques will be applied, to enable the relationships between the various phenomena to be identified, the utilization of resources in stock management, for example, to be optimized, and simulations models to be constructed.

The application of modern management techniques demands the constitution of a pluri-disciplinary team. The most difficult problems are those of recruiting, training, leading and lastly keeping the team. The university will have to offer the team members work as varied as they would find elsewhere, at salaries equivalent to the market rate; or else allow confirmed technicians to work for a clearly specified proportion of their time as 'consultants'. Such an arrangement would assure them of an additional income and of contacts with the market enabling them to keep abreast of technological developments. Those heading the team will have to see that the progress of the work undertaken in the university does not suffer from this diversification of effort.

II. The U.C.L. information system

A. Structure of the system

An integrated information system is made up of different parts which are described, for the sake of convenience, as sub-systems.

A possible way of sub-dividing the university institution is according to its academic and administrative structure, but this relatively rigid classification constantly has to be reviewed. It makes no allowance for the increasingly inter-disciplinary character of both teaching and research. Furthermore, the components of the academic and administrative structure pursue different objectives concurrently, and often use common resources. Thus, they frequently use the same data, which should be combined at a higher level. At this point the general flow chart becomes highly complicated, any alterations and up-datings involve laborious work, and the efficiency of the system is impaired accordingly.

A second approach takes account of the chief elements of the university: students, teachers, buildings, research projects, courses, and so on. This gives too fragmentary a picture, and does not allow the necessary combinations to be made. An information system based on such sub-divisions would in fact constitute a collection of separate files. The production of synthesized data would be difficult, and would require much computer-time. This is not a structure geared to decision-making.

Another possibility would be to classify the system according to the activities carried out at the university. While such a sub-division would be logical, it would not necessarily be operational. Often, commitments and expenditure could be attributed to one particular activity only after breakdown and analysis. Such a structure would therefore determine the presentation of the results of data-processing, but not the lines of organization. The complexity of such a system would render it rigid and unable to progress.

The constraints referred to above indicate that the university information system should be divided into a few general categories corresponding to the basic logic of the data. They should, in fact, correspond to the main components of university life.

The distinction between resources committed and activities carried out to achieve the objectives seems to meet the needs more satisfactorily than the compilation of files according to structure, which is always subject to modification, or according to type of activity, which is too heterogeneous.

The university commits those resources over which it has direct control. These include financial, material (buildings and equipment) and human (academic scientific, administrative and technical staff) means. Other resources represent a demand from the outside world. Students belong to this category; they are at one and the same time raw material and product; it is the university's job to assist their development. Many universities make a selection of candidates for registration, and thus influence the 'input', but U.C.L. does not apply such a policy. The students thus constitute a 'demand' element coming from society, and the university has little control over their numbers. It needs to ensure the optimum combination of the factors at its disposal in order to answer this demand. This special position explains the importance which must be attached to the constitution of a students' information sub-system.

The structure of the information system may be summed up as follows:

    Environment
    Inputs
        (1) Staff
        (2) Buildings and equipment
        (3) Financial means
    Outputs
        (4) Activities
    Input and output category
        (5) Students.

This simple structure makes it possible to co-ordinate the administrative activities and collect the data at the source. Broadly speaking, it takes account of the specialization of the administrative services. The routine work requires few comparisons between the different sub-systems, and this gives the whole system great flexibility.

However, the compilation of each file must be planned with reference to the other elements of the system. The file on teaching activities will therefore contain data concerning the teaching staff, students, buildings and equipment, and the financial resources allocated for such activities and for the different courses.

The 'activities' sub-system is less operational than the others, and less directly useful for 'management'. It is, however, more complete, and entails reference to the other parts of the system. It must be planned to fit the authorities' information requirements. Its implementation depends on that of the other sub-systems, and on the decision-making process which is partly based on it.

The 'activities' files must be classified according to the university's aims. Four sets of files may be suggested:
1. *The teaching file* must contain a record of the courses given, details of the teaching dispensed during the period considered, and data allowing the teaching activities to be projected into the future.

2. *The research file* should contain the current research projects, research projects previously conducted, and publications by members of the university.
3. *'Public service' activities*, i.e. refresher courses, lectures, and so on, must also be recorded in a file if the university wishes to have an accurate picture of its contribution to society.
4. *Extra-curricular activities* should be inventoried. Combined with the teaching activities they make it possible, for example, to calculate how the various categories of students spend their time. The full set of data serves as a basis for decisions on academic policy and the reform of curricula.

The structure of an integrated university data system may be graphically represented as in Figure 1.

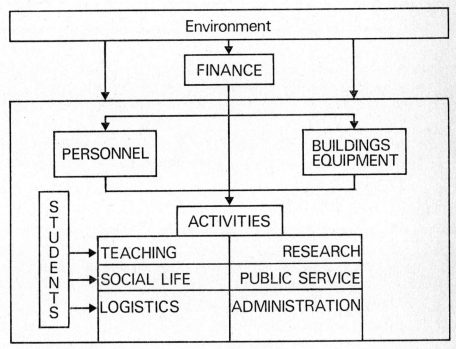

FIGURE 1.   *Structure of an integrated university data system*

It will be noted that the Analytical Unit confines its attention to the university itself, without including the library or the university hospital.

B. Integrated nature of the information system

The integrated nature of the information system is mainly dependent on the following three factors: unified coding system; links between files; and application of PPBS.

1. Unified coding system

All production units (i.e., units consuming and generating resources) were represented by a mnemonic code of not more than four letters, combined with a six-figure numerical code. The mnemonic code permits ease of handling by all concerned (staff, services, students); the numerical code allows all these units to be arranged in a graded structure. In this way, a manageable *structure* of all the production units in the institution is obtained (see Section III).

To this central pivot additional numerical codes are linked, so that the activities going on in the institution can be represented by connecting them to the corresponding production unit (see Section IV). The integration of the various sets of activities is thus implicit in the coding system. On the basis of these key characters, all the elements which go to make up the structure and activities of the institution are identifiable and can be referred to in the files.

The way of obtaining the closest integration would be to set up a data bank, making all the information accessible through the same process, which would permit rearrangement or selection with no further programming. This solution was not applied at Louvain, mainly because the requisite software had not been perfected at the time when the computer system was worked out.

2. Links between files

In the absence of a data base and its management system several files were compiled and an attempt was made to optimize the ratio between the amount of information available (cross-reference between files) and the storage capacity.

The files were as follows:

> elements of structure
> research activities
> study-years
> courses
> students
> budgets (current accounts)
> accounting plan
> personnel
> premises
> equipment
> suppliers

The keys to the first four files being similar, as far as the mnemonic part, representing structure, was concerned, immediate links were available between research, study-years and courses on the one hand, and structure on the other.

Other links between files are obtained by pointers, sometimes with partial duplication of the information (see Figure 2).

Each pointer file can be selected by one of the pointers it contains, and so by the element constituting the key to the file to which it points. Figure 2 shows that:

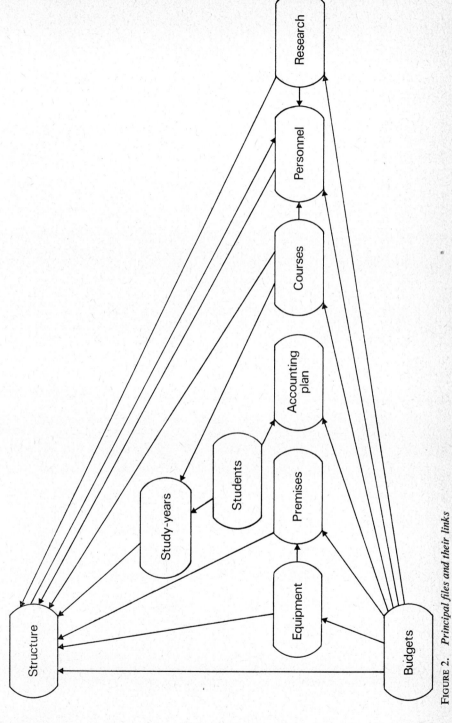

FIGURE 2. *Principal files and their links*

1. All the files can be organized on the basis of the university structure. Courses, study-years, and research are automatically so ordered, given that their keys represent the structure itself. Students are ordered according to years of study. (The accounting plan is a separate structure pursuing a different objective, and the suppliers are not concerned here).
2. The budgets file can be ordered according to any element constituting a key in another file. The various budgets can thus be established by:

   structural element
   item of equipment
   premises
   course
   member of staff (holding an account)
   research activity
   accounting application
   supplier

   Specific problems of analytical accounting can also be solved by additional programming; for example to know the cost of course X in equipment Y, one can select the cross-checks between the budgets allotted to equipment Y and those allotted to course X (see Appendix 6).
3. The links between premises, equipment and students are not clearly revealed; nor are those between budgets and students. This flaw arises directly from the realities of the university system in Belgium. Premises and equipment are linked to teaching activities, that is courses, whereas the students have to register by study-year, which represents a fixed number of courses. For this reason, the automated establishment of the course timetables was not introduced. If the legal concept of study-years was replaced by a more flexible concept of curricula, and students were enrolled per course, not for a set of courses, it would be possible to set up links between students and courses, courses and premises.

   The links between budgets and students also depend on legal constraints. The majority of the university's funds are drawn from State subsidies. These subsidies are granted under several general heads, covering five groups in the academic structure (medicine, veterinary medicine, human sciences, exact sciences, agronomics) and three types of cost (equipment, operating, personnel) according to the number of students enrolled in each of these groups. Financial resources obtained directly from students (registration fees) are attributed to one item in the accounting plan, and each student's financial situation *vis-à-vis* the university is stored in the student file.

   The system as described allows for all the required links between students, personnel, and budgets, within the framework of the structure prescribed by Belgian legislation. In the given context, and with the means available, satisfactory integration was achieved in the U.C.L. information system.

   In a less restricted context, with the advanced software now available, the data of the system would have been controlled like the items in a data bank, with the concept of the file giving place to the concept of the informative element, capable of being handled alone or in conjunction with any other element. Such a sophisticated solution would be valid only for large university complexes; it would, however, secure virtually perfect integration of the institution's various information sub-systems.

3. Application of PPBS techniques

Programme Budgeting is a method of management and decision-making initiated in the U.S. Defense Department and adopted, since 1966, by a number of public bodies. The Planning-Programming-Budgeting-System (PPBS) has several fundamental characteristics:

(a) Overriding importance of objectives. The initial phase of PPBS ignores the existing organizational structure. It concentrates on the definition of the objectives of the institution and its different components, details the measures needed to achieve them, and then fixes the contribution required from each structural unit.

(b) Relationship between measures taken and resources committed. PPBS should make it possible to compare the resources committed with the activities undertaken. Resources should be understood to cover not merely financial resources, but also human and material ones.

(c) Permanent control over a period of several years. If the plans are to retain their interest, they must be kept constantly under review, and the results must be compared with the forecasts. Any departure from the implementation timetable, and any failure to observe the limits, must be at once communicated to the responsible authorities.

(d) Decisive function of analyses. Programme Budgeting is chiefly distinguished by the scope of the systems analyses. The latter take account of the objectives, the alternative approaches, and, in each case, the comparative costs and benefits. The analyses often require the processing of a large stock of information, and its interpretation by quantitative methods.

Programming can be done only after recording and structuring the activities. The thousands of activities pursued in a university have to be grouped by main sectors corresponding to the objectives, and structured at different levels of general application: programmes, sub-programmes and element of programmes.

The programmes constitute a set of activities directed towards the achievement of one of the objectives. Each programme will thus contain activities which are either complementary, or nearly interchangeable in the achievement of the objectives.

Sub-divisions of each programme or sub-programme combine more specific activities directly contributing to the achievement of the programme objectives. The lower level consists of programme elements. Combinations of resources (personnel, buildings, equipment, operating subsidies, etc.) form an integral part of a programme or sub-programme, and have a specific function in this context. The programme elements are assembled to 'furnish' the general structure of the programmes and sub-programmes. Their place in the general structure may sometimes cause certain problems. Some units may be organizationally responsible to a Faculty, for example, but fulfil some of the targets pertaining to another Faculty. The structure of activities should not reproduce the organigram of a university. If the existing situation is seen in perspective, each department's contribution to the achievement of the objectives can be discerned. Duplications or deficiencies in the organization can also be detected. The structure must be exceedingly flexible, so that it can be adapted to any new development in the institution or its environment. The application of PPBS requires complete integration of information concerning the university structure, objectives, resources invested and services expected and obtained. The existence of an integrated information system is thus a condition of the success of a university PPBS. Only the integrated management system can attribute the resources to the thousands of activities and establish links between those activities and objectives assigned to the hundreds of education and research units over time. The integrated management system provides the base needed for analyses, and ultimately for the taking of important decisions.

4. State of the art at U.C.L.

Integration of the information system is effected at the coding stage. This is an operational measure which allows many links to be established between the sub-systems.

The mean computer capacity (128 K) and the rudimentary nature of the software available prevented relations from being established between files by an automated system of pointers. The links are therefore effected through the coding system. The files are, however, so organized that nothing prevents their being adapted later on for more elaborate management software.

At the same time, the inventory of the units and their activities was drawn up in such a way that the objectives of each could be identified, and the management of U.C.L. along PPBS principles could be introduced on a medium-term basis. However, this has not yet been done. Only the first inventory stage has been completed, allowing all the flexibility required for the pursuit of the above objective.

C. Outlines of reform

1. Renovation of the administration

As already stated, the administrative services of U.C.L. were set up between 1967 and 1970. As an illustration, reference may be made to Appendix 1 (page

428), which illustrates the structure of the administration at 1 February 1968 and
1 November 1970. It has obviously expanded.

In addition to the rectorate services and the general administration, account
must be taken of the buildings services (about 60 people), the central clinical
secretariat and the units responsible for the co-ordination of social and cultural
activities. The administrative services have grown over the last two years to keep
pace with the various decision-making bodies at U.C.L., which call upon 39
members with varying frequency: President, Rector, Deans, and so on.

2. Constitution of the analytical unit

The principle of the constitution of an analytical unit was approved by the Bureau
of the U.C.L. Academic Council on 25 October 1967. The first two members of
the unit took up their duties in February and March 1968.

On a long-term view, the work of the Analytical Unit concerns the rationalization of the decision-making process at U.C.L. In a shorter view, its mission is to
improve the existing management techniques at U.C.L. Two-and-a-half years
after their introduction, the Analytical Unit and the data-processing service
employed eighteen people:

    1 head
    2 civil engineers, specialists in industrial management
    1 'business' engineer
    1 civil engineer, specialist in applied mathematics
    2 data-processing specialists
    3 Assembler programmers
    3 Cobol programmers
    1 chief operator
    1 operator
    1 card punch monitor
    2 punch operators.

3. Hardware

The two Louvain universities began operations with one IBM 360/40 and one
IBM 360/44, each of 128 K. The Analytical Unit uses the IBM 360/40, which is
better suited to management applications. It is equipped with 5 magnetic tape
units, 1 card reader-punch and 3 magnetic disc units. In 1971 these units were
replaced by one IBM 2314 to increase the capacity of the disc storage. In 1972
the IBM 360/44 was replaced by a 370/145. An IBM 1050 teletype terminal is
connected to the computer.

The Analytical Unit also has tele-processing equipment connected to the
computer by an IBM 2701. It consists of four IBM 2260 cathode screen terminals
controlled by an IBM 2848 unit.

The Analytical Unit has programmed in Cobol, Fortran, PL_1 and Assembler.
It has also worked out a technique for programme analysis which can be used by

all its members. Analyses and programmes are standardized; the files are drawn up in a standard form which allows them to be consulted by other analysts or programmers.

D. Stages of implementation

The breakdown into sub-systems makes it possible to approach the problems a few at a time, so that gradually an integrated system may be built up.

The following table recapitulates the work of the Analytical Unit. It is by no means set up as a model for the progressive constitution of an information system. In many cases the reorganization of a sub-system is required for special reasons, for instance the interest shown by a head of service in data-processing, the departure of another or the urgent call for statistics needed for policy discussions. The timing will therefore be different in every university, and will reflect each institution's specific demands.

At Louvain, circumstances led us to give priority to the reform of the registration procedure. From 1960 onwards the influx of students' caused a number of problems, and at times the Registrar's office was overwhelmed with work. This meant that thousands of students had to devote several hours to the formalities of registration for studies or for examinations and the productivity of the clerical staff declined as a result of excessive overtime. The Registrar had no solution to offer apart, of course, from the appointment of extra staff, who would have had little to do for long periods at certain times of the year.

The reform of the Registrar's office was carried out in four phases. In 1963 the university improved the amenities for students' registration, to make their wait less irksome. In 1964 the administrative reorganization made it possible to simplify the registration forms and expedite their handling. In 1965 the first mechanized operations were introduced, using four small machines which assembled, sorted, reproduced, and printed the data. This first reorganization enabled the rate of staff recruitment to be reduced, the services of the administration to be improved, and the first Students' file to be constituted. This file was computerized in 1969.

The financial sub-system was the next to be reformed, again in progressive stages. An information system can of course only be planned in successive phases, under an overall plan meeting each institution's specific needs. Each university is a special case. In certain cases some procedures may be useful whereas others may have to be rejected for technical, psychological or administrative reasons. It is not the authors' intention to take the reader through the successive phases of the process at Louvain; he may, however, be interested in the methods used and the long-term objective in view.

Stages of implementation of U.C.L. information system, 1967-70

	Sub-systems					
End of 1967	Adoption of general coding principles and breakdown into sub-systems					
	Activity	Students	Finance	Staff	Buildings	Equipment
June 1968	Inventory of research and teaching units (U.C.L. structure)	First study				
September 1968	Publication of a detailed programme specifying the activities (courses, research, etc.) of each unit (4 Faculties)			Computerization of salary payments		
January 1969			Introduction of new accounting plan			
May 1969			Computerization of budget procedure			
September 1969	Detailed programme for all Faculties	Registration by telephone and tele-processing for 2 Faculties		Integration in the budget		
January 1970	Division of the bilingual data-processing service. Takeover of operations	Utilization of U.C.L. cheques				

[continued overleaf]

345

Stages of implementation of U.C.L. information system, 1967-70 *(continued)*

| Activity | Sub-systems | | | | |
	Students	Finance	Staff	Buildings	Equipment
May 1970		Inception of analysis of the new financial system	Integration into the accounts		
August 1970	Flow model				
September 1970 Form for each course	General introduction of registration by telephone with direct access				
October 1970				Premises file	
November 1970 Introduction of PERT for administrative purposes		Inception of programming of the new system	Inventory by units and publication of list of addresses	Statistics on allocation of premises	

E. Role of the administrative services

1. Responsibility for information

The constitution of an information system renders the administrative services increasingly interdependent. In addition, the mechanization of a large proportion of tasks means that the data-processing unit is the intermediary between the services concerned and the machine. Card-punching, checking and computer handling of the data are potential sources of error, and hence of inter-service conflict.

From the very beginning therefore, one agreed principle of reorganization was that each service should be responsible for the reliability of the data it fed into the computer. This allows for three possibilities in practice:
(a) the service fills in the basic forms for transmission to the card-punch section;
(b) the service handles the card-punching itself, if the volume of operations justifies the full-time use of a card-punch machine;
(c) the service has direct access to the computer.
The third alternative is the best, and this is the one applied by the registration service, which has the use of terminals connected to the computer for several hours each week. Registration staff up-date the information themselves, after which the data-processing service handles it in the appropriate manner.

2. Consultation prior to reform

No alteration is made to existing procedures without prior consultation. Every month the administrative secretaries of the Faculties meet to consider an agenda covering the various projected reforms and the head of the service concerned participates in the meeting. Each reform project is commented on and analyzed, and the minutes of the meeting record the various suggestions made by those present. The following month the item reappears on the agenda, and the amended project is again discussed. After further amendment, if necessary, it is formally adopted, to be put into effect forthwith. This protracted consultation procedure allows the analysts to benefit from the suggestions of the members of the staff with experience of administrative problems, and at the same time it allows the management to form a precise idea of what is needed, and subsequently to convince others of the need to respect the decisions taken.

3. Training of staff

The application of administrative formalities and, in certain cases, the taking of micro-decisions, the introduction of more and more elaborate management methods, the devolution of responsibility and the wide participation in the formulation of reform projects, are all factors which make it essential for the staff to receive appropriate training.

This training should familiarize them with data-processing techniques, particularly with the method of problem analysis worked out in the Analytical Unit. The senior administrators should also be conversant with the content of the data bank and the possibilities and cost of data-processing. Training on these lines is essential if a genuine dialogue is to be established between the administrative services which are the producers and users of the data, and the computer service which is responsible for processing them.

The training may take the form of sessions organized within the university, or of courses arranged by specialized centres in which members of the staff are enrolled. A large part of the training will be acquired 'on the job', that is during the analysis of the problems and the discussion of the reform projects. Throughout this vital phase of the constitution of the information sub-systems, the analysts will take great care never to impose a point of view, especially in technical matters, without informing their hearers of all the reasons behind it. Only by this patient approach can they avoid the ill-feeling provoked by a reorganization prescribed from above. Such a dialogue will allow the administrative staff to become familiar with the technical components of the information system.

F. Technical conditions of success

1. *Coding principles*

To facilitate the identification of the data and of the machine processing, a code has to be adopted, complying with a number of criteria:

univocal character;
legibility;
ease of machine handling, irrespective of the type of machines employed;
flexibility and ease of up-dating;
compatibility with other coding systems;
generalized application, and possibility of referring to other data of the same kind.

These criteria are sometimes contradictory. For instance, the legibility of a code often depends on its length and on the use of letters; but the processing of data expressed in a code of this type will require more computer-time.

The strict application of a single coding system throughout the university makes it possible to integrate the data, use identical media and processing techniques, and finally, constitute a data bank. The Bureau of the U.C.L. Academic Council decided, in September 1968, that 'any proposal for a code, or for the modification of the existing codes, and any transfer of information to the data bank must be submitted to the Analytical Unit for decision'. All codes are kept up to date by the Analytical Unit, and the fact that it processes all the administrative data enables it to have the same coding system applied by all services.

Every sub-system operates with a series of codes identifying the various data, for example types of expenditure and financing services, students and study-years, or buildings and equipment. These items could not, however, be incorporated in a data bank unless they were connected by a common link. The hub of the coding system, and hence of the data bank, is constituted by the 'structure' code, re-representing the organization chart of the university. This four-letter code links up with the codes identifying the activities performed by each unit in U.C.L.'s academic, administrative and social structure.

2 Analysis as a first essential

The name, like the composition, of the U.C.L. Analytical Unit indicates the importance attached to analysis prior to any programming operation. Experience has shown the value of a first investment in analysis. Unless analysis is done the problems are not considered in their entirety, and relationships between files and procedures are taken as given. This approach leads to the juxtaposition of processing sequences which hampers the operation. Furthermore, an efficient management analysis is the basis for an intensive technical analysis. The latter alone can serve as a basis for sub-division of the programmes along the lines best suited to the joint demands of administrative application and computer operation.

3. Modular concept of programming

The success of an information system depends on its flexibility in use and its capacity to adapt to changes in the logic and form of the data. This is the principle which leads the analysts to consider the idea of computer processing, which in fact consists of carrying out arithmetical or logical operations on data recorded in the central processing unit. The results of operations will be included in the same unit, regardless of the source or output of the data. Processing is therefore independent of the configuration of the computers, the compilation of files or the presentation of data.

The flexibility of the system calls for a modular concept of programming. The sub-division of programmes into routine operations of access to the files and processing modules increases their adaptability. A change in configuration, for example, will affect only access to the peripheral equipment. Conversely, a logical correction in processing will leave the structure of the data unchanged. This concept allows a considerable saving in programming time to be made, as a number of modules will be used several times over in a given application. Systems of the OS/360/IBM or SCOPE (CDC) type allow the programmes to be independent of the medium. The use of specialized modules extends this advantage to the compilation of files and access to them.

4. The punched card: an obsolete instrument

The manipulation of punched cards is a considerable source of difficulties, both for programming purposes and for the input of data into the computer.

The adoption of punched cards as a basis for programming offers the temptation of rearranging manually the elements of one active system to form another.

This practice inevitably leads to the cards being put back in their proper order by hand, which is both a source of error and time-consuming. It is therefore preferable to fix the operational processing chains on a magnetic medium, and regard the set of 'files' constituted by them as a fresh information sub-system.

The putting of data on cards involves several preliminary stages:

    answering a questionnaire

    coding the data

    punching the data

    checking on conventional machines

    checking on the computer and listing the errors

    coding the corrected data

    punching the corrected data

    checking the corrected data.

All these tasks, carried out at different times by different people who are not in touch with the source of information, leave room for error at every stage, and entail a lapse of a fortnight to a month between the supplying of the data and the production of results. The risks of loss or destruction of cards or manuscript material which are passed on from one service to another represent a real hazard, which can be considerably reduced by teleprocessing, where

    the data are obtained directly from the source

    checks and corrections are carried out immediately

    the information is available by the end of the day.

The administrative service responsible for keeping the files up-to-date has confidence in the accuracy of the data, as it works with files which reflect the actual position at the time, not with material compiled several days or weeks earlier.

III. The 'structure' file

A. Conception

The 'structure' code represents the general organigram of U.C.L. It constitutes the foundation of the data sub-systems, as activities, appropriations, staff, etc., all come under the same unit, and are therefore identified by the code for this unit. The 'structure' code is the hub around which all the data sub-systems revolve.

The U.C.L. is divided into Faculties, covering groups which represent the major disciplines (history, physics, economics, etc.). The groups are made up of units pursuing more specific objectives, so that there is a three-tier structure. The administrative and social services are built up in the same way.

The U.C.L. structure, like that of other universities, is frequently criticized. The coding system therefore has to be extremely flexible, so as to accommodate eventual modifications without difficulty.

The success of a coding system depends on its adoption not only by the various administrative services involved but also by the academic and scientific staff as a whole, as well as by the students. The first requirement for a code is thus its legibility, even at the expense of the speed of data-processing by machine. The various elements are mnemonically coded, using only letter symbols. Such a coding has the advantage of being both easy to memorize and legible to the uninitiated. In many cases the symbol chosen is already used in the university.

An alphabetical code of not more than four letters was chosen. The classification of the units, groups and Faculties in the non-alphabetical order of the university structure was obtained by translating the four letters into a six-figure code, two figures identifying the element's position in each of the three tiers of the structure. Intervals of two, five or ten places allow new units, groups or Faculties to be inserted into the flow chart. For example:

FACULTY	GROUP	UNIT		
—	—	—		
30	—	—	DROI	Faculty of Law
35	—	—	SESP	Faculty of Econ., Soc. & Polit.
40	—	—	MD	Medicine
45	—	—	FLTR	Faculty of Philosophy & Letters

FACULTY	GROUP	UNIT		
50	—	—	SC	Faculty of Science
	02	—	MATH	Mathematics group
	04	—	PHYS	Physics group
	06	—	CHIM	Chemistry group
	12	—	BOTA	Botany group
		06	CYGE	Cytogenetics unit
		10	ECOV	Plant ecology unit
		15	MOVE	Plant morphology unit
		20	PALY	Palynology unit

The code-books circulated in the various services show only the alphabetical coding. The programme provides for their being printed in 'steps', and combines the heading, code, name of the person in charge and the address of each element in the U.C.L. structure. The lists are issued in alphabetical order of heading, code or name of the person in charge. For example:

ESPO			**FACULTY OF ECONOMICS, SOCIAL AND POLITICAL SCIENCE**
	SESP		*Propaedeutics in economics, social and political science*
	ECON		*Institute of Economics*
		DEMO	Demographic Department
		TRAV	Labour Department
		GRE	Centre for Economic Research
		ANEC	Economic Analysis Unit
	POL		*Institute of Political and Social Science*
		SPOL	Political Science Department
		SSOC	Social Science Department
		SOC	Sociology
		COMM	Social Communications
	ISEA		*Institute of Applied Economics*
		PERF	Centre for Advanced Training in Business Management
	DVLP		*Institute for the Study of Developing Countries*
		DVLS	Social Development Unit
	ACTU		*Institute of Actuarial Science*

One particular unit may be set apart as a reminder in a specific group or Faculty, and marked by an asterisk in the margin. This applies to the inter-disciplinary research centres in several Faculties.

B. Maintenance

The file is periodically up-dated to incorporate new decisions by the authorities. Every month units are set up, disbanded or transferred from one group or Faculty to another.

Several programmes are involved in the up-dating and editing operations. The most important provide for the conversion of numerical codes into alphabetical codes, and vice versa. One of these programmes, known as NUAL, uses a disc whose storage capacity can be varied. The structure can, in fact, be consulted with or without the names of the units. Another programme, NUAK, enables the conversion tables to be recorded on a disc. Up-dating is done by feeding in the whole table. NUAK checks each card, records the data on a disc and prints a message if the card is wrong or doubtful. Once loaded, the table can be used by the NUAL programme which, in turn, gives out error messages in case of inadequate data or erroneous operation.

The structure file is the pivot of the data system; it is consulted in most of the operations already put into the computer, and allows relationships to be established between the data on students, finance, buildings, and so on.

IV. 'Activities' files

A. Activity categories

The components of the university structure may contribute activities of various types. One Faculty, for instance, may include propaedeutics (first-cycle studies), an administrative secretariat, libraries, and so on. All these are covered by the same unit or Faculty, even if a different person is responsible for each activity. The organisation chart of the university has to take account of these sub-divisions, and the U.C.L. activities have therefore been classified in 10 groups.

1 First-cycle education (propaedeutics)
2 Second-cycle education (degrees)
3 Third-cycle education (doctorates, additional degrees, etc.)
4 Fourth-cycle education (refresher courses, etc.)
5 Research
6 Public service (publications, hospitals, consultations, etc.)
7 Social activities (housing facilities, restaurants, theatres, etc.)
8 Logistics (libraries, computing centre, etc.)
9 Administration
0 Non-allocatable.

Each of these groups can be sub-divided; for example:

PSP   Faculty of Psychology and Educational Science
       1O   Propaedeutics
       1M   Propaedeutics tutoring
       1S   Propaedeutics Secretariat.

The thousands of activities dealt with by all the various components of the university structure are identified by a code indicating the 'producer' unit and the activity category. Each activity thus has a coding consisting of the four letters of the 'structure' code, and a coding of four digits.

B. Teaching activities

1. Coding and publication

Teaching activities are organized or contributed to by a specific Faculty or group. They are represented by the symbol of this element of the academic structure, the coding of the appropriate study cycle, and a two-digit number following a numerical sequence; for example:

ECON	2	11	Pure economics
	2	12	Macro-economic analysis
	2	13	Economic analysis: consumption
	2	14	Economic analysis: production and distribution
			etc.

The numbers from 80 to 89 are reserved for the activities classified under the description of 'background teaching'; those from 90 to 99 are reserved for individual work (first-cycle studies, dissertations for a first degree, doctoral theses, etc.).

When a single course is split up because of the excessive number of students attending, the different sections are distinguished by different letters; for example, ECON   214 A.

A start was made with the coding of the 3,300 courses taught in the 10 Faculties and 113 groups in 1968; it was published in the new U.C.L. programme. For each course the following is shown:

the code and name of the course

the professor(s) in charge, deputies, assistants, etc.

an abstract of 75 words covering the purpose of the course and a summary of the compulsory or optional subfects taught

number of hours taken up with theoretical classes, practical classes and seminars, by semester.

study-years, by course.

These various data guide the student's choice of optional courses.

2. Systematizing the file

(a) 'Course' forms

A substantial documentation was built up in 1970. A form was worked out for each course, synthesizing the chief data (see Appendix 2, page 429). The file is held in the Rectorate and each Faculty has at the least the part of the file relating to the courses it organizes. The availability of this information enables the decision-making procedure for teaching activities to be reorganized. The Faculty wishing to make an alteration to a teaching activity uses the 'course' form, which provides for different possibilities of modification.

The decision is based on the data contained in this form, after reference to the competent services. No alterations are made to the curriculum or timetable by any other procedure. This innovation simplifies the formalities involved and throws more light on the administration of the teaching side, which hitherto was not based on full and accurate information.

(b) The basic file
The introduction of a new course is subject to the decision of the Faculty Council and the Bureau of the Academic Council. The same applies to any modifications made to the number of hours, the name of the course, the established teacher in charge.

The same is true for the constitution or modification of a degree-course programme and in such cases the data composing the basic file, which did not in fact become operational until the end of 1971, are reviewed.

3. Utilization

From the teaching activities file the Analytical Unit can draw up:
> (i) List of teaching activities, showing number of hours and number of auditors:
>> by cycle, group and Faculty
>> by teacher
>> by teaching method
>> by scientific discipline
>> by study-year and degree (curricula) without reference to facilities used (timetable)
> (ii) List of appropriations
>> by teaching activity, cycle, group and Faculty
>> by type of expenditure
>> by scientific discipline and cycle.

At the end of 1971 the findings of a survey on teachers' work schedules enabled accounts to be prepared in standard cost per course hour, by discipline, teaching method, etc.
> (iii) Number of auditors per teaching activity
>> Note: The 'evaluation' and 'non-budgetary decisions' files have not yet been compiled.

C. Research activities

It is U.C.L.'s policy to promote research, and the limited resources which it can invest in this field make it essential to have data describing the activities pursued in the various scientific disciplines by the 150 or so research units. These data are published annually in the University programme; after being combined in one way or another, they also serve as a basis for the analyses and decisions of the academic authorities. At the present time the Analytical Unit has one file containing the coding and names of the activities, and data relating to those taking part in the 1,300 or so research activities. The file is up-dated at the beginning of each academic year.

New research activities are introduced upon the decision of the unit responsible, provided that they are approved in principle by the Faculty or academic authorities. A questionnaire is completed by the sponsor, which serves as the base document for punching the cards which constitute the main file. There may be from 5 to 44 cards:

> 1 master card
> 1 to 3 cards on 'name of research activity'
> 1 to 20 cards on 'summary of research activity'
> 1 to 15 cards on 'participants'
> 1 to 5 cards on 'programme for the year'.

After processing, the basic file consists of:

> *(i) Identification file*
>> The items contained in this file define the research activity and the resources allocated to it.
>>> type of research and scientific discipline
>>> name and summary of research activity (with key words) participants, premises, equipment and appropriation.

> (ii) *Decisions file*
>> Provides the authorities with the basic information needed to take decisions both as to the contributions anticipated or promised and the resources employed:
>>> record of decisions taken about the unit
>>> appropriations requested and obtained
>>> programme for the year
>>> evaluation criteria (publication, doctorates, citations, external funds, etc.)
>>> five-year forecasts of staff, facilities, equipment and appropriations.

> (iii) *Results file*
>> Contains data indicating the 'production' of the research unit for the constitution of a file to be communicated, upon request, to the experts periodically required to express an opinion on the functioning of a given unit:
>>> titles and summaries of studies made (with key words)
>>> references of publications, patents, etc.
>>> index of extracts from publications
>>> authors
>>> coding of the scientific discipline.

The U.C.L. Analytical Unit can make available to the academic authorities or researchers, upon request (Items 1 and 4 have already been compiled):

1. List of research activities by unit, group or Faculty. This includes only the coding and names of the activities.
2. List of research activities, by type of research
3. Summary of research activities:

> by member of the academic or scientific staff concerned
> by unit
> (by scientific discipline)
>> National Science Foundation code
>> U.C.L. key-words.

4. List of appropriations for research activities:
   > by activity, unit, group or Faculty
   > by type of research
   > by type of expenditure
   > (by scientific discipline)
5. List of external financing
6. List of participants, by activity or research unit
7. List of results (publications, patents):
   > by research activity
   > by unit
8. Research programme for the coming year, by research activity
9. By scientific discipline
   > inventory of research and teaching activities, to compare the conjunction of efforts in both fields.

D. Social activities

The approach adopted to identify the U.C.L.'s social activities differs from that used for teaching and research activities. The aims pursued by the various units of the U.C.L. social structure are far more easily identifiable than those of the teaching and research units.

Code 7 is reserved for activities of the social structure units, each of which is assigned a coding which corresponds to the objective in view. The code can be sub-divided into programmes.

7.1 *Social aid*
    7.1.1   Individual aid
    7.1.2   Collective aid
    7.1.3   Co-operative services
    7.1.9   Support
7.2 *Hostels and accommodation*
    7.2.1   U.C.L. 'open' residences
    7.2.2   U.C.L. 'closed' residences
    7.2.3   Non-U.C.L. residences
    7.2.4   Accommodation in private homes
    7.2.5   Student initiatives
    7.2.6   Integration of commuters
    7.2.9   Support
7.3 *Restaurants*
    7.3.1   U.C.L. restaurants catering for a general clientèle
    7.3.2   U.C.L. restaurants catering foɪ a specific clientèle

7.3.3 Non-U.C.L. restaurants
7.3.5 Student initiatives
7.3.9 Support

7.4 *Educational and vocational guidance*
7.4.1 Data on secondary-school pupils
7.4.2 Guidance of secondary-school pupils
7.4.3 Relations with heads of secondary schools
7.4.4 Data on students
7.4.5 Consultation with students
7.4.7 Employment bureau
7.4.9 Support

7.5 *Health and sports*
7.5.1 Physical health
7.5.2 Mental health
7.5.3 Medico-social assistance
7.5.5 Sports (generally practised)
7.5.6 Sports (teams and clubs)
7.5.9 Support

7.6 *Cultural and leisure-time activities*
7.6.1 Drama
7.6.2 Music and fine arts
7.6.3 Cinema and photography
7.6.4 Literature
7.6.5 Press and communications media
7.6.6 Recreation
7.6.7 Reception and guidance centre
7.6.9 Support

7.7 *Students' associations and social commitment*

7.8 *Reception and guidance of foreign students*
7.8.1 Social assistance
7.8.2 Residential accommodation and lodgings
7.8.3 Restaurants
7.8.4 Guidance
7.8.5 Health and sports
7.8.6 Cultural activities
7.8.7 Reception and guidance
7.8.8 Language classes
7.8.9 Support

7.9 *General support*
An all-round centre like 'Placet', which offers various facilities for students, will thus be assigned different codings:
PLAC
      7 21 University residence
      7 32 Restaurant open to the public
      7 61 Functioning of the university theatre
      7 66 Recreation
      7 82 Proportion of costs of residence attributable to the presence of foreigners (vacations)
      7 90 Support (secretariat, management).

E. Administrative activities

The inventory of administrative activities is established at two levels. Firstly, one file of activities is constituted which indicates the allocation of responsibility —a very limited file made up on the same lines as the file of teaching and research activities. This is included in the U.C.L. syllabus in order to inform the members of the university about the Administration's activities and the responsibilities of cach service. In addition, the expenditure incurred by each service is itemized by activities, so that the cost of the latter can be calculated.

A much more detailed inventory is at present being drawn up. This serves as the basic file for the application of the Critical Path Method (CPM), one variant of which is known as the Programme Evaluation and Review Technique (PERT). This method is based on the detailed analysis of the tasks to be performed in relation to a given objective, for example, the submission of the university budget. The data relevant to each task are fed into the computer, which maps out the critical path of operations and indicates the 'sensitive' stages where the time required for implementation is longer than or equal to the period allowed.

The Analytical Unit has added three elements to the programme supplied by the I.B.M. library. The first is the use of the 'BETA' distribution to calculate the average duration of an activity, based on the weighted average of three estimated durations for each job. The coefficient 1 is applied to the pessimistic and optimistic estimates, and the coefficient 4 to the middle estimate. After aggregating the data for each job, and dividing by 6, the computer calculates the aggregate number of days needed for a given activity. The second programme calculates the probabilities of accomplishing the sequence of activities along the critical path. The third programme prints the list of the jobs to be performed by each person, specifying the time required in working days and the operations prior or subsequent to the start or finish of each job.

The CPM was first applied to the analysis of budget and nominations procedures for 1971/72. It has the advantage of delimiting responsibilities and of obliging each head of service to take the many implications of each activity into account sufficiently far ahead. Furthermore, it provides the heads of administration with an excellent instrument of co-ordination. It is thus possible to consider the results not merely as a file of administrative activities, but also as the beginning of a management system.

V. 'Students' information sub-system

The 'students' sub-system is of paramount importance in a university information system. Of the five systems, the 'students' sub-system and the research activities file are the hardest to analyze, compile and keep up to date. The former is also one of the most useful and interesting, as full, prompt information about the student population provides the only possibility of choosing the optimum combination of the resources to be employed in a university.

A. Aims

1. Speed and efficiency of registration procedures

The registration formalities represent the student's first contact with the university, and determine its image in his eyes. Considerations of human relations and public service are reinforced by the need to eliminate sources of conflict between the administration and the students. The time spent in waiting and in complying with formalities has to be reduced to the strict minimum.

2. Saving of time and staff

Reorganization of the registration procedures should lead to a reduction in the numbers employed, or at least a drop in the rate at which new staff is appointed.

3. Improving the supply of information to the authorities

Scarcity of information makes the formulation of an academic policy a difficult matter. If statistics on registration numbers and examination results are not produced promptly, the authorities are not equipped to take informed decisions. The rationalization of registration procedures increases the reliability of the basic data, and consequently of the information given to the academic authorities.

4. Appraisal of results

The administration's role is not confined to taking decisions and carrying them out. Supervision and review also form part of the administrative process, and involve the delicate problem of the university's 'productivity'. The success of a study programme, for instance, must be judged not merely from the examination results, but also from the students' development. This entails the study, among other things, of the characteristics of the university population, student 'cultures' and changes in students' behaviour during and after their period at the university. The evaluation of university activities calls for a considerable amount of data, and the need for rapid access to it and the complexity of the processing call for the application of the most up-to-date techniques.

5. External uses

Information on students is essential for any study of the intellectual resources and economic development of a given country or region or sector of industry or trade. In addition, the data produced by the university administration must answer the requirements of the government bodies concerned with higher education.

6. Preparing for the future

The switch to a three- or four-term year entails registrations being accepted three or four times a year. The registration period will therefore have to be curtailed so as not to be spread out over a whole term. Furthermore, the countless alternatives open to students will shortly necessitate registration for each separate course, not merely for each year of study. The adoption of the credit system has increased the volume of data to be handled, and the university is obliged to have the 'students' data machine-processed by a large computer.

When the 'students' sub-system is planned, the team of analysts must therefore look beyond the present situation, and predict future developments; otherwise their efforts may prove worthless if a few years after the introduction of the new system, they are outpaced by events.

B. Stages of the reorganization process

It was considered useful to provide the reader with the timetable of the stages in the 'students' information sub-system, which, initiated in 1968 by the Analytical Unit, reached a very refined level by the end of 1970. In years to come it should be enriched by data on the careers of former U.C.L. students, course by course enrolments, and the marks given by each examiner, as well as data on the cultural and psychological profiles of the students, before, during and after their university period.

1968

July and August	Coding of courses and study-years
Sept. to Dec.	Recording the curriculum on punch cards

1969

January	Allocation of alphabetical code
February	Incorporation of existing data
March	First implementation of the registration procedure for examinations
July	Storage of results and distribution to users
August	Registration for the second examination sessions
September	Registration of new students
	Tele-processing of student registrations for Law and Applied Science (2,000 students)
End Sept. & beg. Oct.	Storage of results of the second session
15th October	Registration of existing students completed
	Production of certificates, etc.
	First attempt at automated information for examiners' meeting

1970

January	Reminder of payments due
March	Registration for first examination sessions
June	Production of statistics on examination results
	Production of statistics on students' socio-economic background
August	Complete automation of processing of data on new students
September	Registration of new students
	Tele-processing of registrations of all students already in the university
November	Completion of reorganization of registrations by study-year
December	Second trial of automated processing of an examiners' meeting

1971

July	Automated processing of examiners' meeting for 800 students
October	Trial registration by course of 500 students.

C. Registration at U.C.L.

1. The Belgian registration system

In Belgium, the students select a discipline upon entering the university. The rigidity of the system may be regrettable, but the analysis has to respect it, while preserving the possibility of introducing greater flexibility later on. In certain cases, the subjects which can be taken during each study-year are prescribed by law. This is so for Law, Medicine, Pharmacy, Applied Science, Philosophy and Humanities, and Science. For disciplines or special courses not covered by the State regulations, the university itself decides in which subjects teaching will be provided. Under this system, the student's choice of courses is very restricted.

Each year, he registers for a set of courses, and not for each course separately. The student has to register for optional courses in the Faculty or Institute concerned. The mechanization of these operations will therefore represent a second stage in the process.

To obtain a degree, the student has to pass the examinations held at the end of each year first of all in a two- or three-year propaedeutics course, and next in a two-, three- or four-year 'second-cycle' course. The first examination sessions are held in June-July each year, with a second session in September for students who failed the first. The student has to pass the examinations held at the end of one year's course before he can register for the next, unless granted a special dispensation.

2. Admission system

Any holder of a secondary-education certificate is admitted to the university, and only the Applied Science Faculty holds an entrance examination for the selection of candidates. The university thus practises an 'open door' policy, applying a selection procedure to foreign students alone.

Consequently, a 'students' sub-system does not need to take account of the 'admission' stage. Furthermore, the student's past performance is not a factor which affects his chances of being registered, provided he possesses a certificate awarded by a secondary school. The same applies to admission to the second cycle of studies; any student holding a first-cycle diploma from a Belgian institution is automatically admitted to another institution in the same discipline.

3. U.C.L. Registrar's office

Up to 1968 the same service was responsible for collecting information on the students in both the French and the Flemish universities, but after the two were split up an entirely new French-speaking staff had to be appointed; the new service, free from tradition, was able to operate on completely new lines from the outset.

In 1970 the Registrar's office employed a director assisted by a secretary, and was mainly concerned with the selection of foreign students. The actual registration service had a staff of five to handle the operations relating to 14,000 students.

Despite its small staff, the service is responsible for registering students for university courses and examinations, keeping the 'Student' accounts up-to-date, issuing certificates, circulating lists, and so on. In addition, the head of the service has the job of keeping up to date and publishing the curricula and timetables of U.C.L. courses. All forms relating to the administration of the teaching side pass through his hands.

The service has the assistance of three punch operators lent by the data-processing service during the registration period.

D. Organization of data

Before any reorganization of the processing procedures was initiated, an inventory was drawn up of the data required by the administrative services and decision-making bodies of U.C.L., and by the government organizations concerned with the universities. The complete list of information relating to students is of little interest here, as it corresponds to the specific needs of each university, but the method employed to identify the relevant information may merit some attention.

The sub-system must contain the information needed to pursue the various aims of the university and to assess the extent to which they are achieved. It must meet the needs of the authorities and the operational requirements of the various services. The structure of the sub-system must be planned with a view to the distribution of information. The analysis will have to work out the information procedures from the source of supply right through to the user: on this logical basis, an inventory of availabilities and requirements can be taken.

The sub-division is made according to the functions to be performed, the information required and the way it is to be communicated. This approach is not, however, satisfactory from the operational standpoint. As soon as the university is open to receive registrations, the various channels are simultaneously supplied with new information; in actual fact, many services must be provided with the same information or data from varying sources. Accordingly, in practice, the different channels will be integrated in a general flow chart.

The procedures will have to comprise at least one stage for the recording and processing of data between their collection and communication; this corresponds to the constitution of the files. This stage has to be organized according to the type of data. The analysis will therefore make up 'information groups' based on criteria of autonomy, coherence and fulness of the data supplied. The information groups will have the advantage of reducing duplication, linking the most active sources of information and grouping data showing certain similarities. They must, in addition, largely satisfy the needs of the management and of the services concerned, otherwise the various components of the university will prefer traditional methods. The management of the administrative services must be so planned as to maximize the efficiency of the flows; this requires the complete remodelling of the information circuits and the formulation of modification procedures.

1. Information groups

The most logical structure for the 'students' data handled by the U.C.L. administrative services provides for nine separate information groups:

(a) Selection documents

The selection procedure applies exclusively to foreign students, and it has not so far proved necessary to incorporate such documents in a 'students' information system. In any event, all students have to comply with the registration formalities.

(b) Registration documents

The information collected from registrations has to be broken down. Mention should be made of the courses followed by each student. This will enable the function of the optional course to be reassessed, and account to be taken of the 'pre-requisites', or compulsory courses to be followed before any registration is permitted for a more advanced course. The detailed data relating to registrations for courses allow the composition of the study programmes and the links between the different disciplines to be analyzed. They provide the basis for projections of staff requirements and buildings with sufficient accuracy to guide the decisions affecting the future of the institution.

The data concerning the socio-economic origins of the students should be included in the university data bank. The same applies to the results of any psychological tests which new students may be required to take. In short, any data which add further details to the general picture of the student population and its activities in the university should be added to the store of information.

(c) Historical data

The students' examination results are an important element of any university data bank; the statistics to be obtained from them may be considered among the most useful. They can provide the academic authority with some idea of the relative value of the different institutions from which the students are drawn, the difficulties encountered by students from different socio-economic backgrounds, the impact of different methods of teaching, and so on. The historical file is a compendium of all the annual files, and is printed each year.

(d) Address file

Any change of address involves an alteration in the U.C.L. file, from which a number of lists are compiled and supplied to the various administrative services.

(e) Accounting information

An account has to be opened in each student's name, showing his financial position vis-à-vis U.C.L. as regards registration fees, attendance fees, fines, acknowledgements of indebtedness, guarantee deposits, and rentals. This enables the university to keep track of defaulting students. Furthermore, access to such information will facilitate the introduction of a loan system, and the admittance to the university of students from new social strata.

(f) Information on extra-curricular activities

This information group is hard to constitute, as the many social and cultural services in the university pursue a variety of objectives. The information should be marshalled under two main headings: first, the financial assistance granted to students, and secondly, the division of students' time among different social and cultural activities.

The university has not hitherto felt responsible for the social and cultural development of its students and it therefore holds little information on the subject.

(g) Medical and health insurance documents

Results of medical examinations, X-ray examinations, and so on, should be included in the data bank, but up to now this comparatively simple information has not been collected, owing to shortage of staff.

(h) Information on courses and curricula

The whole programme of courses should be fed into the computer, as direct access to such data is an essential condition for carrying out an immediate check as to whether the data collected at the time of registration are correct. In addition, the data in this group allow some cross-references between the 'students' sub-system and the 'staff' sub-system. This information group forms the basis of the file of university teaching activities, and thus plays a vital part in the university information system. Its input into the computer is at present under study.

(i) Timetable of courses

This information group provides a link between the 'students', 'staff', 'buildings-equipment' and 'teaching activities' information sub-systems.

The preparation of the timetable of courses was taken over by the joint university body in 1970; it still decides any problems which may arise in connection with the use of lecture-rooms as between the two universities. The current procedure is entirely manual. The person in charge resolves any difficulties about fitting in students' with teachers' timetables, but has not yet attempted to optimize the use of the facilities.

2. Information flows

The sub-systems are based on the essential data required for the achievement of the University's aims. In planning the information flows, one must take account of the essential functions to be fulfilled by the university and by each of its components. The flow procedures may, in fact, be regarded as special systems set up to collect, record, process and communicate the 'students' information, thus taking it right the way through from source to user.

Several services are sources of 'students' information. The U.C.L. secretariat keeps the information collected during the selection procedures, and part of the data collected at the time of registration. Information concerning housing accommodation is held by the Social Centre and the Women's University Centre; Social Security is handled by a Government Department; the Institute of Physical Education is responsible for arranging medical and X-ray examinations. The Social Centre keeps individual data concerning students holding scholarships from the State or from U.C.L. The secretariats of Faculties and Institutes store an appreciable volume of data, in particular examination markings. They regularly remit the overall results for each session and each study-year. Lastly, a research centre collects and records information concerning the socio-economic origin of new students.

The consumers of 'students' information are still more numerous. In the last resort, it may be supposed that every element in the U.C.L. academic or administrative structure must be in possession of information about the students, although requirements differ widely. The sub-system will therefore be based on a reorganization of the information flows between the source and the consumer.

Information flows must allow for new requirements of data. New methods of university administration demand a growing mass of facts, ordered in very specific ways. The application of Programme Budgeting techniques involves the collection of new information. The management of the University must, in fact, have data for each programme element in order to measure the extent to which aims have been achieved. It may be a matter of student numbers, contact-hours between students and teachers, degrees and certificates awarded, student attrition rate, and so on; but it may also be a matter of information obtained to assess the development of the student's personality. The purpose of the university is not merely to produce graduates, but to provide society with well-balanced people, capable of dealing with problems, able to cope with ideas, develop innovations and apply new techniques. The 'students' data bank should therefore contain certain information collected in the course of tests and interviews, not merely at initial registration, but also when the student leaves the University, and even later. Despite the weaknesses of psychological testing, only such information can enable the management of the University to gauge the influence of various study programmes or teaching methods.

The information flows may be classified as follows:

A. Information sub-system
  1. Students

  2. Finance

  3. Buildings & equipment

  4. Staff
  5. Activities
    Teaching
    Social life

    Research
    Public service

B. Decision-making process

'*Students*' *flows*
1. Selection
2. Registration
3. Addresses
4. Accounting and financial data
5. Fellowships and financial assistance
6. Allocation of lecture rooms
7. Libraries (considered as scientific equipment)
8. Planning requirements of facilities
9. Planning staff requirements

10. Registration for examinations
11. Cultural activities
12. Medical and mutual insurance services
13. Employment of students
14. Psychological consultation
15. Housing service

16. Associations of former students

17. Communication of information to the decision-making bodies and transmission of decisions to the various elements of the academic, administrative and social structure (statistics, forecasts).

By the end of 1970 the only information flows to have been radically reorganized were those for registrations, addresses, accounting and financial services and registration for examinations.

3. *Coding of data*

a. *Student's registration number*

The student should be identified by a number which facilitates the retrieval and production of data. Several alternative solutions were considered.

National number	9 characters
Registration number of the	
National Council on Science	
Policy (C.N.P.S.)	
Initials of surname and first name	2 letters
Sequential number	4 digits
	6 characters
Number in the U.C.L. register,	
with prefix indicating the year of first registration	7 digits
Alpha-numerical number	
Position in the alphabet	4 digits
Year of first registration	2 digits
Sequential number	2 digits
	8 digits
Existing number in 1968	
Year of first registration	2 digits
Secondary school attended	4 digits
Sequential number	3 digits
	9 digits

Each method has its advantages and its drawbacks. The present registration number enables statistics to be compiled on the schools supplying the students, and provides a continuity link with the existing documentation. However, the registration of students presents some difficulties; there are wide gaps in the sequence; the length of the number is a source of errors, and makes its oral transmission more difficult.

The U.C.L. registration number is specific and sequential and the series cannot fail to be dense. Attribution is easy, and in fact automatic. Nevertheless, the U.C.L. registration number does not correspond to any useful order. Like the present registration number, it does not allow of automatic alphabetical classification; research in the historical file means going through an alphabetical index which has to be re-made every year.

The constitution of an alpha-numerical series eliminates alphabetical sorting and facilitates research in the historical file; but machine alphabetical classification can never be perfect.

The registration number issued by C.N.P.S. allows of inter-university comparisons; there will, however, be some delay in communicating it, and it cannot always correspond to a strictly alphabetical order.

The number in the national file affords the advantage of having been issued before entrance to the University; it also allows of inter-university comparisons; but unfortunately, this system is not yet operational.

The students' information system will have to provide for the insertion of the national registration number, and will also have to introduce an alpha-numerical series facilitating alphabetical classification. The U.C.L. registration number is of interest only for the accounting system, but it can, perhaps, be used pending the availability of the national number. In view of these considerations, the alphanumerical method was chosen, the number being automatically issued by the computer.

2. 'Study-year' code

U.C.L. students are admitted to about 690 different study-years, the latter being identified by the 'structure' code with the addition of two digits. The first indicates the study cycle, and the second the year in the cycle. One letter may be added to this 6-place code to distinguish between the streams or sections of a single study-year. For example:

PHYS 11 Propaedeutic course in physics
        (first year of the first physics cycle)
HIST 22 Second degree in history
        (second year of the second history cycle).

The grid of the possible alternatives in a single group or Faculty is as follows:

First cycle	*Second cycle*	*Third cycle*
10 General study	20 General study	30 General study
11 1st year	21 1st year	31 1st year
12 2nd year	22 2nd year	32 2nd year
13 3rd year	23 3rd year	33 1st year doctorate
14 4th year	24 4th year	34 2nd year doctorate
15 test for 2nd cycle	25 qualifying exam. for doctorate or "actuariat"	35 specialization
16 graduation	26 graduation	36 —
17 "Agrégation" lower sec. educ.	27 "Agrégation" higher sec. educ.	37 "Agrégation" higher education
18 single test qualif. course	28 single test degree	38 —
18 addit. qualif. course (C, K or Z)	28 addit. degree	38 —
	29 mémoire or thesis	39 mémoire or thesis

    N.B. 05 Propaedeutics test
           07 "Agrégation" for primary education

E. Registration procedure

1. *Principles of organization*

The registration of students is a race against time and there are frequently bottle-necks during the registration period and during the examination sessions:
Reception capacity for students (queues)
Coding of data
Punch-recording and checking data
Up-dating the files in the computer, after checking.
Data can be fed into the computer either by batch processing or by remote processing in real time. The latter method was chosen, for the following reasons:
1. Punching and part of the coding operations are eliminated by the use of terminals.
2. An instant check can be made of the data on the computer, and an error message sent at once, if necessary.
3. There is automatic control of verisimilitude, allowing relatively unskilled temporary staff to be employed.
4. Registration by telephone is possible, avoiding congestion in small offices, while nevertheless allowing direct contact with the student.
5. Day-to-day access to the computerized data, whereas batch processing entails long delay. The accounting system provides an example.

2. *Comparative cost of batch processing and real-time processing*

The annual consumption of computer time for the 'Students' system in real time is made up of 310 hours of production (issue of examination cards, compilation of statistics, printing lists and labels, payments, reminders, etc.) and 130 hours when the terminals are linked to the computer during the registration period. This link is also maintained during the 310 hours of production, and allows all the necessary updating to be made to the 'Students' file. The teleprocessing of data on students does not exclude the execution of other jobs; on the contrary, the pro-grammes are planned with multi-programming in view. The speed of execution of other work is slowed down by only about 10 per cent. The cost of teleprocessing is thus $\frac{(310 + 130)}{10}$ hours, equivalent to 44 computer hours.

The batch processing method would not require the terminals to be linked to the computer, but would demand more computer time, as the configuration of the computer would not permit either multi-programming or the immediate correction of errors. First, the time needed for execution would have to be charged entirely to the 'Students' system, whereas, at present, processing-operations, for example, can be carried out while the terminals are linked to the computer. Secondly, the number of machine runs would be increased by the need to correct errors detected during the initial execution. Lastly, teleprocessing eliminates the printing of some lists, and card reading and punching, which demand a good deal of computer time. With the present configuration, then, teleprocessing allows a saving in computer time which it is hard to quantify accurately. It is therefore assumed, for the sake of clarity, that the consumption of computer time is the same with both methods of data input.

The 'take-off' period was completed at the end of 1970. From 1971 onwards the analysts have needed much less time to complete operations which have become routine.

A comparison between the cost of the system in lot processing and in real time gives the following results.

Cost in a period of normal operation (1971)

	Batch processing		Real time	
	Man-months	B.Frs.	Man-months	B.Frs.
Analysts	1	38 000	1	38 000
Programmers	3	97 000	3	97 000
Operators	6	132 000	4	88 000
Key punchers	6	90 000	1	15 000
Clerks	96	2 450 000	84	2 306 000
Students employed	—	501 000	—	397 000
Equipment	—	125 000	—	1 088 000
Operating costs	—	230 000	—	205 000
Computer time	350 comp. hrs.	1 050 000	350 comp. hrs.	1 050 000
TOTAL		4 713 000		5 284 000
Per student	B.Frs.	344.05	B.Frs.	383.23
	US$	8,00	US$	8,91

The expenditure per student can thus be estimated at Frs. 380 or about US $ 8,91 per year, which does not include the cost of occupying the facilities. This expenditure is largely met by the B.Frs. 500 disbursed by the students each year as registration fees; it covers all the operations relating to the 'Students' sub-system (registration, certificates, examinations, lists, statistics, labels, accounting, etc.).

3. Advantages of real time processing

For equivalent or even lower cost, the adoption of real time processing is greatly preferable for many reasons:

(a) Independence of the U.C.L. secretariat
The direct linking of the U.C.L. secretariat with the computer frees it from the necessity of keeping contact with the analytical, programming and punch operation services. It is entirely responsible for the reliability of the data, but does not

have to depend on intermediaries for access to the information. Teleprocessing thus eliminates the sources of friction frequent in long chains of data transmission.

(b) Improved service provided for students
The adoption of the principle of registration by telephone eliminates the long queues which are a feature of the registration procedure in many universities, and the U.C.L.'s image is improved as a result.

(c) Prompt availability of information
The transmission of data for batch processing delays the up-dating operations. The accounting system provides a typical example On the other hand, there have never been any complaints from users of the 'Students' system.

4. Choice of hardware

(a) Type of terminal
U.C.L. has an IBM 360/40 computer, and the choice of terminals is thus restricted to IBM 1050 or 2740 and IBM 2260. The first two present the information on paper with a printing device; the 2260 uses a cathode-ray tube to throw it on to a screen very similar to a television screen.
The second alternative was chosen, for several reasons:
1. Speed of transfer of the data (14.8 characters/second with a printing device, compared with 120/characters/second with the cathode-ray tube).
2. Logic of the processing system. The information is processed in batches of characters with the 2260, and sequentially (character by character) with the 1050 and 1740. The 2260 requires fewer question-answer messages, and thus permits a higher processing speed to be attained.
3. Rental of telephone lines. The slow transfer of the characters necessitates renting one telephone line for each 1050 terminal, whereas a single line can, in theory, serve up to 48 terminals of the 2260 type.
4. Rental cost. The cost of hiring is lower for the 2260 terminal than for the 1050 whenever the system requires more than 6 terminals.
5. Working conditions. The 2260 is completely silent; the printing device of the 1050 is very noisy.

(b) Processing time
Assuming the use of cathode ray tube terminals, the processing time for one registration is estimated at 135 seconds, covering:
1. The time needed to type on the keyboard an average number of characters, based on a speed of 1.5 characters per second.
2. The time needed to process three or four messages per student registration, comprising the following phases:
      automatic terminal-computer linkage
      transit and recording of the input message
      any waiting time in the input work queue

processing the message
recording and waiting time in the output work queue
connection and returning the answer to the terminal.
These 2 minutes and 15 seconds make no allowance for conversation time between the operator and the student; in practice, the average time needed for the dialogue and recording is 3 minutes.

(c) Number of terminals

The adoption of teleprocessing techniques enables the coding and checking operations to be speeded up, but the manual introduction of the data forms a bottleneck in the processing chain. The capacity of the system depends on the type and number of data-input units.

The choice of the type and number of terminals depends, first, on the volume of information to be transmitted over a given period, and secondly, on the processing time needed for the information contained in each message. The volume of information to be collected for each student is fairly constant and can therefore be expressed in number of student registrations. The relationship between these different variables may be set out as follows:

$$x = k \frac{N. \, t}{J. \, H. \, 60}$$

where x is the number of terminals required
  N the number of students to be registered
  t the processing time per student (in minutes)
  J the number of days in the registration period
  H the number of working hours per day
  k a coefficient taking account of the non-uniform distribution of telephone calls.
As k has a value of 2 and H a value of 5:

$$x = 2 \frac{7,000 \times 3}{30 \times 5 \times 60} = 4.5 \text{ terminals.}$$

F. Registration of new students

The registration formalities for new students differ from those for students already enrolled in the following respects:
  a larger quantity of information has to be collected
  a registration number has to be allocated
  new items have to be recorded in the 'Students' file.
New students have to attend the University in person for an identity check.
  A sequential registration number, to identify the student, is allocated on a pre-punched card. The student completes two forms, one for optical scanning which groups the information required for the sociological survey, the other

recording all other information. The forms are memorized on a card-data carrier, and stored by the computer within a fortnight. After the initial loading, their processing requires no further action by the card-punching service, and follows the sequence of students already registered.

G. Registration procedure by telephone

The student who is already a member of the university gives the telephonist his registration number, surname and first name. These data are conveyed by the terminal to the computer, which sends back for checking the registration number, surname and first name, home address, civil status, nationality, and coding of the proficiency diploma. The telephonist reads the information, enquires about any changes to be made, and puts it into the computer storage. The computer throws on to the screen the courses attended by the student the year before, and his results. The student states the main and secondary subjects for which he wants to be enrolled for the new academic year, and any reductions in fees he is entitled to. After storage of these data, the computer confirms their reception, checks the accuracy of the data and calculates the amount to be paid by the student.

All new information is stored on a magnetic disc, and transferred to a sequential file recapitulating the day's operations. This file represents a precaution against loss of information, and is used to produce the printed records at the end of the day.

The accounting data take note of the operations connected with the registration formalities; registration fees, attendance fees and examination fees, and so on. The student may point out that he is entitled to a reduction. The terminal sends a code message to the computer, which takes this into account in calculating the sum to be paid.

The student subsequently sends in the documentary proof, which enables the Registrar's office to communicate the scholarshipholders' results to the official quarters. The amount due by the student is calculated automatically, with no possibility of interference by the operator. There is thus no room for human error. Subsequent payments are recorded by a special message which is not sent at the time of registration. The computer does, however, issue a message when the student has not paid the total amounts due for the previous academic year.

In January a reminder is printed by the computer, and sent out to those in arrears. In June the Registrar's office receives a list of unpaid accounts, and asks for the settlement of outstanding debts before entering the students concerned for the examinations.

During the telephone call the operator enquires whether the student has changed his address. If so, the information is stored, and thus appears on all documents communicated by the secretariat. To save time in recording the data, and to save space on the recording disc, the name of the district in Louvain is not stored. Consequently, to draw up a list a translation table has to be consulted, based on the cantonal postal code.

H. Programmes and files

The organization of the files must allow them to be checked instantly and leave room for possible changes in the data. Direct access to the Students file is therefore essential. The information will accordingly have to be stored on magnetic discs, and classified by an indexed sequence or by direct access.

All the data relevant to students will previously have been put into storage. The university has to arrange for the collection of any data which may have changed, namely:

new registrations
new address at Louvain (40 % modification)
new home address (6 % modification)
new civil status (2 % modification)
new nationality (less than 1 % modification).

The operation of the system is controlled by three 'jobs'. The first confirms the execution of the prior operations. In the case of partial or total destruction of the file, the latter is reconstituted from the master tape, then brought up to date with the information stored in the 'back-up disc'.

The data concerning the development of the programme are recorded as it proceeds, and the recording indicates, after any stoppage, the type of interruption experienced. This enables the effects to be corrected, and indicates to the operator the manipulations to be carried out.

The second job follows the execution of the actual processing. The priority section of the computer central unit contains the QTAM (Queued Telecommunication Access Method) programmes, regulating the input and output of messages and queueing them up on a disc. The following section contains the message processing and control programme. Each message can be processed in four different ways.

The first message normally allows the registration number to be introduced. Using this key, the computer transmits the data concerning identity, address, etc. Modifications are shown on the screen underneath the original information. When the information group concerned is put into storage, the computer selects the processing *ad hoc*, and stores the new information, while not as yet bringing the disc up to date. It selects the subsequent processing phase, and throws the information relevant to the study courses on to the screen. When the message comes back, the computer checks the spelling and existence of the 'study-year' code, and corrects minor misprints. When all the information is accurate, the computer loads it on to the Students disc and on to the transactions file. It is then ready to receive another first message, i.e. the registration number of another new student.

In the last stage of processing, the third job retrieves the students file and the transactions file and stores them on magnetic tape. It is also responsible for putting on disc all modifications which have come in on card during the day, e.g. registrations of new students. The sequence of operations is automatically determined by the computer, but can be modified by the operator.

The information required for processing and back-up is loaded on five files:

1. *The Students file* is organized in order of registration numbers (sequentially indexed). It holds all the data liable to annual modification, and thus constitutes a part of the 'historical' tape-recorded file. Each student has one or two recordings of 235 characters, according to the number of annual courses for which he is enrolled. The on-line updating of this file may thus involve some new recordings being made. This is done in real time, and a number of controls are needed to avoid the destruction of information simultaneously scrutinised by another terminal.

2. *The 'study-year' file*, with direct access, incorporates the coding and text 'in words' for the approximately 690 annual sets of courses followed by students at U.C.L.

3. *The 'nationality' file* is organized for direct access, and provides a translation 'in words' of the code contained in the recording.

4. *The 'queues' file* stores the computer's input and output of messages.

5. *The 'transactions' file* is compiled sequentially, and exactly reproduces the information transmitted on the Students disc. It faithfully records the day's operations, allows the Students disc to be brought up to date in case of breakdown, and at the end of the day serves as the basis for the preparation of the documents remitted to students.

Unlike other well-known applications, the teleprocessing carried out at U.C.L. allows of something more than the simple remote consultation of files. The system enables the files to be up-dated in real time. This involves a strict check on the accuracy of the data accepted in the core storage.

The checking is partly visual and partly automatic.

1. Automatic check on the existence of a registration number and transmission of an error message if there is no such number.

2. Continuous check to detect any modification made to the initial registration number.

3. Visual check on a sequential number given by the student as issued in 1968/69 and displayed on the screen.

4. Automatic check on the existence of a study-year, correction of minor typing errors and display of an error message.

5. Visual checking of prior data, i.e. study-years whose successful completion is a condition of registration, is now automated; the basic information is recorded in the 'study-year' file. The 'study-year 'code was in fact planned with this type of application in mind.

I. Staff and equipment

Four IBM 2260 terminals with television screens have been installed, with control unit and modulation and demodulation units, for telephonic transmission. Four telephone lines are installed in the registration offices; one telephone line hired for the transmission of data is linked to the computer three kilometres away. Four operators work on a rota system, five hours a day for thirty days, and use the terminals to feed information into the computer. They receive very little training. It is, in fact, a very simple matter to handle the alphabetic codes identifying the courses and study-years. In addition, the operators are familiar with these codes, which they deal with for the rest of the year in the accounts departments or in the card-punching unit. One great advantage of the system is that it simplifies the registration operations and promotes the mobility of staff.

J. Examination results and record sheets

(a) Objectives
1. To compile the necessary information to verify registration and the satisfaction of prior conditions and exemption from lectures and to constitute record sheets.
2. To regroup elements for measuring the achievement of the aims of education.
3. To produce statistics of examination results.

(b) Organisation
The examination results procedure is an extension of the registration procedure; one taking its data from inside the University and the other from outside. The general flow-sheet of the procedure is given in Appendix 3.

(c) First stage: examination registrations
This stage requires verification of the conditions for registration. Students must be in good financial standing, must have had an X-ray and medical examination and must not have been turned down by the Faculty. These particulars have been stored in the computer which punches one card per entrant. These cards are distributed to the students through the class stewards; their return after signature is equivalent to registration for the examination. Students who are not in order are not given a card and must attend the University Secretariat in person.

(d) Second stage: establishing the list of candidates
The Faculties receive a set of punched cards, which enables them to change the order of the list of candidates, to authorise changes and to issue the first and last numbers. These punched cards are returned to the University Secretariat for the printing of candidates' lists and examination schedules.

(e) Third stage: notification, storage and communication of examination results
The Faculties and Institutes receive a punched card for each examinee. The result of the examination is indicated by mark-sensing on the card. The computer stores this new information. This procedure minimises errors by eliminating all coding or punching. Finally, the computer prints the examination lists which constitute the official document signed by the Secretary of each Board of Examiners. It also prints a record sheet for each student.

K. Documents produced by the system

(a) Service to students
After registration, the student receives, printed automatically:
    a debit note for the amount of registration fees
    a certificate of registration
    certificates for the Students Mutual Fund and the railways
    since 1971, the student's card.
Later, he will receive
    a national service certificate
    a payment reminder, if necessary.

(b) Service to the Registrar's office
The Registrar's office receives a daily statement of students' accounts. Periodically it receives:
    a summary of the balance of student accounts
    a forecast of receipts from the 'students' sector
    alphabetical lists, both general and by study-year
    an alphabetical list of foreign students, by nationality
    an address list
    a general historical record.

(c) Service to Faculties
    a general alphabetical list
    alphabetical lists by study-year
    an address list
    the list of examination entries
    the list of examination results
    a historical record.

(d) Service to secondary schools
    list of alumni with study-years and addresses
    examination results of alumni

(e) University Foundation
    magnetic tape containing all the information needed to compile national statistics

(f) Associations of students and alumni
    printing lists, records and adhesive labels.

L. Information transmitted to the authorities

Summarized information is transmitted to the authorities at regular intervals dealing with registrations, examination results and the social and economic composition of the student body.

1. Registration statistics

Registration statistics are published on 1 November and 1 February each year. They make it possible to measure the trend of the number of students by faculty and by study-year, sex and nationality. A useful distinction is drawn between new students and students already in a course of study. Statistics are also produced by *commune* and *arrondissement*, giving the origin of students by region of the country.

There is nothing very original about the registration statistics and they call for no special comment.

2. The social and economic characteristics of the student body

The U.C.L. authorities have made a contract with the Social Sciences Department under which an assistant is studying the social origin of students. This work has elicited the social and economic characteristics of students entering university for the first time in 1970.

On the completion of a first study conducted by the Department of Social Sciences, the student body was divided into fifteen categories by father's occupation.

A more detailed analysis was made of a sample of 500 students which provided valuable conclusions on the correlation between social background, choice of secondary studies and rate of participation in higher education and on the correlation between social background and choice of University studies.

3. Statistics of examination results

The most interesting data are those of the successes and failures of students. An extremely complex programme provides these statistics:

> by study-year
> by cycle and by faculty
> by institute and faculty
> for the whole of the University
> by nationality
> by school of origin
> by *arrondissement* and region of the country
> by social category

For each of these categories the programme distinguishes, in absolute numbers and percentage:

> the number of students enrolled;
> the number of students taking the examination, for each of the three sessions and in total;
> the total successes and failures, detailing the ten possible results (pass, distinction, etc.).

Within each major category (faculty, nationality, etc.), the programme provides the following details:

male and female;
Belgians and foreigners;
scholarship-holders and others;
newcomers to Belgian higher education;
newcomers to U.C.L.;
resident in Louvain or commuting;
married or unmarried;
enrolled for the first or second time, etc.
enrolled for one or two study-years, etc.
by social category.

The programme of statistics of examination results, STAREXA, is an interrogation programme which makes it possible to select the population to be studied and to give precise answers to questions about it. Once this interrogation technique has been perfected, it will be applied to other sectors.

Appendix 4 gives an output of statistics of examination results for all in their first study-year at U.C.L.

4. *The automation of procedures for examiners' meetings*

The discussions of examining boards are very time-wasting: teachers sit for hours coming to decisions which could largely have been programmed and suggested by the machine. Furthermore, the allocation of marks by teacher or by subject may lead to important decisions both as to the procedure itself and to the weighting of the different subjects. The following procedure has been worked out to simplify examining procedures.

The data are fed into the machine in the form of punched cards; the marks have been noted in soft pencil, either by the examiners or by the faculty secretariat. Computer processing provides, in diminishing order of success, the list of students with the marks received in each examination and a general average. In addition, after this first processing, the computer provides the statistics of marks awarded by each examiner in the form of a histogram and calculates the dispersion of marks (Appendix 5). This information indicates how an examiner assesses students' work.

This system was worked out in 1969 and tested on a population of 600 students. Its general adoption depends on the absorption capacity of the computer.

M. Model of student flow

The availability of two years' history of registrations made it possible to construct a simulation model of the student flow. The principle of calculation is that of Markoff chains. For each student, the computer makes a comparison between registrations during the year t and those of the year $t + 1$. Regrouping the registrations by curriculum for the year t the probabilities of registration in the different curricula for the year $t + 1$ are determined. On the basis of information relating to the student body by programme of studies and the rate of promotion from one year to another, it is easy to multiply the matrix successively and to obtain the population for the years $t + 1, t + 2$, etc.

The only element which has to be put into the system is a forecast of the annual number of new students in the form of an equation with three parameters, so as to give a variety of forms to the forecasting curve.

The construction of this model makes it possible to go beyond the stage of information systems into the stage of management systems. In practice, this precision tool permits the testing of the incidence of recruitment assumptions or selection policy decisions. It will later serve as the basis for a more general model covering the other sub-systems. It is therefore the first step towards a management system.

VI. The financial sub-system

A. Objects

The financial sub-system expresses in financial terms the different fields of university administration. It has two aspects: the budget, the financial expression of a plan, and the accounts, the financial expression of the commitment of resources allocated to the activities provided for in the plan.

1. Improvement of service to users

The administration must provide rapid and reliable service so that the academic and scientific staff are provided with adequate information and are thus free to devote more time to their primary function. This saving of the time of highly qualified staff is in fact a saving of money, even if it is hard to quantify.

The speed of operations will improve the public image of the University; suppliers will be particularly sensitive to it. Regular payments may even give the University the benefit of better terms from contractors who are prepared to allow a discount for prompt settlement.

Sound financial administration will induce the holders of external funds to entrust their accountancy to the University. The University will thus have a larger cash flow and by that very fact will reduce its financial costs.

2. Saving of staff and of administrative costs

First, the methods of compiling and processing information by the finance department must be as efficient as possible so as to minimise the proportion of university resources allocated to management functions. The setting-up of a financial system should therefore be preceded by economic analysis of the proposed reform.

Secondly, the efficiency of the central finance department has a direct influence both on the administrative work done in faculties and units and on the quality of decisions taken at different levels. This element should be taken into account when a new system is being worked out.

3. Aid in decision-making

Most decisions taken, both in profit- and non-profit-making institutions, are based on information relating to financial criteria. However, the comparison of activities of different kinds is difficult in a University which is not sensitive to notions of profit, but the authorities nevertheless need the fullest possible information. The information system should therefore be capable of digesting information of all kinds and, as far as possible, translating it into financial terms.

A unit account holder needs to be informed of the trend of expenditure: in the light of this information he administers available funds and prepares applications for futher monies. He should also have access to the breakdown of resources among the various teaching or research activities of the unit. This will enable him to review the allocation of resources in the light of objectives. At a higher level, major decisions call for rapid and reliable information based on the collection of thousands of data derived from all the academic and administrative units. Only experience, coupled with thorough analysis, can identify the relevant information. An inventory of information needs at all levels is therefore a pre-requisite to the introduction of a new financial system.

B. The financial departments

The financial system may be broken down into several sectors:
    preparation of budgets
    pre-audit
    treasury and financial management
    accounts
    post-audit
    economic analysis
University structure differs from one university to another. At Louvain there are three administrative departments with financial responsibilities. Their working methods are laid down by the Directorate of Administration, which is, moreover, the only level at which the financial departments are co-ordinated.

1. The Accounts Department

(a) Functions
The Accounts Department provides and processes the information necessary to each phase of decision-making and financial transaction. It pre-audits expenditure and the commitment of funds by comparing the amount of invoices and estimates of expenditure with the available credit balance and submits any queries to the administrator of the funds. Financial management is based on information supplied by the Accounts Department. Post-audit of expenditure is also integrated into the Department, which keeps budget accounts. Finally, economic analysis is obviously based on accounts data; it brings out their full significance by com-

paring the costs which they reflect with elements which are used to assess the level of activity which is a result of the resources committed.

The Accounts Department thus provides the necessary infrastructure for the various operations of the financial system. Its functions can be summed up under four heads:

to act as paying agent;

to record financial transactions with a view to justifying them to third persons;

to provide an instrument of diagnosis in the form of budget accounts;

to provide information for decision-making.

(b) Scope

The Accounts Department records all financial transactions concerning the activities of the University. These are very varied and cover teaching and research, the social and cultural sector, the University clinics, the administration of the university assets and of the Pensions Fund. Each sector has its own separate accounts, kept either by the central Accounts Department or at the headquarters of distant units such as the University clinics or social and cultural centres.

There are two accounts showing movements between these sub-accounts and the central accounts. In the case of the clinics, for example, the central accounts include a 'clinics current account' and a 'clinics capital account', while each clinic has a 'university current account' and a 'university capital account'.

This form of organisation has the advantage of leaving the different sectors of the University considerable autonomy of management. The year-end accounts or an interim account in the course of the year give an overall picture of the activities of the University. This, however, calls for perfect compatibility between the accounting systems adopted by the different units.

The sphere of activity of the accounting service must be extended to the management of external funds. Several members of the academic staff receive grants from public or private sources to finance part of their research. Very often, these funds are administered directly and exclusively by the beneficiaries themselves. This reduces the scope of the Accounts Department and limits the view which the academic authorities have of university activities. The authorities, therefore, encourage members of the academic body to entrust the administration of these funds to the central Accounts Department. The Department will only be able to satisfy these 'customers' in so far as it can provide a perfect service, like a bank. In this way, researchers will be freed from administrative duties and the authorities will have more complete information.

(c) Organisation

The U.C.L. Accounts Department has a staff of ten:

Head of Department	1
Invoice Office (reception, checking, assigning invoices)	4

> Financial Transactions Office   2
> (checking incoming
> and outgoing funds
>
> Social Bodies and debtors' accounts   1
>
> Secretariat   2
> (typing and filing)

The volume and speed of processing, the need for accurate data, and the need to limit staff commitments call for the use of the most modern information processing techniques and accounting procedures. Since 1 January 1969 all accounting operations have been computerised.

2. The Ordinary Budget for Operating Expenditure

(a) Functions
The Operating Expenditure Budget Department is responsible for preparing and implementing decisions about the allocation of financial resources. In this connection, it has various functions:
> to estimate the amount of university resources;
> to make proposals for their allocation;
> to collect information and prepare budget documents;
> in the course of the year, to estimate the cost of new decisions
>   and to keep the reserves account updated;
> to open and keep accounts (transfers etc.);
> to exercise budgetary control;
> to issue U.C.L. cheques;
> to make financial analyses.

(b) Scope
The Operating Expenditure Budget Department limits its field of action to funds allocated by the U.C.L.. It intervenes only rarely in the administration of funds granted to members of the U.C.L. by outside organisations. The availability of information nevertheless results in the Head of Department often being consulted in other fields.

(c) Organisation
The Department has a staff of three, the Head of Department, an assistant and a secretary. It benefits from the co-operation of the Data-processing Department, indispensable during the budget preparation period or in issuing chequebooks.

3. The Capital Expenditure Budget

The obligation of the U.C.L. to move the Faculty of Medicine to Brussels and all its other faculties to Ottignies involves expenditure of the order of 17 billion

Belgian francs. A specialised department is responsible for preparing the construction budget.

This Department, with a staff of three, has inventoried the U.C.L.'s space needs between 1970 and 1980. After estimating the cost of construction on a basis of detailed norms, a budget was drawn up and, as with the Operating Expenditure Budget Department, accounts opened once the plans had been approved by the academic authority. Within the defined limits of their funds, the Construction Department can then enter into contracts with contractors and with the building trades subject to the approval of the authorities.

C. The reform of the financial system

On 1 January 1969 the Accounts Department common to the two universities was officially divided. The new director was able to take a few liberties with the traditional rules which had governed the old service. The common data-processing service, however, was still responsible for processing accounts information and the new service did not therefore have a great deal of freedom. This restraint was eliminated at the beginning of 1970. During that year the Analysis Unit took over the old system and devoted most of its efforts to creating a new system, better adapted to the functioning of the service and of the University.

1. Fundamentals of the financial system

(a) The accounting method
Accountants are divided into two main schools of thought, the advocates of income and expenditure accounting (or cash accounting), and the advocates of double entry accounting.

The first method is limited to recording cash movements. It is often accompanied by an analysis of income and expenditure, and is used by public bodies and by many universities. It simply shows cash variations without allowing for debts or claims or for any items of assets. The difference between income and expenditure results in a debit or credit cash balance, with no possibility of analysing changes in assets.

No distinction is made between income from the sale of a building, the recovery of a claim or the award of a grant. Yet the first two items represent a change in the nature of the assets and the third an increase in wealth. Furthermore, cash accounting merely records transactions having an immediate effect on cash on hand. No account can therefore be taken of depreciation in the value of assets.

Double entry accounting shows both the current state of affairs (difference between assets and liabilities) and the management situation (difference between costs and earnings). This method is applied in industrial and business firms. It is the only one which allows an exact economic analysis of the position and management of the enterprise; in fact, it takes account of all transactions, including those which have no direct effect on the cash position.

The accounts of the University of Louvain have hitherto been cash accounts. In order to make them an instrument of management, it was decided to introduce double entry accounting. This reform implies:

1. The existence of debit and credit accounts, with the balance carried forward to the next year.
2. The existence of income and expenditure accounts, the balance of which is transferred at the end of the year to an operating account, showing in the balance sheet the increase or diminution in assets in the course of the past year.
3. The existence of reconciliation accounts showing separately income received but not due in respect of the relevant period and conversely income due but not received during the period. For example, at the end of the year, the account 'income from students' fees' should be credited with the whole amount due from students. The difference between the amounts actually received and the amount initially due will be debited to a credit account 'claims for students' fees'. The same applies to costs. The cost accounts must be debited with the amount payable for the relevant period. The difference between the amount payable and the amount actually paid must be shown as a debit or credit in a reconciliation account, 'charges paid in advance' for a credit and 'charges payable' for a debit.
4. The existence of amortization accounts and provision for depreciation. For the purpose of financial analysis, the purchase cost of equipment should be spread over its useful life. This proportion will be charged to the running costs of departments. The need to constitute a provision to finance the replacement of fixed assets is open to discussion. In the case of buildings, this measure seems justified in every instance. Its application requires an inventory and valuation of the university buildings. Provision should also be made for the depreciation of other assets, if the amounts involved warrant it. Provision could be made for *doubtful debts*, depreciation of portfolio investments, etc.
5. The existence of inter-department transfer accounts. Various departments of the University perform services for other departments. These internal services do not generally give rise to any cash movement. In order to obtain an exact picture of the income and expenditure of a department, however, it is essential to show these services in the accounts. Such accounts would also make it possible to judge the efficiency of certain internal services compared with services performed by outside contractors. Finally, this technique avoids the waste of services, since they will no longer be free, but will be effectively charged against each consumer department.

    Under this principle, the following should be shown in the accounts:
    deliveries of products from one department to another;
    services rendered by one department to another (graphic work, reproduction of documents, etc.);
    logistical services (computer, central library, etc.);
    academic services, e.g. the cost of lectures given to the students of one department by a teacher from another.

In conclusion, the accounting method adopted should provide for the recording of all features of university life. It should be emphasized that this method should cover not only the funds controlled by the University, but also those at the disposal of members of the academic body but outside the control of the university departments. The application of this principle conditions the effectiveness of accounting as an instrument of management and financial analysis.

(b) The accounting system
The U.C.L. accounts have been designed as centralised accounts based on specialised sub-accounts.

Student registration accounts. The University Secretariat records the sums due and payments made by students and any reductions allowed by the academic authorities. It calculates the amounts still unpaid and reports the totals to the central accounts department each month. These are entered in the general accounts to the credit of the 'student income' account for amounts paid, and to the debit of the 'claims for students' fees' account for amounts outstanding.

Personnel accounts. The Personnel Department calculates the amount payable to each member of the University and pays what is due. Each month the total emoluments, the tax payable and social security contributions are shown in the general accounts and charged to each sector.

Puchasing accounts. On the basis of requisition vouchers, the Purchasing Department makes out the purchasing orders, which are entered by the Accounts Department on a list of commitments. Commitments are not shown in the general accounts but are nevertheless, subject to audit. Purchasing orders must be approved by the Director of Accounts and recording them makes it possible to forecast estimated expenditure. The invoice office, a section of the Accounts Department, records and checks invoices and keeps the daybook and suppliers' ledger accounts. The totals are entered in the general accounts each month.

Building accounts. These accounts have not been organised: the U.C.L., in fact, owns very few buildings. Ultimately, however, the technical departments will prepare maintenance bills, the cost of which will be charged to the relevant building. At the end of the month, the list of maintenance costs will be drawn up for each building and the totals entered in the general accounts.

The same applies to water, gas, fuel and similar costs for each building. In the case of major maintenance costs, the invoices must be checked against available credits and recorded by building site rather than by building. The building site is in practice a subdivision of a building. The totals will be shown in the general accounts at the end of the month.

Income accounts. It is extremely important to keep a close watch on the trend of university income. The main sources of income can be classified as follows:

> government subsidies
> students' fees
> research grants
> donations
> sales
> recovery of claims
> loans
> income from assets

Each of these categories of income requires its own separate account. The semi-public research organisations require some account of the use of their funds; donations call for letters of thanks and an account for each donor. The same applies to loans and the recovery of claims. In each case, a special account is opened so that the movement of each category of income can be easily followed.

General and budget accounts. These accounts are in three parts:

> department accounts
> general accounts
> budget accounts

The accounts of each department are made up identifying income and expenditure by type. The monthly summary of department expenditure covers the following main headings:

> personnel costs
> administrative costs
> scientific costs
> share of costs of premises

A monthly list of the specific income of the department is also drawn up. The headings of income and expenditure may be as varied as in the general accounts. The monthly table of expenditure is completed by a summary of purchases of capital equipment by department. It is extremely useful to combine budget accounting with department accounting. At the beginning of the year, the expenditure account is credited and the income account is debited with estimates. Actual income and expenditure during the year is recorded normally and interim balance sheets may be drawn up by department and by account.

It should be stressed that this budget accounting is geared to departmental accounts and not to general accounts. This method has the advantage of emphasising the responsibility of departments, whereas budget accounting does not pinpoint the responsibility of the account-holder in the event of any overspending.

(c) Accounting procedure

Since 1 January 1969 all accounting transactions are recorded on punched cards and computerised. Accounting machines have therefore been abandoned except for the general accounts. There are many reasons for this change in technique:

1. The large storage capacity of the computer allows the constitution of an information system. The same phenomena can thus be expressed in both financial and real terms. The interpretation of the information provided by the accounts

will be more revealing and will, in fact, increase the value of the information. This factor influenced the decision to abandon the traditional accounting machines and to replace them by the computer, the central organ for the processing of all information.

2. The computer with its very fast working speed and its complete independence of the information medium affords wide possibilities of sorting, classification and combination. The analysis of accounts data can be extremely sophisticated. With the computer, information need be recorded only once on punched cards, and can be sorted according to the criteria demanded; the Accounts Department can obtain any statements it needs without additional work.

3. In general, the computer processes data faster. This is important if accounting is to be anything more than an instrument for recording data. The speed with which information is processed enables it to be kept fully up to date and the accounts can thus provide a sound basis for decision-making. Computerisation was therefore dictated by the role assigned to accounts. In view of the volume of the data, it was necessary to have information-recording and processing equipment more powerful than the traditional machines in order to achieve high standards of efficiency.

2. The organisation of information

The quality of the basic data dictates not only the functioning of the financial services, but also the quality of the information transmitted to the authorities. Extreme care must therefore be taken in identifying and codifying them and in updating the various files.

The most important information concerns the cost centres identified in the university structure. The conception of this file has already been commented on above.

(a) Type of income or expenditure
Belgian law requires state-aided establishments of higher education to submit to the state in a prescribed form an annual budget and accounts vouching for the use of grants. The U.C.L. accounts are used not only in this way but also, and above all, as an instrument of management. The U.C.L. accounting system therefore goes beyond the statutory requirements.

The new accounting system must meet the needs of all departments of the University. Many headings will, moreover, be used by certain departments only. Even if the accounts are kept outside the central office, it is always possible to aggregate the year-end accounts and in this way to keep an overall view of university activities. A uniform accounting system allows valuable comparisons of the cost of the different departments of the institution. The Accounts Department and the Budget Department should adopt the same presentation by type of income and expenditure and use the same codes. In this case, there is no difficulty in comparing expenditure commitments with the balance of available credits. It is indeed the uniformity of the accounting system which makes it possible to keep budget accounts.

SUMMARY OF THE ACCOUNTS PLAN

(1) Balance sheet accounts

A 100 - 999 Fixed capital
B 100 - 999 Cash in hand and at bank
C 100 - 999 Land and facilities
D 100 - 999 Acquisition of books (libraries and collections)
E 100 - 999 Equipment
M 100 - 999 Merchandise and products in stock (university genera stores)
T 100 - 999 Third party accounts, non-university
X 100 - 999 Third party accounts, university
Y 100 - 999 Operating results
Z 100 - 999 Suspense accounts

(2) Expenditure accounts

F 100 - 999 Operating costs
L 100 - 999 Facilities costs
N 100 - 999 Student costs
P 100 - 999 Personnel costs
V 100 - 999 Subscriptions and donations

(3) Income accounts

R 100 - 999 Income

(b) Sources of finance

The indication of the source of finance makes it possible to justify the use of funds coming from the various sources. It also makes it possible to integrate all operations regardless of the source of the funds which finance them. Statistics can be compiled on this basis breaking down the source of funds by type of activity, research centre, building constructed and so on.

CLASSIFICATION OF SOURCES OF FINANCE

1000 - 1999 Operating budget: Belgian public sector
2000 - 2999 Operating budget: Belgian private sector
3000 - 3999 Operating budget: U.C.L. operations
4000 - 4999 Operating budget: Foreign countries
5000 - 5999 Operating budget: Public international bodies
6000 - 6999 Operating budget: Extra-university credits
7000 - 7999 Capital budget: Belgian public sector
8000 - 8999 Capital budget: Belgian private sector
9000 - 9999 Transfers to capital budget

(c) Suppliers file

The list of 2,500 U.C.L. suppliers was drawn up at the beginning of the reform of the financial system. The supplier's code number is shown on each entry, so that questions from the University's creditors can be rapidly answered. It is an alphabetical list; each supplier is assigned a code number according to the place of his name in the general alphabetical order.

(d) Account-holders

From the beginning, the account-holder was identified by his personal registration number. This system, however, created a number of difficulties. First, the same person might hold more than one account in various capacities as Dean of a Faculty or as director of a unit, for example. Identification by his personal number did not enable the system to take account of these distinctions. This shortcoming led to confusion in entering items and in despatching and classifying documents. The turnover of university directors is, moreover, fast and the file was therefore rarely up to date. The account-holder is therefore now identified by his function in the cost centre. The file of functions by cost centre gives the personal number of the individual concerned, thus giving the key to the name, title, address, etc. of the account-holder.

D. The reform of budget procedure

1. The limits of the reform

(a) The shortcomings found in 1969

An analysis of the procedure in 1969 led to the following conclusions:

1. The budget is not the financial expression of a plan. It is arranged by categories of expenditure and not according to the objectives pursued by the institution. As a rule, moreover, the overall budget of a unit is not subject to examination. Decisions relate to each category of expenditure without any study being made of their interdependence.

   The numerous activities carried out by the 250 or so units which form the University are not regrouped and structured around the major themes underlying U.C.L. policy. It is therefore impossible to estimate the cost of achieving the different objectives pursued at institutional level.

2. Except in the case of the Scientific Development Fund, the automatic renewal of credits limits the power of decision of the authorities to increases in expenditure.

3. The services rendered are not subject to any cost-effectiveness analysis.

4. The budget cycle is limited to a year, which is not long enough to achieve any significant part of the objectives of the institution.
   The creation of the Scientific Development Fund has nevertheless gone some way towards filling this gap.

5. Decisions on a proposal relate to a single course of action only. The various alternative ways of achieving the same objective are not taken into account. This limits the information given to the authorities and hinders their decision-making.

6. Decisions are normally taken in purely financial terms without reference to the services to be performed by those receiving funds. The criteria for the achievement of objectives have never been the subject of research. The budget therefore gives a fairly vague picture of the activities financed by the University.

7. The financing of university activities from external sources is not taken into

account. It nevertheless forms an important element in the life of those academic departments which benefit from it.

8. The mode of submitting requests lays very little stress on the interactions between the operating and the capital budgets.

9. Requests are very often submitted individually by members of the academic and scientific body and this reflects the low level of efficiency of the existing structure. Requests submitted through the groups or faculties are rated on a scale from 0 to 20. In practice, owing to the shortage of resources, requests rated below 20 are turned down by the academic authorities. The rating procedure therefore scarcely fulfils its function.

The capital budget, external financing and the medium- or long-term effects of decisions are scarcely integrated in the existing budget procedure. The budget gives the authorities only a fragmentary view of the University and of the numerous groups which make it up. Furthermore, the budget sets limits to the commitment of expenditure without reference to the concrete services to be rendered by those who receive the funds.

(b) Improvements made in 1969 and 1970

By rigorous action, it has been possible to improve the presentation of the budget through the mechanisation of data-processing. The following improvements have been introduced:

1. All credits have been regrouped by unit, department and faculty.

2. A first integration of information of an academic and of a financial character has been achieved by doing away with budget and account numbers, and identifying credits by unit and holder.

3. The reorganisation of the budget procedure guarantees the reliability of information. Data are compiled and checked by the ten administrative secretaries of faculties. The information is then transmitted to the central authorities, transcribed on to basic documents, punched and recorded. Twelve machine-instruction programmes allow the preparation of budget documents.

4. The faculties have acquired greater freedom within their total budget.

5. Mechanisation has made it possible to integrate the Budget Department and the Accounts Department. The budget initiates the accounting on 1 January each year.

In spite of the improvements made in the form and procedure of the budget, criticisms have not yet been followed up. The main cause of difficulties is the instability of Belgian university financing. It is difficult in practice to draw up five-year budgets when financing is ensured for a year at most and there is no indication of the growth rate of government grants.

2. Budget documents

(a) Collection of data

Data are collected on the basis of a number of application forms:

      (1) Applications for operating and equipment expenditure;

(2) Census of academic, scientific, administrative and technical personnel;
(3) Applications for promotion and appointments;
(4) Candidates for vacant Chairs.

(b) Constitution of basic file

Applications for promotion and for operating and equipment expenditure and for the purchase of books as well as applications for special credits (financial interest, maintenance of premises, etc.) are recorded on basic documents, giving the following particulars:

(1) Code and title of unit;
(2) Code of activity;
(3) Nature of expenditure (2 positions);
(4) Serial number by nature of expenditure;
(5) Applicant's registration number;
(6) Source of finance;
(7) Nature of application;
(8) Amount;
(9) Positions reserved for any remarks.

(c) Reference to other files

The machine-instruction programmes make use, in printing budget documents, of the following files:

(1) Structure of U.C.L.;
(2) Teaching activities;
(3) Research activities;
(4) Personnel;
(5) Facilities.

(d) Budget documents

The information compiled in the course of the budget procedure gives rise to the following:

(1) Personnel structure by unit, category and grade;
(2) List of credits applied for and granted, by holder, unit, department or faculty;
(3) List of credits by nature of expenditure and holder;
(4) Statistics of distribution of expenditure;
(5) Double entry table showing amount of expenditure by unit, department and faculty, by category of activity (teaching in the four cycles, research, etc.) and nature of expenditure (operating, equipment, personnel);
(6) Magnetic tape containing budget information used by Accounts Department to check expenditure;
(7) Letter informing applicants of the official reply of the authorities.

3. Issue of U.C.L. cheques

The budget is approved at the end of May. Equipment and operating credits are approved later, probably in November. Not later than 31 December, credit-holders must have the documents available which will enable them to tell the Accounts Department the account against which they want their expenditure charged. In practice, certain holders belong to more than one unit and at the same time exercise administrative functions, such as that of dean. A number of accounts have therefore been opened in their name.

To deal with this point, it was decided to run the financial system like a bank. Holders would have a chequebook for each account opened in their name. Each invoice sent to the Accounts Department for payment would have to be accompanied by a cheque issued by the Budget Department and giving the information enabling the invoice office to make the entries needed to process the accounts.

These chequebooks were issued for the first time at the beginning of 1970 in proportion to the size of each account. They look like a bank chequebook and each cheque (50 to a book) gives the following information:

In words:
  name of unit;
  name and first name of holder;
  designation of activities directed by holder;
  nature of expenditure (capital or operating).

In code:
  alphabetical code of unit;
  personal number of holder;
  budget year;
  serial number of nature of expenditure;
  source of finance;
  code of activities directed by holder.

Boxes reserved for Accounts Department:
  building code;
  inventory code;
  number of order form;
  supplier's number;
  number of U.C.L. invoice.

The holder proceeds as follows:
  (1) Marks with a cross:
    the activity to which the expenditure or commitment should be charged;
    the nature of expenditure.
  (2) Amount
    indicates the amount in the case of an invoice;
    strikes out the amount space in the case of a requisition note (in any event the amount will be estimated by the purchasing office).
  (3) Dates;
  (4) Signs;

(5) The cheque is attached:
    to every invoice to be paid by the Accounts Department;
    to every requisition note transmitted to the purchasing office;
    to every requisition note presented to the U.C.L. stores.

The cheque is treated not only as an information medium but also as a means of payment. Several shops in the town, approved by the University, accept direct settlement by cheques of not more than B.Fr. 5,000; the invoice, accompanied by the cheque, is then sent to the U.C.L. Accounts Department which pays the amount without requiring further formality.

4. Budget control

Budget control is carried out by the computer in the course of processing the accounts.

Any irregularity detected in the course of processing is reported by the Accounts Department to the Budget Department, which looks into the case. The Budget Department, therefore, works only 'by exceptions' and refrains from making a budget check before each operation. The attention of the Department is attracted by the messages emitted by the system during the phase of budget check, such as 'exceeds credit granted' or 'invoice number faulty', etc.

5. Modifications and transfers in the course of the year

The approved budget is subject to a number of modifications in the course of the year. Most frequently, they arise out of new decisions financed from reserves. The Budget Department must therefore ascertain the state of reserves before each meeting of the decision-making bodies, must investigate new applications in order to estimate their cost, and must record decisions. It informs the Accounts Department of the opening of new accounts or the modification of existing ones.

In the course of the year, holders may make transfers. Transfers of up to B.Fr. 25,000 within the same unit require no external sanction. The sanction of the dean is necessary for transfers from one unit or department to another. Application must be made to the Budget Department when the amount to be transferred exceeds B.Fr. 25,000. After a decision, the Budget Department informs the Accounts Department of the modification.

E. The reform of the processing of accounts information

1. Objectives of reform

The new system should be designed to improve:
    (a) The flexibility of operations;
      the possibility of working with budgets covering several years;
      integration of operating and capital budgets;

possibility of internal invoicing;
possibility of working in debit as well as in credit.
(b) The speed of operations both in the Accounts Department and on the machine;
(c) The automation of operations;
counterpart accounts should be automatically debited or credited.
(d) Inter-departmental relations;
the possibility of integrating data such as suppliers' delivery date;
the transmission of information necessary to the sound operation of the budget.
(e) Clarity of information;
readable extracts of accounts with explicit reference to transactions;
periodic progress schedules for transmission to the authorities.
(f) Staff working conditions;
(g) Details of information;
the introduction of analytical accounting detailing the cost of each activity or series of activities as a basis for a budget by programmes and objectives.

2. Inquiry in the department

The Accounts Department was divided into a number of sectors:
Invoice office
Cash
Administration of credits
Treasury
General accounting
Social debtors
Non-social debtors
Financial control
The head of each section listed the events occurring within his field of competence. An event was defined as any fact having a financial significance and requiring recording. Each event, such as the arrival of an invoice, sets off a certain number of operations, such as arithmetical checking, checking tax, checking exchange rates, verifying the date of the invoice and so on. The head of section indicates on a form the data needed to carry out these operations and the file on which they are recorded.

This procedure enabled a complete inventory to be made of the activities of the Department, the information needed for its functioning and the interrelations between activities and information. It also had the advantage of enabling the staff to participate in the analysis and of allowing analysts and accountants to talk a common language.

3. Types of account

The analysis revealed the existence of several types of account which had not previously been separately treated. Many operating difficulties arose out of this confusion.

The criteria for distinguishing between types of account are:
the source of finance;
the existence of an official decision;
the fixing of a ceiling;
the term of any repayment.

On this basis, a distinction is drawn in the operating and capital budgets of U.C.L. between:

ordinary accounts, opened by decision of the academic authorities, for a specified amount, with no possibility of overspending;

advances with no fixed ceiling or term of repayment; they relate only to small amounts;

repayable credits opened authorized by the authorities, for a specified amount without a fixed term for repayment;

loans of a specified amount repayable within a time fixed by official decision.

4. Identification of accounts

The next stage in the analysis was the identification of accounts. It was accepted at the outset that operations relating to the operating and the capital budget should be integrated. The identification of these two types of account should therefore follow the same logic. Furthermore, the identification of the account should include a reference to all the information needed to process the accounts and to produce management information.

The identification number of the account provides the following information:

cost centre (structure code)	4 digits
number of activity or overall credit (lot) for capital expenditure	4
number of account holder (function code)	2
source of finance	4
order number	5
nature of expenditure	2
serial number of nature of expenditure	2
opening date	5
closing date	5
	33 digits

This 33-digit identification number is obviously too long to be used between the holder and the finance departments, and in practice, it is condensed into a 5-digit account number.

Thanks to this unique identification number, identical in type for all accounts, accounting operations are greatly simplified. In practice, all follow the same procedure and give rise to information processed by the same programme.

5. Identification of movements

Each account is subject in the course of the year to a succession of movements. Several events giving rise to movements in accounts can be identified:

Credit movements: 'Increase by decision of Council....' 'Your repayment of 12 August 1970, paid on invoice number 14787 on cash advance of 30 June 1970', etc.

Nil movements: 'Supplier DUPONT, order note no. 12345'
'Available balance insufficient, order note refused', etc.

Debit movements: 'Supplier DUPONT, invoice no, 12345 of 23 September 1970'
'Supplier DUPONT, part invoice no. 12345 of 23 September 1970, for DM 120, order no. 54321', etc.

The precise determination of all movements capable of modifying an account is a long job. The reform of the processing of accounts information could not start until after this decisive stage.

6. Documents issued by the department

The Accounts Department is in contact with all units of the U.C.L., with suppliers and banks, and with the other administrative departments. Information also moves between the different sections of the Department. The list of documents to be issued is established from the collation of these different links. Each of them must in fact be reflected in the communication of information, generally in printed form.

The documents issued before funds are administered can be distinguished from those issued by the computer afterwards.

(a) Before budget control

The Accounts Department carries out a number of checks before feeding the data into the system, and in the event of error or doubt, sends a document to the supplier or account-holder. Verification concerns:

> the signature of the holder or his authorised representative or representatives by comparison with the list of authorised signatures;
> the attachment of a properly made out cheque;
> the accuracy of the invoice (tax, arithmetical check, etc.)
> the placing of an order through the purchasing office in the event of the purchase of equipment.

(b) Documents issued after budget control

Once an invoice has been accepted, the Accounts Department makes out a basic document. Most of the information needed is already on the cheque issued by the Budget Department and signed by the account-holder and attached to the invoice. Once the data have been punched, they are fed into the computer. The information-processing programme could be drawn up only after a decision on the documents to be printed in the subsequent stage. The destination of these documents can be summarized as follows:

DESTINATION OF FINANCIAL DOCUMENTS

| | | Information | | Payment | |
| | | Records | | | |
Destination	Extract	Invoices	Commitments	Transfers	Bank list
Holder	X				
Budget office			X		
Accounts department authorities	X	X	X	List	X
Banks and suppliers				X (Tape)	
Purchasing Office			X		
State		Accounts			

(1) The extract of account

This document is the most important output at the basic level. It is sent to account-holders for their own records. It shows the date and serial number of operations. The Accounts Department keeps a copy and a copy is sent, where appropriate, to the administrative secretariat of the faculty or institute.

The extract shows the account number and indicates the structural unit to which the account is assigned. This last datum is given in words and is followed by the name of the account-holder.

The extract starts with an up-to-date statement of account. Space is provided for printing the description of the operations which have affected the account. Then follows the amount of payment or commitment corresponding to the operation described. The same extract may refer to about six operations, which is ample, since an extract is sent to the holder every time the situation of his account changes appreciably. If weekly or monthly statements had been chosen, this would have meant a long list of operations in some cases and a long form which would be largely unused in most cases. It was thought better therefore to adopt an irregular frequency which would allow the holder to be informed more rapidly and would have the advantage of a less cumbersome format.

The last entry on the extract is the balance remaining after subtraction of the amount of the last payments and commitments. With this information at his disposal, the account-holder can incur new expenditure without fear of over-spending his budget.

To facilitate contacts between account-holders and the Accounts Department staff, each operation is given a code number indicating the section responsible and the date of the event. By referring to this number, the account-holder can immediately contact the person best able to answer his questions. This system also has the advantage of defining responsibilities.

(2) Invoice office statement
This list, issued after each processing or twice a week, summarizes all invoices by the supplier's number. It gives the following information:

supplier's number
invoice number
date of invoice
date of arrival of invoice
supplier's references
account-holder's number
cost centre
number of any order note
due date
date of technical check
date of budget check
date of payment authorisation
date of payment
unit of currency (foreign exchange)
amount in Belgian francs
amount to be paid in Belgian francs.

The invoice office statement also gives, by supplier, the total amount already paid during the year and the outstanding balance on his invoices. This document gives the head of the invoice office all the information he needs to answer questions by suppliers or account-holders.

(3) Credit office statement
The credit office statement takes the form of two tables:

(a) State of credits by holder
holder's number, in alphabetical order
name and forenames
credit number
cost centre (unit)
designation of credit
initial amount of credit
amount of increases or reductions during the year
total expenditure
balance

(b) Commitments or invoices accepted or refused
These lists summarize, by faculty, the budget control operations carried out by the computer.

(4) Daybooks, ledgers and consolidated account
Each month the tapes containing information relating to the invoice office, the emoluments of academic and scientific staff and of administrative and technical staff and the tapes summarising all the corrections made to the system are processed to produce the corresponding auxiliary daybooks. In the last phase of the reorganisation of accounting the printing of these auxiliary daybooks will, in fact, become superfluous; the reliability of the system will in fact make it possible to do without these daybooks which are at present used as a basis for checking.

After the printing of these auxiliary daybooks, the tapes are sorted and combined to produce a single tape. This, in turn, produces the main daybook, listing daily operations in succession.

After printing the monthly daybook, the tape is again processed. The information is classified by nature of expenditure, cost centre and date of operation. The consolidated account for the month is then printed.

The last stage in this monthly processing of accounts information is the combination of the last monthly tape with the tapes giving the information for the preceding months. At the end of the year, the existence of this tape makes it very easy to print the consolidated account for the year.

(5) Summary of the consolidated account
The accounts for each month are balanced at the beginning of the following month. The combination of all the information is completed during the first week. Four programmes make it possible to condense information relating to the accounts operations of the past month.

The computer at present prints four lists showing total operations:
    by nature of expenditure and source of finance;
    by cost centre, nature of expenditure and source of finance;
    by source of finance, cost centre and nature of expenditure;
    by source of finance and nature of expenditure.
Thanks to these documents, the accounts and budget departments can answer the most diverse questions without resorting to extra processing of information. This regular output therefore saves valuable time which can be devoted to compiling information, preparing special programmes and additional computerisation.

These documents answer questions such as 'How much has been spent on books?' 'What has been the income of such-and-such a faculty, excluding credits granted by the University itself?' 'What is the main appropriation of funds coming from external sources of finance: personnel, equipment, operating?' 'What have been the cost centres (research units) which have benefited from contracts from such-and-such a firm or foundation?'

In addition to their intrinsic value, the monthly account documents contain information essential to the preparation of progress schedules summarizing information from both the Accounts Department and the Budget Department.

(6) Transfers
The U.C.L. works with three banks. These banks provide the data-processing

service with transfer forms in a standard format suitable for machine processing.

The task of the analysts here is therefore very simple since the user himself designs the document he needs from the University.

By the end of 1971, communications between the U.C.L. Accounts Department and its main banker no longer used the medium of transfer forms but took place through the exchange of magnetic tapes. This reform saved many hours of computer time previously spent on printing transfers.

(7) Detail of expenditure by activity
The use of 'U.C.L. cheques' enables account-holders to indicate the research or teaching activity to which each item of expenditure should be charged. In certain cases, account-holders may inform the Accounts Department that the expenditure cannot be broken down.

At the beginning of the year, all the operations carried out in the preceding year are broken down by unit, activity, source of finance and nature of expenditure. The document detailing this information enables research unit heads to make better estimates of the cost of research projects to be submitted to foundations and other sources of finance. It also affords an opportunity of judging the real appropriation of resources within a unit. Within the near future, information compiled on the occupation of facilities and on the breakdown of staff time will be incorporated in the system and will also be shown on this document. This will give an even more detailed picture of the cost of each activity. An example of the document is given in Appendix 6.

At this stage, the analytical accounting which should provide data for analysis gets under way.

(8) Reports to central government
The accounting system designed by the central government for the use of the universities is based on the functional and economic classification adopted by the public sector in the Benelux countries, and university accounts are integrated in central government accounts and thereby in the national accounting.

While the economic and functional classification has advantages at macro-economic level, it is not well adapted to such a special institution as a university. Compatibility between the university accounting system and the Belgian government accounting system is therefore catered for by a conversion programme, transferring the items under each heading to the appropriate heading under the other system. This operation is preceded by sorting out the sources of finance so as to take account of information relating to government grants only.

7. Arrangement of data

The content and form of the documents to be circulated to users determine the data to be fed into the system. The different 'files' or sets of similar data must be recorded on cards, tapes or discs, according to the technical possibilities, the frequency of consultation and the time allowed for each consultation. The following table details the mode of recording files.

PARTICULARS OF FINANCIAL FILES

Files	Volume	Medium (IBM 2314)
Events	8 000/month	Disc
Structure	600 cards	Disc
Activities	4 900 cards	Disc
Source of finance	150 cards	Disc
Accounting system	1 800 cards	Disc
Current balances	—	
Invoices	4 500/month	Disc
Personnel	1 200 personnel	Disc
Functions	400	Disc
Suppliers	2 500	Disc
Buildings	3 000 cards	Disc
Inventory	—	Disc

8. *Modular structure of the system*

The new programmes for the processing of accounts information have been designed on the modular plan. Each phase of processing corresponds to a sub-programme stored until the next phase. This procedure makes it possible to reduce the size of programmes and to break down the work of programming as well as making it easier to update programmes. Thorough technical analysis also makes it possible to automate the transition from one phase to another. The system will automatically call up the modules as the processing advances. It will do the same with the files or, where appropriate, will tell the operator when to place a particular disc on the appropriate spindle.

The first processing module sorts the data fed into the system in bulk. This safeguard greatly cuts down the time needed to prepare for machine-processing. The cards need no longer be fed in strict order. On the contrary, the system will put the data into the required order, list the missing data, calculate the size of files according to the number of data and, within each account, will fix the operations to be processed in a priority order.

Another phase of processing will be devoted to checking the reliability of each item of information. The system will verify the existence of the operation indicated, the source of finance, the unit, the person responsible, the nature of the expenditure, the order, the supplier and so on. It will also check the balance of the account to which the operation is to be assigned. These first checks will be backed up by audit checks. Finally, the system will ensure the existence of certain duplications which are themselves designed to increase the reliability of the information.

The sorting and checking of data is followed by the processing phase. During this phase, changes are made in accounts according to the instructions given for each operation. The system will automatically find the counterpart account to be debited or credited with the amount of the operation. In this way the accounts staff are relieved of half the bookkeeping work. The head of the invoice office checks the account to which the operation must be assigned and determines the movement affecting the account. The computer does the rest, observing the priorities set during the first phase. For example, an account will be credited before it is debited. An invoice will be paid before an order is taken into account; the University is already committed by the invoice, but not yet committed by the order.

The last and longest phase of processing accounts information is the printing of statements, extracts of accounts and transfers. Fortunately, multiple programming allows this work to be combined with other work which does not rely on central storage. It should be noted that before printing transfers the system sorts them according to the date on which they fall due. The 'treasury' section of the Accounts Department is therefore in no danger of paying invoices before they are due. This may be particularly useful at moments when there is not a great deal of ready money available.

9. *Access to information*

In normal periods accounts information can be processed by the machine twice a week. In vacation, weekly processing is sufficient. In spite of the great speed of processing, the classical procedure of feeding in data is very clumsy. In practice, it requires coding, punching and checking, and the transfer of data to tape or disc before any processing. Secondly, the information must be presented in the required form or it is rejected. These two factors illustrate the rigidity of the conventional procedures for recording and processing information. Furthermore, once stored, the data are accessible only if one goes through the whole reading procedure. In any event, the information is not available for some hours, given the timetable of machine occupation.

Recourse to teleprocessing reduces the excessive rigidity of these procedures. In the concrete case of U.C.L. accounts, consultation and, where appropriate, modification by direct access would have a number of advantages:
1. The credits administrator could test the computer reactions and immediately visualise the state of an account. In this way, he would be forewarned of the rejection of an invoice by the computer and — an additional advantage — would know the reasons why.
2. Information rejected by the computer could be fed in manually by the operator. This procedure would afford a solution for complicated cases such as the breakdown of expenditure, partial invoices, and so on. It would save valuable time and would allow payment orders, etc., to be made out by hand. This is the only way of bypassing the computer in urgent or complicated cases. It eliminates the domination of the machine which can at present be approached only through the medium of a rigid and complicated procedure.
3. The Department can give an immediate answer to inquiries from accountholders, and this would mean an appreciable saving of time.

The teleprocessing of information reduces the effects of distance. The U.C L. occupies two new campuses at a distance of twenty and thirty kilometres from each other. The consultation of accounts information by direct access cou'd be extended to the new campuses. Only this mode of consultation allows the maintenance of real central accounting and means that the decentralised accounting units do not need a staff of more than two.

Teleprocessing is therefore advantageous from several points of view. Its flexibility and the decentralisation and saving of machine-time which it allows compensate for the extra cost of machine rentals and programming. The use of distant consultation or teleprocessing should, however, be used only for the processing of exceptions, even though they may be numerous. The mass of information will still be recorded on card or tape and fed into the system in 'batches'. The immediate consultation of information and modifications made from a distance will be limited to the prior checking of doubtful cases, and to the manual introduction through the terminal of complex data, with the possibility of bypassing too rigid normal procedures in urgent cases.

As things are at present, constraints of machine-time, the size of the central storage and cost are delaying the application to accounts of the teleprocessing techniques already successfully applied in the field of enrolments.

F. Functioning of the Capital Budget Department

The accounts financed by the capital investment budget are identified in the same way as the operating expenditure budget accounts. Budget control will be carried out in the same way as in the case of operating credits. It will relate both to 'lots' and to expenditure.

(a) Control of lots
An aggregate budget is opened for each building or construction to be undertaken. This forecast budget is broken down into a certain number of lots or aggregate commitments, generally representing distinct types of work, such as main structure heating, electricity, etc.

Orders may be assigned to each of these lots. The first budget control takes place at this level. Total orders cannot exceed the amount allocated to a lot.

(b) Control of expenditure
Each order accepted creates a credit account to which invoices may be immediately assigned up to the amount of the order. The invoices stamped by those responsible for the buildings are submitted to the Accounts Department.

(c) Economic analysis of expenditure
An important function of the Capital Budget Department is to analyse expenditure and compile consolidated information on building costs, unit costs per square metre or cubic metre, by type of building or construction process and so on. This

407

information will be used in preparing future budgets and drawing up specifications. It is compiled after the accounts processing.

G. Consolidation of the budget and accounts information

The computerisation of budget and accounts information produces an imposing mass of documents. This volume of information cannot be assimilated by the university administrators. The data, therefore, had to be condensed into an informative summary. This process was long and difficult. The progress schedule for the operating budget went through no fewer than five versions, while that for the capital budget is not yet finished.

1. Operating budget income and expenditure

The information needed to construct the progress schedule comes from the four summaries printed each month after balancing the accounts for the previous month. It is enough to compare the budget figures with total expenditure to get an idea of the state of the budget.

The progress schedule is placed on the monthly agenda of the Executive Committee of the Board, whose members can thus assess the financial administration of the U.C.L. The schedule is in two parts: the first deals with income and expenditure on teaching and research financed by the University, the second with social activities financed by *ad hoc* grants from the Ministry of Education.

In 1972 the construction of this schedule was automated, thus saving valuable time which the Accounts Department staff can devote to interpreting the figures. The document is attached in Appendix 7.

2. The capital budget progress schedule

While the U.C.L. has the advantage of two years' experience in administering an operating budget, it still has only fragmentary information on the capital budget. It is, in fact, only quite recently that the government has made grants to enable it to undertake new building. A progress schedule must be constructed for each of the two campuses and summarized in a third schedule.

3. Other summaries

The system is designed to regroup the most diverse information. It would be easy to summarize the data relating to:

sources of finance;
the breakdown of expenditure by nature;
purchases, by supplier, in order to claim rebates;
year-end balances, in order to launch reporting procedure;
income, in order to speed up collection, etc.

The difficulty lies not in the production of information but rather in the capacity of the departments to analyse and of the administrators to assimilate.

H. Treasury reform

1. Objectives

The autonomous status of the U.C.L. means that the University administers the funds placed at its disposal to meet operating and investment needs. The aim of the treasury section of the Accounts Department is to get the best return on liquid funds by cutting down the interest payable on University debts and increasing the interest received by the University on surplus funds invested with financial institutions.

2. Establishment of a cash budget

Receipts from the various sources of U.C.L. finance are pooled in the University treasury, which thus enlarges its working capital and minimises the need to resort to bank financing. The administration of funds deposited with the treasury requires the establishment of an overall budget centralising the data of the various budgets of the institution. This cash budget distributes income and expenditure over time.

3. Documents

(a) Cash statement

The treasury section makes out the official cash statement every two days. This official statement is accompanied by a forecast statement setting out the instructions already communicated to the financial bodies which will affect the accounts. This document, with very brief comments, is communicated twice a week to the general administrator of the U.C.L. and is given in Appendix 8.

(b) Monthly forecasts

Short-term forecasts allow investments for a month. By giving a better view of the situation, they give the director of accounts the possibility of checking and postponing certain disbursements when cash is very tight, provided of course that the payment date is not obligatory, as for example in the case of staff salaries.

The one-month forecast is based on a timetable made up partly of information about staff pay and partly of data compiled from invoices submitted for payment. In Belgium, in practice, invoices are payable thirty days or sometimes sixty days 'after the end of the month' in which the invoice is made out by the supplier. This information is completed by information about repayments and the payment of loan interest, rent of premises, payments under contract and so on.

Estimates of revenue are based on information from the ministries concerned. They are completed by information from the students' account section and capital assets section of the U.C.L.

(c) Six-month and twelve-month forecasts

These forecasts enable the director of accounts to make medium-term investments, to take action in connection with commitments and to obtain credits from finance houses. The twelve-month forecast makes it possible to act upon the different budgets and upon university policy.

The technique of constructing six-month and twelve-month forecasts is a little different from that used for one-month forecasts. In practice, information about future maturities is totally lacking. Even forecasts of operating and capital expenditure are based on the experience of the previous years. Variations in monthly expenditure are in fact cyclical in character. The recurrence of phenomena may therefore be counted upon. As in the case of short-term forecasts, information relating to staff emoluments is perfectly reliable. Forecasts of building costs are drawn up by the services concerned and reflect the timetable of works.

It is even harder to forecast income on a monthly basis. Government grants are not paid on any fixed date, but according to the state of financial affairs in the treasury or even sometimes according to political events.

4. Cash budget control

The treasury section processes the debit and credit notes of the finance departments everyday. This information allows the actual situation to be compared with the forecasts and any necessary corrections can be made.

VII. The building and equipment sub-system

The analysis unit has not yet had the time to achieve any major results in the administration of buildings and equipment. At best, it has an inventory drawn up by the common services of the two universities and checked by the administrative secretariats of the U.C.L. faculties. It has been possible to extract some statistics from this mass of information, but they relate solely to the facilities with no reference to the equipment installed.

1. Inventory of facilities

The 6,000 or so different types of space occupied by the U.C.L., the K.U.L. and the services common to the two universities have been inventoried. Each building, floor and room is now identified by a code. The 'facilities' data base contains the following data:

> By site:
>> commune in which located
>> code
>> number of buildings
>> form of tenure
>> area
>> taxation and purpose codes
> By building:
>> reference of site
>> code
>> area
>> address
>> date of commencement and date of occupation
>> gross area by floor
>> net area by floor
> By room:
>> reference of building
>> code
>> use (university, faculty, unit)

purpose

net area

capacity (in number of persons)

The 'purpose' code identifies lecture-rooms, teaching or research laboratories and administrative and technical facilities. Each of these major headings is broken down into a certain number of subdivisions giving more or less precise particulars which identify the type of facility; classrooms with fixed or movable seats, seminar rooms, lecture rooms, projection rooms and so on.

2. First statistics

A programme for processing these data produces statistics giving the number of rooms and net area occupied by each faculty and unit, broken down by building, type of room and purpose.

3. Renting of facilities

As from 1 January 1971 the U.C.L. has paid the K.U.L. rent for the whole of the space it occupies in Louvain. The occupation statistics enable the cost of using the facilities to be charged against each unit. This heading has, therefore, been included since the 1972 budget.

VIII. The personnel sub-system

Attempts to organise the personnel subsystem have been limited to improving the functioning of the administrative services. They have not yet reached the stage of producing statistics or management information.

1. The personnel departments

A department with a staff of four is responsible for updating administrative files and for the renumeration of academic and scientific staff. It has a small NCR computer and provides the Analytical Unit with punched cards used to make out payment orders for the 1,600 or so members of the U.C.L. academic and scientific staff.

The administrative and technical Personnel Department keeps the files of 1,500 staff. The Analytical Unit is responsible for computerising the data originating from this Department.

2. Documents

The Department issues the usual documents:
> payment order to the bank;
> statement of taxes and vacation allowances;
> statement of social security contributions;
> list of addresses;
> breakdown of salaries subsidised by external sources of finance.

3. Information

In order to produce the documents needed to keep administrative files, the Department has the following information, recorded on disc:
> personal number (serial number in alphabetical order);
> name and forenames;
> name of husband or wife;
> date of birth, marriage, birth of first child, joining and leaving the service, retirement, termination of contract;

unit or units in which the teacher or researcher works;

percentage of time spent in each unit;

function in each unit;

working hours;

nationality, civil status, sex, title;

staff category, grade, scale, seniority;

official residence, usual residence, professional address or addresses, street, number, commune, postal canton, telephone;

pension fund, social security, identity card, personnel register, bank account and postal cheque account numbers;

system of group insurance, family allowances (number of dependents);

source of finance.

IX. Projects

The constitution of an information system is a dynamic process. Furthermore, it is not an end in itself but rather a means which should contribute with others towards rationalising the decision-making process. Its implementation should therefore serve as a support for the many decisions taken at every level. It will, therefore, be subject to continual change in order to keep pace with the changing activities of the University and the relevant decisions.

A. Extension of the data base

The attentive reader will have detected the present weaknesses of the U.C.L. information system. The file of teaching and research activities still needs enriching with numerous data. Student registrations should take account not only of level of studies but also of the courses followed. The personnel file is very summary and merely meets the operating needs of the departments concerned. It should take account of the distribution of the time of teachers and researchers among their different activities; should also contain information about the *curricula vitae* of staff members and provide management information such as rate of turnover, replacement of teachers and researchers by discipline and seniority and so on. The list of gaps is a long one and proves that to arrive at even the first stage of an information system is a long task.

B. Improvement of certain procedures

Several important fields have not yet been tackled, since we did not want to disperse the efforts of the Analytical Unit. Examples of these fields would be the distribution of lecture rooms, stock control, checking the regular maintenance of equipment, the automatic printing of certain documents such as course timetables, the communication of decisions in the matter of credits and nominations, treasury administration, the charging of maintenance and repair costs.

Progressively and according to certain priorities the corresponding departments will be able to benefit from the data base to integrate their own data and to apply modern management techniques so as to increase their efficiency.

C. Production of strategic information

The various sub-systems should produce summaries consolidating a great many data and indicating to those responsible the evolution of the University and the extent to which the aims are being achieved. After thirty months of work, the first summaries were available in two sectors only. They have been described in the chapters on the students system and the financial system. The other sets of files are being organised in turn to produce the information needed to master the problems. The reader in search of a list of strategic information can usefully refer to the documents published by the IIEP[1], where he will find details of the staffing formula, the budget time of teachers, the rate of staff turnover, unit costs and so on.

In 1970 the U.C.L. laid the foundations of analytical accounting but it included only operating and capital expenditure. In 1971 the rent of areas occupied by research and teaching units was included, and in 1972 the breakdown of staff time to serve as a basis for assigning resources in time and space to each research and teaching activity was also added. Analytical accounting can now provide valuable information about the resources invested in each activity or group of activities, and on this basis a technique for unit costs can be developed.

Up to now, only easily measurable variables have entered into the constitution of an information system which is therefore limited to expressing relations between concrete units such as areas, hours, francs or very specific activities. It can be said that the very essence of higher education eludes this first effort at quantification. The training of men by teaching and research defies description of this kind. A university information system, if it is to be complete, should therefore be enriched with data on the intellectual and social development of students and the psycho-sociological characteristics of their background. The students should therefore be tested qualitatively before, during and after their time at the University. The tests would relate to their affective and cognitive characteristics. Scales of attitudes should provide an assessment of their critical spirit, their creativeness, their capacity for self-learning and the strains to which they are subjected, for example. These data would complete the detailed information derived from enrolments and examination results. Psychological tests and interviews afford the only means of measuring the evolution of the members of the university community. These techniques, however, are still imperfect, and moreover time-consuming.

The measurement of research results is even more difficult. It is, however, necessary to be able to assess the contribution of the University to the different disciplines so as to be in a position, where appropriate, to reallocate the resources invested. In addition to the inventory of publications, the information system

1. *Planning the development of universities,* Paris, The Unesco Press, 1971-74. (Full details of the series are given at the beginning of this volume.)

should be able to supply particulars on patents or inventions based on work done at the University, and on researchers' development and so on.

The contribution of the University to the society which surrounds it should also be specified. The collection of data would deal both with public services rendered by the University in the matter of hospitals, advice to firms and its contribution to economic growth through the training of graduates.

The determination of the relevant information in these numerous fields is conceivable only in the long term. Its collection and processing will also raise many problems. The constitution of an information system is therefore not a short-term concept, but rather one of the long-term objectives of a University which aims to rationalise its management.

D. The system at the service of the basic unit

Too often, the application of management techniques is reserved for the top level of the institution. Nevertheless, faculties, departments and units take decisions every day which, in the long term, have a profound influence on the allocation of resources and on the achievement of the objectives of students, researchers and teachers. The university administration must certainly satisfy the management needs of the University as a whole. This objective is, of course, essential, but not sufficient. The U.C.L. Analytical Unit therefore devotes part of its efforts to research into the most appropriate management methods as instruments of decision for members of the university community in the context of basic units.

One of the decisions frequently formulated at the base and needing final sanction at university level is the creation or modification of a curriculum. The decision-making process must be rapid if the curriculum is to be adapted to the needs of students and of society and to the evolution of knowledge in different disciplines. It is, therefore, essential to be able to test rapidly the work of those who work out new curricula.

It can be noted, however, that the very magnitude of the work of reform delays the adjustment of curricula to needs. The cumbersome character of the process of change in fact prevents original reform. It also stops the students from taking an effective part in this work and from assessing the results of reforms. These various findings have induced the U.C.L. Analytical Unit to set about formulating a method of decision-making suitable to teaching units.

1. Decentralised decision

We consider that the formulation of a curriculum is a decentralised decision. It is at the level on which they have their being that curricula should be established, modified and evaluated. This presupposes, in particular, that the level responsible has its own overall budget within which it has an adequate freedom of choice.

The *objectives* of the curriculum must conform to the general objectives of the University.

417

The *resources* allocated to the curriculum are the indication of its integration in the University as a system of means; the cost of all the resources must therefore be evaluted and economic reasoning must be an integral part of the work of the group; the information system must provide data calculated to inform about different choices and to test their financial and even educational incidence.

The *content* of the curriculum will be co-ordinated with that of other curricula so as to avoid duplication. This is a horizontal co-ordination corresponding to the vertical co-ordination envisaged under the preceding points, and is one of the concerns of higher authority in the event of curriculum changes. Here again, the university information system is an essential intermediary.

2. Basic assumption

Any method of decision-making in the matter of curricula must be based on an idea of what an educational situation involves. In the absence of such a concept, the administrative system might be led to impose its own values on the educational system.

The problem of educational activities is generally seen as the search for the most appropriate educational method of imparting a certain content which is, moreover, little open to challenge. A content, however, is not self-defining; it must be related to the objective which is, or should be, its *raison d'être*. In other words, there should be an objective underlying every educational activity. The objective will be the subject of discussion and a condition of the control and self-regulation of the system. Even so, the objective must be precisely defined. To learn the history of art is not a precise objective; it can cover the training of tourist guides or psychological research on the evolution of modes of expression.

The fixing of the objective is a prerequisite to all educational action, and therefore to any study of the educational methods to be used. It should be the result of concerted agreement among all those concerned.

After the objective, the two other essential characteristics of an educational activity are (a) the *content*: more often defined as 'courses' or 'subjects'; and (b) the *teaching methods*, i.e. the educational means used to impart the content (formal lectures, tutorials, practical exercises, etc.)

It seems essential to regard the content as a means of achieving the educational objective. It is, in practice, too often identified or confused with the objective. Too often, also, for this very reason, evaluation systems strive to ascertain how far the content has been assimilated, when they should really be looking at the objective.

The choice of content and teaching methods will be conditioned by a clear and precise definition of objectives. Educational self-management is not a myth if the person to be educated can choose with full knowledge of the facts, that is to say, if he is encouraged to formulate his objectives and take them into account.

The soundness of a method of determining curricula will, therefore, depend on the possibility of clearly formulating the objectives and fixing their relative importance. Similarly, the value of a curriculum will depend on the adjustment of the content and teaching methods to the objectives of the learners.

To sum up, the approach should:

1. Direct the thinking of the responsible group towards the formulation of objectives and enable it to discern the consequences of its choice.
2. Then, determine content and methods, ensuring their adjustment to the objectives.
3. Allow great freedom of choice and innovation.

This method of decision presupposes the assignment of a budget to each teaching unit and this 'resources' aspect should be treated almost automatically. Thanks to a flexible and effective instrument, the members of the unit will envisage a great many alternatives and look at them in terms of objectives. The method should also take into account the human, financial and material resources needed to achieve the objective.

3. Description of the method

Two types of work will be closely linked:

1. The work of the group building up the curriculum, centred solely on the definition of objectives, content and methods, their adjustment to the objectives and, finally, on the evolution of the proposed curriculum.
2. The automated work; essentially the following:
   (a) determining resources by a simulation model of the cost of teaching activities;
   (b) determining the optimum curriculum on the basis of the resources of the group (linear programming, simplex method);
   (c) the distribution of the aggregate 'teaching' budget among the different curricula in the light of the 'outputs' expected and general university policy (linear programming);
   (d) the five-year forward budget to establish future needs according to the different resources (overall simulation model).

4. Work of the responsible group

The group responsible for drawing up the curriculum should consist of students with common objectives, assisted by teachers, researchers and, where appropriate, representatives of outside interests. Obviously, the views of new students will emerge only progressively in the course of studies. The importance of advisers will, therefore, be preponderant at the outset; a whole semester of induction would even be advisable.

Aims

       to draw up an ordered list of objectives;

       to determine a set of content and methods which will make it possible to achieve these objectives;

       to judge the adaptation of content and methods to the objectives formulated;

in a later phase, to criticise the optimum curriculum furnished by linear programming, and where necessary, to revise judgments passed in the first phase.

Working methods

The adoption of Delphi type techniques will obviate the disadvantages of group work (tendency to agree with the views of the strongest personalities, digressions on points of detail, etc.).

> each participant will be invited to give his views individually, in writing;
> the extreme judgments (first and last quartile) will then be analysed in group;
> each member will be invited to review his judgment, and so on until a final consensus is reached.

Output

The work of the group will take concrete form in:

> a list of objectives with a weighting reflecting the priorities assigned by the group;
> a list of contents;
> a list of educational methods;
> a matrix of markings reflecting the contribution of different contents to the achievement of each objective;
> a matrix of the same type establishing the relations between educational methods and objectives.

5. Costs simulation model

Costs simulation makes it possible to introduce economic reasoning into the formulation of the curriculum and to determine the resources needed to carry out the teaching activities.

The curriculum should be defined with the utmost freedom. Costing should therefore be adapted to the widest diversity, avoiding clichés such as 'classes', 'tutorials', and so on. The members of the group, moreover, cannot be expected to concentrate their attention on complicated calculations. A flexible and simple method of calculation must be found to bridge the gap between educational language and economic reasoning.

The costs model has two inputs and two outputs:

1. The input for the use of the groups takes the form of simple questions grouped on two standard sheets. These are the *variables* of the activity.
2. The input for the use of the overall model is a set of *parameters* which are included in: (a) the module converting the activity into various categories of resources, and (b) the module converting resources into francs.
3. The output for the use of the groups takes the form of a table of costs related to number of hours of activity and number of students.
4. The output for the overall model is a file summing up the variables and the resources needed for each activity.

6. *Optimisation of curriculum*

The optimum curriculum is the one which best achieves the objectives of the group, while obeying a certain number of restraints, the main one of which is clearly the budget available. It is, therefore, necessary to determine the time to be devoted to each of the content-method combinations which best satisfy the aspirations of the students.

This comparison of the degrees of achievement of the objectives is made through the medium of an objective function.

The objective function
This function reflects both the priorities assigned to the different objectives and the degree to which methods and contents are adjusted to the objectives. The product of the two matrices, content-objective and objective-method will, therefore, constitute the objective function.

The number of hours to be devoted to each subject under each method of teaching is an unknown quantity. It is, therefore, necessary to find all the combinations which maximise the objective function.

The restraints
The overall budget of the curriculum will be obtained by adding the fixed costs of each method and the hourly costs multiplied by the number of hours devoted to each activity. The amount should not exceed the budget allocated to the curriculum.

The time restraints are of several kinds:

(a) Total time
The resource 'student-time' is not unlimited. The total work required by the curriculum must be contained within a certain number of hours (T).

(b) Subject time
The time devoted to each subject, whatever the method used, must also be kept within certain limits ($m_i M_i$).

(c) Method time
The same remark applies as in the case of subjects ($n_j N_j$).

(d) Preliminaries
In each subject, certain teaching methods can be used only at a certain stage. It is obvious, for instance, that the revision of content by programmed teaching must be preceded by an exposition which may be by means of lectures, personal study, group investigation under the leadership of a senior student and so on.

If there are M subjects
          n methods
          r objectives

Mathematical expression:

Let i be the subject index

j the method index

k the objective index

At the outset, we have:

the matrix $A = aik$ adjustment of subject to objective

the matrix $B = bjk$ adjustment of method to objective

and the diagonal matrix $P = pkk$ priority of objectives.

The unknowns are Xij, the number of hours to be devoted to subject i by method j.

The objective function $F = \sum_{ij} C_{ij} X_{ij}$

where the matrix $C = A.P.B$

The restraints are:

- *Budget*

The simulation model supplies equations of the cost of methods in the form:

$$T_j = f_j + v_j h_j$$

where T_j is the total cost

f_j the fixed costs

v_j the cost per hour of activity

h_j the total number of hours of activity

of which $h_j = \sum_i X_{ij}$

The budget restraint will therefore be expressed:

$$\sum_j (f_j y_j + v_j \sum_i X_{ij}) \leqslant \text{Budget allocated}$$

with

$$y_j = 1, \text{ if } \sum_i X_{ij} > 0$$

$$y_j = 0, \text{ if } \sum_i X_{ij} = 0$$

To enable a check to be made, we shall add constraints of the type:

$$T y_j = \sum X_{ij} \geqslant 0$$

Total time:

$$\sum_{ij} X_{ij} \leqslant \text{maximum total time}$$

Subject time:

$$M_i \leqslant \sum_j X_{ij} \leqslant M_i$$

Method time:

$$N_j \leqslant \sum_i X_{ij} \leqslant N_j$$

Preliminaries:

$$X_{ij} \geqslant t_{ij}$$

Solution:

The whole of the problem can therefore be expressed in the form:

$$\text{MAX F} = \sum_{ij} C_{ij} X_{ij}$$

Subject to the restraints:

$$\sum_{j} (f_j y_j + v_j \sum_{i} X_{ij}) \leqslant \text{Budget}$$

$$T_y = \sum_{j} \sum_{i} X_{ij} \qquad \geqslant 0$$

$$\sum_{ij} X_{ij} \qquad\qquad \leqslant \text{Total time}$$

$$M_i \leqslant \sum_{j} X_{ij} \leqslant M_i$$

$$N_j \leqslant \sum_{i} X_{ij} \leqslant N_j$$

$$X_{ij} \geqslant T_{ij}$$

The problem is therefore one of linear programming, and a solution can be found in the simplex method.

The optimum curriculum which results is submitted to the group for criticism or acceptance. In the event of criticism, the initial positions of the group must be reviewed and if necessary, reformulated.

7. Curriculum budget

The allocation of a budget by the academic authorities should result, first, from a forecast of the services and needs of the basic unit, and secondly, from the general policy of the University. The integration of all these decisions is one of the research projects in hand.

Ideally, an overall objective function should be constituted by the weighted sum of the objective functions of each curriculum. The coefficients of weighting would reflect the determination to promote certain curricula. With this approach, a curriculum would no longer be optimised for a determined budget value, but for a whole series of budgets within a 'bracket'. This bracket would be determined by two extreme values; the minimum budget essential to satisfy the minimum restraints and the maximum budget after which the objective function ceases to grow. At this point, the available time becomes the predominant restraint. Thanks to the parametrisation of the budget restraint, the optimisation programme provides the law which links the optimum satisfaction of students with the budget allocated to their curriculum. The sum of the individual budgets should not exceed the total budget allocated to teaching.

Current research is designed to solve the two problems raised by the practical achievement of this integration. The first is due to the dimension of the linear programme. The capacity of the present computer does not allow the use of the simplex algorithm for several hundred curricula each involving a great many variables and restraints. The Wolfe and Dantzig algorithm seems much more appropriate.

The second problem arises out of the volume of data to be processed. It will have to be solved in terms of the organisation and integration of information. The formulas proposed by the manufacturers have proved to be too cumbersome for the achievement of an information system on the scale of a large university. Current research should lead to a more effective solution.

8. Overall simulation model

The overall simulation model is designed to bring out the consequences of general policy options. It should provide medium-term forward budgets by type of resource. This model should make it possible to test the incidence of decisions such as:

> promotion of post-graduate studies;
> conversion to the three-term system;
> improved staffing ratio;
> promotion of new teaching methods (e.g. by computer or television);
> reduction of the size of groups taking part in practical exercises.

The model will, therefore, be inspired by the following logic:

1. Forecast of the number of students by programme of studies (operational in 1970).
2. On the basis of the curriculum activities file, translation and regrouping by method of teaching.
3. Through the costs simulation model, translation of methods of teaching into terms of resources and consolidation of this information.
4. Overall budget by type of human and material resources, and by subtracting existing availabilities, identification of long-term needs.
5. Translation into financial terms of the needs for human and material resources, i.e. the establishment of medium-term ordinary and extraordinary budgets.

The reliability of this model depends on the soundness of the forecasts of the student population, the pertinence of the analysis of teaching methods and the choice of parameters for the cost simulation model.

Conclusion

The establishment of an information system is a prerequisite to the introduction of modern management techniques, and to the rationalisation of decisions taken in the University. It is also an essential condition for participation. The latter is, indeed, conceivable only on the basis of a dialogue sustained by a constant flow of information.

U.C.L. has had some success, both in overall planning and in working out the 'students' and 'finances' sub-systems. Our study will have familiarized the reader with the administrative and computer techniques used in this context.

Some technical difficulties remain to be solved. University management, indeed, requires an enormous volume of information to be available. The programmes worked out by the computer manufacturers do not allow for easy handling of all the files. In addition, the achievement of such complex administrative applications as accounting and registration demand the collaboration of qualified experts.

The real problems arise, however, over the identification of the strategic information to be supplied to the responsible parties. The choices in fact depend on the objectives assigned to the institution as a whole, as well as to its many components. Universities are at present distinguished by a manifest lack of policy and they do not seem particularly inclined to reconsider the objectives of the past and readjust the allocation of their resources in the light of new needs.

The acceptance of new procedures also raises some problems. Their adoption should therefore be visualized only after a trial period, during which the old methods remain in use side by side with the new. The views of the administrative heads should be sought on each occasion; the ideal arrangement is to constitute, as at Louvain, a standing administrative committee to which all new projected reforms are submitted. The acceptance of changes by the teaching staff involves further obstacles, usually due to the inadequate information available to the professors, absorbed as they are by their teaching and research responsibilities. Personal contact cannot be established in every case. Any decision on a proposed reform should, however, take into account the 'reconversion' effort which the teachers would have to make, even if the new formula has undeniable advantages over the old one. It is, therefore, desirable for any administrative procedure implying the participation of teachers and researchers to be fully explained, at the Faculty or University Board level for example.

The biggest psychological obstacle is not, perhaps, to be found among the administrative staff, nor among teachers and researchers. Lack of interest on the part of the authorities will kill initiative more surely than any form of hostility. Efforts to bring in an information system will come to nothing if, on the one hand, the academic authorities do not suggest what information should be produced, and on the other hand, they do not use that information as the basis for their decision-making process.

Apart from these difficulties, the University should ensure stability of the staff in charge of the administrative procedures and the handling of information. It will therefore have to guarantee salary scales and career prospects equivalent to those found in industry. The University will also have to provide such staff with varied, interesting work.

Universities will consider the establishment of an information system in the light of the direct advantages it offers in the form of efficiency of administrative procedures and statistical information. Each University is, of course, a unique case; the decision to launch the university administration on the track of an information system should therefore be preceded, each time, by a detailed cost-effectiveness analysis of the project. The results of this analysis will guide the choice of the problems to be allotted priority, as well as the selection of working methods, equipment, and the people responsible for implementing the system.

After the stages of administrative reorganisation and the data base, the University will be able to contemplate going to the heart of the matter. In doing so, it will arouse the interest of those responsible for the management of the faculties and departments. The habit of handling strategic information will make them familiar with the system; they will then expect more of it, and will want to use the available information to improve the quality of their decisions. It is at this point that the resources invested in the constitution of a system will show their highest return.

The *raison d'être* of an information system is its contribution to decision-making. Even so, it is essential that the responsible parties make use of the instrument placed in their hands, and try themselves to rationalise the management of their University. The fundamental problem lies at this level, not in the data equipment or human resources needed to constitute an information system. Without the express intention of the responsible persons to act in strict conformity with it, it would be useless to enter upon the long, costly and often arduous course which leads to the achievement of a university information system.

Appendixes

APPENDIX 1.

Rectorate

SECTION		Cabinet office	Scientific secretariat	Third World secretariat	Scientific and academic personnel	External relations	TOTAL
1968	Office staff	1	4	3	1	3	11
	Administrators		3	3		3	11
1970	Office staff	2	3		3		11
	Administrators	2	3	1	4	4	14

General administration

Administration

SECTION		Cabinet office	Management	Student secretariat	Ordinary budget	Extraordinary budget	Accounts	Analysis unit	Data processing	TOTAL
1968	Office staff		1	1	2	1	1			6
	Administrators	1	1	1	2	2	1	6		14
1970	Office staff	1	1	4	1		4			11
	Administrators	2	3	7	2	2	9	6	5	36

APPENDIX 2.
Form for curriculum changes

FORM FOR CURRICULUM CHANGES	*Reserved for the rectorate*
RECTORATE VISA	
	Total number of hours
FACULTY VISA	1st Semester: / / Note:_____ 2nd Semester: / /
Signature Name _____ Date _____ Date of entry to rectorate Decision of Board	PRELIMINARIES STUDY YEARS BY COURSES code code ob op lg code ob op lg

I. DELETION   YES – NO (1)

II. SUBDIVISION   YES – NO (1)

     Note: in the event of subdivision, open a new file and cite the references
               of the new course below

     code   Designation_____

III. CHAIR VACANT (3)   YES – NO (1)

       new course *(justifications to be annexed)*
       retirement
       death
       resignation   (2)

IV. PROPOSALS

     1) New designation

     2) Established staff, deputies, etc.

       to be deleted

Name	Forenames	Duties	Personal number

Financial incidence   **Decisions**

(1) *Strike out as appropriate*   (2) *Mark in the appropriate box*   (3) *Annex the syllabus of the course*

continued overleaf

APPENDIX 2 *(continued)*

					Financial incidence	Decisions

to be added

Name	Forenames	Duties	Personal number

to be renewed

Name	Forenames	Duties	Personal number

3) Total number of hours   Theory   Practical or tutorial

     1st semester

     2nd semester

Two-year course (1)
This course will be held every two years
Length of course to be decided
This course will be held in

4) New code   TOTAL

5) Preliminaries

     code   code

     to be added   to be deleted

6) Study years by courses

     code   ob op lg   code   ob op lg

     to be added   to be deleted

V. NUMBER OF EXAMINEES: 1st session 1970   2nd session 1970
                                  1971   1971

VI. REFERENCES TO EARLIER DECISIONS

ACAD. CNCL.	EXEC. BD.	FAC. CNCL.	INST. CNCL.			

(1) *Strike out as appropriate*

APPENDIX 3.

Flow charts of examination procedure

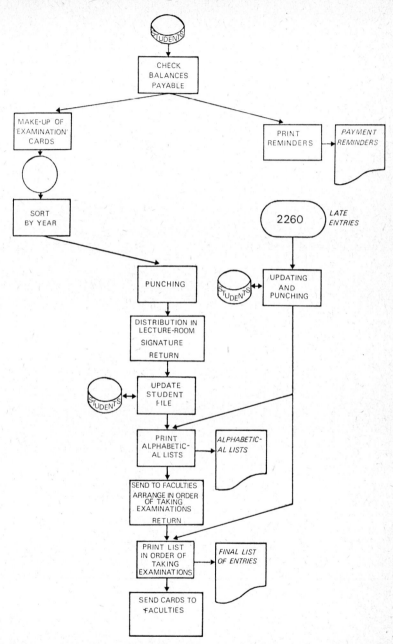

1. *Enrolments*

APPENDIX 3 *(continued)*

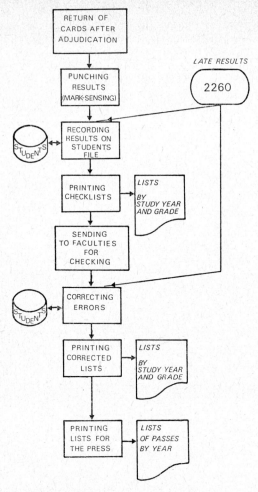

2. *Statistics of examination results:
   daily processing*

APPENDIX 3 *(continued)*

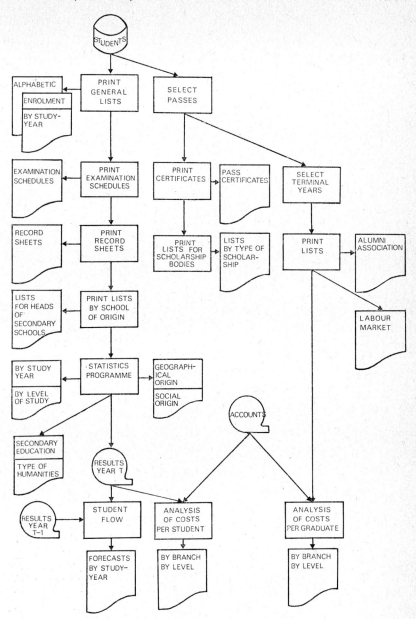

3. *Statistics of examination results: terminal processing*

APPENDIX 4

Output of statistics of examination results (part only)

```
              ****              ****              ****1969-70 ***
           Entries    Sat.    Feb    June    Sept    Pass    Fail
```

		Entries	Sat.	Feb	June	Sept	Pass	Fail
Total	N	13593	11321	338	10251	4119	8855	2466
100.00	%	100.00	83.29	2.49	75.41	30.30	65.14	18.14
100.00	%		100.00	2.99	90.55	36.38	78.22	21.78
Men	N	9235	7712	193	7068	2923	5938	1774
67.94	%	100.00	83.51	2.09	76.53	31.65	64.30	19.21
68.12	%		100.00	2.50	91.65	37.90	77.00	23.00
Women	N	4358	3609	145	3183	1196	2917	692
32.06	%	100.00	82.81	3.33	73.04	27.44	66.93	15.98
31.88	%		100.00	4.02	88.20	33.14	80.83	19.17
Belgian	N	10971	9390	262	8566	3337	7438	1952
80.71	%	100.00	85.59	2.39	78.08	30.42	67.80	17.79
82.94	%		100.00	2.79	91.22	35.54	79.21	20.79
Foreign	N	2622	1931	76	1685	782	1417	514
19.29	%	100.00	73.65	2.90	64.26	29.82	54.04	19.60
17.06	%		100.00	3.94	87.26	40.50	73.38	26.62
Non-scholarship.	N	10310	8739	231	8023	3207	6779	1960
75.85	%	100.00	84.76	2.24	77.82	31.11	65.75	19.01
77.19	%		100.00	2.64	91.81	36.70	77.57	22.43
Scholarship	N	3283	2582	107	2228	912	2076	506
24.15	%	100.00	78.65	3.26	67.86	27.78	63.23	15.41
22.81	%		100.00	4.14	86.29	35.32	80.40	19.60
New 1st Gen	N	144	124		120	63	69	55
1.06	%	100.00	86.11		83.33	43.75	47.92	38.19
1.10	%		100.00		96.77	50.81	55.65	44.35
Former Univ.	N	13449	11197	338	10131	4056	8786	2411
98.94	%	100.00	83.26	2.51	75.33	30.16	65.33	17.93
98.90	%		100.00	3.02	90.48	36.22	78.47	21.53
New UCL	N	3336	2854	6	2753	1220	1754	1100
24.54	%	100.00	85.55	.18	82.52	36.57	52.58	32.97
25.21	%		100.00	.21	96.46	42.75	61.46	38.54
Former UCL	N	10257	8467	332	7498	2899	7101	1366
75.46	%	100.00	82.55	3.24	73.10	28.26	69.23	13.32
74.79	%		100.00	3.92	88.56	34.24	83.87	16.13
Kotteurs	N	9861	8396	189	7709	3029	6606	1790
72.54	%	100.00	85.14	1.92	78.18	30.72	66.99	18.15
74.16	%		100.00	2.25	91.82	36.08	78.68	21.32
Navette	N	3732	2925	149	2542	1090	2249	676
27.46	%	100.00	79.38	3.99	68.11	29.21	60.26	18.11
25.84	%		100.00	5.09	86.91	37.26	76.89	23.11
unmarried	N	11886	10320	256	9448	3808	8030	2290
87.44	%	100.00	86.82	2.15	79.49	32.04	67.56	19.27
91.16	%		100.00	2.48	91.55	36.90	77.81	22.19

```
** U.C.ᴸ. *****        CATHOLIC UNIVERSITY OF LOUVAIN    *****  *****      *****
```

G.D.	GR.D	Dist.	Satis.	Accepted	Post-poned	Absent	Refused	Reus'	A.N-M
107	557	2310	5202	679	2164	139	163	17	6
.79	4.10	16.99	38.27	5.00	15.92	1.02	1.20	.13	.04
.95	4.92	20.40	45.95	6.00	19.11	1.23	1.44	.15	.05
84	386	1518	3533	417	1551	95	128	10	4
.91	4.18	16.44	38.26	4.52	16.79	1.03	1.39	.11	.04
1.09	5.01	19.68	45.81	5.41	20.11	1.23	1.66	.13	.05
23	171	792	1669	262	613	44	35	7	2
.53	3.92	18.17	38.30	6.01	14.07	1.01	.80	.16	.05
.64	4.74	21.95	46.25	7.26	16.99	1.22	.97	.19	.06
96	494	1997	4423	428	1739	92	121	10	4
.88	4.50	18.20	40.32	3.90	15.85	.84	1.10	.09	.04
1.02	5.26	21.27	47.10	4.56	18.52	.98	1.29	.11	.04
11	63	313	779	251	425	47	42	7	2
.42	2.40	11.94	29.71	9.57	16.21	1.79	1.60	.27	.08
.57	3.26	16.21	40.34	13.00	22.01	2.43	2.18	.36	.10
78	413	1704	4198	386	1738	82	140	10	4
.76	4.01	16.53	40.72	3.74	16.86	.80	1.36	.10	.04
.89	4.73	19.50	48.04	4.42	19.89	.94	1.60	.11	.05
29	144	606	1004	293	426	57	23	7	2
.88	4.39	18.46	30.58	8.92	12.98	1.74	.70	.21	.06
1.12	5.58	23.47	38.88	11.35	16.50	2.21	.89	.27	.08
1	2	12	49	5	47	2	6		
.69	1.39	8.33	34.03	3.47	32.64	1.39	4.17		
.81	1.61	9.68	39.52	4.03	37.90	1.61	4.84		
106	555	2298	5153	674	2117	137	157	17	6
.79	4.13	17.09	38.32	5.01	15.74	1.02	1.17	.13	.04
.95	4.96	20.52	46.02	6.02	18.91	1.22	1.40	.15	.05
16	79	392	1148	119	961	25	114	6	1
.48	2.37	11.75	34.41	3.57	28.81	.75	3.42	.18	.03
.56	2.77	13.74	40.22	4.17	33.67	.88	3.99	.21	.04
91	478	1918	4054	560	1203	114	49	11	5
.89	4.66	13.70	39.52	5.46	11.73	1.11	.48	.11	.05
1.07	5.65	22.65	47.88	6.61	14.21	1.35	.58	.13	.06
80	413	1695	3893	520	1581	95	114	12	4
.81	4.24	17.19	39.48	5.27	16.03	.96	1.16	.12	.04
.95	4.98	20.19	46.37	6.19	18.83	1.13	1.36	.14	.05
27	139	615	1309	159	583	44	49	5	2
.72	3.72	16.48	35.08	4.26	15.62	1.18	1.31	.13	.05
.92	4.75	21.03	44.75	5.44	19.93	1.50	1.68	.17	.07
86	494	2084	4849	517	2027	106	157	13	4
.72	4.16	17.53	40.80	4.35	17.05	.89	1.32	.11	.03
.83	4.79	20.19	46.99	5.01	19.64	1.03	1.52	.13	.04

APPENDIX 5
Histogram of dispersion of marks

Faculty of Economics and Political and Social Sciences

First candidature, July 1969

Course: Infinitesimal calculus

Section : A Prof.

****

Graphic representation of results

Values to be noted:

Numbers: 71

Arithmetical mean: 10,22

Standard deviation: 3,11

Students unmarked: 8

Graph : Ordinates : Number of students in %

Maximum represented 46%

Abscissae : Marks from 1 to 20

▓▓▓ = one class

APPENDIX 6
Summary of expenditure by activities

Université Catholique de Louvain

SERVICE DE COMPTABILITE
de Croylaan, 52
3030 HEVERLEE TEL. 349.31

SUMMARY OF EXPENDITURE BY ACTIVITIES

From / /   To / /

No	DESIGNATION OF ACTIVITIES	Source of Finance	Disbursements	Current Commitments Frs	TOTAL Frs

Total Operating	Total Equipment (E)	Total Premises	Total Personnel (P)		Total Disbursements	Total Commitments	Grand Total

Breakdown by financing : U.C.L. :   NON U.C.L. :

0 10 001 2599

APPENDIX 7
Operating budget progress schedule

	INCOME AND EXPENDITURE UNDER THE ORDINARY BUDGET OF THE TEACHING AND RESEARCH SECTOR (as of 30 October, 1970)				
	1970 budget before amendment	1970 budget after amendment	Accounts 30/10/70	Rate of execution	1971 budget
I. INCOME					
II. EXPENDITURE					
- Personnel					
- Operating					
- Financial charges					
- Equipment					
- Depreciation					
- Grants to clinics					
- Contribution to UCL-KUL administration:					
a) personnel					
b) operating					
c) equipment					
d) financial charges					
e) sundries					
f) depreciation					
- Refund of costs incurred by KUL:					
a) personnel					
b) operating					
c) minor maintenance					
d) major maintenance					
e) improvements					
f) sundries					
- Provisions:					
a) FFR					
b) Deaths during year					
c) Faculty reserve					
d) FDS					
Total expenditure					
III. BALANCES OF SECTOR					
UCL action on behalf of KUL :					
- convention: Annex 14, art. 34					
NEW BALANCE					

APPENDIX 8
Official cash statement

CASH POSITION OF CENTRAL ADMINISTRATION AT _____					No
SIGHT ACCOUNTS	SITUATION AT____	SITUATION AT ____	Movements		COMMENTS
			IN	OUT	
Cash in hand					
SGB No. 44040					
SGB No. 44080 "endowments"					
SGB No. 45500 "enrolments"					
-					
BB No. L/00/12300					
CCP No. 666666					
CCP No. 334.306 "enrolments"					
C.G.E.R.					
TOTAL DISPOSABLE					
TERM ACCOUNTS					
SGB No.					
-					
-					
C.G.E.R.					
TOTAL DISPOSABLE					
GRAND TOTAL					
MEDICAL SECTOR					
FORECAST					
Current payments					
Current Income					

IIEP book list

The following books, published by the Unesco Press, are obtainable from the Institute or from Unesco and its national distributors throughout the world:

Educational cost analysis in action: case studies for planners (1972. Three volumes)

Educational development in Africa (1969. Three volumes, containing eleven African research monographs)

Educational planning: a bibliography (1964)

Educational planning: a directory of training and research institutions (1968)

Educational planning in the USSR (1968)

Financing educational systems (series of monographs: full list available on request)

Fundamentals of educational planning (series of monographs: full list available on request)

Manpower aspects of educational planning (1968)

Methodologies of educational planning for developing countries by J. D. Chesswas (1968)

Monographies africaines (five titles, in French only: list available on request)

New educational media in action: case studies for planners (1967. Three volumes)

The new media: memo to educational planners by W. Schramm, P. H. Coombs, F. Kahnert, J. Lyle (1967. A report including analytical conclusions based on the above three volumes of case studies)

Planning the development of universities (see list of titles at the beginning of this volume)

Planning the location of schools (series of monographs: full list available on request)

Population growth and costs of education in developing countries by Ta Ngoc Châu (1972)

Qualitative aspects of educational planning (1969)

Research for educational planning: notes on emergent needs by William J. Platt (1970)

Systems approach to teacher training and curriculum development: the case of developing countries by Taher A. Razik (1972)

The following books, produced in but not published by the Institute, are obtainable through normal bookselling channels:

Education in industrialized countries by R. Poignant
   Published by N.V. Martinus Nijhoff, The Hague, 1973

Managing educational costs by Philip H. Coombs and Jacques Hallak
   Published by Oxford University Press, New York, London and Toronto, 1972

Quantitative methods of educational planning by Héctor Correa
   Published by International Textbook Co., Scranton, Pa., 1969

The world educational crisis: a systems analysis by Philip H. Coombs
   Published by Oxford University Press, New York, London and Toronto, 1968